PRAISE FOR *THE FOUNDING MYTH*

"Seidel, a constitutional attorney, provides a fervent takedown of Christian Nationalism in his furious debut. After support by far-right Christian nationalists helped Donald Trump win the U.S. presidency, Seidel worries that Evangelical political influence is increasing and dangerous. He argues that America was not founded as a Christian nation on Judeo-Christian principles, and thus Christian nationalists are inherently wrong. . . . His well-conceived arguments will spark conversations for those willing to listen."

—Publishers Weekly

"In *The Founding Myth*, Andrew Seidel examines the beliefs and values of the founders of our nation and the framers of our Constitution to demonstrate that, contrary to the beliefs of many Americans, our nation was *not* founded as "a Christian nation." . . . As he explains, those who established our nation were generally skeptical of traditional Christianity and were deeply committed to the separation of church and state. At a time when too many religious and political figures trumpet the notion that the precepts of traditional Christianity were built into our national values, Seidel persuasively demonstrates that such an assertion is simply unfounded. This is an important insight that Americans of every political and religious stripe should understand and embrace."

—Geoffrey R. Stone, Edward H. Levi Distinguished Professor of Law,
University of Chicago, and author of *Sex and the Constitution:
Sex, Religion, and Law from America's Origins to the Twenty-First Century*

"What if ['Judeo-Christian'] values are not only not the foundation of our country but are actually in conflict with America's bedrock principles? That is the stunning thesis of Seidel's new book— and it's one he backs up with ample evidence. This book is a game-changer. I can think of several politicians (and would-be politicians) who would greatly benefit from reading it."

— **Robert Boston**, Senior Adviser/Editor of *Church & State*,
Americans United for Separation of Church and State

"By meticulously dissecting the concept of a Judeo-Christian America, Andrew Seidel exposes it for what it is: a fabrication of those who would define America according to their own religious views, a political tool for those who see the Wall of Separation as a troubling obstacle rather than a foundational structure of our democracy. This book is a valuable resource for understanding the struggles of American secularism in modern times."

— **David Niose**, author of *Fighting Back the Right:
Reclaiming America from the Attack on Reason*

"Andrew Seidel does a marvelous job debunking the 'Christian nation' myth. He reminds us that we're not a country founded on Biblical principles and we should all be grateful for that. This book should be required reading for every member of Congress."

— **Hemant Mehta**, editor of *Friendly Atheist*, and author of
I Sold My Soul on eBay: Viewing Faith through an Atheist's Eyes

"Andrew Seidel's *The Founding Myth* is a profoundly necessary book for our times. Armed with a thoroughly researched knowledge of history, Seidel adeptly picks apart the lie that the United States was founded on Judeo-Christian values. Moreover, he demonstrates how American values present an open affront to biblical values, and why Founding Fathers like Jefferson and Franklin believed so strongly that no religion—including Christianity—should have any influence in public and political affairs. Seidel builds his arguments meticulously, fact by fact, resulting in a riveting and helplessly compelling read."

— **Ali A. Rizvi**, author of *The Atheist Muslim: A Journey from Religion to Reason*

"In a powerfully rendered account of the true principles grounding the nation, Seidel reveals the shameful extent to which religious interest groups distort and deface our secular heritage. Combining far-ranging scholarship with lively prose, this book is indispensable reading for lawmakers, activists, and all citizens alarmed at religious encroachment in our politics and revisionism of our history."

— **Sarah Haider**, Director of Outreach for Ex-Muslims of North America

"There are legal experts on the Constitution and faith-based 'experts' on the Ten Commandments. Andrew Seidel is a legal expert who has brilliantly shown that the two systems of law are incompatible and mostly contradictory. After reading this well-documented book, you will not only cringe when you hear a politician or preacher refer to "the biblical principles on which our Constitution is based," but you will also have no trouble debunking such claims."

— **Herb Silverman**, founder of the Secular Coalition for America, and author of *Candidate Without a Prayer: An Autobiography of a Jewish Atheist in the Bible Belt*

"With wit and brio, Seidel demolishes the Christian nationalist talking point that the United States was somehow founded on 'Judeo-Christian' principles (or on a list of nine or ten often offensive 'Commandments' allegedly delivered by a Near Eastern deity a few millennia ago). Along the way, his wide-ranging and well-researched narrative offers a much more inspiring vision of the American experiment than the bigoted exceptionalism of today's mythmakers."

— **Matthew Stewart**, author of *Nature's God: The Heretical Origins of the American Republic*

"Andrew L. Seidel takes readers on an informative and accessible journey through the thicket of maneuvers by which Judeo-Christian theocrats attempt to exert their influence on American society. *The Founding Myth* is a potent exposé of how those who most want to impose biblical values on Americans are often the ones who least understand or follow the Bible."

— **Dr. Hector Avalos**, biblical scholar and Professor of Religious Studies, Iowa State University

THE
FOUNDING
MYTH

Why Christian Nationalism Is
UN-AMERICAN

ANDREW L. SEIDEL

foreword by SUSAN JACOBY

preface by DAN BARKER

STERLING
New York

STERLING
New York

An Imprint of Sterling Publishing Co., Inc.
1166 Avenue of the Americas
New York, NY 10036

ISBN 978-1-4549-3327-4

Distributed in Canada by Sterling Publishing Co., Inc.
c/o Canadian Manda Group, 664 Annette Street
Toronto, Ontario M6S 2C8, Canada
Distributed in the United Kingdom by GMC Distribution Services
Castle Place, 166 High Street, Lewes, East Sussex BN7 1XU, England
Distributed in Australia by NewSouth Books
University of New South Wales, Sydney, NSW 2052, Australia

For information about custom editions, special sales, and premium and corporate purchases,
please contact Sterling Special Sales at 800-805-5489 or specialsales@sterlingpublishing.com.

Manufactured in the United States of America

6 8 10 9 7 5

sterlingpublishing.com

Interior design by Susan Welt

Picture credits – see page 338

"It has been the misfortune of history that a personal knowledge
and an impartial judgment of things, can rarely meet in the historian.
The best history of our country therefore must be the fruit of contributions
bequeathed by co-temporary actors and witnesses, to successors who will
make an unbiased use of them. And if the abundance and authenticity of
the materials which still exist in the private as well as in public repositories
among us should descend to hands capable of doing justice to them, then
American History may be expected to contain more truth, and lessons
certainly not less valuable, than that of any Country or age whatever."

—James Madison,
in a letter to Edward Everett, March 19, 1823[1]

"From the totalitarian point of view, history is something to
be created rather than learned. A totalitarian state is in effect
a theocracy, and its ruling caste, in order to keep its position,
has to be thought of as infallible."

—George Orwell "The Prevention of Literature," 1946[2]

Contents

PART I

THE FOUNDERS, INDEPENDENCE, AND THE COLONIES

PART II

UNITED STATES v. THE BIBLE

PART III

THE TEN COMMANDMENTS v. THE CONSTITUTION

PART IV

AMERICAN VERBIAGE

Foreword

Andrew Seidel's *The Founding Myth: Why Christian Nationalism Is Un-American* could hardly arrive at a more propitious moment, as a nation based upon the world's first secular Constitution—a document that never mentions any god and derives its authority from "We the People"—must cope on a daily basis with an administration in thrall to what is best described as Christian nationalism. President Donald J. Trump never displayed any intense interest in religion of any kind in his public persona before he began running for the nation's highest office. But he owes his election to far-right Christian nationalists, whom he has rewarded with an unprecedented number of cabinet appointments and judgeships galore (the latter certain to outlast Trump).

Who will ever forget former attorney general Jeff Sessions's biblical rationalization for Trump's policy of separating migrant children from their parents? Sessions turned to a passage from Paul's Epistle to the Romans, in which Christianity's first great proselytizer admonished every soul to be "subject to the governing authorities; because there is no authority except that which God has established." (A federal judge thought otherwise, however, and ordered the government to reunite the families—thereby deciding that the Constitution, not a first-century evangelist, is a higher authority on the making of public policy.) And let us not overlook Betsy DeVos, the secretary of education, who was raised a strict Calvinist and has devoted much of her lifetime and her family's fortune to promoting private over public schools. When DeVos made a trip to New York City, which has the nation's largest public school system, she did not visit a single public school but put in an appearance at two Orthodox Jewish schools and a fundraising banquet where she was introduced by New York's Roman Catholic cardinal Timothy Michael Dolan. Above all, there is Vice President Mike Pence (who, presiding over an evenly divided Senate, cast the deciding vote for DeVos's confirmation), whose far-right evangelical rectitude is so stringent that he will not attend any event if alcohol is served unless he is accompanied by his wife. Nor will he dine alone with a woman except his wife—even for business purposes. Indeed, Trump chose Pence as his running mate precisely because he does wear his moral purity (as defined by the religious right) on his sleeve and therefore provides an antidote to the president's record of well-publicized serial affairs and serial marriages. I would be remiss, given the head-spinning turnover of Trump appointees, not to mention the possibility that any cabinet member might be gone by the time Seidel's book is published. Pence will definitely be around, since presidents cannot fire their elected vice presidents. In any case, it is assured that any new Trump appointees, given their boss's immense political debt to the religious right, will continue their attempts to privilege religion, especially Christianity, in as many public programs as possible.

This political environment, in which the separation of church and state is treated as a kind of heresy rather than the real rock upon which our government stands, is what makes the timing of Seidel's book so fortuitous.

As an attorney for the Freedom From Religion Foundation, an organization dedicated to battling all attempts to breach the wall of separation between church and state, Seidel is well acquainted with the legal and political battles over the entanglement of religion and government, ranging from Washington to small towns across the nation. The great virtue of his book, however, is that he focuses not on the individual battles but on the overarching myth that the United States is a nation founded not on Enlightenment values and our secular Constitution but on "Judeo-Christian values" as embodied in the Bible.

Seidel makes a powerful argument that the term "Judeo-Christian" is basically a twentieth-century, post-Holocaust, made-in-America formulation designed to sound more inclusive than it is for those who really pay attention only to the "Christian" half of the hyphenated fabrication. This subject is seldom discussed, because it can make both Christians and Jews uncomfortable in a society wishing to pretend that all religions (and ethnic backgrounds) are equal. What makes a believing Jew a Jew and a believing Christian a Christian is that the former does not acknowledge Jesus as the son of God, God, or the Messiah and the latter does. Or, as Philip Roth noted in a speech 1961, "The fact is that, if one is committed to being a Jew, then he believes that on the most serious questions pertaining to man's survival—understanding the past, imagining the future, discovering the relationship between God and humanity—he is right and the Christians are wrong." Seidel, who, like many freethinkers of many generations, has taken the trouble to learn a great deal about various religions and their sacred books, takes pains to discuss the ways in which the Ten Commandments (which actually *are* a part of shared Judeo-Christian tradition) emphatically do *not* form the basis of American law. If the founding fathers had observed the first commandment's prohibition against graven images, for example, we would have no portraits to tell us what these august "Judeo-Christians" looked like. Just kidding. The founders—all of Christian descent, insofar as genealogical research reveals—were mainly deists. They believed in a divinity (often called Providence) who set the universe in motion but subsequently takes no part in the affairs of men. Many of these deists were freethinkers who might call themselves agnostics or atheists today but who definitely did not believe in the civil primacy of any religion. (The word "agnostic" was not coined until the nineteenth century. Some of the most prominent deists among the founders, like Thomas Jefferson, were called atheists by their contemporary political opponents because deists rejected the supernatural and did not belong to any church.)

The essential argument of *The Founding Myth* is that one might as well describe the United States as a nation founded on Hammurabic-Judeo-Christian-Hindu-Buddhist-Muslim-humanist values as on the values of the Hebrew and Christian bibles. This is, of course, a ridiculous statement—but not as obviously ridiculous to many Americans as a claim to national legitimacy based on the oxymoronic Judeo-Christianity. All religions and all societies have laws against murder, for instance, but the big problem—now playing out in the American debate over legal abortion and physician-assisted suicide—is that different religions and different cultures define murder differently. You may think abortion is murder and I may think it is a legitimate medical choice, but the commandments handed down on Sinai will not help us resolve the question of how this issue is to be decided in a modern democratic society defined by religious pluralism.

Another important point of *The Founding Myth* is that many of the pieties Americans now take for granted and attribute to the founders are really artifacts of the late nineteenth and twentieth centuries. I know, from having spoken at many universities throughout the nation during the past twenty years, that large numbers of students attribute the Pledge of Allegiance to the revolutionary era. In fact, the pledge was written in 1892, and the phrase "under God" was not added until 1954, at the height of the McCarthy era. The addition was intended to draw a distinction between pious America and atheistic communism. I well remember the nuns in my parochial school telling us that Russian children could be shot for simply saying the word "God." Seidel recounts the history of the relatively recent origins of the public sanctimony that many Americans now take for granted, including the routine use of the phrase "God bless America" at the end of presidential speeches—something that was not a commonplace when I was growing up in the 1950s.

The entire book is on solid legal ground because of Seidel's experience as an attorney fighting attempts to introduce religion into public institutions—from the promotion of Bible-reading in public schools to attempts by many right-wing religious groups to obtain public funds for faith-based institutions. The author recounts the legal issues in a lively, lucid fashion accessible to readers unfamiliar with the fine points of either the Bible or the Constitution. Above all, he makes the vital point that when faith is politically weaponized, religion itself is "weakened and tainted." He recalls Benjamin's Franklin's argument—as incisive today as it was more than 200 years ago—that when "a Religion is good, I conceive that it will support itself; and when it cannot support itself, and God does not take care to support [it], so that its Professors are oblig'd to call for the help of the Civil Power, 'tis a sign, I apprehend, of its being a bad one."

Amen.

— SUSAN JACOBY
August 1, 2018

Preface

I met Andrew Seidel in 2010. He came to a speech I gave at Metro State College in Denver, where I told my personal "preacher to atheist" story and described the work of the Freedom From Religion Foundation to keep state and church separate. Andrew remembers that I compared Christian nationalists to those territorial animals who mark off their boundaries, howling "The capitol is ours! The statehouse is ours! City halls, police departments, public schools—the whole country is ours!"

After the speech, Andrew introduced himself. I remembered his name because he had been a winner of FFRF's 2010 Graduate Student Essay Contest on "Why we need to get God out of government." He had written about the danger of mixing government and religion.

We met for breakfast the next morning, and I quickly saw that Andrew is one smart and interesting guy. He had been a Grand Canyon guide—ask him how many basketballs it would take to fill that vast gulf—and had done legal work with environmental law clinics working to take down polluters. But he spent most of the breakfast asking me about FFRF. I didn't realize until later that he was conducting a job interview in reverse.

We were all so impressed with Andrew that about a year later, we hired him. He and his wife, Liz Cavell—also a lawyer—moved to Wisconsin. Andrew started work on October 31, 2011 (Halloween, appropriately enough). Liz joined FFRF's legal department about a year later.

FFRF prefers to solve most problems without going to court. In 2018, our legal staff sent out more than 1,000 complaint letters to public officials around the country, resulting in more than 300 victories.

But we do file lawsuits. We usually have about a dozen cases in the works at any time in various stages of development in state and federal courts. We litigate over religious symbols on government property (mostly Ten Commandments, Christian crosses, and nativity scenes), religion in public schools, taxpayer money to repair churches, prayer at public meetings, chaplaincies, and other violations of the First Amendment. We are currently suing the IRS in two different cases involving preferential benefits to ministers and religious organizations. In the first two years of Trump's presidency, we racked up an impressive record of sixteen victories (decisions or positive settlements) and only two losses. Andrew was a big part of that.

As I write this, one of those losses is on appeal, and it involves me personally. When a member of Congress asked the chaplain of the US House of Representatives to invite me to open Congress with a secular invocation as a guest chaplain, the congressman was told no. Since an atheist does not believe in a Higher Power, I am not qualified to solemnize the workings of government, though the Supreme Court has said otherwise. Andrew Seidel and FFRF attorney Sam Grover conceived the case and worked on it along with outside litigators. The district court in *Barker v. Conroy* ruled on procedural grounds that we could not sue the chaplain because although I was indeed injured, the violation of my constitutional rights was not "traceable" to the chaplain. He is simply following the orders of Congress.

Believing that the House of Representatives should be representative, we appealed. In October 2018, Andrew gave the oral arguments in the US Court of Appeals for the DC Circuit, and he did a masterful job. Andrew has always advocated deep research, and it showed. As the judges hammered him with questions, he calmly replied with facts, history, legal precedent, specific citations, and clear logic. All those weeks of preparation, including two arduous moot courts, paid off handsomely. His fondness for research and preparation show in this book.

Andrew is now FFRF's Director of Strategic Response, a jack-of-all-legal-trades, and, on top of this workload, he has persistently been writing and researching for this book—a project he started before we knew him. When it was taking shape, I suggested it could be called *America is not a Christian nation: And it's a good thing it isn't!* Because that is exactly what Andrew has proved in *The Founding Myth*.

— DAN BARKER
Co-president, Freedom From Religion Foundation

Illustration by Gustave Doré, *Moses Breaks
the Tables of the Law*, 1866.

Introduction: Prelude to an Argument

"When I think of all the harm the Bible has done,
I despair of ever writing anything equal to it."

—Oscar Wilde[3]

God bequeathed the Ten Commandments to Moses, or so the story goes. It's a tale believed by millions of pious churchgoing Americans, including former judge James Taylor of Hawkins County, Tennessee. Taylor also believes that America was founded on those commandments and that America's "founders were religious people whose faith influenced the creation of this nation, its laws, and its institutions of government."[4]

Elected to higher office in 2011, Judge Taylor ached to use his new power to proclaim these great truths. He insisted that the Ten Commandments be displayed in his courthouse. The holy exhibit would edify citizens and show that Judeo-Christian principles shaped the development of American law and government. It would demonstrate that his religion birthed America. Taylor commissioned a Ten Commandments plaque, elegantly lettered and struck in bronze; it read as shown in this replica:

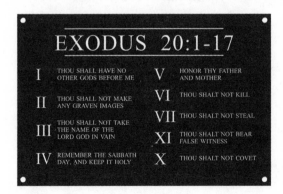

Not shy about using a public office to promote his personal religion, Taylor promised to showcase other items of civic piety, including the national motto, "In God We Trust"; the Pledge of Allegiance ("one nation, under God"); and a picture of Washington praying in the snow at Valley Forge. But the commandments were to be the centerpiece. The complete message was unmistakable: Judeo-Christian principles influenced America's creation, its laws, and its government.[5]

This widespread belief is unexamined and, like Judge Taylor's plaque, unable to withstand scrutiny. Look closely at the wording on that plaque. Taylor lists nine commandments, not ten, omitting the adultery stricture. He also mislabeled his ninth commandment as the eleventh—XI. Hypocritically, Taylor pocketed donations meant to finance the commandments display and had stolen money from his clients. One former staffer filed a $3 million sexual harassment and retaliation lawsuit against the married Taylor.[6] All told, Taylor pled guilty to multiple felony theft charges, was sentenced to four years in prison, had to pay $71,783 in restitution and serve six hundred hours of community service, and was disbarred.[7]

Taylor struggled to obey his beloved commandments, but that does not necessarily mean that he was wrong about their influence. Was he right? Do the Ten Commandments, "In God We Trust," Washington's prayer, and the other evidence show that America was founded on Judeo-Christian principles?

What Are Judeo-Christian Principles?

Taylor's claim that America was founded on Judeo-Christian principles is common—so much so that people accept it as true without asking simple questions: What is a Judeo-Christian principle? Where do Judeo-Christian principles come from? Are they handed down from on high, like the Ten Commandments? The few attempts to answer these questions are unsatisfying because they are often as vague as the term "Judeo-Christian principles" itself. One reason the "nation founded on Judeo-Christian principles" claim has not been fully examined is that the vagueness of the term insulates that claim from scrutiny.

The term "Judeo-Christian" is difficult to pin down because it is something of a fabrication.[8] From a scholarly standpoint, as noted in a 1992 *Newsweek* article, "the idea of a single 'Judeo-Christian tradition' is a made-in-America myth."[9] One Jewish theologian stated the problem plainly: "Judaism is Judaism because it rejects Christianity, and Christianity is Christianity because it rejects Judaism."[10] "Judeo-Christian" is slippery because it is more a political invention than a scholarly description. It originated at the close of World War II when Christian exclusivity was too threatening. After "the Nazi death camps, a phrase like 'our Christian civilization' seemed ominously exclusive," explained Prof. Mark Silk.[11] But the term didn't gain prominence until the fight against communism, during which some religion, *any religion*, was better than atheistic communism. Eisenhower was probably the first president to use the term, explaining to a Soviet general in 1952 that the American "form of government has no sense unless it is founded in a deeply felt religious faith, and I don't care what it is. With us of course it is the Judeo-Christian concept."[12]

These indistinct principles can be sharpened somewhat by looking to the books that embody Judeo-Christianity: the Hebrew Bible, or Old Testament, and the Christian Bible, or New Testament. Taylor, the "nine commandments judge," and others who claim that America is "founded on Judeo-Christian principles" confirm this approach. For instance, when running for president, Woodrow Wilson said, "America was born a Christian nation. America was born to exemplify that devotion to the tenets of righteousness which are derived from the revelations of Holy Scripture."[13] President Harry Truman stated, on more than one occasion, that "the fundamental basis of all government is in this Bible right here, and it started with Moses on the Mount," and "the fundamental basis of our Bill of Rights comes from the teachings we get from Exodus and Saint Matthew, from Isaiah and Saint Paul."[14] The ill-defined term becomes clearer in light of these statements; Judeo-Christian principles can be derived from Mosaic Law, such as the Ten Commandments, and the rest of the bible.

The term has the benefit of sounding inclusive to a broad audience while actually speaking directly to conservative Christians who hear only the second part of the term, "Christian." Robert Davi, the actor, Bond villain, and frequent contributor to the conservative website Breitbart.com, gave this game away. Writing about the imaginary

"War on Christmas," Davi argued that removing a nativity scene from government property is part of "a systematic attack on Judeo-Christian values that our country was founded on."[15] Davi surely knows that the nativity scene features the birth of Jesus as savior, something Judaism rejects. The nativity is Christian, not Judeo-Christian.

It's not just celebrities who inadvertently admit the singular, not dual, nature of the term. The Judeo-Christian Voter Guide website[16] provides local guides and resources, but, prior to the 2016 election, they were nearly all Christian. In the state with the highest number and percentage of Jewish citizens, New York,[17] the state voter guide linked to groups such as the Christian Coalition and the American Family Association, whose goal is "to be a champion of Christian activism."[18] It did not link to a single Jewish group. The site even had an identical twin, the "Christian Voter Guide" website, which was the same in every respect except that it lacked that crumb of inclusion: "Judeo-."[19] The Family Research Council (FRC), whose "mission is to advance faith, family, and freedom in public policy and the culture from a Christian worldview," was once featured heavily on these two sites.[20] Tony Perkins, the head of the FRC, inadvertently showed the irrelevance of the "Judeo-" in "Judeo-Christian" when chastising the Daughters of the American Revolution for telling its members not to pray in Jesus's name (a claim the group denied): "This signals a dramatic change in the strong Judeo-Christian roots of the DAR. After all, this is a service group meant to perpetuate the memory of the American Revolution and the values for which we fought. Like it or not, those values and our nation's identity were rooted in the Christian tradition."[21] One sentence later, Perkins's inclusive affectation had evaporated.

John McCain was a bit more honest when he claimed that "this nation was founded primarily on Christian principles,"[22] but McCain's more honest phrasing is less inviting. "Judeo-" is a sop, a fig leaf, tossed about to avoid controversy and complaint. It is simply a morsel of inclusion offered to soften the edge of an exclusionary, Christian movement.

That exclusionary movement is Christian nationalism. As a modern American movement, it is fully described by Michelle Goldberg in her 2006 book, *Kingdom Coming: The Rise of Christian Nationalism*.[23] Christian nationalists are historical revisionists bent on "restoring" America to the Judeo-Christian principles on which they wish it were founded. They believe that secular America is a myth, and under the guise of restoration they seek to press religion into every crevice of the government. They not only think it appropriate for the government to favor one religion over others, but also believe America was designed to favor Christianity. To them, America is a Christian nation founded on Christian principles, and promoting that belief is a religious duty.[24]

History had proven to the framers of the US Constitution that religion is divisive. They separated religion from government to avoid the mistakes of past regimes. "The Framers and the citizens of their time intended . . . to guard against the civic divisiveness that follows when the government weighs in on one side of religious debate; nothing does a better job of roiling society," wrote the Supreme Court in 2005 when examining the origins of the religion clauses of the First Amendment.[25] Christian nationalism's fabricated history conceals an important historical truth: that religion and government are best kept on either side of an impregnable wall, as the founders intended. This book seeks to expose that fabricated history and tell the greater truths.

Is Christian Nationalism Really a Problem? Is It Influential?

It is because of Christian nationalism that "President Donald Trump" is a phrase that reflects reality and not reality television. Before Trump, Christian nationalism tended toward the corrupt and inept. It was an odd, impotent curiosity. But the 2016 election changed that. Trump won because of Christian nationalism. The movement is still based on lies and myths, but a Christian nationalist was elected president of the United States, and he was elected *because of*, not in spite of, his Christian nationalism.

The single most accurate predictor of whether a person voted for Donald Trump in the 2016 election was not religion, wealth, education, or even political party; it was believing the United States is and should be a Christian nation.[26] Researchers studied this connection and were able to control for other characteristics to ensure that Christian nationalism was not simply a proxy for other forms of intolerance or other variables related to vote choice.[27] They concluded, "The more someone believed the United States is—and should be—a Christian nation, the more likely they were to vote for Trump."[28]

Trump rode a wave of Christian nationalism, fostered by fables and myths about America's founding, to the most powerful office in the world. "Once Christian nationalism was taken into account," the researchers explained, "other religious measures had no direct effect on how likely someone was to vote for Trump. These measures of religion mattered only if they made someone more likely to see the United States as a Christian nation."[29] Put another way, "Christian nationalism provides a metanarrative for a religiously distinct national identity."[30] That identity depends on the historical myths exposed in this book. Those myths are the glue that unites the Christian part of this identity with the American part of the identity. Without the bond provided by these myths, the identity and political power begin to crumble.

Christian nationalism is, at least in this sense, more important than religion, political party, or any other factor in American life.

ONLY AFTER THE SHOCK of the 2016 presidential election subsided could we begin to fully understand the power of Christian nationalism. During the election and before, Christian nationalists themselves underestimated their power. Few expected Trump to win, let alone win because of his Christian nationalism. Christian nationalists had caught the presidential tiger by the tail and were unprepared. Playing catch-up, in February 2016 a loose coalition of conservative religious groups and Christian nationalists launched "Project Blitz," a curious sobriquet given its historical connotations. The goal was to elevate "traditional Judeo-Christian religious values" and "to reclaim and properly define the narrative which supports such beliefs."[31]

Project Blitz encapsulates the problem Christian nationalism poses. First, it seeks to alter our history, values, and national identity. Then it codifies Christian privilege in the law, favoring Christians above others. Finally, it legally disfavors the nonreligious, non-Christians, and minorities such as the LGBTQ community, by, for instance, permitting discrimination against them in places of public accommodation or in employment.

This legislative push, ongoing as this book goes to press, includes three categories of bills that reflect these steps, all of which promote Christian nationalist myths and lies. The first category centers on "Our Country's Religious Heritage." These bills "recognize the place of Christian principles in our nation's history and heritage [and] deal broadly with our national motto, history, and civics, including their Judeo-Christian dimensions."[32] They attempt to prove what Judge Taylor's nine commandments display was meant to prove, that "religion, and particularly our Judeo-Christian heritage, have played a large part in the founding and history of this country."[33] The second category, which includes measures such as a proclamation recognizing Christian Heritage Week, "focus[es] more on our country's Judeo-Christian heritage," though more on the Christian and less on the Judeo.[34]

Christian nationalist myths are central to the Blitz because they are meant to provide a legislative rationale, historical precedent, and legitimacy. Category 1 bills are supposedly less controversial but promote many of those myths, including a bill that mandates displaying "In God We Trust" in all public schools, libraries, and buildings and on license plates,[35] and a "Religion in Legal History Acts" bill that requires "public displays of religious history affecting the law," including the Mayflower Compact, the Declaration of Independence, and George Washington's Farewell Address.[36]

Category 2 bills include proclamations recognizing "Christian Heritage Week," "the Importance of the Bible in History," and "the Year of the Bible." There is even one for "Recognizing Christmas Day," because we would all forget otherwise.[37] These proclamations list historical evidence to support their claims, including a claim that "the first act of America's first Congress in 1774 was to ask a minister to open with prayer" and another that "Biblical teachings inspired concepts of civil government that are contained in our Declaration of Independence and the Constitution of the United States."[38]

These seemingly mundane bills are the tip of Christian nationalism's sword. More dangerous bills will follow. Category 3 bills grant a license to discriminate against LGBTQ Americans, atheists, unmarried couples, and others in the name of Jesus. These bills will allow religious adoption agencies to refuse to put children in loving homes because the bible says that gay couples are an abomination. They seek to give businesses and places of public accommodation the right to discriminate against customers of a different religion or even skin color (though Christian nationalists would be unlikely to admit the latter). This discriminatory agenda cannot be furthered without the seemingly innocuous bills that first warp our sense of who we are as a nation.

The goal is to redefine America according to the Christian nationalist identity and then reshape the law accordingly. As of the end of April 2018, Project Blitz has resulted in more than seventy proposed bills nationwide.[39] Christian nationalism's identity is built on the foundational myths underlying these bills; this inescapable point is reflected in their legislative strategy. If these myths can be exposed and eviscerated, the aim of this book, so can Christian nationalism's legal and legislative agenda.

Who Are the Christian Nationalists?

The most vocal Christian nationalists are, as you'd expect, religious leaders. James Dobson founded Focus on the Family and thinks "that we have been, from the beginning, a people of faith whose government is built wholly on a Judeo-Christian foundation."[40] Moral Majority co-founder Jerry Falwell wrote that "our Founding Fathers established America's laws and precepts on the principles recorded in the laws of God, including the Ten Commandments . . . [and any] diligent student of American history finds that our great nation was founded by godly men upon godly principles to be a Christian nation."[41] Jimmy Swaggart preached that America has "the greatest freedoms of expression the world has ever known. . . . Those freedom are based squarely on the Judeo-Christian principle, which is the Word of God."[42] The late Billy Graham and his son Franklin Graham have preached that America "was built on Christian principles."[43]

Christian nationalism is not solely about religion. It's an unholy alliance, an incestuous marriage of conservative politics and conservative Christianity. According to *ABC News*, the Council for National Policy is one of the most powerful political organizations you've never heard of,[44] and it exemplifies this alliance. The *New York Times* described it as "a little-known club of a few hundred of the most powerful conservatives in the country."[45] It was founded by prominent Christian nationalist Tim LaHaye, and its secretive membership roll is filled with Christian nationalists from the religious and government sectors, including many repeatedly cited in this book.[46] The group's vision statement declares its Christian nationalist mission: to "restore . . . Judeo-Christian values under the Constitution."[47]

Politicians are some of the most vocal Christian nationalists. Presidential candidates seem particularly fond of repeating Christian nationalism claims. In the run-up to the 2016 election, Donald Trump was asked, point blank, "Do you believe that America was founded on Judeo-Christian principles?" He replied in his prolix, disjointed fashion: "Yeah, I think it was. . . . I see so many things happening that are so different from what our country used to be. So religion's a very important part of me and it's also, I think it's a very important part of our country."[48] After winning office with 81 percent of the white evangelical vote, Trump became slightly more adept when deploying Christian nationalist rhetoric. As president, he has often claimed that "in America we don't worship government, we worship God."[49] He supports this line, so popular with his base, by trotting out some of the favorite Christian nationalist talking points, including:

- That "the American Founders invoked our Creator four times in the Declaration of Independence."
- That the pilgrims at Plymouth were religious and prayed.
- That "our currency proudly declares, 'In God we trust.'"
- That "Benjamin Franklin reminded his colleagues at the Constitutional Convention to begin by bowing their heads in prayer."
- That presidents take the oath of office and "say, 'So help me God.'"
- That "we proudly proclaim that we are 'one nation under God' every time we say the Pledge of Allegiance."[50]

This book will address all of these anemic talking points.

While campaigning in 2016, Trump's primary opponents joined him in promoting these myths. Without bothering to support his position, Senator Marco Rubio argued, "If you don't believe that Judeo-Christian values influenced America, you don't know history."[51] After winning the Iowa primary, Senator Ted Cruz told CNN, "This is a country built on Judeo-Christian values."[52] He also vowed, ironically given the election's outcome, to defend—against Trump—the GOP platform, which was the manifestation of "Judeo-Christian principles, the values that built this country."[53] Ohio governor John Kasich promised to create a new federal agency "that has a clear mandate to promote the core Judeo-Christian Western values."[54] Kasich asserted that "it's essential . . . to embrace again our Jewish-Christian tradition rather than running from it, hiding from it."[55]

Most of the Republican presidential primary candidates in 2012 also bent toward Christian nationalism. Rick Perry—former Texas governor, *Dancing with the Stars* contestant, and now secretary of energy—rambled on about "our values—values and virtues that this country was based upon in Judeo-Christian founding fathers"[56] and said that "our founding fathers, they created this country, our Constitution, the foundation of America upon Judeo-Christian values, biblical values. . . . They didn't shy away from referencing Him, using the values he brought and the message of his son Jesus Christ to build the system that we as a society have enjoyed for more than two hundred years."[57] Senator Rick Santorum was infamously introduced at a campaign rally in Baton Rouge by a pastor who howled "Get out!" at all the non-Christians in America because America "was founded as a Christian nation."[58] Santorum was forced to distance himself from those remarks.[59] Representative Michele Bachmann argued that "American exceptionalism is grounded on the Judeo-Christian ethic, which is really based upon the Ten Commandments. The Ten Commandments were the foundation for our law."[60] During the Florida debate, Mitt Romney was asked how his Mormon religion might influence his presidency. He dodged, saying "ours is a nation which is based upon Judeo-Christian values and ethics. Our law is based upon those values and ethics."[61]

Christian nationalism surfaces in the US Congress. Representatives Louie Gohmert, Doug Lamborn, and Steve King are some of its most strident proponents.[62] Representative King of Iowa, known for his racism and xenophobia, proclaimed that our nation "was founded on Judeo-Christian principles, which means we need less law enforcement than anybody else in the world"[63]—a fallacy we'll explore later on. Texas representative Louie Gohmert declared in a December 2017 floor speech, "The Supreme Court looked at all of the evidence and declared in an opinion that the United States was founded as, and is, a Christian nation." He added to this gross misstatement by insisting that "the only way any people can truly have freedom of religion is if they have a constitution that is founded on Judeo-Christian principles."[64] The opposite is true.

Former Virginia representative Randy Forbes, who founded the Congressional Prayer Caucus, gave a 2015 sermon claiming: "President George Washington, John Adams, Thomas Jefferson, Andrew Jackson, Abraham Lincoln, William McKinley, Teddy Roosevelt, Woodrow Wilson, Herbert Hoover, Franklin Roosevelt, Harry Truman, Dwight Eisenhower, John Kennedy, Ronald Reagan all indicated how the Bible and Judeo-Christian principles were so important in this nation. So if in fact we were a nation based on those principles, what was that moment in time when we ceased to so be?"[65] In 2010, Michele Bachmann invited one of the most deceitful historical revisionists, David Barton—a man who used erroneous historical quotations,[66] misrepresented Jefferson and his views on the separation of state and church,[67] and wrote a biography of Jefferson so full of bad history that the publisher pulled it off the shelves[68]—to teach a class to Congress on the Christian history of the Constitution.[69] Two-time presidential hopeful and former Arkansas governor Mike Huckabee expressed the belief that "all Americans should be forced—forced at gunpoint no less—to listen to every David Barton message."[70] Forbes's Congressional Prayer Caucus once introduced a resolution in the House of Representatives to recognize "the first weekend of May as Ten Commandments Weekend to recognize the significant contributions the Ten Commandments have made in shaping the principles, institutions, and national character of the United States."[71] The resolution also claimed that the Ten Commandments are "an elemental source for United States law."[72] Not quite. Forbes and Barton founded and run the groups (the Congressional Prayer Caucus Foundation and

Wallbuilders, respectively) leading the Christian nationalist push discussed earlier, Project Blitz.

Politicians and political parties have elections to win, so their words can be discounted; but some scholars have also made these claims. Michael Novak, a former United States Ambassador to the United Nations Commission on Human Rights and a professor at Stanford, Syracuse, and Notre Dame, agreed with eighteenth-century jurist Sir William Blackstone that the Law of Moses is the "font and spring of constitutional government."[73] (Thomas Jefferson thought the idea that the Ten Commandments or Christianity was the foundation of English Common Law an "awkward monkish fabrication" and a "fraud."[74]) Anson Phelps Stokes—a priest and former secretary of Yale—wrote in his three-volume work on church and state in America that the "ideal of the Declaration [of Independence] is of course a definitely Christian one" that is clearly based on "fundamental Christian teachings."[75] Less scholarly examples include judge-turned-television-personality Andrew Napolitano, who thinks that "we have a Constitution and a Declaration of Independence that embodies Judeo-Christian moral values."[76]Author and disgraced Fox News host Bill O'Reilly advocates teaching Christian nationalism in public schools: "Kids need to know what Judeo-Christian tradition is, because that's what all of our laws are based on. That's what the country's philosophy is based on . . . because that's what forged the Constitution."[77] Even the Museum of the Bible, which claims to be fair-minded, "is preoccupied with the question of whether America is a biblically rooted nation," according to *The Atlantic*, which added, "While the exhibits portray some conflicting views, the message is clear: The country was forged through Christianity."[78]

PATRIOTISM HAS NO RELIGION. The Christian nationalist's argument seeks to change that and is, at its core, a fight about what it means to be an American. A disturbing number of Americans already believe that Christian and American identities are one and the same. The Pew Research Center found that about 32 percent of "people in the U.S. believe it is very important to be Christian to be considered truly American."[79] Some are vocal about it. When Mike Pence accepted the Republican vice-presidential nomination, after a few formalities, he repeated one of his favorite lines: "I'm a Christian, a conservative, and a Republican—in that order."[80] The Christian nationalism ideal fuses two identities, Christian and American, so that to be one, you must also be the other. And if you're not both, you can, as Santorum's preacher screamed, "Get out!" President Trump's infamous travel bans embodied this idea.

Throughout the presidential campaign, Trump promised to impose "extreme vetting" on immigrants. Vague in the particulars, he promised to admit only those people who "loved our country."[81] In his second week in office, Trump signed a controversial and unconstitutional executive order that banned travel from seven Muslim-majority countries. The order also favored immigration for Christians. Anyone who is oppressed for their beliefs should be welcome in this country—it shouldn't depend on what those beliefs are (a point Trump essentially conceded in the wording of the first revised immigration order, issued on March 6, 2017, even if its implementation did not concede the point). But for Trump, there is no difference between favoring Christians and testing to see if potential immigrants love America, something he reiterated during the signing ceremony.[82] Trump used Christianity as a proxy for loving America. He explained this with his typical circumlocution while campaigning at an evangelical stronghold, Liberty University, in Lynchburg, Virginia. Almost precisely one year before he signed the order, Trump declared, "We're going to protect Christianity. And I can say that. I don't have to be politically correct. We're going to protect it."[83] He then made his infamous "Two Corinthians" gaffe, saying "Two Corinthians" instead of "Second Corinthians." The verse to which Trump was referring, 2 Corinthians 3:17, says that "where the Spirit of the Lord is, there is liberty" and confirms the point. After that telling slip, Trump continued, "If you look at what is going on throughout the world, if you look at Syria, if you are a Christian, they are chopping off heads. . . . Christianity is under siege. I'm a Protestant, Presbyterian to be exact. . . . Very, very proud of it. We have to protect [Christianity] because very bad things are happening."[84] Incidentally, Syria was one of the seven countries whose citizens Trump banned from the United States in his first order. Syrians were also banned in the two subsequent immigration orders.

For Trump and Christian nationalists, to be an American is to be a Christian. The two have fused. Conservative columnists, such as Diana West, opined on Breitbart.com in 2015 that "the Trump [immigration] plan is absoutely [*sic*] essential to any possible return . . . to America's constitutional foundations and Judeo-Christian principles. I actually think of it as our last shot."[85] West penned this before the Iowa Caucus, when Trump was still a candidate proposing a "complete and total shutdown of Muslims entering the country."[86]

Christian nationalists use the language of revival and return, but that itself is misleading. They are not seeking to return, but to redefine. They want to redefine our Constitution—they want to redefine what it is to be an American—in terms of their religion.

Christian nationalism has already had a massive impact on our government and its policies, including foreign policy. When Trump moved the US embassy to Jerusalem, Christian nationalist mouthpieces on Fox News declared that he had "fulfilled . . . biblical prophecy" and related the move back to "the foundation of our own Judeo-Christian nation."[87] Christian nationalism affects immigration policy, as we've just seen. Its effects on education policy could be felt for decades, and not just because Secretary of Education Betsy DeVos was a dream appointment for the Christian nationalist goal of dismantling public schools through vouchers and school choice. It has denigrated our concept of equality, including by meddling with the legal definition of discrimination and attempting to redefine religious freedom as a license to discriminate, and it has sought to restrict women's rights and even the social safety net. And, of course, Christian nationalism features heavily in the culture wars.

Correcting the record is important. The political theology of Christian nationalism, the very identity of the Christian nationalist, depends on the myths exposed in this book. Christian nationalism's hold on political power in America rests on the claim that America was founded as a Christian nation. Without historical support, many of their policy justifications crumble. Without their common well of myths, the Christian nationalist identity will wither and fade. Their entire political and ideological reality is incredibly weak and vulnerable because it is based on historical distortions and lies. In this right-wing religious culture, the lies are so commonplace, so uncritically accepted, that these vulnerabilities are not recognized. The purpose of this book is simple, if lofty: to utterly destroy the myths that underlie this un-American political ideology.

What I'm Arguing and Who I Am

This objective is particularly important because history is powerful. George Santayana's warning that "those who cannot remember the past are condemned to repeat it" rings true because the past influences the present.[88] Unfortunately, history's power does not depend on its accuracy. A widely believed historical lie can have as much impact as a historical truth. President John F. Kennedy explained to Yale's graduating class of 1962 that "the great enemy of the truth is very often not the lie—deliberate, contrived, and dishonest—but the myth—persistent, persuasive, and unrealistic. Too often we hold fast to the clichés of our forebears. . . . We enjoy the comfort of opinion without the discomfort of thought."[89] Powerful historical falsehoods are particularly harmful in constitutional republics such as the United States. Courts may uphold practices that would otherwise be illegal by relying on comfortable myths instead of legitimate history. Legislators might promulgate laws based on historical clichés instead of reality. Each law or court decision based on revisionist history provides a new foundation from which the myth can be expanded. The myth feeds off itself, lodging more firmly in our collective consciousness.

When James Madison protested Patrick Henry's proposed three-penny tax to fund Christian ministers, he wrote a landmark in American history and law: the "Memorial and Remonstrance against Religious Assessments" (1785). Madison's arguments overwhelmed Henry and convinced Virginians to strike down the proposed tax. Madison argued that even small, seemingly insignificant battles to uphold our rights must be fought on principle; otherwise the infringements become authority for future violations of our rights:

> It is proper to take alarm at the first experiment on our liberties.
> We hold this prudent jealousy to be the first duty of Citizens, and
> one of the noblest characteristics of the late Revolution. The free

men of America did not wait till usurped power had strengthened itself by exercise, and entangled the question in precedents. They saw all the consequences in the principle, and they avoided the consequences by denying the principle.[90]

Because of history's power, myths can endanger our liberty. It is our duty as citizens to guard the truth and prevent these myths from becoming tangled in legal and legislative precedents. When Christian nationalists are permitted to use the machinery of the state to impose their religion on us all, even if they do so during times when dissent is punished, these constitutional violations are remarkably tenacious. Christian nationalism operates like a ratchet or a noose, with each violation tightening its hold and making it more difficult to undo. Worse, the violations are used to justify other violations, so the tightening proceeds apace.

Unfortunately, there are two Christian nationalist myths we failed to guard against. These two myths encompass all the lesser myths that Trump and Project Blitz feed into. The first is that America was founded as a Christian nation. The claim is demonstrably false as revealed by any number of documents from the time, including America's godless Constitution, Madison's Memorial, or the Treaty of Tripoli, which was negotiated under President George Washington and signed by President John Adams with the unanimous consent of the US Senate in 1797, and which says that "the Government of the United States of America is not, in any sense, founded on the Christian religion."[91] Most people with even a modest grasp of US history, law, government, or politics can debunk this divisive fabrication.

This book does not depend on the specific language of a single treaty, however applicable it may be—"not in any sense founded on the Christian religion" is admirably clear. Nor will it focus on the first myth, that America is a Christian nation. According to Bertrand Russell, religious apologists "try to make the public forget their earlier obscurantism, in order that their present obscurantism may not be recognized for what it is."[92] So do Christian nationalists.[93] They abandon their earlier obscurantism, the first myth, in favor of a new one: the subtler argument that our nation is founded on Judeo-Christian principles. Christian nationalism hinges on this second myth and, unlike the first, it is broadly accepted.

This second myth is the focus of this book because it pervades all other Christian nationalist arguments. If America is not founded on Judeo-Christian principles, it is not a Christian nation. If America is not founded on Judeo-Christian principles, Christian nationalists are wrong. And although other authors have refuted the first fiction, the second remains untouched. This book seeks to change that by comparing the principles of Judeo-Christianity and the principles upon which the United States of America was founded. By focusing on the central tenets, the core ideas, of America and Judeo-Christianity, the first myth—America as a "Christian nation"—will necessarily be tested, as will the relevance of the founding fathers' personal religious choices. But those issues are subsumed in the second, greater question, the question the "nine commandments" judge never had to answer: did Judeo-Christian principles positively influence the founding of the United States?

No, they did not. America was not founded on Judeo-Christian principles. In fact, Judeo-Christian principles, especially those central to the Christian nationalist identity, are thoroughly opposed to the principles on which the United States was built. The two systems differ and conflict to such a degree that, to put it bluntly, Christianity is un-American.

Not only is it fair to say that Judeo-Christian principles are un-American, we must. The word "un-American" might make some squeamish because of the value judgment inherent in it. But America is in a fight for its values—its soul, if you prefer—and Christian nationalism is warping and torturing those values, dragging this country down a dark hole. To hesitate to describe this identity with apt phrases because they may be unpleasant is to cede the American identity to an imposter. To refuse to label that which is antithetical to America is to watch Christian nationalists hijack our nation.

Previous books offered gentle corrections to the Christian nationalist: Here's what history tells us, here's what the founders actually meant, here's what the founders actually said. And they've left it at that. But correction is not enough—otherwise we wouldn't have a President

Trump. No, pointing out errors is insufficient. This book does so, but then it takes the next step. It goes on the offensive. This book is an assault on the Christian nationalist identity. Not only are Christian nationalists wrong, but their beliefs and identity run counter to the ideals on which this nation was founded.

This book is an assault, but it's also a defense, a defense of that quintessentially American invention, the "wall of separation between church and state." I am a watcher on that wall. As a constitutional attorney with the Freedom From Religion Foundation, I defend the First Amendment to the US Constitution by ensuring that government officials do not use the power of a public office to promote their personal religion. It is my duty to take alarm at the first experiment on our liberties. We handle thousands of state/church complaints every year. Without fail, recalcitrant violators and their vocal supporters argue that they can impose prayer on kindergartners or pass out bibles in public schools or display the Ten Commandments on public property because this is a Christian nation founded on Christian principles. In short, I rebut this claim for a living, and I've dedicated my career to this fight because it is so important.

What I'm *Not* Arguing

It is important to understand the arguments this book is not making. Our country's government and laws are distinct from its society and culture. It is the difference between our constitutional (or legal) identity and our popular (or social, or cultural) identity. This book does not argue that religion is absent from our culture. Indeed, some of the founders thought religion was necessary for an ordered society (as we shall see, this belief was both elitist and mistaken). However, this book will argue that religion is absent from our constitutional identity and that much of the Christian religion conflicts with that identity.

That constitutional identity is not fully realized, and this book does not argue otherwise. Many of America's founding principles are aspirational, or were for a long time. Since the American founding, successive generations have failed to fully implement the values, leaving it to their children to conquer human tragedies like slavery, segregation, and the subjugation of half the American population. We've made progress toward including all people in "We the People" and have made strides toward genuine equality, but there is still work to be done. Those as-yet-unmet goals do not alter America's founding principles; rather, they speak to our ability and appetite to realize those principles.

This book will also not revisit that well-trod territory of Judeo-Christianity's role in important campaigns like the abolitionist and civil rights movements. Many books have been written about religion's role in those movements while seeming to ignore religion's contribution to the need for those movements in the first place. It's a bit like praising a child for cleaning up his messy room. Religion helped perpetuate slavery in the first place, as we'll see in chapters 17 and 24. Religion did not create slavery—war, economics, racism, poverty, and many more explanations for slavery have been advanced. But religion did provide a moral justification for American slavery. Plenty of historians and authors have focused on the cleanup while ignoring who made the mess. It may seem that this book blames all of society's ills on religion, but that is simply because I am focusing on the side of the ledger that is typically ignored. Religion has much to answer for.

In short, this book considers the accepted narrative of America's founding from a new angle, one that does not assume religion is a positive influence on the world. I am an atheist with reasoned, thoughtful objections to religion. I do not think religious beliefs should be immune from criticism, even when analyzed from a historical perspective. Religious beliefs are ideas like any other, though they are defended more fervently and can often seem immune to reasoned argument. This book will treat religion like any other idea: not with contempt, but not with undue respect either. Christian nationalism has succeeded in part because of Americans' ingrained unwillingness to offend religious sensibilities. But catering to these sensibilities limits our search for the truth, as does religion itself. There is strength in throwing off those self-imposed restraints.

Of course, irreverence is not enough. This book presents the facts. The endnotes are extensive, though the important substance is in the text, not the citations. Wherever possible for the founding era, citations are to original sources. If no original source could be found, the point cannot be found in this book.

One of the paradoxes of writing a book like this is that simply stating facts and relating history from original sources will be seen as an attack on Judeo-Christianity. The destruction of a beloved myth is no more persecution than the erosion of an unwarranted privilege. Many conservative American Christians fail to grasp these distinctions and, as a result, they are gripped by a morbid persecution complex. Every new instance of equality—every time a Christian government employee is told to obey the Constitution, every unconstitutional religious display removed from government property—becomes another talking point of the persecuted majority: the same majority that is over-represented at every level of American government. When Trump told the Values Voter Summit in 2017, "We are stopping cold the attacks on Judeo-Christian values," he was referring as much to books like this as he was to store clerks not saying Merry Christmas.[94] *The Founding Myth* is not a work of academic history but an argument, an attack. Specifically, it is an attack on Christian nationalism.

The Argument in Brief

This book takes seriously JFK's warning about holding fast to the clichés of our forebears. It is time to subject the second myth—that America was founded on Judeo-Christian principles—to the discomfort of scrutiny.[95] This book will analyze Judeo-Christian principles and compare them to American principles to see if there is agreement or positive influence.

First, we examine America's pre-constitutional era, beginning with the founders. We will not attempt to provide an in-depth examination of the founding fathers and their religion, which would be a book itself, but some discussion is inevitable. In looking at the founders' personal views on religion, which are largely irrelevant, and their views on religion's role in society, which were largely misguided, we find that the Christian nationalist's argument is both wrong and disrespectful to those founders. The founders' beliefs about the separation of state and church and political science, not their personal religious beliefs, are most important.

The Declaration of Independence and even its quasi-religious language, examined next, are opposed to biblical law. Then we'll step back and survey colonial history, where we find true Christian nations—the colonies—founded on Christian principles. Those Christian governments were so tyrannical that they became examples for the founders of how *not* to build a nation.

Next, we turn to the bastion of Judeo-Christian principles, the bible, and compare some of its fundamental principles—the Golden Rule, obedience to god, crime and punishment, original sin, redemption through Jesus's sacrifice, faith, and biblical governments—to America's founding principles. The comparison is disastrous for Christian nationalists.

Then we scrutinize each of the Ten Commandments to see how they stack up against America's founding principles. The few principles that appear both in the decalogue and in America's judicial and legislative system—the prohibitions on murder, theft, lying—are not uniquely or originally Judeo-Christian. The exclusively Judeo-Christian principles are actually opposed to American principles.

The book concludes with a look at some unavoidable American verbiage: "in God we trust," "one nation under God," and "God bless America." These are not founding principles, but simply relics of Christian nationalists' using government offices to promote their religion during times of fear, strife, and diminished civil rights.

Usage Note

Capitalization was used deliberately in this book, not as a way to slight religion, but as a way to accurately reflect how we ought to write about religion. The founders overused capital letters, often adhering to a personal style that befuddles the modern reader. I will try to avoid that mistake.

There are many different bibles, thesauri, and dictionaries. There is *Roget's Thesaurus*, the *Oxford English Dictionary*, the King James Bible, and the New Revised Standard Version. But there is no Bible with a capital *B*, just as there is no Thesaurus or Dictionary. For this book, I chose to quote the New Revised Standard Version. When a particular bible is written about, its name will be capitalized; otherwise it will not. Nor should it be. Despite the word's ancient Greek root (*biblia*, plural of *biblion*, book), the bible is not *the* book. It might be for some, but certainly not for all. The mechanics of writing and grammar should not be dictated by the edicts of one religious sect.

The same is true of the word *god*. While I may be writing of *your god*, I would not capitalize *your husband, your wife, your mother, your father,* and so forth. If I were to name that god—YHWH, Jesus, Allah, Thor, Vishnu, Apollo, Hermes, Zeus, and so on—the initial capital would be appropriate. It is proper mechanics to not capitalize the title *president* unless one is naming a specific president—President George Washington. Refusing to capitalize *god* is not a mark of disrespect; it is simply an assumption that one religion is not more true than another. It treats religions equally.

When quoting others, I will capitalize as they did.

The phrases *founders, founding fathers,* and *framers* are loaded terms, but are difficult to avoid when writing a book of this kind. (Note: these terms will also be lowercase in this book.) Take each use with a healthy dose of skepticism. For the sake of simplicity and at the expense of accuracy, we tend to group the founders as a homogeneous unit. The term *founders* itself assumes what was rarely true—that all the founders agreed. But they disagreed on nearly every issue. The political divisions in George Washington's cabinet crystallized into America's first two political parties. Jefferson and Adams—two men so pivotal in uniting the colonies and declaring independence—became such bitter political opponents that they did not write to each other for twelve years. (Happily, they resumed their correspondence and friendship, leaving us a wealth of correspondence from 1812 until their death on the same day, the fiftieth anniversary of July 4, 1776.) The terms are also politically loaded. *Founding fathers* was popularized in religious campaign speeches by President Warren G. Harding: "I must utter my belief in the divine inspiration of the founding fathers. Surely there must have been God's intent in the making of this new-world republic."[96]

Using this terminology also presents a host of questions that are rarely answered. Who qualifies to rank among the founders? Does the pantheon include everyone who signed a founding document? If so, which document or documents? The Declaration of Independence or the Constitution? Only six men signed both. What about the Articles of Confederation? What about the people who were present for the debates on those documents but who did not sign or who refused to sign? What about those who had an important contribution and impact, like Thomas Paine, but who neither debated nor signed? Should greater weight be given to those who were more instrumental—for instance James Madison, who wrote most of the Constitution, defended it in *The Federalist Papers*, and was the force behind the Bill of Rights? What about someone like Vice President Aaron Burr, who was an active politician and altered our history, but contributed less to the development of ideas and the debates that shaped our country?

So please do not abandon reason when reading that term in this book. Assume that I'm referring to the major founders or a majority of the founders, and by all means, disagree with me.

PART I

THE FOUNDERS, INDEPENDENCE, AND THE COLONIES

"There is a fierce custody battle going on out there
for the ownership of the Founding Fathers."
—Joseph Ellis, historian and author[1]

"From the beginning men used God to justify the unjustifiable."
—Salman Rushdie, *The Satanic Verses*, 1988[2]

1

Interesting and Irrelevant, the Religion of the Founders

"The foundation of our Empire was not laid in the gloomy age
of Ignorance and Superstition, but at an Epoch when
the rights of mankind were better understood and more
clearly defined, than at any former period."

— George Washington circular, June 8, 1783[3]

"Washington, you know is gone!"[4] announced Mason Locke Weems, an Episcopal priest, to his Philadelphia publisher. The indecent glee of Weems's exclamation point was matched by the unseemly haste with which he wrote, penning his note in mid-January, a month after Washington's death on December 14, 1799.

In that exclamatory note, Weems told his publisher: "Millions are gaping to read something about him. I am very nearly prim[e]d & cock[e]d for 'em."[5] In an earlier exchange, Weems proposed publishing biographies of the American Revolution's military stars, which would "without doubt, sell an immense number."[6] Weems had reason to know. In addition to preaching, Weems sold schoolbooks, almanacs, and popular literature as he wandered the new United States.[7] He also published salacious tracts on gambling and masturbation: "God's Revenge Against Gambling" and the apparently ribald tract entitled "Onania."[8] Historian Sylvia Neely has observed that Weems "recognized the money-making potential of schoolbooks and wanted to produce exciting stories of adventure and romance that young people would devour."[9] Weems was interested in profit, not accuracy.

When Weems published *A History of the Life and Death, Virtues and Exploits of General George Washington* in 1800, it was a commercial venture. He wrote what people wanted to read. And it worked. Far more sensationalist than truthful, the book sold well, going through some eighty editions.[10] Weems expanded the initially small pamphlet in those subsequent editions. One addition is the book's most well-known story—that Washington couldn't tell a lie about a cherry tree. Ironically, given its moral, the story is untrue.[11]

By the seventeenth edition, another Weemsian fable was added: General Washington praying in the Valley Forge snow.[12] According to Weems's story, "in a dark natural bower of ancient oaks," Washington was discovered praying aloud, "on his knees at prayer."[13]

The story was repeated and reprinted with no regard for truth; its proliferation accelerated during the nation's religious revival from 1820 to 1860. That revival, referred to as the Second Great Awakening, was itself an indication that the founding generation was not as religious as Christian nationalists often argue: only those who are asleep can awaken.

For decades, America's best-selling school textbooks, the McGuffey Readers, edited by educator William Holmes McGuffey (and later reprinted by Henry Ford), included the Valley Forge story, ensuring that it would be read by millions of children.[14] McGuffey was also an ordained Presbyterian minister and used his textbooks to inculcate religion. For McGuffey, Christianity was "the religion of our country. . . . On its doctrines are founded the peculiarities of our free institutions."[15] He warned teachers and parents to avoid "teaching to our pupils the crude notions and revolutionary principles of modern infidelity."[16] As Edward G. Lengel, editor of Washington's papers, noted, "In retelling Weems's stories, McGuffey simplified their morals and turned them into generic Sunday school lessons, putting Washington's piety on constant display."[17] McGuffey's work led to other displays of Washington's conjured piety.

The Valley Forge prayer scene has been painted by Lambert Sachs (c. 1854); Henry Brueckner (c. 1866); J. C. Leyendecker (1935); and Arnold Friberg (1975). It appeared on stamps in 1928 and in 1977. The George Washington Memorial Chapel was founded in Valley Forge in 1903 partly to commemorate "the inspiring image of a solitary and steadfast Washington kneeling in the snow at Valley Forge."[18] The US Capitol's Congressional Prayer Room, built in 1955 (see page 280), features a stained-glass window depicting the scene. Ronald Reagan called the image of Washington kneeling in the snow at Valley Forge "the most sublime picture in American history."[19]

For all its ubiquity, there is no historical evidence to support the tale. Weems designed the story to portray a devout Washington. In Lengel's enlightening book *Inventing George Washington*, he writes, "Over and again, Weems emphasized Washington's Christian upbringing, frequent prayers, and spiritual dependence on God."[20] But historical facts tell us of a different Washington. He was a man of little or no religion with a strong character that, had he been religious, would have prevented showy religious displays. Washington "avoided referring to Jesus Christ in his letters, attended religious services irregularly, did not kneel during prayer, and often dodged out of church before communion," according to Lengel.[21]

On the rare occasions when Washington actually attended church (perhaps twelve times a year pre-presidency and only three times in his last three years), Washington refused to take communion, even though his wife did.[22] Bishop William White officiated in some of the churches Washington occasionally attended. When asked specifically if Washington was a "communicant of the Protestant Episcopal church," White wrote, "truth requires me to say, that Gen. Washington never received the communion, in the churches of which I am the parochial minister. Mrs. Washington was an habitual communicant."[23] The bishop concluded in another letter that no "degree of recollection will bring to my mind any fact which would prove General Washington to have been a believer in the Christian revelation."[24]

Washington refused to have a priest or religious rituals at his deathbed, a startling lapse if he were truly devout. As historian Joseph Ellis put it, "there were no ministers in the room, no prayers uttered, no Christian rituals offering the solace of everlasting life. . . . He died as a Roman stoic rather than a Christian saint."[25]

If he was religious, Washington was exceedingly private about those beliefs, even in personal letters and papers. He mentions Jesus perhaps once in ninety volumes of letters and papers, and never in private correspondence.[26] The ostentatious show Weems invented is simply not in keeping with Washington's strong, silent character. As

Ron Chernow, Washington's Pulitzer Prize–winning biographer, notes in *Washington: A Life*:

> Some of Washington's religious style probably reflected an Enlight-
> enment discomfort with religious dogma, but it also reflected his
> low-key personal style. He was sober and temperate in all things,
> distrusted zealotry, and would never have talked of hellfire or dam-
> nation. He would have shunned anything, such as communion,
> that might flaunt his religiosity. He never wanted to make a spec-
> tacle of his faith or trade on it as a politician. Simply as a matter
> of personal style he would have refrained from the emotional lan-
> guage associated with evangelical Christianity. This cooler, more
> austere religious manner was commonplace among well-heeled
> Anglicans in eighteenth-century Virginia.[27]

One of the many interpretations of the Valley Forge prayer
story: a lithograph by Frederick Heppenheimer titled
Washington at Valley Forge, c. 1853.

The Weemsian myth is disrespectful, particularly when one understands how Washington worked ceaselessly to perfect his own character, because the fable reflects Weems's character, not Washington's. As W. W. Abbot, another editor of Washington's papers, explains, "More than most, Washington's biography is the story of a man constructing himself."[28] Washington worked tirelessly to better himself. He woke early, studied etiquette and sought to improve his own manners, deliberately mastered elegant penmanship, fastidiously attended to his personal appearance, and carefully weighed options before deciding. He personified measured self-control, silence, and thoughtful deliberation, though he was apparently a sight to behold when he lost his temper. The character Weems portrays is a shade. Those who would honor Washington ought to condemn these myths and remember what Abigail Adams said on his death: "Simple truth is his best, his greatest eulogy."[29]

The prayer story, as historian François Furstenberg notes, "almost certainly sprung from Weems's imagination."[30] But Weems was not writing to capture Washington's true character.[31] He wanted to capitalize on the name and death of a greater man, to write about what people wanted to buy. But the story survives for reasons other than Weems's initial pecuniary interest: by imbuing Washington's hard-won character with the kind of ostentatious piety he shunned, it dragged the incomparable leader down to an imitable level. "Perhaps sensing something too stern and difficult about the real Washington, Weems tried to humanize him through treacly fables," suggests Chernow.[32] This facile, reflected glory is why the fraudulent scene hangs in the Capitol prayer room, why Reagan gushed over a lie, and why all a politician need do is claim to be a prayerful Christian and he is suddenly Washington's equal.

Weems's salvo began a long written war between authors and historians over the founders' religiosity. George Washington, Benjamin Franklin, Thomas Jefferson, John Adams, James Madison, and others are invoked in the attempt to claim this nation as Christian because they were Christian. This spiritual wrangling has a checkered history, with each generation repeating the falsehoods of the earlier, including Weems's.[33]

Though interesting, the battle over what the founders personally believed is irrelevant to the claim that our nation was founded
on Judeo-Christian principles. That the founders had personal beliefs
about religion and god does not prove that they used those principles to found a nation. Nor should we make the mistake of assuming
that their religious beliefs were static throughout their lives. People's
beliefs change. Two of my good friends, authors Dan Barker and Jerry
Dewitt, were once preachers and are now atheists. It is unlikely that at
age fifty-eight Washington had the same beliefs he'd held at eighteen.
Even were we to concede, for the sake of argument, that the founders
were all Christian, the logic required to prove the Christian nationalist
argument is flawed:

> *Major Premise* The founders were all devout, Jesus-has-risen
> Christians.
>
> *Minor Premise* The founders established this nation.
>
> *Conclusion* Therefore, this nation is a Christian nation founded on
> Judeo-Christian principles.

One's personal theistic beliefs do not "own" the other ideas gen-
erated by one's mind. By that same logic, blue jeans would be "Jewish
Blue Jeans" because the inventors of the pants, Jacob W. Davis and Levi
Straus, happened to be Jewish. If we follow this illogic—that a person's
religion informs all their other ideas—why limit it to religion? Why
not argue that America is a nation of hair-powderers and wig-wearers?
And why limit the logic to suggesting that religion informs the nation?
Why not claim that the founders built a Christian outhouse or planted
a Judeo-Christian vegetable garden? Of course, designing a nation is
different from designing a pair of jeans, but religion cannot be assumed
to influence either. Those religious beliefs must be examined and compared against the principles that informed the design. To argue that
the founders were Christian is irrelevant because it does not answer the
ultimate question about Christianity's influence on America's founding. And even if the founders were all Christian and this fallacious logic
held, we *know* that they never cited biblical principles during the constitutional convention and ratifications, as we'll see in Chapter Six.[34]

The religious faith of the founders is irrelevant for another reason: they made it irrelevant when they erected a "wall of separation" between religion and the government they created.[35] The Constitution deliberately rejects commingling religion and government. The Constitution severed religion's power from the government to limit the danger it would pose; separates church and state;[36] prohibits a religious test for public office;[37] and, as Alexander Hamilton put it, gives the president "no particle of spiritual jurisdiction."[38] The same is true of Congress; it has limited, enumerated powers, no scintilla of which are religious.[39]

Two facts illustrate the founders' intentions to build this wall. First, our Constitution is deliberately godless. There are no references to gods, goddesses, or divine intervention.[40] The omission was not an oversight. Supernatural power was rejected in favor of the natural power contained in the first three words: "We the People." Civil War colonel, author, and orator Robert Ingersoll best captured the deliberate beauty of this omission:

> They knew that to put God in the constitution was to put man out. They knew that the recognition of a Deity would be seized upon by fanatics and zealots as a pretext for destroying the liberty of thought. They knew the terrible history of the church too well to place in her keeping, or in the keeping of her God, the sacred rights of man. They intended that all should have the right to worship, or not to worship; that our laws should make no distinction on account of creed. They intended to found and frame a government for man, and for man alone. They wished to preserve the individuality and liberty of all, to prevent the few from governing the many, and the many from persecuting and destroying the few.[41]

The second fact is that our Constitution's only references to religion are exclusionary. It excludes the state from involving itself in religion (the First Amendment's "free exercise" clause) and excludes religion from involving itself in the state (the First Amendment's "establishment" clause: "Congress shall make no law respecting an establishment of religion"). The separation of state and church was woven into the constitutional design even before the First Amendment was drafted. The prohibition on religious tests in Article VI, Clause 3—"No religious test shall ever be required as a qualification to any office or public trust under the United States"—was the only mention of religion in the original document. The Constitution often uses malleable language, but this prohibition is "the most emphatic statement in the document."[42]

"No . . . shall . . . ever . . . any." These words are a mandate. Joseph Story, Supreme Court Justice from 1812 to 1845, wrote the first definitive commentaries on the Constitution. He explained that the clause was "not introduced merely for the purpose of satisfying the scruples of many respectable persons, who feel an invincible repugnance to any religious test." According to Story, "It had a higher objective: to cut off for ever every pretence of any alliance between church and state in the national government."[43]

Divorcing religion from government offices was so important that the US Congress edited the word god out of its oath of office. The first bill Congress passed under the Constitution that President George Washington signed into law in June 1789 was "An Act to regulate the Time and Manner of administering certain Oaths." As originally proposed, it had two clauses mentioning god: "in the presence of Almighty GOD" and "So help me God."[44] Neither made the final cut, and the oath remains godless until 1862 (see chapter 24).

The federal experiment with state-church separation was so successful that the states began to follow along. Other than New York and Virginia, arguably the two most important, the original states had religious tests for public office, and none had godless constitutions.[45] But they also all predated the federal Constitution. As they updated and amended those constitutions, the states began to follow the federal model of state-church separation, abolishing religious tests for public office, prohibiting taxpayer funds from flowing to churches and houses of worship, and, with this separation and secularization, guaranteeing the freedom of religion. There is no freedom of religion without a government that is free from religion.

The idea of government separate from religion was floating around during the Enlightenment. John Locke, Montesquieu, Voltaire, Denis Diderot, and the greats of the day discussed it. But while other ideas in political science had real-world antecedents on which the founders could rely, there was no example of a truly secular government. No other nation had sought to protect the ability of its citizens to think freely by separating the government from religion and religion from the government. Until the theory was put into practice, true freedom of thought and even freedom of religion could not have existed. The United States realized those concepts because it embarked "upon a great and noble experiment . . . hazarded in the absence of all previous precedent—that of total separation of Church and State," according to President John Tyler.[46] America was the first nation to try this experiment; it invented the separation of state and church. Pulitzer Prize–winning author Garry Wills put it nicely:

> That [separation], more than anything else, made the United States a new thing on earth, setting new tasks for religion, offering it new opportunities. Everything else in our Constitution—separation of powers, balanced government, bicameralism, federalism—had been anticipated both in theory and practice. . . . But we invented nothing, except disestablishment. No other government in history had launched itself without the help of officially recognized gods and their state-connected ministers.[47]

Americans should celebrate this "great American principle of eternal separation."[48] It's ours. It's an American original. We ought to be proud of that contribution to the world, not bury it under myths.

The founders' private religious beliefs are far less important to the Judeo-Christian question than their views on separating state and church and the actions they took to divorce those two institutions. They were as close to consensus on separating the two as they were on any subject. In the first volume of *The Decline and Fall of the Roman Empire*, published the same year that America declared independence, historian Edward Gibbon wrote that "the various forms of worship, which prevailed in the Roman world, were all considered by the people to be equally true, by the philosopher as equally false, and by the magistrate as equally useful."[49] Most of the founders agreed with Gibbon and recognized that religion can be exploited for political gain and that religion, when it has civil power, is often deadly. These beliefs were common among the founders, but not universal. Benjamin Rush, a signer of the Declaration, believed that "the Christian religion should be preferred to all others" and that "every family in the United States [should] be furnished at public expense . . . with a copy of an American edition of the BIBLE."[50] However, in spite of, or likely because of, their divergent religious beliefs and backgrounds, the founders thought that separation made sense.

George Washington promised "that no one would be more zealous than myself to establish effectual barriers against the horrors of spiritual tyranny. . . . Every man . . . ought to be protected in worshipping the Deity according to the dictates of his own conscience."[51] A few weeks after issuing the nation's first Thanksgiving proclamation—at Congress's official command—Washington responded to a letter from Presbyterian ministers in Massachusetts and New Hampshire. They expressed their approval for the Thanksgiving proclamation and their dismay that "some Explicit acknowledgement of the only true God and Jesus Christ" was absent from the American Magna Carta—the Constitution.[52] In his response, Washington observed "that the path of true piety is so plain as to require but little political direction. To this consideration we ought to ascribe the absence of any regulation, respecting religion, from the Magna-Charta of our country."[53] He continued, writing of piety, "To the guidance of the ministers of the gospel this important object is, perhaps, more properly committed."[54]

Washington thought that religion was best left to the private sphere. He defended the Constitution's godlessness. The government would "give every furtherance" to "morality and science," which might incidentally advance religion, but religion was a personal, not a government matter.[55]

The Constitution separated state and church even before the First Amendment reinforced that separation, as Alexander Hamilton explained in *The Federalist*. Advocating ratification of the Constitution, Hamilton compared the powers of the new office of president of the United States to the powers of the king of Great Britain. "The one has no particle of spiritual jurisdiction; the other is the supreme head and governor of the national church!" he exclaimed.[56] Hamilton "sounded a theme that was to resonate straight through the Revolution and beyond: that the best government posture toward religion was one of passive tolerance, not active promotion of an established church," according to Ron Chernow, who is Hamilton's biographer as well as Washington's.[57]

Jefferson wrote the very metaphor our courts use to interpret the government's relation to religion: "I contemplate with sovereign reverence that act of the whole American people [the First Amendment] which declared that their legislature should 'make no law respecting an establishment of religion, or prohibiting the free exercise thereof,' thus building a wall of separation between Church & State."[58] Jefferson also authored the Virginia Statute for Religious Freedom, upon which the First Amendment would be based. That law, along with the University of Virginia and the Declaration of Independence, were the only achievements he wanted inscribed on his gravestone. The statute guaranteed religious freedom by guaranteeing a secular government. In the statute, Jefferson skewered "the impious presumption of legislators and rulers, civil as well as ecclesiastical, who being themselves but fallible and uninspired men, have assumed dominion over the faith of others, setting up their own opinions and modes of thinking as the only true and infallible, and as such endeavouring to impose them on others."[59] The law ensured:

1. that there would be no governmental support of religion ("to compel a man to furnish contributions of money for the propagation of opinions, which he disbelieves is sinful and tyrannical");

2. that the government could not take away a citizen's rights because of their opinion on religion ("our civil rights have no dependence on our religious opinions any more than our opinions in physics or geometry"); and

3. that religious tests for public office were prohibited ("proscribing any citizen as unworthy [of] the public confidence, by laying upon him an incapacity . . . unless he profess or renounce this or that religious opinion, is depriving him injuriously of those privileges and advantages, to which . . . he has a natural right.")

In 1785, six years after Jefferson first proposed the statute for religious freedom, Madison shepherded it through the state legislature
(as he would later push the First Amendment through the House),
making Virginia the first state to separate government and religion.
The statute was unique in another respect. It was less a declaration
of positive law and more a declaration of a natural right: "the rights
hereby asserted, are of the natural rights of mankind, and that if any
act shall be hereafter passed to repeal the present or to narrow its operation, such act will be an infringement of natural right." Relying on
natural law to protect rights was a Jeffersonian motif, as we shall see in
chapters 3 and 4 on the Declaration of Independence.

Madison is not only the Father of the Constitution and the Father
of the Bill of Rights, but also perhaps the greatest advocate for the
separation of state and church. "Every new & successful example therefore of a perfect separation between ecclesiastical and civil matters,
is of importance;" he wrote in 1822, adding, "And I have no doubt
that every new example, will succeed, as every past one has done, in
showing that religion & Govt. will both exist in greater purity, the less
they are mixed together."[60] Madison argued that the separation existed
as much to protect religion as to protect government. In response to a
sermon he received from a New York clergyman, Madison wrote that
"the United States is a happy disproof of the error so long rooted in the
unenlightened minds of well-meaning Christians, as well as in the corrupt hearts of persecuting usurpers, that without legal incorporation of
religious and civil polity, neither could be supported."[61]

As president, Madison vetoed two bills granting land to churches.
He set down the reason for his vetoes in an 1811 letter to several Baptist churches in North Carolina. He wrote that he had "always regarded
the practical distinction between Religion and Civil Government as
essential to the purity of both, and as guaranteed by the Constitution
of the United States."[62] For Madison, the tendency of government and
religion to mix and corrupt each other is so great "that the danger
cannot be too carefully guarded against."[63]

James Madison also wrote the greatest defense of the wall of separation. His anonymously published essay of 1785, "Memorial and
Remonstrance against Religious Assessments," convinced the people

of Virginia to vote against the bill giving financial support to Christian ministers. The Supreme Court consistently cites the "Memorial" when interpreting the religion clauses of the First Amendment. "Pride and indolence in the Clergy, ignorance and servility in the laity, in both, superstition, bigotry and persecution" were the "fruits" of fifteen centuries of established Christianity, Madison wrote.[64] Echoing Gibbon, he observed, "Rulers who wished to subvert the public liberty, may have found an established Clergy convenient auxiliaries."[65] But it wasn't just about keeping religion out of government. Madison urged the government not to legislate religious matters either. Doing so "implies either that the Civil Magistrate is a competent Judge of Religious Truth; or that he may employ Religion as an engine of Civil policy. The first is an arrogant pretension . . . the second an unhallowed perversion of the means of salvation."[66] Separation benefits all sides.

Incidentally, according to the Episcopal bishop of Virginia, William Meade, who knew the Madison family, James Madison's "religious feeling" was "short lived" because of "his political associations with those of infidel principles, of whom there were many in his day."[67] According to the bishop at least, infidel principles, not Judeo-Christian principles, influenced the Father of the Constitution.

THAT THE FOUNDERS SOUGHT TO BUILD this wall of separation does not necessarily mean that they were personally irreligious. One can be religious and endorse this separation. Indeed, many minority religious sects favored separation at the founding. Madison's 1811 letter to Baptist churches in North Carolina explaining his church land grant veto was actually a reply. Those churches had written first to congratulate Madison for vetoing "a grant of public land to the Baptist Church at Salem Meeting House, Mississippi Territory." Baptists were objecting to public land going to Baptists and thanking the president for vetoing the deal. In that reply, Madison commended the Baptist sect for favoring separationism: "Among the various religious societies in our Country, none has been more vigilant or constant in maintaining that distinction [i.e., the separation] than the Society of which you make a part, and it is an honorable proof of your sincerity and integrity, that you are as ready to do so in a case favoring the interest of your brethren as in other cases."[68] Even some Roman Catholics were for strict separation. When the First Congress was debating the First Amendment, one of only three Catholics in Congress, Representative Daniel Carroll of Maryland, was "very much in favor" of the separation because "the rights of conscience are, in their nature, of peculiar delicacy, and will little bear the gentlest touch of governmental hand."[69] (Senator Charles Carroll of Maryland and Representative Thomas Fitzsimmons of Pennsylvania were the other two Catholics, out of ninety members.)

Regardless of their personal religious beliefs, the founders chose to safeguard liberty by "building a wall of separation between Church & State."[70] And according to Supreme Court Justice Felix Frankfurter, writing an opinion in 1948, "Separation means separation, not something less. Jefferson's metaphor in describing the relation between Church and State speaks of a 'wall of separation,' not a fine line easily overstepped."[71] Separation is not a one-way street that allows religion to influence government while preventing government from influencing religion; it is a wall preventing religion from tainting government as well. State and church "will both exist in greater purity, the less they are mixed together," as Madison explained.[72]

2

"Religion and Morality": Religion for the Masses, Reason for the Founders

"In regard to the furtherance of morality, [religion's] utility is, for the most part, problematical. . . . Of course it is quite a different matter if we consider the utility of religion as a prop of thrones; for those where these are held 'by the grace of God,' throne and altar are intimately associated."

—Arthur Schopenhauer, *On Religion: A Dialogue*, 1891[1]

"It is in our lives, and not from our words, that our religion must be read."

—Thomas Jefferson, letter to Mrs. Samuel H. Smith, Monticello, August 6, 1816[2]

Whatever religion, if any, the founders believed in, they agreed that those beliefs were personal, not for public display or political benefit. The founders were not perfect and sometimes expressed their views with language that confuses Christian nationalists. For instance, John Adams seemed to be relying on reason and faith when he wrote in 1787: "The experiment is made, and has completely succeeded; it can no longer be called in question, whether authority in magistrates and obedience of citizens can be grounded on reason, morality, and the Christian religion, without the monkery of priests, or the knavery of politicians."[3] "Eureka!" the Christian nationalist might exclaim, here's a Christian founder talking about a government based on Christianity. But that conclusion lacks the discerning subtlety of the founders. By "Christian religion," Adams meant something like what Jefferson meant when he used similar phrases—the ideals of Jesus, his philosophy, without organized religion—hence Adams's pejorative qualifier "without the monkery of priests." But quotes like these, which pull in two directions, lead to the inevitable aspect of this fight: the religion, or lack thereof, of the founders. We may never know to which group they belonged because, like Washington, many kept their religion to themselves. This reticence may have arisen from the idea that even if they themselves were not orthodox in religion, they thought others should be.

Christian nationalists assert that Christianity was the source of the founders' morality, and that, as a democratic republic, our nation needs religion because it needs a moral people[4] (see page 44). These claims are not only illogical, but also disrespectful on two fronts.

First, the nationalists credit Christianity for the triumph and sacrifice of thoughtful, committed individuals—the men and women who fought the American Revolution and implemented a theory of self-government with its accompanying rights. America is quintessentially a human achievement. The glory and recognition should go to the individuals who realized previously theoretical ideals. God is not responsible for America. Washington, Jefferson, Adams, Madison, Franklin, Hamilton, and thousands more earned that honor. Attributing to a god the sacrifice of that generation diminishes the sacrifice. To call our government "God-given democratic institutions,"[5] as Billy Graham and so many other religious leaders and pandering politicians have done, denigrates the founding generation.

Giving undue glory to a god is nothing new. Within a month of the Battles of Lexington and Concord, Ethan Allen and a nominally in-command Benedict Arnold led Allen's Green Mountain Boys to Canada and captured Fort Ticonderoga. Colonel (later, general) Henry Knox brought more than fifty cannons from the fort to Boston so that Washington could bombard the British blockade. When the British awoke to find Dorchester Heights manned and gunned courtesy of Allen and Knox, they retreated. Together, Washington, Knox, Allen, and the rest of the colonial irregulars had lifted the British Empire's siege of Boston. Shortly after the Ticonderoga victory, the Reverend

Jedediah Dewey preached a long sermon thanking God and giving him credit for the victory. Ethan Allen rose and shouted, "Don't forget, Parson, that I was there!" But Dewey refused to recognize the human side of the accomplishment. He harangued Allen as a "bold blasphemer" for daring to take credit.[6]

But other founders agreed with Allen. Franklin touched on the idea in *Poor Richard's Almanack*: "God helps those who help themselves."[7] (Though not original to Franklin,[8] this advice does not, as three-quarters of Americans believe, come from the bible.[9]) John Jay wrote, "Providence seldom interposes in human affairs but through the agency of human means."[10] And John Adams thought, "Miracles will not be wrought for us. . . . If we will have government, we must use the human and natural means."[11]

The blood and treasure spilled and spent by the founding generation was their own. Abigail Adams, daughter of a clergyman and a founder in her own right, was a religious woman, but refused to ascribe the patriot sacrifice to heaven. In a letter to her husband, she likened the peace after the Revolutionary War to a blanket of freedom: "The garb of this favorite of America, is woven of an admirable texture and proves the great skill, wisdom, and abilities, of the master workmen."[12] But she would not give credit to god, the French, or the English. The peace and liberty were American achievements: "It was not fabricated in the Loom of France, nor are the materials english, but they are the product of our own American soil, raised and Nurtured, not by the gentle showers of Heaven but by the hard Labour and indefatigable industry and firmness of her sons, and watered by the Blood of many of them."[13]

The second reason the claims are inappropriate is that they exclude from the founding pantheon, almost by definition, the contributions of the many founders who were not Christian.[14] Entire shelves of books explore the founders' religious beliefs, with conclusions all over the spectrum.

"It is in our lives, and not from our words, that our religion must be read," Jefferson wrote.[15] If this is true, we should look less to out-of-context quotes and more to the actions of the founders. We've seen that George Washington rarely prayed, attended church, or mentioned Jesus in his correspondence and that he shunned priests at his deathbed. Many people tried to pry some religious endorsement or personal religious information from Washington, but "the old fox was too cunning for them," as Jefferson merrily recalled.[16]

Jefferson rewrote the New Testament using a razor, editing out the supernatural and salvaging what he considered worthy lessons from a mortal man. By his own admission, he excised "the immaculate conception of Jesus, his deification, the creation of the world by him, his miraculous powers, his resurrection and visible ascension, his corporeal presence in the Eucharist, the Trinity, original sin, atonement, regeneration, election, orders of Hierarchy, etc."[17] It was, Jefferson wrote, like pulling "diamonds" from "dunghills."[18]

Gouverneur Morris spoke more than any other delegate to the Constitutional Convention (173 times[19]) and actually penned much of the final wording of the Constitution, including the poetic preamble. He also had sex with a married woman . . . in a convent, hardly respecting the nunnery as a believer would. The peg-legged bon vivant was the US minister plenipotentiary to France in the early 1790s. While there, he carried on a tryst with Adélaïde-Emilie Filleul, Marquise de Souza-Botelho (later Madame de Flahaut). Morris and Adele, as he called her, "had each other whenever they could," notes one biographer, including "in his carriage; and in the visitors' waiting room of a convent in Chaillot where Adele's old governess lived as a nun."[20] On another occasion, Morris visited the married woman and, as he put it, "we perform[ed] the first Commandment given to Adam, or at least we use the means."[21] That is, they didn't actually bear fruit and multiply, but they went through the motions. He got to know her in the biblical sense while violating biblical principles. Another biographer captured Morris's sexual escapades nicely. Flahaut "and Morris were eventually so 'wanton and flagrant' that they engaged in intercourse 'in the passage . . . at the harpsichord . . . down stairs . . . the doors all open,' and in a coach with the coachman staring straight ahead."[22]

Morris's roguery was not merely the result of passion kindled by this particular woman. Morris lost his left leg below the knee after a carriage accident in Philadelphia. According to one story, likely apocryphal and perhaps encouraged by Morris himself, he was fleeing a wrathful husband he had cuckolded at the time of the accident.

Morris's womanizing was so rampant that it led John Jay, one of the more pious founders, to remark that instead of losing his leg in a carriage accident, Jay wished Morris had "lost something else."[23]

Washington's, Jefferson's, and Morris's actions are hardly those of devout, bible-believing Christians.

A MORE INSIDIOUS RATIONALE underlies the Christian nationalist claim about the founders: the myth that only Christians are moral. The argument is that the United States was created by Christians for Christians because only they are moral,[24] that Christianity is required for a moral society. There are two falsehoods tangled up in this claim. The first conflates religion with morality, and the second assumes that the founders did the same.

Religion gets its morality from us, not the other way around. Even today, many people mistakenly believe that morality cannot exist outside of religion.[25] The founders certainly did not make this mistake, as we'll see in a moment. However, some founders did think that religion was necessary, not for themselves, but for the rest of society. This elitist belief does not equate religion and morality or suggest that religion is a prerequisite for moral behavior, but it is often mistakenly read as such by Christian nationalists. For many founders, religion was not the *source* of morality; they thought it was a *substitute* for morality: a substitute for those who didn't have the time and education to discover moral truths on their own. Often, when the founders spoke of "religion and morality," they were speaking not of one thing, but of two separate phenomena—religion for the people, morality for them.

A cursory reading of George Washington's 1796 Farewell Address might give the impression that he thought religion was necessary for society to succeed:

> Of all the dispositions and habits which lead to political prosperity, religion and morality are indispensable supports. . . . Whatever may be conceded to the influence of refined education on minds of peculiar structure, reason and experience both forbid us to expect that national morality can prevail in exclusion of religious principle.[26]

"National morality" here means something akin to societal or collective morality, as opposed to the government as a moral agent. Alexander Hamilton wrote these lines, not George Washington.[27] Hamilton was not referring to the government needing divine aid or religion requiring governmental aid, but to society requiring a morality Hamilton thought religion provided.

This was also less a moral exposition than a political attack on Jefferson's new Republican party. Biographer Ron Chernow has pointed out that these comments "arose from [Hamilton's] horror at the 'atheistic' French Revolution."[28] Interestingly, although Washington included this sentiment in his final speech, he omitted Hamilton's next sentence: "does it [national morality] not require the aid of a generally received and divinely authoritative Religion?"[29] Washington's edit suggests that he believed that any religion, not just Christianity,

An engraving titled *Leaders of the Continental Congress* depicts, from left to right, John Adams, Gouverneur Morris, Alexander Hamilton, and Thomas Jefferson, c. 1894.

could replace morality. The Farewell Address conceives of religion and morality as two separate, distinct things—not as synonyms expressing the same thought, though Christian nationalists misread it that way.

Like Washington and Hamilton, John Adams spoke of religion and morality as distinct. As president, Adams wrote, "Our Constitution was made only for a moral and religious people. It is wholly inadequate to the government of any other."[30] In a later missive to Jefferson, he hypothesized about a world in which the masses were not checked by religion: "Without religion this world would be something not fit to be mentioned in polite society—I mean hell."[31] Though religion would check the masses, Adams did not believe "in the total and universal depravity of human nature, I believe there is no individual totally depraved. . . . While conscience remains there is some religion."[32] This letter, which is worth reading in full, goes on to lament people's credulity, and Adams himself was incredulous that people ever submitted "to be taxed to build the temple of Diana at Ephesus, the pyramids of Egypt, Saint Peter's at Rome, Notre Dame at Paris, [or] St. Paul's in London." Like Washington, Adams suggested that any religion, not only Christianity, can replace morality.

Jefferson did not confuse religion and morality. He organized his library into three major divisions by subject: memory or history, philosophy or reason, and imagination or fine arts. There were numerous subcategories, including ethics. Ethics was further broken down into morality and moral supplements. Religion was assigned to the moral supplements section, along with law (see note for link to original image of his divisions outline).[33] Religion was not morality, but a substitute or supplement. He wrote explicitly about this distinction: "On the dogmas of religion as distinguished from moral principles, all mankind, from the beginning of the world to this day, have been quarreling, fighting, burning and torturing one another, for abstractions unintelligible to themselves and to all others, and absolutely beyond the comprehension of the human mind."[34] (Note: what's left of Jefferson's personal library is now housed in the Library of Congress. It has been partially recreated after a fire, but is similarly organized.)

Washington, Adams, Jefferson, and even Franklin and other founders did not think that religion was the source of morality, but its substitute. Madison, in *The Federalist* number 10, differentiates the two. "If the impulse and the opportunity [to create majority factions] be suffered to coincide," he wrote, "we well know that neither moral nor religious motives can be relied on as an adequate control."[35]

These founders were not saying that religion is the source of morality or that an individual's morality cannot exist without religion. They were claiming that religion is necessary for societal morality.

And they were wrong.

The educated elite, including the founders, achieved morality independent of religion, but they failed to extend the possibility of that achievement to others. They thought religion was needed for the commoners. The enlightened could use reason to discover morality, so they needed no religion other than a bare deism or theism, to which many luminaries ascribed. John Stuart Mill thought that "the world would be astonished if it knew how great a proportion of its brightest ornaments—of those most distinguished even in popular estimation for wisdom and virtue—are complete sceptics in religion."[36] He might have been writing of the founders.

The Pulitzer Prize–winning historian Gordon Wood voiced this view in his book *Revolutionary Characters: What Made the Founders Different* (2006). Wood noted that "one would be hard put to demonstrate the ways [Thomas] Paine's rationalistic religion or deism differed from the religious views of his contemporaries Franklin or Jefferson" and that such views "were common among the liberal-thinking gentlemen of the era."[37] While Paine was open about his views, expounding them in *The Rights of Man*, "Jefferson and other elites" confined their views to that elite circle, fearing that spreading them might undermine society's moral order.[38] While "gentlemen" such as Washington, Jefferson, Madison, Adams, and Franklin were "free of the prejudices, parochialism, and religious enthusiasm of the vulgar and barbaric," the laity was not.[39] Their attitude toward plebeians was patrician, as Wood points out. Washington referred to the masses as the "grazing multitude," Adams spoke of the "common herd of mankind" or "common persons" with no idea of "Learning, Eloquence, and Genius," and Gouverneur Morris thought they had "no morals but their own interests."[40]

Elsewhere Wood observes, "At the time of the Revolution most of the founding fathers had not put much emotional stock in religion, even when they were regular churchgoers. As enlightened gentlemen, they abhorred 'that gloomy superstition disseminated by ignorant illiberal preachers' and looked forward to the day when 'the phantom of darkness will be dispelled by the rays of science, and the bright charms of rising civilization.'"[41]

The founders may have been influenced by Enlightenment thinkers on this subject. We know that both Baruch Spinoza and John Locke profoundly influenced the founders' thinking. Berated as an atheist and drummed out of Jewish society in Holland, Spinoza thought religion "in the highest degree necessary for the common people who lack the ability to perceive things clearly and distinctly."[42] Locke thought that for the "vulgar" and the "mass of mankind" it was better to have divine rules than to "leave it to the long, and sometimes intricate deductions of Reason, to be made out [by] them. Such trains of reasonings the greatest part of mankind have neither the leisure to weigh; nor, for want of education and use, skill to judge of."[43]

Franklin is the most explicit on this point in an undated, unaddressed letter discussing a manuscript that criticized religion—possibly Thomas Paine's *Rights of Man*. Franklin suggested that the letter's recipient, who was also the manuscript's author, "burn this piece before it is seen by any other Person."[44] He explained that he thought religion necessary to ensure that the "weak and ignorant" act ethically.

> You yourself may find it easy to live a virtuous life without the assistance afforded by religion; you having a clear perception of the advantages of virtue, and the disadvantages of vice, and possessing a strength of resolution sufficient to enable you to resist common temptations. But think how great a portion of mankind consists of weak and ignorant men and women, and of inexperienced, inconsiderate youth of both sexes, who have need of the motives of religion to restrain them from vice, to support their virtue, and retain them in the practice of it till it becomes habitual, which is the great point for its security.[45]

Even if the founders were correct in this elitism and people really did need religion to prevent them from running amok, it does not follow that we are a nation founded on Judeo-Christian principles. That a republic requires morality and therefore a moral people, and therefore a religious people, does not mean it requires Christians. The founders' guarantee of religious freedom for all makes it clear that they did not think so either. In fact, these Enlightenment thinkers and the founders they influenced shared an important constant: they did not view religion as valuable because of its truth claims or as a source of morality, but simply as a means of producing good behavior without a reasoned moral analysis. This is a severe blow to the Christian nationalist. Any religion would do; Judeo-Christianity was not special. Montesquieu, the political theorist the founders may have relied on more than any other, perhaps said it best: "even a false religion is the best security we can have of the probity of men."[46]

WHEN REVIEWING THAT IRREVERENT MANUSCRIPT, Franklin rhetorically asked, "If Men are so wicked as we now see them *with Religion* what would they be if *without it?*"[47] [emphasis in original] Here, Franklin's imaginative mind failed him. To be fair, Franklin and the other founders did not have the data we possess today. Social science now unequivocally shows that the less religious a society is, the better off it is. We now *know* that religion is not necessary for a society to succeed.

In a metastudy examining this very question, sociologist Phil Zuckerman explains, "Murder rates are actually lower in more secular nations and higher in more religious nations where belief in God is deep and widespread. And within America, the states with the highest murder rates tend to be highly religious, such as Louisiana and Alabama, but the states with the lowest murder rates tend to be among the least religious in the country, such as Vermont and Oregon. Furthermore, although there are some notable exceptions, rates of most violent crimes tend to be lower in the less religious states and higher in the most religious states. Finally, of the top 50 safest cities in the world, nearly all are in relatively nonreligious countries, and of the eight cities within the United States that make the safest-city list, nearly all are located in the least religious regions of the country."[48]

Additionally, sociologists and Holocaust scholars, "in their studies of heroic altruism during the Holocaust, found that the more secular people were, the more likely they were to rescue and help persecuted Jews."[49] In fact, when any given factor of societal health or well-being is measured, the less religious countries score better. The *least religious* countries:

- Have the lowest rates of violent crime and homicide
- Are the best places to raise children and to be a mother
- Have the lowest rates of corruption
- Have the lowest levels of intolerance against racial and ethnic minorities
- Score highest for women's rights and gender equality
- Have the greatest protection and enjoyment of political and civil liberties
- Are better at educating their youth in reading, math, and science
- Are the most peaceful
- Are the most prosperous
- Have the highest quality of life.[50]

This pattern also exists within the United States. Those states that are the *most religious* have more societal ills, and tend to:

- Have the highest rates of poverty
- Have the highest rates of obesity
- Have the highest rates of infant mortality
- Have the highest rates of STDs
- Have the highest rates of teen pregnancy
- Have the lowest percentage of college-educated adults
- Have the highest rates of murder and violent crime.[51]

This, of course, does not prove that religion causes immoral behavior, but it confirms that religion is not required for people to behave morally.

Author Michael Gaddis relates a story that answers Franklin's fearful question about the wickedness of a human race without religion. In fifth-century Egypt, a Christian monk named Shenoute denounced a local pagan magnate, ransacked his house, and smashed his idols. The pagan accused Shenoute of banditry and he responded, "There is no crime for those who have Christ."[52]

People who believe they are acting in accord with a higher law are giving themselves a license to do anything. That is, as the physicist Steven Weinberg observed, the real danger of religion: "With or without it you would have good people doing good things and evil people doing evil things. But for good people to do evil things, that takes religion."[53]

The founders should have paid more attention to Thomas Paine, who was closer to the mark. Paine wrote, "Accustom a people to believe that priests or any other class of men can forgive sins, and you will have sins in abundance."[54] Sins that can be "forgiven" without real punishment, without the victim's consent, without involving the civil law, are more likely to be committed. (Perhaps this is one reason the Catholic Church is failing so abominably to protect the children in its charge.)

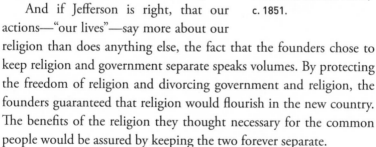

Portrait of Thomas Paine, c. 1851.

And if Jefferson is right, that our actions—"our lives"—say more about our religion than does anything else, the fact that the founders chose to keep religion and government separate speaks volumes. By protecting the freedom of religion and divorcing government and religion, the founders guaranteed that religion would flourish in the new country. The benefits of the religion they thought necessary for the common people would be assured by keeping the two forever separate.

IF THE FOUNDERS BELIEVED THAT RELIGION was important to ensure moral behavior for the masses but not for themselves—the educated elite—it means the founders were moral without religion. It means they built a government using their own morality, not religion. And this eviscerates the Christian nationalist claim.

That the founders did not look to the bible or religion turns out to be an important character trait for the formation of America. The prime movers among the founders showed a liberality and unorthodoxy in religion, a characteristic that often leads one to question other established "truths" such as the legitimacy of a monarchy. There is a strong correlation between reformers and religious heterodoxy.[55] People who are more likely to question the political status quo are more likely to question religion, and vice versa. If the founders had been bible-beating believers, they might never have thought to revolt against an empire and declare independence.

3

Declaring Independence from Judeo-Christianity

"This radical change in the principles, opinions, sentiments, and
affections of the people, was the real American Revolution."
—John Adams, letter to Hezekiah Niles, February 13, 1818[1]

Christian nationalists often argue that the Declaration of Independence embodies Judeo-Christian principles.[2] And, as it is one of our founding documents, they claim that our nation is Judeo-Christian because of the Declaration's religious language—specifically the four references that many read as invoking a supernatural power: "the Laws of Nature and of Nature's God," "endowed by their Creator," "Supreme Judge of the World," and "divine Providence." The truth is both subtler and more exciting.

"The independence of America, considered merely as a separation from England, would have been a matter of but little importance," wrote Thomas Paine.[3] He is correct: the Declaration was not just about political separation. Nor did it establish a new country. Rather, independence was important, as Paine again correctly observed, because it was "accompanied by a revolution in the principles and practices of governments."[4] The Declaration of Independence gave voice to the most important shift in political thought in history, but it did not establish a new nation, a government, or a legal system.[5] The Declaration "dissolve[d] the political bands" that connected the colonies to Great Britain. It did not create; it severed, which is far simpler than nation-building. "It is much easier to pull down a Government, in such a Conjuncture of affairs as We have seen, than to build up," remarked John Adams.[6] The Constitution, not the Declaration, created our government and laws.[7]

In fact, the Declaration cannot even properly be said to have severed the connection with Great Britain. It simply *announced* the separation. Two days before the Declaration was adopted, the Continental Congress approved Richard Henry Lee's resolution, which John Adams had seconded, that "these United Colonies are, and of right ought to be, free and independent States, that they are absolved from all allegiance to the British Crown, and that all political connection between them and the State of Great Britain is, and ought to be, totally dissolved."[8] The vote that approved Lee's resolution (12–0 with New York abstaining) actually severed the political ties.

If the Declaration of Independence didn't create a new nation and it didn't technically declare independence, what was its point? Nearly fifty years after he drafted it, Jefferson wrote about "the object of the Declaration of Independence."[9] It was "[n]ot to find out new principles, or new arguments, never before thought of" or "to say things which had never been said before."[10] It was meant "to place before mankind the common sense of the subject, in terms so plain and firm as to command their assent."[11] It did not aim "at originality of principle or sentiment."[12] Put simply, "it was intended to be an expression of the American mind."[13] Carl Becker, the American historian who wrote the book on the subject—*The Declaration of Independence: A Study in the History of Political Ideas* (1922)—thought that "the primary purpose of the Declaration was not to declare independence, but to proclaim to the world the reasons for declaring independence. It was intended to formally justify an act already accomplished."[14]

It was a justification, and as part of that justification it laid out a political philosophy. That philosophy was not new, but Jefferson's formulation of it was more beautiful, simpler, and more powerful than any previously, and perhaps since, written. The central pillar of this political philosophy—that governments are instituted for and by the people—had never been put fully into practice. But it would be enshrined in the first three words of the Constitution eleven years later and then carved into the American mind forever: "We the People."

The Declaration of Independence had several purposes, but above all, it was written to persuade. It needed "to convince a candid world that the colonies had a moral and legal right to separate from Great

Britain," according to Becker.[15] It also needed to unite the colonies, to meld them into one people by influencing public opinion. Independence would also allow the colonies to treat and trade with other countries. Finally, it may have been a bit of an attempt to convince a king, who believed himself to be a Christian hero and the spiritual head of a church, to end hostilities—not to reconcile, but to stop the war. And it, or at least the philosophy it laid out, was something of a repudiation of the divine right of kings.

The first two purposes—severing the connection with Great Britain and unifying the colonies—are best understood if treated together, because Jefferson accomplished both by explaining the American political philosophy and applying that philosophy to the colonial situation. He took the theoretical construct and put it into concrete terms involving real people. The bulk of the Declaration's 1,300-plus words is dedicated to listing the grievances against the king. But before Jefferson indicted George, he described the logic and the political theory on which the case against George would rest.[16]

The theory is twofold. First, despotic governments can and should be overthrown. Second, people are the source of governmental power and must consent to their government. This is a philosophy of rebellion against arbitrary power, and of self-government. Jefferson wanted the Declaration to be "the signal . . . to burst the chains under which monkish ignorance and superstition had persuaded [men] to bind themselves, and to assume the blessings and security of self-government."[17] As that language indicates and as we'll see, that philosophy makes the Declaration thoroughly anti-biblical. These two philosophical prongs, rebellion and self-government, line up nicely with the Declaration's primary purposes—severing political ties and uniting the colonies.

After spelling out these "truths," Jefferson then fit the British-American relationship within this two-prong philosophy. The first 274 words, beginning with "When in the Course of human events" and continuing until "it is their right, it is their duty, to throw off such Government, and to provide new Guards for their future security," say nothing about Britain or the colonies. Neither is mentioned until the end of the second paragraph, after the philosophy has been laid out. As

Professor Stephen Lucas has observed, the Declaration argues by syllogism. Jefferson argues his major premise first and Britain's violation of that premise second:[18]

> ***Major Premise*** Because governments are instituted to protect citizens' rights, people have a right and a duty to throw off despotic governments and to create "new guards" for those rights.
>
> ***Minor Premise*** The British government is despotic, as the following 28 charges show.
>
> ***Conclusion*** Therefore, the American people have a right and a duty to throw off British rule.

The heavy lifting is done up front. The catalog of crimes validates the end result, but the important ideas and legal rationales come first.

Those are the revolutionary purposes of the Declaration. But there were other purposes as well, including gaining foreign recognition and support. Two years of embargoes and war were destroying the American economy and trade. "Most of the delegates to the Continental Congress regarded the Declaration as a ceremonial confirmation of what had already occurred," writes Pulitzer Prize–winning historian Joseph J. Ellis, adding, "its chief practical value, apart from publicizing a foregone conclusion in lyrical terms, was to enhance the prospects of a wartime alliance with France, and all the revolutionary leaders understood the French alliance to be the urgent issue at the time."[19] After all, who were the colonies? They were distant, rebellious outposts of a vast, powerful empire. At least, that is what other monarchs and countries would believe. What ruler would treat or trade with a group of rogue colonies? Virginia Continental Congressman George Wythe raised this issue a few months before July 1776:

> But other things are to be considered, before such a measure is adopted; in what character shall we treat?—as subjects of Great Britain,—as rebels? Why should we be so fond of calling ourselves dutiful subjects? If we should offer our trade to the Court of France, would they take notice of it any more than if Bristol or

Liverpool should offer theirs, while we profess to be subjects? No. We must declare ourselves a free people.[20]

Samuel Adams worried about this as well: "no foreign Power can consistently yield Comfort to Rebels, or enter into any kind of Treaty with these Colonies till they declare themselves free and independent."[21] The colonies' instructions to delegates at the Continental Congress in Philadelphia show that acquiring foreign aid was an important aim of the Declaration. North Carolina empowered its delegates in April 1776 to "concur with the delegates of the other Colonies in declaring independency and forming foreign alliances."[22] If the colonies wished to continue the war, if they wished to restore and revive trade, they needed a treaty with a foreign power.[23] Negotiating one required declaring independence and achieving legitimacy as a state. The Declaration helped accomplish the first. And Jefferson started the process in the first sentence, when he listed the British and Americans as two separate people: "necessary for *one people* to dissolve the political bands which have connected them with *another*."[24] That treatment, the obvious yet somehow subtle differentiation between two peoples, was a powerful announcement to the world.

Yet one more purpose was to unite the colonies in the war against Britain. In 1776, the citizens who would come to be known as the American people were divided. Some were committed to independence, some were opposed, and some were wavering despite the convincing arguments in Thomas Paine's *Common Sense*. King George issued an ultimatum: "The colonies must either submit or triumph."[25] There was no turning back. If Patrick Henry did, in fact, proclaim "give me liberty or give me death," he was right: the choice was to win or die.[26] Or, as Franklin put it: "Join, or Die." But the people had to be convinced. Adams, Jefferson, Washington, Franklin, and other founders were traitors in the eyes of the king. The Declaration essentially put every citizen on the enemies list. As Franklin may have said, "we must, indeed, all hang together, or most assuredly we shall all hang separately."[27]

Looking back on the revolution forty years later, John Adams wrote about why unification was such a monumental task: "The colonies had grown up under constitutions of government so different, there was so great a variety of religions, they were composed of so many different nations, their customs, manners, and habits had so little resemblance, and their intercourse had been so rare, and their knowledge of each other so imperfect, that to unite them in the same principles in theory and the same system of action, was certainly a very difficult enterprise. The complete accomplishment of it, in so short a time and by such simple means, was perhaps a singular example in the history of mankind. Thirteen clocks were made to strike together—a perfection of mechanism, which no artist had ever before effected."[28]

THE DECLARATION MAY ALSO HAVE BEEN AN ATTEMPT to convince the man who was both a Christian king and the head of the Church of England to stop an unjust war. King George III was not only the titular head of the Church of England, but also a faithful and active supporter.[29] Ecclesiastical debates raged in England during the 1770s, and they helped to bind George's religiosity to his political views, particularly with respect to the American colonies.[30] His opposition to the Revolutionary War stemmed, at least in part, from his opposition to religious heterodoxy.[31]

George conflated morality with "the ideal of a Christian people led by a Christian king," according to biographer Jeremy Black.[32] Throughout the Revolution, George believed that his god would give him strength and protection, writing, "I begin to see that I shall soon have enfused some of that spirit which I thank Heaven ever attends me when under difficulties. . . . I trust in the protection of the Almighty, in the justness of the cause, the uprightness of my own intentions."[33] Black explains that George "took his role and God-given responsibilities as Supreme Governor of the Church very seriously."[34] He was devout, was known for his personal piety, and thought that his god intervened in this world, so he governed according to what he saw as his god's will.[35]

In theory, the divine right of kings was abandoned in England when the Glorious Revolution (1688–89) dethroned the Stuarts. James Wilson—Scottish émigré, founding father, and one of the original six Supreme Court justices—said as much in the Pennsylvania ratifying convention: "Is the executive power of Great Britain founded on representation? This is not pretended. Before the [Glorious] revolution, many of the kings claimed to reign by divine right, and others by hereditary right."[36] Thomas Hobbes, John Locke, and Algernon Sidney had all penned devastating critiques of the divine right, but the idea was still embraced in many quarters. As Becker notes, "In that day kings were commonly claiming to rule by divine right, and according to this notion there could be no 'right' of rebellion."[37] The more religious a monarch, the more likely he would be to think a god had assigned him his rightful place as ruler.

The idea that all people are created equal is not a religious idea; the idea that some people are special or chosen is one that various religious groups have embraced throughout history. The entire Hebrew Bible is about the chosen people. Religion promotes elitism, not equality. So too, the divine right of kings elevated one individual or family over an entire nation. In the Declaration, Jefferson wrote that when a government becomes despotic, "it is the Right of the People to alter or to abolish it, and to institute new Government, laying its foundation *on such principles* and organizing its powers in such form, as to them shall seem most likely to effect their Safety and Happiness." But, despite the Christian nationalists' arguments to the contrary, self-government and revolution against tyranny are not principles derived from Christianity or the bible.

THE DECLARATION OF INDEPENDENCE is an anti-Christian document with snippets of religious-sounding language as window dressing. If Jefferson and the other revolutionaries had been devout Christians, they never would have rebelled, the Declaration would never have been written, and America's political relationship to the United Kingdom today would resemble Canada's. The Christian bible stands directly opposed to the Declaration's central ideas, including that it is "the Right of the People to alter or to abolish [their government], and to institute a new Government."

Paul's letter to the Romans demonstrates this opposition:

Let everyone be subject to the governing authorities, for there is no authority except that which God has established. The authorities that exist have been established by God. Consequently, whoever rebels against the authority is rebelling against what God has instituted, and those who do so will bring judgment on themselves.[38]

Paul claims that governments are instituted for men by god and that rebelling against the government is rebellion against his god. Paul continues, and again he is explicit:

> For the one in authority is God's servant for your good. But if you do wrong, be afraid, for rulers do not bear the sword for no reason. They are God's servants, agents of wrath to bring punishment on the wrongdoer. Therefore, it is necessary to submit to the authorities, not only because of possible punishment but also as a matter of conscience.[39]

Paul could not have been clearer. Rulers, like King George III, must be obeyed as a matter of conscience. The colonies would have nothing to fear so long as they obeyed their ruler. With such threats, it is a wonder that the divine right of kings was ever overturned. If the ruler is not obeyed—if the people revolt—then they will be killed.

Such passages are not outliers; there are more in both the Christian and Hebrew bibles. In the Christian bible we learn that the biblical god must be obeyed first and earthly rulers second: "We must obey God rather than any human authority."[40] But that god is also telling followers to obey earthly rulers. The Hebrew bible says, "By me [God] kings reign, and rulers decree what is just; by me rulers rule, and nobles, all who govern rightly."[41]

This theology is alive and well in Christian nationalism. In what one journalist labeled "a stunning expression of Christian nationalism," President Donald Trump's closest evangelical advisor, Paula White, reiterated these passages to diffuse the constant and justified criticism that Trump is vulgar and undignified: "They say about our president, 'Well, he is not presidential.' Thank goodness . . . he is not a polished politician. In other words, he is authentically—whether people like it or not—has been raised up by God. Because God says that He raises up and places all people in places of authority. It is God who raises up a king. It is God that sets one down. When you fight against the plan of God, you are fighting against the hand of God."[42]

White's words and these bible verses exhibit a servility entirely foreign to the Declaration of Independence, which embodies *contrary* ideas. The political philosophy on which the Declaration is based says people have a "duty to throw off" absolutist governments. Altering the government is at once a "necessity," a "duty," and a "right." Jefferson says that it is "necessary for one people to dissolve the political bands which have connected them with another" and speaks of "the necessity which constrains them to alter their former Systems of Government." Rights, necessities, and duties, not obedience, sin, and submission.

John Adams put it with his customary bluntness in Article 7 of the Massachusetts Constitution's Declaration of Rights: "The people alone have an incontestable, unalienable, and indefeasible right to institute government; and to reform, alter, or totally change the same."[43] Not a god, but the people alone.

Enemies of colonial independence relied on the divine authority of governments. John Lind, an English barrister, refuted the Declaration in a 1776 pamphlet. Lind pointed out that the Declaration does not, indeed cannot, rely on "any law of God":

> What difference these acute legislators suppose between laws of Nature, and of Nature's God, is more than I can take upon me to determine, or even to guess. If to what they now demand they were entitled by any law of God, they had only to produce that law, and all controversy was at an end. Instead of this, what do they produce? What they call self-evident truths, 'All men' they tell us, 'are created equal.'[44]

Jefferson could not rely on any law of god because the laws of god opposed the principles he relied on.

Robert Boucher was an Anglican minister and a Maryland loyalist who moved to England before independence. Like Paula White, he relied on the bible to support the divine right of kings, writing that it is "the uniform doctrine of the Scriptures, that it is under the deputation and authority of God alone that kings reign . . . far from deriving their authority from any supposed consent or suffrage of men, they receive their commission from Heaven; they receive it from God, the source . . . of all power."[45] And he relied on the bible to argue against American independence. Declaring independence was against his god's law because "Obedience to government is every man's duty" though "it is particularly incumbent on Christians, because . . . it is enjoined by the positive commands of God; and therefore, when Christians are disobedient to human ordinances, they are also disobedient to God."[46] No matter how repressive the government, Boucher argued, "it is our duty not to disturb and destroy the peace of the community, by becoming refractory and rebellious subjects, and *resisting the ordinances of God*."[47] According to Boucher, the bible never even discusses government except to say that it must be obeyed, not rebelled against: "The only circumstance relative to government, for which the Scriptures seem to be particularly solicitous, is in inculcating obedience to lawful governors."[48]

The bible undercut the American cause.

The Declaration does not require blind obedience; the bible and the biblical god do. God takes away everything Job has—he kills his children, bankrupts him, sets his skin afire with boils. Job bears this train of abuse by continuing to worship god. This is precisely the opposite of what the Declaration demands: "When a long train of abuses and usurpations, pursuing invariably the same Object evinces a design to reduce them under absolute Despotism, it is their right, it is their duty, to throw off . . ." For the founders, King George III was akin to the biblical god in this situation, abusing the colonies and expecting blind obedience in return.

Religions, particularly established religions or religions to which a majority of the population ascribe, will nearly always oppose revolution because revolution upsets the status quo in which they are powerful. This also means that religions will usually fight progress, as can be seen across history, from flat-earthers to geocentrists to young earth creationists; from the index of prohibited books to book burnings to declaring one—and only one—book the book of truth; from outlawing pain relief during childbirth to banning contraception to preventing women from taking control of procreation; from exorcisms to opposing vaccines and stem cell research; from validating slavery to enslaving women in the home to prohibiting same sex marriage; to the religious persecution of Socrates, Hypatia, Galileo, Giordano Bruno, Spinoza, and Charles Darwin. Progress threatens religion—this was true for and well known to the founders.

The founders had firsthand experience here. Ben Franklin was renowned in his time for snatching "lightning from the sky and the scepter from tyrants."[49] Until he invented the lightning rod, ringing church bells specially baptized with water from the Jordan River were used to ward off lightning.[50] This practice, which required humans to grasp a connection to a hunk of metal atop the highest structure in a town, killed more than 120 bell-ringers from 1750 to 1784, but was still believed to be effective.[51] Many Christians did not believe humans had a right to defend themselves from divine attacks. Abbe Nollett, a man of the church, deemed it "as impious to ward off Heavens' lightnings as for a child to ward off the chastening rod of its father."[52] Franklin retorted that "the Thunder of Heaven is no more supernatural than the Rain, Hail, or Sunshine of Heaven, against the Inconvenience of which we guard by Roofs & Shades

Portrait of Benjamin Franklin at his desk in front of a window; outside, lightning is shown striking a building, c. 1780.

without Scruple."[53] When organized Christianity failed to stop the spread of the useful invention, it blamed other natural phenomena, such as the 1755 Boston earthquake, on Franklin's rods.[54] John Adams condemned the religious opposition to Franklin's rods, writing that they "met with all that opposition from the superstition, affectation of

Piety, and Jealousy of new Inventions, that Inoculation to prevent the Danger of the Small Pox, and all other useful Discoveries, have met with in all ages of the World."[55] Franklin's unholy invention was a blessing to humanity from the mind of a man, and religion fought it at every step.

Scientific, political, and social progress all threaten religion, which is why the bible demands blind obedience—"do not revile the king, even in your thoughts"[56]—first to its god, and then to the state. God, even as only an idea, is a millstone around the neck of society, not an engine of progress.

Abigail and John Adams's first son, John Quincy Adams, may have best reinforced the Declaration as embodying the people's right—their duty—to rebel against tyrannical governments in a speech before Congress. As a member of the House of Representatives from Massachusetts, an office he held for nine terms after only a single term as president, Adams waged a lonely war against slavery. In 1836, the slaveholding states had successfully imposed a gag rule (the origin of that term) in the House, which essentially prohibited mentioning slavery. Adams rebelled against the rule as much as against slavery itself. On behalf of some constituents in 1842, he submitted a petition to dissolve the "Union of these States" over southern slavery. Harlow Giles Unger tells the story of the ensuing parliamentary conflict in his biography of the younger Adams:[57]

> Kentucky Congressman Thomas Marshall . . . moved to censure John Quincy for having "committed high treason when he submitted a petition for dissolution of the union."
>
> "Sir," John Quincy shot back, "what is high treason? The Constitution of the United States says what high treason is. . . . It is not for the gentleman from Kentucky, or his puny mind, to define what high treason is and confound it with what I have done." John Quincy then ordered the clerk to read the first paragraph of the Declaration of Independence. . . .
>
> "When in the course of human events it becomes necessary for one people to dissolve the political bands which have connected

them with another and to assume among the powers of the earth, the separate and equal station to which the Laws of Nature and of Nature's God entitle them, a decent respect to the opinions of mankind requires that they should declare the causes which impel them to the separation–"

"Proceed!" John Quincy thundered. "Proceed! Down to 'right' and 'duty'!"

The clerk continued: "It is their right, it is their duty, to throw off such government."

"Now, sir, if there is a principle sacred on earth and established by the instrument just read, it is the right of the people to alter, change, to destroy, the government if it becomes oppressive to them. There would be no such right existing if the people had not the power in pursuance of it to petition for it. . . ."

"I rest that petition on the Declaration of Independence!" John Quincy boomed.

John Quincy Adams was more orthodox than many of the founders, yet even he noted that the Declaration, not the bible, established the sacred principle of rebellion.

THE BIBLE AS A WHOLE—and Paul's epistle to the Romans in particular—contradicts the Declaration and the Constitution in another respect. It holds that governments are "established by God."[58] "By me," meaning by the biblical god, "kings reign" and "rulers rule," says the bible.[59] The Declaration of Independence is based on a different idea: that "Governments are instituted among Men, *deriving their just Powers from the consent of the governed.*" This is the very foundation of the self-government ideal and an explicit rejection of a god-given government. That rejection is embodied (and rather heavily emphasized) in the first three words of the Constitution, "We the People." People give the government power and legitimacy, not gods. The Constitution and the Declaration directly contradict Christian principles of governmental authority.

The Declaration emphasizes people while minimizing the divine or supernatural. The first sentence alone proves the Declaration's concern for humanity:

> When *in the Course of **human events***, it becomes necessary ***for one people*** to dissolve the political bands which have ***connected them with another***, and to assume among the ***powers of the earth***, the separate and equal station to which the Laws of Nature and of Nature's God entitle them, a decent respect to ***the opinions of mankind*** requires that they should declare the causes which impel them to the separation.

The Declaration concerns human events, the powers of the earth, and the opinions of humanity; the only possible mention of the divine or supernatural in the above sentence, "Nature's God," is—as discussed at length in chapter 4—not supernatural at all. "When in the course of human events," as the political philosopher Matthew Stewart points out, "alerts us that the event to be announced does not arise from any divine intercourse."[60] The human and decidedly unsupernatural bent continues with one people severing a political connection with another people, and taking their place "among the powers of the earth." Not heaven, the earth. Stewart again gets it right: "In this graceful opening sentence, the Declaration makes clear that the event to unfold and the reasons with which it will be explained are entirely circumscribed within the experience of this world."[61] The entire document enshrines a political philosophy that is, as Abraham Lincoln referred to it in the Gettysburg Address, "of the people, for the people, and by the people."[62]

If we look at just the first two paragraphs, the emphasis on "mankind" and this world is evident. Set against the "Nature's God" and "their Creator" references, the humanity embedded in the Declaration is overwhelming:

> . . . human events . . . one people . . . another . . . mankind . . . powers of the earth . . . the opinions of mankind . . . all men . . . Governments are instituted among Men . . . consent of the governed . . . it is the Right of the People . . . to them . . . their Safety

and Happiness. . . . all experience hath shewn, that mankind . . . to which they are accustomed. . . . their right . . . their duty . . . their future security. . . these Colonies . . . tyranny over these States . . . a candid world.

The Declaration was written not to justify the separation to a god; it was written because the founders held "a decent respect to the opinions of mankind" and wished to change those opinions. Becker taught us that the founders and their forebears focused on human endeavor and accomplishment, elevating both:

> This is precisely what the eighteenth century did: with the lantern of enlightenment it went up and down the field of human history looking for man in general, the universal man, man stripped of the accidents of time and place; it wished immensely to meet Humanity and to become intimate with the Human Race. If it could find Humanity it would have found man in general, the natural man; and so it would have some chance of knowing what were the rights and laws which, being suited to man in general, were most likely to be suited to particular men, everywhere and always.[63]

The Declaration, the principles it embodied, and the political philosophy it outlined, are truly and thoroughly opposed to Judeo-Christian principles.

This is not to say that American preachers and religious leaders of the time did not advocate independence and revolution; some did.[64] But they did so in spite of biblical constraints. Robert Boucher, the Anglican minister opposed to independence, chastised his godly brethren for this crime: "Let a minister of God, then, stand excused if . . . he seeks not to amuse you by any flowery panegyrics on liberty. Such panegyrics are the productions of ancient heathens and modern patriots: nothing of the kind is to be met with in the Bible."[65] Preachers tortured biblical passages to fit their arguments, including independence; that is the preacher's job. But in truth, ministers preaching independence relied on natural—not supernatural—law, just like the Declaration's author, Thomas Jefferson.

4

Referrals: The Declaration's References to a Higher Power

". . . the Laws of Nature and of Nature's God . . .
. . . their Creator . . .
. . . the Supreme Judge of the world . . .
. . . divine Providence . . . "

—Declaration of Independence

The Declaration repudiates Judeo-Christian values in its purpose, principles, and even taken as a whole. But because it contains quasi-religious language, Christian nationalists cite it regularly. As shown above, the Declaration makes four references that supposedly support the Judeo-Christian principles myth. In full, they read as follows (the language of Jefferson's rough draft is included as well):[1]

FIRST REFERENCE

Final "When in the Course of human events, it becomes necessary for one people to dissolve the political bands which have connected them with another, and to assume among the powers of the earth, the separate and equal station to which *the Laws of Nature and of Nature's God* entitle them, a decent respect to the opinions of mankind requires that they should declare the causes which impel them to the separation."

Draft "When in the course of human events it becomes necessary for a people to advance from that subordination in which they have hitherto remained, & to assume among the powers of the earth the equal & independant station to which *the laws of nature & of nature's god* entitle them, a decent respect to the opinions of mankind requires that they should declare the causes which impel them to the change."

SECOND REFERENCE

Final "We hold these truths to be self-evident, that all men are created equal, that they are endowed by *their Creator* with certain unalienable Rights, that among these are Life, Liberty and the pursuit of Happiness."
Draft "We hold these truths to be sacred & undeniable, that all men are created equal and independent, and from that equal creation they derive rights inherent and inalienable, among which are the preservation of life, and liberty, and the pursuit of happiness."
Alteration likely suggested by Franklin and/or Adams.[2]

THIRD REFERENCE

Final "We, therefore, the Representatives of the united States of America, in General Congress, Assembled, appealing to *the Supreme Judge of the world* for the rectitude of our intentions, do, in the Name, and by Authority of the good People of these Colonies, solemnly publish and declare, That these United Colonies are, and of Right ought to be Free and Independent States . . ."
Draft "We, therefore, the Representatives of the united States of America, in General Congress, Assembled do, in the Name, and by Authority of the good People of these Colonies . . ."
Alteration likely suggested by Franklin and/or Adams.[3]

FOURTH REFERENCE

Final "And for the support of this Declaration, with a firm reliance on the protection of *divine Providence*, we mutually pledge to each other our Lives, our Fortunes and our sacred Honor."
Draft "And for the support of this Declaration, we mutually pledge to each other our Lives, our Fortunes and our sacred Honor."
Alteration suggested by the Continental Congress.[4]

The Continental Congress assigned five men to a committee tasked with drafting the Declaration: Thomas Jefferson, Ben Franklin, John Adams, Robert Livingston, and Roger Sherman. The committee then gave Jefferson the job. Franklin and Adams commented and suggested edits on two of Jefferson's drafts before the draft went to the whole Continental Congress.

The political philosophy Jefferson laid out in the Declaration depended only on the first reference, "the Laws of Nature . . ." This should be self-evident because he fully explained that philosophy in his original draft, which did not include the other three pseudo-religious references. Those three were added to the final draft either by Franklin and Adams or by the Continental Congress as a whole. Jefferson laid the foundation, built the structure, raised the walls and roof, put in the plumbing, wired the framework to give it life, and installed the other guts—the important stuff. The Continental Congress selected the color palette and trim. The Congress's later changes did not alter the fundamental nature of Jefferson's draft or the political philosophy it enshrined. Still, Jefferson complained of these mutilations to Richard Henry Lee. Lee sincerely wished "that the Manuscript had not been mangled as it is. . . . However the Thing is in its nature so good, that no Cookery can spoil the Dish for the palates of Freemen."[5] In other words, the principles of the Declaration were so sound that no veneer, religious or otherwise, could spoil it. Because the first reference was the one included in the original structure of the document, it did all the philosophical and rhetorical heavy lifting; it contributed most significantly to the document's principles and requires more attention.

But before looking at the references individually, note that some observations apply to all four. Neither the content nor the wording of these references supports the Judeo-Christian principles myth. Not a single reference mentions Jesus Christ, Yahweh, or a specifically Christian god. The references specify, at most, a broad deism or, possibly, a narrow theism in the "Supreme Judge" reference. Deism is the belief that a god or supernatural being created the universe but has played no role in events since, rather like a watchmaker who made the universe and set it in motion; deism has no organized or structured religion—it is simply this one belief. Theism is a belief that a god or gods play an active role in current events, tinkering with the watch's gears, perhaps even after we die. Jefferson, Adams, and Franklin and the Continental Congress *could* have chosen to root the entitlements, endowments, appeals, and protections in Jesus Christ or any other specific god, but they did not. Instead, they carefully selected references that do not specify any religious denomination or sectarian belief. These were deliberate men who knew they were drafting a monumental and historic document; they chose their words carefully. As University of Chicago constitutional scholar Geoffrey Stone put it, "in acknowledging Nature's God, the Creator, and Divine Providence, the Declaration carefully and quite consciously eschewed any invocation of the Christian religion."[6]

That the four references are broad may actually explain why Christian nationalists claim them as their own. Naturally, readers with such a worldview assume that the Declaration is referring to *their* god, especially since a claim to hold the ultimate, exclusive truth necessarily entails a belief that that truth is superior to others. But sectarian claims to these references are unsupported by the Declaration's language.

The references are not biblical. At the time, there were about eleven major English versions of bibles that the founders could have borrowed verbiage from.[7] Two of the phrases, "divine Providence" and "Nature's God," do not appear in any of those bibles. Nor does the phrase "Supreme Judge of the World," though the bible does occasionally speak of its god as a judge. More likely, this juridical phrase came from John Locke, who used "Supreme Judge of all Men" to refer to the biblical god in his *Second Treatise of Government* (1690),[8] something the founders certainly read. And, of course, the Judeo-Christian god is described as a creator—in Genesis and at least five times outside the Genesis story[9]—but every religion that describes a creator-god and deism is defined solely by a belief in a cosmic creator-god. Scholars can argue forever about whether the references are deist or theist, but we can all be sure that they are not Christian.

This was almost not the case. Jefferson's rough draft *did* contain a mention of the Christian religion—in a section condemning the slave trade. But the Continental Congress removed this passage from the final version. The omitted paragraph helps illuminate another phrase, "the Laws of Nature and of Nature's God." In the list of King George's crimes, Jefferson wrote:

he has waged cruel war against human nature itself, violating its most sacred rights of life & liberty in the persons of a distant people who never offended him, captivating & carrying them to slavery in another hemisphere, or to incur miserable death in their

transportations thither. This piratical warfare, the opprobrium of
infidel powers, is the warfare of the CHRISTIAN king of Great
Britain. Determined to keep open a market where MEN should
be bought & sold, he has prostituted his negative [his veto] for
suppressing every legislative attempt to prohibit or to restrain this
execrable commerce . . .[10]

That was the only mention of Christianity in the whole document—that the *Christian* king is a slaver while "infidel powers" loathe
the slave trade. This effectively chastises Christianity's monopoly on
morality, with handwritten emphasis on its shortcomings. It's the only

Detail of Thomas Jefferson's "original Rough draught" of the
Declaration of Independence, written in June 1776, showing his
emphasis of the word "Christian."

explicit reference to Christianity, and it is highly critical. However, it didn't make the final cut. (That Jefferson could write of freedom so eloquently and condemn slavery in fervent and revealing terms here and elsewhere, while at the same time owning slaves and fathering children with the slaves, who then became slaves themselves, is a paradox of cowardice. He was one of America's greatest intellects, excelled at communicating grand ideas in simple and poetic terms that enthrall us centuries later, but failed utterly and in terrible ways to practice some of those ideas.)[11]

Jefferson, Adams, and Franklin knew about George III's pious nature, especially given that it was in such stark contrast to the bent of his predecessors.[12] Including some religion in an argument that is meant to convince a devout Christian king that he's wrong in the eyes of a god is rhetorically intelligent. Indeed, appealing to a higher power may have been necessary to change the devout king's opinion. After all, if you believe a god put you on earth to rule, to whom would you answer but a god? One constitutional scholar, Jeffry H. Morrison, has aptly labeled these added references "strategic piety."[13]

Finally, there is no reason to believe that the four terms "Nature's God," "Creator," "Supreme Judge," and "Providence" were capitalized to lend gravity, respect, or specificity to the Declaration. Jefferson used minimal capitalization in his rough drafts and often did not capitalize—including the first words of most sentences—as you can see in the passage on the opposite page. The founders left the task of capitalization to the engrosser, Timothy Matlack, and to printers John Dunlap[14] and Benjamin Towne. Writers of the time capitalized many words, mostly nouns, that are not capitalized today. The list of words capitalized in the Declaration, other than those claimed by Christian nationalists, those that were then considered proper nouns (such as "King of Great Britain," "United States of America," "States," and "Colonies"), and words beginning sentences, includes all the following:

Course, Laws of Nature, Rights, Life, Liberty, Happiness, Governments, Men, Powers, Form of Government, Right, People, Government, Safety, Happiness, Governments, Object, Despotism,

Government, Guards, Colonies, Systems of Government, Tyranny, Facts, Assent to Laws, Governors, Laws, Assent, Laws, Representation, Legislature, Records, Representative Houses, Legislative, Annihilation, People, State, States, Laws for Naturalization of Foreigners, Appropriations of Lands, Administration of Justice, Assent to Laws, Judiciary, Judges, Will, New Offices, Officers, Standing Armies, Consent, Military, Civil, Assent, Acts, Legislation, Quartering, Trial, Murders, Inhabitants, States, Trade, Taxes, Consent, Trial by Jury, Seas, System, Laws, Province, Arbitrary, Boundaries, Colonies, Charters, Laws, Forms of our Governments, Legislatures, Government, Protection, War, Coasts, Lives, Armies, Mercenaries, Cruelty, Head, Citizens, Captive, Seas, Arms, Country, Brethren, Hands, Indian Savages, Oppressions, We, Petitioned, Redress, Petitions, Prince, Tyrant, We, Separation, Enemies in War, Peace, Friends, Assembled, Name, Authority, People, That, Right, Absolved, Allegiance, Power, War, Peace, Alliances, Commerce, Acts, Things, Lives, Fortunes, and Honour.

Becker wrote that the fact that the engrossed Declaration's "capitalization and punctuation follo[w] neither previous copies, nor reason, nor the custom of any age known to man, is one of the irremediable evils of life to be accepted with becoming resignation."[15]

First Reference: "*the Laws of Nature and of Nature's God*"
The first reference is the only one Jefferson employed when crafting the political philosophy of the Declaration. With this language, Jefferson invokes natural law, not the Judeo-Christian god.

In 2011, Michael Peroutka, founder of the Institute on the Constitution, tried to argue that evolution, a scientific theory, is anti-American because of the Declaration of Independence. Peroutka paraphrased what he believed to be the Declaration's political philosophy: "There exists a creator God. He is the God of the Bible. He is not Allah, nor any of the million Hindu deities, nor is he the God that is the wind or is in the trees or some other impersonal force. He created us."[16] Peroutka has it backward: it's not true that the creator mentioned is the god of the bible, and the only "god" mentioned is "Nature's

God"—a concept considerably closer to the "God that is in the wind or in the trees" than the biblical god.

This argument also ignores, as most Christian nationalists do, the first part of the term "the Laws of Nature." And if one is going to ignore the natural law reference and inject religion where it does not belong, there is no reason that that religion should be Christianity. Because nature is referenced twice in the first reference and pagan religions revere nature and the natural world, *paganism* would be a more appropriate choice. But any "pagan nation" claim is as untenable as the "Christian nation" claim, even though the natural law aspects of the Declaration dominate.

The oft-ignored initial four words of the first reference are the most important. There are two basic categories of law: positive law and natural law. Positive law is "promulgated and implemented within a particular political community by political superiors," according to *Black's Law Dictionary*.[17] Positive law is the law we make. Natural law is defined as a "philosophical system of legal and moral principles purportedly deriving from a universalized conception of human nature or divine justice rather than from legislative or judicial action."[18] Natural law is the law that *is*. To achieve what *ought to be*, one must either change positive law with legislation or a constitutional amendment or invoke natural law.[19] Early twentieth-century Harvard Law School dean and legal scholar Roscoe Pound preferred to call natural law "philosophical jurisprudence."[20] Voltaire defined it as "The instinct by which we feel justice."[21] But as the definition in *Black's Law Dictionary* points out, there are two views of natural law. The first is founded on universal human nature, the second on divine justice.[22] William Blackstone, an accomplished English jurist, is a favorite of Christian nationalists because they believe he defined the law of nature as the revelations of the Christian god.[23] Blackstone preceded the founders and influenced their legal thought. But he was anti-republican, and his influence on the founders' *revolutionary* ideas, such as natural law, revolution, and self-government, was minimal. The founders mostly disagreed with him on those important points.[24] Jefferson blamed Blackstone for the "degeneracy of legal science."[25] Blackstone was not only anti-republican, but had "done more towards the suppression of the liberties of man than" Napoleon Bonaparte, wrote Jefferson in 1814.[26] Blackstone was not a man Jefferson was likely to agree with, particularly when outlining a political philosophy of rebellion and republicanism.

The Declaration invoked natural law because the founders needed a legal basis to justify revolting against the positive law imposed by Parliament and George III. Natural law demands the abolition of inequality and privilege, so it is perfect for arguing against oppressive positive law.[27] Again, Becker helps us understand: "When honest men are impelled to withdraw their allegiance to the established law or custom of the community . . . they seek for some principle more generally valid, some 'law' of higher authority, than the established law or custom of the community. To this higher law or more generally valid principle they then appeal."[28]

But which natural law did Jefferson invoke in the Declaration: natural or supernatural? According to Alan Dershowitz, "'Natural Law' based on divine revelation—the source of Christian natural law for Aquinas—was anathema to Jefferson."[29] Jefferson's own words—within the Declaration and in writings penned before and after—support this conclusion. Seventeen years after the Declaration, as secretary of state, Thomas Jefferson wrote *Opinion on the French Treaties*. In it, he espoused natural law based in human nature: "Questions of natural right are triable by *their conformity with the moral sense & reason of man*. Those who write treatises of natural law, can only declare what *their own moral sense & reason* dictate in the several cases they state."[30] The Declaration, a pinnacle of natural law, is built on humans' moral sense and reason. Two years before that document, in *A Summary View of the Rights of British America*, Jefferson, in a precursor to the Declaration's litany of crimes, listed the grievances against the king:

> with that freedom of language and sentiment which becomes a free people claiming their rights, as derived from the *laws of nature*, and not as the gift of their chief magistrate. . . . To give praise which is not due might be well from the venal, but would ill beseem those who are *asserting the rights of human nature*. They know, and will therefore say, that kings are the servants, not the proprietors of the people.[31]

Rights are not bestowed, not even by kings. Rights are asserted, not given. Rights come from human nature, not divine nature. Most of all, natural law is a product of "liberal and expanded thought," not of divine revelation.

In the draft language of the Declaration that condemned the "Christian king," Jefferson wrote that violations of natural law, such as slavery, are not violations of divine law; rather, they amount to "cruel war against *human nature* itself, violating its most sacred rights of life & liberty."[32] In the Declaration, Jefferson appealed to a natural law founded in human nature and discoverable by human reason to justify a revolution against tyrannical positive law.

The human nature interpretation of "the Laws of Nature" is favored over the divine justice interpretation elsewhere in the discourse of American independence. George Mason wrote Virginia's Declaration of Rights in May 1776, and the Virginia convention ratified it that June. Jefferson relied on Mason's charter for the Declaration's opening, and it also influenced the Bill of Rights more than a decade later. The first right Mason declared was "That all men are *by nature* equally free and independent and have certain inherent rights . . . namely, the enjoyment of life and liberty, with the means of acquiring and possessing property, and pursuing and obtaining happiness and safety."[33] The similarities are obvious, and religion is nowhere to be found. This passage simply codifies the social compact theory of government and rights that had recently been explained by Hobbes, Locke, and Jean-Jacques Rousseau. Mason is relying on the natural law centered on humanity, not the supernatural natural law of Blackstone and Christian nationalism.

The First Continental Congress published its "Declaration and Resolves" on October 14, 1774. It too rested on natural, not supernatural, law: "The inhabitants of the English colonies in North-America, by the immutable *laws of nature*, the principles of the English constitution, and the several charters or compacts, have the following RIGHTS."[34] Samuel Adams wrote a famed circular on behalf of Massachusetts to other colonial citizens that discussed natural rights in 1768. Sam Adams was one of the more orthodox founders, but he still rested rights on nature and not the Christian god. He wrote that the right to property "is an essential, unalterable right *in nature*, engrafted into the British constitution, as a fundamental law, and ever held sacred and irrevocable by the subjects."[35] The right is "in nature, engrafted" and held "sacred and irrevocable by the subjects." It is not god-given.

Matthew Stewart, in *Nature's God: The Heretical Origins of the American Revolution* (2014), has shown conclusively that the Enlightenment view of "the Laws of Nature and of Nature's God" enshrined in the Declaration was not religious in any Judeo-Christian sense.[36] As Stewart points out, Nature's God, "the presiding deity of the American Revolution, is another word for 'Nature.'"[37] This makes sense. After all, the full phrase is "the laws of Nature and of Nature's God." Thomas Paine agreed: "As to that which is called nature, it is no other than the laws by which motion and action of every kind, with respect to unintelligible matter, are regulated. And when we speak of looking through nature up to nature's God, we speak philosophically the same rational language as when we speak of looking through human laws up to the power that ordained them."[38]

This phrase invokes no religion, though it may evince a belief in the unorganized and heretical idea called deism. One of America's unsung founders, Dr. Thomas Young, wrote, "That the religion of Nature, more properly stiled the Religion of Nature's God, in latin call'd *Deus*, hence *Deism*, is *truth*, I now boldly defy thee to contest."[39] Jefferson and Adams agreed. Adams explicitly tells Jefferson that a belief in "Nature's God" is deism, not Christianity: "We can never be so certain of any prophecy, or the fulfilment of any prophecy, or of any miracle, or the design of any miracle, as we are from the revelation of nature, that is, nature's God, that two and two are equal to four."[40] Nature's God is a law, like math. Adams continues, noting that organized religions, like Christianity, misunderstand the nature of god:

Is [god] ambitious? Does he want promotion? Is he vain, tickled with adulation, exulting and triumphing in his power and the sweetness of his vengeance? Pardon me, my Maker, for these awful questions. My answer to them is always ready. I believe no such things. My adoration of the author of the universe is too profound and too sincere. The love of God and his creation—delight, joy, triumph, exultation in my own existence—though but an atom, a *molécule organique* in the universe—are my religion.[41]

One can't be much clearer than that—Nature's God is not the Christian god. Jefferson also wrote to Adams about Nature's God, remarking that "of the nature of this being we know nothing."[42]

Church authorities declared natural law as ordained by "Nature's God" to be heretical. They had been saying so for decades. Churches and theologians raged against the enlightened thinkers who would influence the founders: Bruno, Pierre Gassendi, Lucilio Vanini, Galileo, René Descartes, Spinoza, Shaftesbury, and even Locke, to name a few. Priests condemned as "new Epicureans" those who believed that "there is no other divinity or sovereign power in the world except NATURE," that "God is Nature, and Nature is God."[43]

Natural law centered on humanity was so foreign and antithetical to Christianity that the church considered it atheism. Royal Chaplain Richard Bentley of Trinity College at Cambridge opposed "the modern disguised Deists . . . [who] cover the most arrant atheism under the mask and shadow of a deity, by which they understand no more than some eternal inanimate matter, some universal nature, and soul of the world."[44] If the theological scholars of Jefferson's generation thought invoking "Nature's God" was "arrant atheism," we can safely conclude that Jefferson's usage was not Judeo-Christian. The laws were not the biblical god's—they were Nature's, fixed from the beginning, physically impossible to transgress, and discoverable through the application of reason and science.[45] Becker was correct: "Since nature was now the new God, source of all wisdom and righteousness, it was to Nature that the eighteenth century looked for guidance, from Nature that it expected to receive the tablets of the law."[46]

Christian nationalists claim that the phrase "the Laws of Nature and of Nature's God" refers to a Christian god, but there was nothing of Judeo-Christianity in Jefferson's invocation of natural law.[47]

Second Reference: *"their Creator"*

Americans are not terribly familiar with the Declaration. On the first Fourth of July of Trump's presidency, National Public Radio tweeted the entire text of the Declaration of Independence, 140 characters at a time. Many Trump supporters lost their minds. They assumed that NPR was calling for a rebellion against Trump when NPR tweeted passages like this: "A Prince, whose character is thus marked by every act which may define a Tyrant, is unfit to be the ruler of a free people." These die-hard patriots didn't recognize the words of the Declaration and they assumed the tyrant was Trump, not King George III, which says something about how they truly view their populist champion.[48]

Unsurprisingly, this ignorance extends to the phrase "their Creator." Many people change the phrase to something else, such as "our Creator." Fox News host Sean Hannity makes this mistake often.[49] In one illustrative interview in 2009 with Newt Gingrich and Karl Rove, Hannity was complaining about President Obama saying "that we are not a Christian nation," and he argued, "We *are* founded on Judeo-Christian principles." Gingrich, who has a PhD in history, and Rove then trotted out "our Creator" and "your Creator" to support Hannity's Christian nationalism.[50] Former Fox News host Bill O'Reilly is fond of the mistake too,[51] as are members of Congress. US Representative Mac Thornberry of Texas broke down the "full meaning" of "each phrase" of the Declaration in an essay on his website; he quoted the wrong phrase, using "our Creator" instead of "their Creator."[52] US Senator for Kansas Sam Brownback made the switch on the Senate floor.[53] And it's not just the Christian nationalists who make this mistake. Well-meaning but misinformed people make it all the time—Senator Joe Lieberman, for instance.[54] Presidential candidates are fond of the our-for-their substitution as well.[55]

But the founders' choice of language in the second reference is telling. The clause refers not to *our* Creator or even to *the* Creator, but to *their* Creator. If Jefferson, Adams, and Franklin wished to refer to a specifically Judeo-Christian creator, the word *their* was not the best choice.

Three other possibilities, none adopted by the drafters, offer more specificity.

First, they could have written "Men are endowed by *the* Creator." *The* is a definite article with specifying effect, which says that there is one view on the subject, ours, and we're right.

Second, they could have expressed a shared view, choosing "*our* Creator" as some might say "*our* savior." Choosing "their" over "our" diminishes the possibility of a shared view of a creator, though not excluding it altogether. However, the shared view possibility is even more unlikely given that the Declaration was written to the entire "world." The world had suffered never-ending religious conflict, which Jefferson, Franklin, and Adams were acutely aware of—indeed, that was one of the reasons they chose to separate state and church.[56]

And of course, the best option for referring to a specific god would be to specify a particular "creator" by name—Jesus, Yahweh, YHWH, Our Christian Lord and Savior. This seems most likely if they had intended to invoke the Judeo-Christian god. They *could* have named a specific creator, but these deists did not name Christ. Any generic creator god to whom they referred was beyond organized religion.

"Their" is also a possessive pronoun—"their rights as individuals." In this context it indicates a choice, that individuals have their own, valid view of "their Creator." Readers are meant to interpret this phrase as referring to whichever creator—god or otherwise—they believe in. This is probably why Christian nationalists believe the phrase refers to the Christian god.

Of course, the wording may have been chosen simply for clarity because Jefferson is speaking of two sets of people: "**We** hold these truths to be self-evident, that ***all men*** are created equal, that ***they*** are endowed by ***their*** Creator . . ." The first set of people, "We," is the Continental Congress. The second set is "all men," all humanity. But even so, Judeo-Christian specific wording could have been selected. It was not. Even the word "Creator" is not unique to Christianity. Nearly all religions, even deists, have a creator-god.[57] In fact, that's all deists have. Given the phrase's proximity to Nature's God, we can be fairly certain that the framers were referring to natural laws and forces. This clause is either invoking a concept that is not Judeo-Christian or, with the simple and elegant use of the word "their," recognizing the right to freedom of thought and belief that Jefferson protected in the Virginia Statute on Religious Freedom.[58] Perhaps both. Neither supports the Judeo-Christian foundation myth.

UNDER NATURAL LAW, individuals possess natural rights—inherent and unalienable. But this phrase, "endowed by their Creator," leads many Christian nationalists to argue that our rights are god-given, that without a god, there would be no rights. Answering an atheist's question during a town hall meeting, Florida Senator Marco Rubio argued, "This nation was founded on the principle that our rights come from our Creator."[59] But this translation of our founding philosophy is dangerous and something the Declaration avoided. The biblical ideal of political authority—Jesus "will give authority over the nations; to rule them with an iron rod . . . as [he] received authority from my Father"[60] to give but one example—is refuted in the Declaration. The bible is interpreted and enforced by men. And if rights are given by a god, they can be taken away by the men claiming to speak for that god. This is the idea Jefferson rebelled against when he wrote that "the mass of mankind has not been born with saddles on their backs, nor a favored few booted and spurred, ready to ride them legitimately, by the grace of god."[61] Claiming that a god plays a role in human equality lets people who claim to know god's will be "more equal than others,"[62] to borrow from George Orwell.

Jefferson and Madison were incredibly critical and suspicious of organized religion and "the priests of the different religious sects."[63] Jefferson not only cut up the bible, removing all the supernatural nonsense, but he also observed, when discussing religious opposition to the newly founded University of Virginia, that priests "dread the advance of science as witches do the approach of day-light; and scowl on the fatal harbinger announcing the subversion of the duperies on which they live."[64] As we've seen, Madison thought that "Rulers who wished to subvert the public liberty, may have found an established Clergy convenient allies."[65]

Jefferson would probably have disagreed with any religious connotation "their Creator" may have had. In *A Summary View of the Rights of British America* (1774), he wrote: "Our ancestors, before their emigration to America, . . . possessed a right, *which nature has given to all men*, of departing from the country in which chance, not choice has placed them."[66] In *Notes on State of Virginia*, written five years after the Declaration, Jefferson might at first appear to side with the god-given rights idea. But he's as sly as ever. Discussing slavery, he writes:

And can the liberties of a nation be thought secure when we have removed their only firm basis, a conviction in the minds of the people that these liberties are the gift of God? That they are not to be violated but with his wrath? Indeed I tremble for my country when I reflect that God is just: that his justice cannot sleep for ever.[67]

A mangled version of this quote even appears on the Jefferson Memorial in Washington, DC. A careful reading of the original shows that this passage is not as religious as it might first appear. Jefferson does not say that rights are a gift from god, but that rights are secured by "a conviction in the minds of the people" that the rights are a gift from god. This actually supports the idea discussed in Chapter 2: that religion is not the source of, but a substitute for, morality. Jefferson is saying that most people are not sophisticated enough to ponder moral questions, so they should adhere to religion. This belief actually undercuts the Christian nationalists' claims because it means that Jefferson, as a member of the elite, along with the other founders, did not need religion and would not have needed it to draft the Declaration. Jefferson was also writing in poetic terms. He used the biblical language of a wrathful god to prophesy a Civil War over slavery. Langston Hughes would express the same sentiment 150 years later, in "Warning," a beautiful poem that likened retributive justice to the wind, not a deity.

Rights are agreed on by humans and enforced by society. This is the social contract the founders enshrined in the Constitution. In *The Federalist Papers*, those letters written to the citizens of New York by James Madison, Alexander Hamilton, and John Jay to explain the virtues of the newly proposed Constitution, Jay wrote, "Nothing is more certain than the indispensable necessity of government, and it is equally undeniable, that whenever and however it is instituted, the people must cede to it some of their natural rights in order to vest it with requisite powers."[68] That we agree on rights is evident because we also agree that rights can be taken away in certain circumstances. We can take away your rights if you fail to adhere to the social contract by violating another's rights. The bible neglects to note that "the people" are the source of power, instead placing that firmly in the divine plan. It has no mention of "consent of the governed."

More importantly, Jefferson did not include "their Creator" in his original language, which read, ". . . that all men are created equal and independent, and from that equal creation . . ." (see page 69). The creator language, if it is indeed the radical change the Christian nationalists suggest, could not have been a substantial or integral part of Jefferson's underlying philosophy. It might glaze a religious veneer over parts of that philosophy, but that hardly makes it a founding principle.

THE DECLARATION WAS NOT WRITTEN IN A VACUUM. Statements on American independence were common during the years and months surrounding July 1776. Given that Jefferson did not describe rights as god-given in his draft, it is instructive to see what others did at the time.

We already saw that the Continental Congress's 1774 declaration, Samuel Adams's circular letter, and George Mason's declaration[69] all relied on natural law and inalienable rights by birth, not on god-given rights. Pennsylvania's Constitution (September 1776), authored with help from Benjamin Franklin and likely Thomas Paine, said that certain human rights were assumed: "That all men are born equally free and independent, and have certain natural, inherent and inalienable rights."[70] The Massachusetts Constitution (1780), which John Adams drafted, declared that "All men are born free and equal, and have certain natural, essential, and unalienable rights."[71] New Hampshire's Bill of Rights (1784) was similar: "All men are born equally free and independent," and "All men have certain natural, essential, and inherent rights."[72] James Wilson's 1774 pamphlet, *Considerations on the Nature and Extent of the Legislative Authority of the British Parliament*, laid out the humanity and birthright foundation of government: "All men are, by nature, equal and free: no one has a right to any authority over another without his consent: all lawful government is founded in the consent of those who are subject to it."[73] Wilson was one of the more influential founders, speaking more at the Constitutional Convention than any other person except Gouverneur Morris.[74] Wilson thought there were two indispensable rules for government and society: "that all men are naturally equal; and that all men are naturally free."[75]

The founders understood that human rights are more powerful, absolute, and universal than god-given rights. God-given rights depend on geography, varying drastically for residents of Indiana, India, and Iran. God-given rights depend on those claiming to speak for god, as shown by Mohammad, Martin Luther, and Martin Luther King Jr.'s interpretations of their respective gods' will. Women and the LGBTQ have fewer rights in almost every religion because of god's will. The abolition of slavery, women's rights, the end of segregation, marriage equality—progress in each was opposed by those claiming to know god's mind and executing god's will. Human or natural rights are far less susceptible to the whim of preachers. Simply by virtue of being human, of being born, you have certain inherent, inalienable rights. [76]

The god-given rights fallacy is also moral relativism masquerading as moral absolutism. Moral relativism, bemoaned by religious scholars and Christian nationalists, is the idea that morality might change with time or the situation. They believe in moral absolutes handed down from on high. To take an oversimplified example, the moral absolutist might believe it is always immoral to kill because god says so. The moral relativist, on the other hand, might believe it is acceptable to kill in some circumstances, to save innocent lives, for instance. The religious system of absolute morality is actually moral relativism in disguise, but with an alarming alteration: God-given rights depend solely on a particular individual's interpretation of god's word. Perhaps that individual adheres to the interpretation of a higher authority, such as a pope or an author of a holy book. But at the end of the line, a human being is claiming to know "God's will." One person's moral belief is given the authority of divine law. That relativism is far more dangerous because it involves a fallible human being claiming divine sanction. In our example, the moral absolutist believes killing is unacceptable because god said so; therefore, if god changes his mind and orders someone to kill their child, as he did with Abraham and Isaac, or to fly a plane into a building, the moral absolutist must listen. If they balk at murdering their son, as any decent human ought, they are exercising their own morality and moral relativism. In other words, what most religions label absolute morality is simply their personal morality given divine sanction. It is far better to premise human rights on the simple fact of being human, as the founders did, than to put them into the hands of people claiming to speak for a supernatural being that does not exist.

This masquerade was laid bare as believers, and especially evangelical Christians, supported Donald Trump as scandal after immoral scandal broke over his candidacy and presidency. Numbers highlight the pretense. In 2011, a mere 30 percent of white evangelicals thought that an elected official who committed an immoral act in their personal life could still behave ethically and fulfill their public duties. Things had changed by the 2016 presidential race and no group had shifted more than those moral absolutists, the white evangelicals, who swung 42 points, with 72 percent believing that an immoral person could be a moral public figure.[77] Evangelicals' view of Trump actually became *more* favorable over the scandal-ridden first eighteen months of his presidency. A year and a half after the election, 75 percent of white evangelicals had a favorable of Trump, about ten points higher than on Election Day.[78]

Franklin Graham, son of and heir to Billy Graham's evangelical empire, put a face on these statistics less than a month after the numbers were released. In a May 2018 Associated Press interview, Graham said that Donald Trump's affair with porn star Stormy Daniels and the subsequent hush money was nobody's business: "That's for him and his wife to deal with. I think when the country went after President Clinton, the Republicans, that was a great mistake that should never have happened. And I think this thing with Stormy Daniels and so forth is nobody's business."[79] But this was a change for Graham. Almost exactly twenty years earlier, he went after President Clinton. In a 1998 *Wall Street Journal* op-ed entitled "Clinton's Sins Aren't Private," Graham wrote, "The God of the Bible says that what one does in private does matter. Mr. Clinton's months-long extramarital sexual behavior in the Oval Office now concerns him and the rest of the world, not just his immediate family. If he will lie to or mislead his wife and daughter, those with whom he is most intimate, what will prevent him from doing the same to the American public?"[80] It turns out that what the biblical god says depends on the point Graham is trying to make. Deep down, the evangelical concern was not over morality, but over being able to claim a divine sanction for whatever was considered moral. This conception of morality and of human rights is dangerous.

God-given rights are not sacred, self-evident, or inherent: they are fragile, exclusive, and used to favor the chosen few. That was not the intent or legacy of the Declaration.

Third and Fourth References: *"Supreme Judge of the world"* and *"divine Providence"*

The third and fourth references are similarly not specific to Judeo-Christianity or any other religion. Nor can they be found in bibles contemporary to the founding. Like the second reference, these were added during the drafting process and are not integral to the intellectual or philosophical structure of the Declaration's underlying principles. They are poetic, more akin to Thomas Paine's assertion that King George can "unfeelingly" hear of the "slaughter" of Americans and "composedly sleep with their blood upon his soul," though less moving.[81] And however poetic, the references are not Christian. Although some scholars think these mentions are more specific to a particular religion, they do "not definitively identify this God as uniquely Christian," as evangelical Christian and historian John Fea notes.[82]

Garry Wills once wrote that to read the Declaration as dogmatic or theological is to misread it.[83] It is difficult to read the Declaration and think these final two references are anything but superfluous—late additions forced into their respective sentences. Professor Steven Green is correct when he observes that these two "rhetorical appeals . . . come too late in the document to redo the Declaration's overall Enlightenment framework."[84] The truants interrupt the flow of beautiful sentences and detract from the impact rather than add to it.

The jarring nature of the slapdash religious interjections is perhaps most evident when looking at the Declaration's final paragraph as a whole. Like the first paragraphs, it has nothing to do with religion or the supernatural. This paragraph is solely concerned with this world, with people and governments:

We, therefore, the Representatives of the united States of America, in General Congress, Assembled, appealing to the Supreme Judge of the world for the rectitude of our intentions, do, in the Name, and by Authority of the good People of these Colonies, solemnly publish and declare, That these United Colonies are, and of Right ought to be Free and Independent States; that they are Absolved from all Allegiance to the British Crown, and that all political connection between them and the State of Great Britain, is and ought to be totally dissolved; and that as Free and Independent States, they have full Power to levy War, conclude Peace, contract Alliances, establish Commerce, and to do all other Acts and Things which Independent States may of right do. And for the support of this Declaration, with a firm reliance on the protection of divine Providence, we mutually pledge to each other our Lives, our Fortunes and our sacred Honor.

"We . . . the Representatives of the united States . . . our intentions . . . in the name and by the authority of the good People of these Colonies . . . ." The paragraph is bent to this world—to here, not to the hereafter—and written on the people's authority, not that of a divine judge. According to the language, "the Supreme Judge" is judging "the rectitude of our intentions." Basically, the Continental Congress was saying that their intentions were good, as any who knew their genuine intentions would understand. Even if this language had been in the draft and could therefore be considered integral, it is not part of a statement on self-government or political philosophy. It's window dressing. "We promise we're telling the truth" is all it amounts to. It's strategic piety calibrated to appeal to a candid, credulous world and a pious king.

As a justification to a candid world, the writers were wise to choose language that would take advantage of the majority's religiosity but still remain wholly nonsectarian. The language drew in a broader audience instead of alienating those who would be made outsiders by its expressing a religious preference. One historian labels this "equivocal religiosity" and asserts that it is specifically "designed to be acceptable to deists and orthodox believers alike."[85]

When the Continental Congress relied on "divine Providence," they did so to make a pledge. But they did not pledge to that god— they pledged *to each other*. They pledged their lives, their fortunes, and their sacred honor. There is something stirring about the group of rebels pledging all they had and all they were to one another and not to a supernatural deity. They acted on Franklin's exhortation to "Join, or Die" and supported Henry's demand for liberty or death, and they rebelled against the most powerful nation on earth together. The strength of fifty-six of the most brilliant minds on a continent were bent toward one object: self-government. Their honor—their *word*— was sacred, not their religion.

Our nation would continue this trend of pledging to each other, to people, in the Constitution and in the first law Congress ever passed. The presidential oath, despite modern trends, does not actually mention god or include a request for a god's help. The words "so help me God" never appear and were not first used to alter the words of the constitutional oath by a president until nearly 100 years later. The first law that Congress ever passed prescribed congressional oaths for office, and all gods were deliberately edited out of it.[86] The presidential oath remains godless, though modern political piety and a disrespect for the Constitution has marred it.

"The closing sentence [of the Declaration] is perfection itself," wrote Becker, continuing, "Congress amended the sentence by including the phrase, 'with a firm reliance upon the protection of divine Providence.' It may be that Providence always welcomes the responsibilities thrust upon it in times of war and revolution; but personally, I like the sentence better as Jefferson wrote it. 'And for the support of this Declaration we mutually pledge to each other our lives, our fortunes, and our sacred honor.'"[87] I agree with Becker. The congressional edit cheapens the document. Jefferson would probably have agreed as well. In the last letter he would ever write, penned less than two weeks before he died, Jefferson recorded some final thoughts on the Declaration. He was politely declining an invitation to a fiftieth anniversary celebration of American independence. Jefferson was too weak to make the trip, but offered this reflection on the legacy of his Declaration:

May it be to the world, what I believe it will be, (to some parts sooner, to others later, but finally to all,) the Signal of arousing men to burst the chains, under which monkish ignorance and superstition had persuaded them to bind themselves, and to assume the blessings & security of self-government. That form which we have substituted, restores the free right to the unbounded exercise of reason and freedom of opinion. All eyes are opened, or opening, to the rights of man. The general spread of the light of science has already laid open to every view. The palpable truth, that the mass of mankind has not been born with saddles on their backs, nor a favored few booted and spurred, ready to ride them legitimately, by the grace of god.[88]

Both Jefferson and John Adams would die on the same day, July 4, 1826, the day their fellow citizens celebrated bursting the chains of monkish ignorance and superstition and shedding the saddles enforced by god's grace. If the Declaration they authored is at all theological, its theology is anti-biblical and anti-Christian.

Exercising poetic license does not make the Declaration religious; nor does it establish a religion. The genius of the document and its poetic language is that readers may read into it what they will. Christians will see the religious references as being about their god, and atheists like me will think "divine Providence" simply means luck. In psychological terms, the founders were playing to people's confirmation bias—our innate selection and interpretation of evidence to support our existing beliefs. But to claim a national, legal, or governmental foundation on such persuasion or poetry is specious. The references are tools of persuasion, not expressions of a founding faith. Franklin, a pragmatic persuader, would later serve as an ambassador to France to win its support for America's war of independence. To play upon the French people's romantic ideas about Americans, Franklin wore a coonskin cap around France.[89] He would do anything to win support, even play a little dress-up. And he succeeded in soliciting French aid, which eventually helped win the war. To the extent that these four references are religious, they are the coonskin cap of the Declaration.

5

Christian Settlements:
Colonizing the Continent,
Not Building a Nation

"History began on July 4, 1776.
Everything before that was a mistake."

—**Ron Swanson**, a fictional character on
the NBC show *Parks & Recreation*[1]

"It was this great struggle that peopled America.
It was not religion alone, as is commonly supposed; but it
was a love of universal liberty, and a hatred, a dread, a horror,
of the infernal confederacy before described, that projected,
conducted, and accomplished the settlement of America."

—**John Adams**, describing the struggle against
the confederacy of "ecclesiastical and civil tyranny."[2]

America's colonial history does include governments established
on Christian principles and the bible, but it is a mistake to
argue that the United States is a Christian nation from those
early examples. Some colonies had Christian governments—indeed,
some were settled for that purpose. But when the founders were
inventing America, they rejected the example of colonial governments
established on Judeo-Christian principles, viewing them as examples
of what to avoid.

Colonial governments were often overtly and officially religious.
This is hardly surprising. Every colony was part of the British Empire,
subject to the Christian king who headed the Anglican Church. Every

colony had an established church, and English common law made heresy—a crime interpreted and defined by ecclesiastical judges—a capital crime, punished by burning in some colonies.[3] The problem for Christian nationalists is that colonial history precedes the adoption of a US Constitution that separated state and church. Much of the history that Christian nationalists cite comes from a time when the United States of America was not a nation, but a British outpost.

This was a different time, and citizens of the British Empire had a different outlook. The Declaration of Rights of the Stamp Act Congress (1765)—which met eleven years before independence and twenty-two years before the Constitution—provides a glimpse into the pre-Revolutionary colonial mindset. That declaration was issued by devoted royal subjects and Englishmen, not Americans:

> The members of this congress, sincerely devoted, with the warmest sentiments of affection and duty to His Majesty's person and government, inviolably attached to the present happy establishment of the Protestant succession, and with minds deeply impressed by a sense of the present and impending misfortunes of the *British* [emphasis of "*British*" in original] colonies on this continent; having considered as maturely as time would permit, the circumstances of said colonies, esteem it our indispensable duty to make the following declarations, of our humble opinions, respecting the most essential rights and liberties of the colonists.[4]

The Stamp Act Declaration was not about the United States or American States, but about "British colonies." The tone is humble, supplicating, and very different from that used in the Declaration of Independence. A full reading of this important document shows that religion and god were not factors motivating the resolution, but that rather, the central motivation was the colonists' rights as Englishmen.[5] Historian John Fea makes a useful distinction between the colonies, which were "planted" on the North American coast, and the "founding" of the United States of America.[6]

Christian nationalists have a stable of colonial history and quotes they cite in support of their myth.[7] But by definition, each argument relies on a time when the United States was but an outpost of a Christian king's estate. Two hackneyed, yet well-accepted "proofs" are:

1. The Continental Congress prayed; therefore America was founded on Christian principles, and

2. The Pilgrims came to this continent seeking religious freedom and established a Christian duchy; therefore America is a Christian nation.

Even though these are pre-American myths, they are so popular and so integral to the Christian nationalist identity that they must be addressed individually.

ATTENDEES AT THE FIRST CONTINENTAL CONGRESS appointed a chaplain to pray in September 1774, when the colonies were still subjects of the British king and had not declared independence. That assembly spent a considerable amount of time discussing reconciliation with Britain, not independence. The battles at Lexington and Concord were still six months away. This is a seminal meeting in American history, but it was fifteen years before our country invented the separation of state and church. There was no United States of America and there was no Constitution, let alone a First Amendment to that Constitution. Stating that the Continental Congress prayed is like stating that part of the British empire prayed: unremarkable. But still, Christian nationalists point to the chaplain's appointment and his prayer as evidence of America's having been founded on Judeo-Christian principles. The US Supreme Court, in an ill-advised decision in 1983, even declared that modern-day prayers at government meetings are not subject to the First Amendment partly because dependent British colonies prayed in 1774.[8] (More on that case on pages 96–97.) As president, John Adams issued calls for prayer and thanksgiving, but thought they might have been responsible for his failed 1800 reelection bid: "Nothing is more dreaded than the National Government meddling with Religion."[9]

Without the benefit of that hindsight, Adams participated in the chaplain's appointment and that prayer in 1774. He wrote Abigail a brief account when the Continental Congress first met:

Mr. Cushing made a Motion, that it should be opened with Prayer. It was opposed by Mr. Jay of N. York and Mr. Rutledge of South Carolina, because we were so divided in religious Sentiments . . . so that We could not join in the same Act of Worship. Mr. S. Adams arose and said he was no Bigot, and could hear a Prayer from a Gentleman of Piety and Virtue, who was at the same Time a Friend to his Country. He was a Stranger in Phyladelphia, but had heard that Mr. Duché . . . deserved that Character, and therefore he moved that Mr. Duché, an episcopal Clergyman, might be desired, to read Prayers to the Congress, tomorrow Morning.[10]

Relying on *any* religious colonialism for a Christian nation claim is a bit beside the point, because the colonies were still colonies; but pointing to the appointment of Jacob Duché as chaplain and the prayer he gave as an example of our Christian founding is fruitless for three more reasons: (1) The prayer was opposed; (2) The prayer was a political gambit, not a statement of religion in a founding principle; and (3) Duché's whole story (see pages 95–96) shows the appointment to have been a mistake and tends to undercut the Christian nationalist claim.

First, John Jay and John Rutledge opposed the prayer motion. Jay and Rutledge would become the first and second chief justices of the Supreme Court. Their opposition should not be ignored nor their reason: that this land is religiously diverse. The more diverse the company, the greater division religion will cause. In such cases, the best policy is to remove religion from the equation.

Second, the important qualifier of Sam Adams's acquiescence to Duché, "who was at the same Time a Friend to his Country," gets left out of the Christian nationalist retelling of this story. This proposal was political, not religious. The Adamses were enlisting clergy to help spread the fire for independence. The proposal was less about joining together in an act of worship, and more a political move designed to manipulate a large, relatively unsupportive sect. As legal scholar Christopher C. Lund has explained: "The Continental Congress desperately needed help ingratiating the revolutionary movement with the Anglican clergy and laity (who would be overwhelmingly Loyalist when the Revolutionary War came). Duché's selection thus was a way to move

Anglican clergy into supporting the cause for liberty—or at least not opposing it so vigilantly."[11]

Christian nationalists see this prayer as evidence of a deeply religious body doing god's work, but it was strategic piety. John Adams recorded that Joseph Reed said, "We never were guilty of a more Masterly Stroke of Policy, than in moving that Mr. Duché might read Prayers."[12] Policy, not piety. The Continental Congress was a political body debating politics, not religion. And just like the strategic piety in the Declaration, this pious move has no bearing or influence on our founding principles. When writing the US Constitution, *the* founding document, strategic piety was not necessary to score political points, and the founders shunned religious political theater. They did not pray during the Constitutional Convention. The delegates thought the sole motion for prayer so "unnecessary" that they didn't even bother to vote on it.[13]

Finally, the Adamses' faith in the clergy was misplaced. True to the flexibility of religious ethics, Duché abandoned the Revolution. John Adams concluded the above letter to Abigail by noting a contradiction in Duché's occupation and politics. He was, as Adams put it, a member of "the Episcopal order, upon this Continent—*Yet* a Zealous Friend of Liberty and his Country."[14] *Yet* is an important qualifier. Despite being an Episcopal clergyman, Duché supported independence. At least while it was convenient. Three years later John wrote to Abigail, "Mr. Duché I am sorry to inform you has turned out an Apostate and a Traytor. Poor Man! I pitty his Weakness, and detest his Wickedness."[15]

When the British took Philadelphia in 1777 and threw Duché in jail, he switched sides, pledging his allegiance to the Crown. He spent only one night in jail because of this apostasy.[16] After defecting to the British, Duché wrote George Washington a letter condemning American independence, explaining that the only reason he accepted the chaplaincy was self-interest.[17] Duché was not a true believer in self-government or independence, but was merely using his position as a political "expedient," just as the Adamses were using him. Duché told Washington that independence was impious, a form of idol worship, and asked, "Are the dregs of Congress then still to influence a mind like yours?"[18] After attacking Congress as "illiberal and violent men," Duché turned his pen on the army, calling them unprincipled cowards:

"Can you, have you the least confidence in a set of undisciplined men and officers, many of them have been taken from the lowest of the people, without principle, without courage . . ."[19] Duché begged Washington to convince the Congress to end the war and rescind "the hasty and ill-advised declaration of Independency."

Washington forwarded this craven letter to the Continental Congress, noting that Duché might have been "induced" into the "ridiculous–illiberal performance."[20] As to coercion, Duché himself dismissed the idea: "The sentiments I express, are the real sentiments of my own heart, such as I have long held."[21]

Duché is the man Christian nationalists choose as a standard bearer for claiming that our country belongs to their god—a man who abandoned American independence, labeled our soldiers cowards, and slandered the founders. But to the Christian nationalist, facts matter less than being able to claim that at one time, when the colonies were still colonies, an Anglican preacher was selected for political reasons to say a prayer for the same men he would later denigrate.

The better argument for Christian nationalists is to point to what happened after Duché. Not immediately (after reaping the political benefit of the first prayer, the Continental Congress had no further prayers for eight months[22]), but Duché's legacy of chaplains in the US House and Senate continues to this day. In the poorly reasoned 1983 case mentioned on page 93, *Marsh v. Chambers*, the Supreme Court relied on two things to exempt government prayer from the First Amendment: Duché colonial prayers and the bill that the First United States Congress approved for congressional chaplains. I explained why this second rationale is unsound in the 2014 Supreme Court *amicus* brief I authored for the Freedom From Religion Foundation, in which I argued *Marsh* should be overturned.[23]

The Supreme Court tends to heed Madison's First Amendment advice, but, curiously, it relegated Madison's legal opinion on the chaplains to a footnote.[24] Madison condemned "the chaplainship to Congress" as "a palpable violation of equal rights, as well as of Constitutional principles."[25] He's correct, but the court instead highlighted his vote for the appropriations bill that included two chaplain salaries.[26] That bill was not really about chaplains—it authorized salaries for government officials, including the congressmen voting on it.[27] Because of that bill, the *Marsh* court concluded that "the First Amendment draftsmen . . . saw no real threat to the Establishment Clause arising from a practice of prayer."[28]

The more reasonable conclusion is that the members of Congress missed the threat in their rush to secure their own salaries and build the US government from the ground up. Congressmen had been serving at their own expense, most far from home. Salaries and travel allowances were more important than the legality of the chaplaincy buried in the fourth of seven sections in an appropriations bill. This seems even more likely given how few seemed to care about the prayers, which were sparsely attended. A scholar sympathetic to the Christian nationalist perspective wrote in 1950, "One of the chaplains for eight years from 1792 on, complained of the thin attendance of members of Congress at prayers. He attributed the usual two-thirds absences to the prevalence of freethinking."[29] He also noted other complaints that the "Congressional Chaplaincy was not always treated with respect," including that congressmen nominated freethinkers like Thomas Paine to fill the chaplaincy.[30] Not exactly a pious group.

It's also not true that the First Congress "saw no real threat" to the First Amendment, though that would be understandable if only because the amendment had just been written and would not have any legal effect until it was ratified two years later. Madison specifically condemned the chaplaincy when looking back on the bill, writing in 1822 that "it was not with my approbation, that the deviation from it took place in Congress when they appointed Chaplains, to be paid from the National Treasury."[31] Those who did ponder the legality of government prayer, in the form of presidential thanksgiving proclamations, thought it unconstitutional and a threat of the kind the court dismissed. In a debate following this appropriations bill, prayer opponents relied on the Constitution and the law, while proponents relied on the bible and Duché's prayers. Representative Thomas Tucker of South Carolina thought government calls to prayer "a business with which the Congress have nothing to do; it is a religious matter, and, as such, is proscribed to us."[32] Roger Sherman of Connecticut countered with "holy writ" and "the solemn thanksgivings and rejoicings which took place in the time of Solomon," an example he thought worth imitating.[33] The only other pro-prayer speaker, Elias Boudinot of New Jersey—who would go on to found the American Bible Society—relied on Duché's prayers.[34]

As we've seen, Christian nationalism operates like a ratchet or a noose; once the separation of state and church is violated, it tightens its hold and the violation becomes nearly incurable. It is then used to justify other violations, which has happened here. Congress ignored sound legal analyses and did what it was accustomed to before state and church were separated. Currently, Congress pays close to a million dollars a year for two clergymen and their staff, whose only job is to pray once a day over their proceedings.[35] This is unconstitutional, as the only framers, including Madison, Father of our Constitution, to offer a legal opinion on government prayer argued.

ALTHOUGH IT IS QUITE POPULAR, the second Christian nationalist argument from America's colonial history is somewhat convoluted and rarely spelled out. The Pilgrims and the Puritans are often conflated into one sect, when in fact they were two distinct groups. The Pilgrims established Plymouth in 1620, having first fled to Holland. John Winthrop and the Puritans established Boston and the Massachusetts Bay Colony in 1630. In 1691, the colonies were combined. As historian Nancy Isenberg has explained,[36] our popular conception gives these two colonies disproportionate weight largely because New England historians dominated the nineteenth century and shaped the American myth-making by focusing on their genetic and geographic neighbors. The Christian nationalist claim gives these colonies even more weight and goes something like this:

1. Christian settlers came to North America seeking religious freedom and established Christian governments—Christian nations—to protect that religious freedom;

2. The United States also has religious freedom;

3. Therefore, America is a Christian nation with a Christian government.[37]

The Christian nationalists are arguing that a Christian nation is the basis of religious freedom—that a Christian nation is not only compatible with religious freedom, but also a prerequisite. In truth, religious freedom is not possible in a Christian nation or any other theocracy. The concepts are mutually exclusive; each destroys the other.

The danger a Christian nation poses to religious liberty is exemplified in an aspect of America's religious colonial heritage that is often warped and misrepresented. Many Americans, not just Christian nationalists, romanticize the continent's first European colonists, claiming that they fled persecution in England in search of religious freedom.

This is not quite true. Fleeing religious persecution is not the same as seeking religious freedom.

The Plymouth Pilgrims and the Massachusetts Puritans were *not* seeking religious freedom. They were seeking the ability to form a government and a society dedicated to *their* particular brand of religion. This distinction is crucial. Religious freedom allows citizens to practice any religion so long as it doesn't infringe on another's rights. The *Mayflower* settlers were looking for a place to practice their religion *and* force others to practice it too. That is not freedom. It is dissent from the ruling religion and a desire to impose your own. They wanted a theocracy. As Jefferson explained 150 years later, the first English settlers may have been fleeing persecution, but when they gained power "they shewed equal intolerance in this country."[38]

This distinction is underscored by the Pilgrims's path to Plymouth. The Pilgrims—Church of England Separatists—left England and fled to Amsterdam and then Leiden in several waves between 1608 and 1609. They spent more than a decade in Holland, and most stayed for good. Some sailed for the new world aboard the *Mayflower* and the *Speedwell* and founded the Plymouth colony in 1620 (leaks forced the *Speedwell* to quickly return to England, never to sail again).

The Pilgrims had religious freedom when they settled in the Netherlands after fleeing persecution in England. James Madison described Holland's civil relationship to religion well: "Holland ventured on the experiment of combining a liberal toleration, with the establishment of a particular creed."[39] This is not the freedom we would expect today, but at that time, the Netherlands was the most tolerant, religiously diverse country in Europe. The Pilgrims *selected* Holland for the free-dom it promised.[40] It was where the oppressed fled and were welcomed. Spinoza, Locke, Pierre Bayle ("atheism does not necessarily lead to the corruption of morals"[41]), Descartes, Hobbes, and Baron d'Holbach all found a Dutch haven from religious persecution, or Dutch printers willing to publish their revolutionary ideas. During the 1600s, the Netherlands published about half of all books produced worldwide.[42] Bertrand Russell found it "impossible to exaggerate the importance of Holland in the seventeenth century, as the one country where there was freedom of speculation."[43] Freely practicing, or not practicing, one's religion was a right the Dutch extended to all. This freedom meant that the Pilgrim elders could not enforce their beliefs with the help of civil law. And living with ungodly non-Pilgrims degraded their followers' faith. They wanted religious uniformity, not freedom. They wanted a government based on their god, on their religion, and to meld the civil and religious authority into one alliance. They wanted theocracy—they just wanted the "right" theocracy.

The dichotomy between religious freedom and a religious govern-ment is conspicuous in the history of the Massachusetts Bay Puritans too. They banished Roger Williams—who would go on to establish the Rhode Island colony, which actually practiced tolerance—and Anne Hutchinson, among many others, for theological disagreements. Hutchinson was banished for believing in salvation through grace when orthodox doctrine claimed salvation through works. Such dis-agreements can be fatal under a religious regime. The Puritans executed Mary Dyer, William Robinson, Marmaduke Stephenson, and William Leddra on Boston Common for the terrible crime of being Quakers. The Puritans also waged a holy war on the Pequots, setting fire to a village on the Mystic River, killing 700 Native men, women, and chil-dren. The survivors were sold into slavery. The genocide was like some-thing out of the Book of Joshua. And indeed, the Puritans saw it that way. They saw themselves as instruments of their god's holy will: "Such a dreadful Terror did the ALMIGHTY let fall upon [the Natives'] Spir-its, that they would fly from us and run into the very Flames, where many of them perished."[44] According to John Mason, the Puritan mili-tia commander, his god laughed while he murdered: "But GOD was above them, who laughed his Enemies and the Enemies of his People to Scorn, making them as a fiery Oven. . . . Thus did the LORD judge among the Heathen, filling the Place with dead Bodies!"[45]

When religion, the Christian religion included, unites with the civil power, this kind of violence is typical: a recipe for genocide, land theft, and consigning the enemies of a god to a "fiery Oven." A tendency toward theocracy is also a tendency toward violence.

Christianity used fire and the sword to purify citizens elsewhere in colonial America. In 1565, Spanish admiral Pedro Menéndez de Avilés, founder of St. Augustine, Florida, and his zealous Catholic missionaries slaughtered 111 French Huguenots on the Florida coast for refusing to convert to Catholicism. Two weeks later, Menéndez slaughtered another 134 Huguenots, again for refusing to convert. Lest anyone doubt the religious motives of the murderers, Menéndez hung the corpses from trees with a sign proclaiming that they were killed, "not as Frenchmen, but as heretics."[46] Pope Pius V personally commended Menéndez for doing "all that was requisite" to extend "our Holy Catholic faith, and the gaining of souls for God" and also for converting "the Indian idolaters."[47] In the American Southwest, conquistadors and Franciscan monks forcibly converted thousands of Natives while trying to extend the "Holy" Catholic faith by extirpating the Native religion. European settlers were not practicing religious freedom, but religious violence.

WHEN THE PURITANS AND PILGRIMS FLED LEIDEN, they escaped the liberalizing effects of Dutch tolerance, but not completely.[48] Two hundred miles south of their new Massachusetts home, the Dutch colony of New Amsterdam, which would become New York, was thriving. John Adams observed that the Netherlands—which gave the fledgling, newly independent colonies their first loan in 1782 thanks to Adams's hard work—and America were two republics "so much alike, that the history of one seems but a transcript from that of the other; so that every Dutchman instructed in the subject, must pronounce the American revolution just and necessary."[49] The principles Americans are so proud of today have far more in common with the liberal Dutch colony that would become New York City than with the Puritans, the Pilgrims, Menéndez, the conquistadors, and their religious intolerance. In particular, two American principles that contrast severely with Puritan ideals can be traced to Dutch liberalism: diversity, and freedom over intolerance.

The Puritans' "grim theocratic monoculture," to borrow a phrase from historian Russell Shorto, was the antithesis of the thriving, diverse Dutch communities farther south.[50] New England's enforced uniformity stood opposed to what would become an important American principle: strength through diversity. Manhattan, on the other hand, was America's first melting pot. Shorto's *Island at the Center of the World* (2005), a history of the Dutch colony on Manhattan, eloquently recaptures an era that was lost when the less progressive English took over in 1664. Amsterdam was the most liberal and tolerant city in Europe, perhaps the world, and New Amsterdam, renamed New York by the English in 1664, took after its parent city. It was liberal and diverse, a character it has maintained. A marker of the city's early diversity is that in 1646, one observer counted at least eighteen languages while strolling the streets.[51]

Religion in the city was as varied as nationalities and tongues. A later English governor, Thomas Dongan, listed fourteen denominations in the newly English colony, including "Singing Quakers, Ranting Quakers, Sabbatarians; Antisabbatarians, . . . Jews, [and] Independents." He concluded his list by observing, "of all sorts of opinions [denominations] there are some, and the most part of none at all."[52] In stark contrast to New England's rigid homogeneity, most of Manhattan was nonreligious.

Pride in American diversity was enshrined in America's de facto original motto, *E pluribus unum*, "from many, one" or "out of many, one" (see page 274). From many people, one nation; from many colonies, one country. That melting pot became an American ideal. J. Hector St. John de Crèvecoeur, an author and French émigré, wrote about this in *Letters from an American Farmer* (1782), asking,

> What then is the American, this new man? He is . . . [a] strange
> mixture of blood, which you will find in no other country. I could
> point out to you a family whose grandfather was an Englishman,

whose wife was Dutch, whose son married a French woman, and whose present four sons have now four wives of different nations. *He* is an American, who leaving behind him all his ancient prejudices and manners, receives new ones from the new mode of life he has embraced, the new government he obeys, and the new rank he holds.[53]

(Crèvecoeur also approvingly observed that American children were "more indifferent in matters of religion than their parents. The foolish vanity, or rather the fury of making Proselytes, is unknown here; they have no time.")[54]

Melting pots require toleration or they boil over. Captain William Byrd of Virginia traveled to New York in the 1680s and seconded Dongan's observations on the absence of religion. He found it remarkable that the citizens were "not concerned with what religion their neighbor is, or whether he hath any or none."[55] This is not to say that Holland or New Amsterdam reached the modern ideal of religious freedom. But even a "grudging acceptance" from the authorities was hard to come by anywhere else.[56] The distinction between tolerance and true freedom, neither of which the Puritans practiced, is another important one. But the distinction did not exist until America became the first country to separate civil government from religion. That invention is the key to genuine religious freedom.

Both tolerance and intolerance claim the power to crush dissent and heresy. Intolerance wields that power, tolerance does not. But claiming to have this power, even if the powerful hand is stayed, is problematic. Thomas Paine explained this in *The Rights of Man*:

> Toleration is not the opposite of intoleration, but is the counterfeit of it. Both are despotisms. The one assumes to itself the right of withholding liberty of conscience, and the other of granting it. The one is the Pope, armed with fire and faggot, and the other is the Pope selling or granting indulgences. The former is church and state, and the latter is church and traffic [as in trade or commerce].[57]

George Washington expressed the same thing in his 1790 letter to the Touro Synagogue in Connecticut. This letter is justly famous for Washington's declaration that "the Government of the United States . . . gives to bigotry no sanction, to persecution no assistance." But Washington also noted that that government cast aside "toleration" in favor of a natural right: "It is now no more that toleration is spoken of, as if it was by the indulgence of one class of people, that another enjoyed the exercise of their inherent natural rights."[58] True religious freedom comes only when state and church are completely separate, when the government has no power over the human mind at all, neither to prohibit nor to allow thought.

Intolerance looks like the Plymouth and Massachusetts Bay theocracies. A government practicing tolerance *might* look like New Amsterdam or Roger Williams's colony at Rhode Island. Calvinism technically governed New Amsterdam. But Shorto explains that "in the records of the colony expressions of piety are overwhelmed by accounts like that of a woman who, while her husband dozed on a nearby chair, 'dishonorably manipulated the male member' of a certain Irishman while two other men looked on. Excessive rigidity (of the moral kind) was not the sin of New Amsterdam's residents."[59] And of course, when tolerance waned in New Amsterdam, "Religion was the root of it: [Governor Peter] Stuyvesant despised Jews, loathed Catholics, recoiled at Quakers, and reserved special hatred for Lutherans."[60] When Stuyvesant tried to prevent twenty-three Jewish refugees from entering the colony because they were part of a "deceitful race" that would "infect" the island, his superiors back home overruled him, enforcing tolerance and requiring that "each person shall remain free in his religion." [61]

Although tolerance might be adopted as a Judeo-Christian principle in some enlightened circles, religious freedom cannot be. Religion at its heart is a claim to hold the ultimate truth. Christianity holds that truth to the exclusion of all others, with an eternal reward if you accept the truth, and eternal punishment if you do not. Such a worldview can never coexist with true freedom. It will always use its power to promote its truth claim either by the stick (Paine's "fire and faggot") or the carrot (Paine's "traffic" or indulgences).

The Puritans's founding principle was intolerance, not tolerance, let alone religious freedom. They understood and even admitted this. One Puritan preacher, Urian Oakes, later president of Harvard, called toleration the "first-born of all abominations."[62] Another, Thomas Shepard Jr., preached that it is "Satan's policy to plead for an indefinite and boundless toleration."[63] John Cotton helped banish the heretics Anne Hutchinson, who was once Cotton's acolyte, and Roger Williams. In 1647, Cotton published *The Bloudy Tenent, Washed and Made White in the Bloud of the Lambe* as a response to Williams's 1644 book *The Bloudy Tenent of Persecution, for Cause of Conscience*, which had called for a "hedge or wall of separation between the garden of the church and the wilderness of the world." Cotton claimed that "it was toleration that made the Church anti-Christian and the Church never took hurt by the punishment of heretics."[64] This from a man who fled England because Charles I was persecuting Puritans like himself.

The Pilgrims of Plymouth were no better. The Mayflower Compact is often used to show America's Christian principles, but it actually shows Christian intolerance.[65] The Separatists aboard the *Mayflower* referred to themselves, with no apparent vanity, as "Saints." The original Mayflower Compact is lost, but historians have reconstructed it from several copies. Rendered in modern English, it makes evident that the Pilgrims' monolithic religion was foremost in their minds and their purpose. Unlike the United States' godless Constitution, the Compact begins with a mention of the "Saints'" god; their god or their religion is mentioned a total of six times in the Compact's four sentences:

> In the name of God, Amen. We, whose names are underwritten, the Loyal Subjects of our dread Sovereign Lord King James, by the Grace of God, of Great Britain, France, and Ireland, King, defender of the Faith, &c. Having undertaken, for the Glory of God, and Advancement of the Christian Faith and Honour of our King and Country, a Voyage to plant the first Colony in the northern Parts of Virginia; Do by these Presents, solemnly and mutually, in the Presence of God and one another, covenant and combine ourselves together into a civil Body Politick.[66]

The Puritans and the Pilgrims wanted—and got—Christian nations. They established pure theocracies: strongly religious governments able to stamp out heresy, execute schismatics, and banish all but the meekest.

Few settlers wanted to permanently join this harsh monoculture after experiencing it. One of the pillars of the Dutch settlement at New Amsterdam, a young lawyer named Adriaen van der Donck, wrote about an English refugee, a clergyman, who "came to New England at the commencement of the troubles in England, in order to escape them, and found that he had got out of the frying pan and into the fire. He betook himself, in consequence, under the protection of the Netherlanders, in order that he may, according to the Dutch reformation, enjoy freedom of conscience, which he unexpectedly missed in New England."[67]

The Puritans imposed the death penalty for worshipping other gods, blasphemy, homosexuality, and adultery.[68] It is out of this society and this mindset that the terrible idea of a Christian nation founded on Christian principles lodged itself in the American psyche. And it is this intolerant legacy that must be abandoned. That is what a Christian government looks like: exclusive, exclusionary, divisive, hateful, severe, and lethal. It resembles modern theocracies in the Middle East. The insufferable Puritan theocracy declined after King Charles II revoked the colonial charter and passed the Toleration Act of 1689.

All of this happened more than 100 years before the American Revolution and the drafting of the US Constitution. When the framers, like James Madison, surveyed history, they eschewed theocracy and intolerance, condemning the "torrents of blood" spilled in the name of religion.[69] Jefferson looked back on the "millions of innocent men, women, and children, since the introduction of Christianity, [who] have been burnt, tortured, fined, imprisoned; yet we have not advanced one inch towards uniformity."[70]

When the framers wanted to convince the people to ratify the Constitution, they didn't turn to the sword, but to the pen. In the first of *The Federalist Papers*, Alexander Hamilton wrote, "For in politics, as in religion, it is equally absurd to aim at making proselytes by fire and sword. Heresies in either can rarely be cured by persecution."[71]

The early history of theocratic settlements in the New World gave the founders examples to avoid. Jefferson observed that those fleeing persecution "cast their eyes on these new countries as asylums of civil and religious freedom; but they found them free only for the reigning sect."[72] He lambasted Virginia colonial laws that outlawed Quakerism and mandated baptizing children.[73] He invoked the execution of Mary Dyer and the others persecuted in New England as something to shun: "If no capital execution took place here, as did in New-England, it was not owing to the moderation of the church, or spirit of the legislature, as may be inferred from the law itself; but to historical circumstances which have not been handed down to us."[74] After surveying this bloody history, the founders decided to build a wall that would forever separate state and church. They disestablished religion and abolished religious tests for public office. They invented the secular state.

When our nation was founded, it rejected the intolerance theocracy breeds. We had, as Jefferson would say in his inaugural address, "banished from our land that religious intolerance under which mankind so long bled and suffered."[75] One of our founding principles is religious freedom. And a Christian nation is hostile to that ideal. A Christian nation would destroy that which has made America so strong, as it did in these Christian colonies. America's foundation deliberately eliminated religious intolerance. But it also shied away from tolerance, reaching instead for a higher ideal—true freedom.

PART II

UNITED STATES v. THE BIBLE

"We the People of the United States, in Order to form a
more perfect Union, establish Justice, insure domestic
Tranquility, provide for the common defence, promote the
general Welfare, and secure the Blessings of Liberty to
ourselves and our Posterity, do ordain and establish this
Constitution for the United States of America."

—US Constitution, preamble

"[The bible] is a book that has been read more, and
examined less, than any book that ever existed."

—Thomas Paine, in a letter to Lord Thomas Erskine, 1797 [1]

"Is government a science or not? Are there any principles
on which it is founded? What are its ends? If indeed there is
no rule, no standard, all must be accident and chance.
If there is a standard, what is it?"

—John Adams, in a letter to Thomas Brand Hollis, 1788 [2]

6

Biblical Influence

"I find many passages of fine imagination, correct morality,
and of the most lovely benevolence; and others again of so much
ignorance, so much absurdity, so much untruth, charlatanism, and
imposture, as to pronounce it impossible that such contradictions
should have proceeded from the same being."

—**Thomas Jefferson to William Short**, on the bible, 1820[3]

"Those men, whom Jewish and Christian idolaters have
abusively called heathens, had much better and clearer ideas
of justice and morality than are to be found in the
Old Testament, so far as it is Jewish; or in the New."

—**Thomas Paine**, *The Age of Reason*, 1794–1807[4]

Our investigation into the founders, the Declaration, and colonial America have not fully answered a central question: Did biblical principles influence the founding of the American nation, government, or legal system? Part II will tackle this query head on.

But first, it is important to understand that the bible's indisputable linguistic or literary influence does not answer this question. The bible's first English translation was both courageous and transformative. John Wycliffe, William Tyndale, and the work of King James's bishops are as influential as Shakespeare in terms of the language and idioms we use. Perhaps even more so, although Shakespeare offers far greater insights about humanity—"Suspicion always haunts the guilty mind"; and better rules for living—"This above all; to thine own self be true."[5]

Like Shakespeare's plays and poetry, Aesop's fables, and the legends of Greek and Roman mythology, the bible has provided a common stock of stories for the English-speaking world. Unlike Shakespeare's body of work and these other influential collections, which stood on their own merits to gain renown, the bible's reputation was imposed and propagated for millennia with the sword, fire, and mandatory reinforcement sessions held weekly—church. Well-known stories influence communication: "slow and steady wins the race," "sour grapes," "a man reaps what he sows." They provide a common well to draw on to make complicated ideas more digestible. Using biblical stories to communicate an idea does not necessarily indicate that biblical theology influenced the underlying idea or that the speaker adheres to a biblical religion. Evangelical historian Mark Noll put it this way: "The Bible was not so much the truth above all truth as it was the story above all stories."[6]

Lincoln's use of the "house divided" metaphor when he accepted the Republican nomination to be Illinois's senator is a perfect example: "'A house divided against itself cannot stand.' I believe this government cannot endure, permanently, half slave and half free."[7] According to Lincoln's law partner and biographer, Henry Herndon, Lincoln chose the metaphor, which appears several times in the Christian gospels, because he "want[ed] to use some universally known figure expressed in simple language as universally well-known, that may strike home in the minds."[8] Lincoln didn't quote the bible because he believed it to be divine revelation. One Springfield resident recalled Lincoln saying it was "a pleasure to be able to quote lines to fit any occasion" and noting that the bible was the richest source of pertinent quotations.[9] He simply reached for a convenient, comfortable, familiar allusion to ease the acceptance of a hard truth. (In any event, Lincoln "read Shakespeare more than all other writers together," according to his secretary, John Hays.[10])

Politicians and statesmen like Lincoln may regularly quote from and allude to the bible, but this does not necessarily indicate an underlying religiosity. Ethan Allen, of Green Mountain and Fort Ticonderoga fame, read the bible because it was the only book available during his bucolic childhood. According to Matthew Stewart, he read it "over and over again, until its parables took up residence in every foxhole of his mind, always ready to sally forth to defend a friend or threaten a foe."[11] But neither Lincoln nor Allen can be considered Christian merely because they read and quoted the bible. Many atheists do the same and, according to studies, know the book better than Christians.[12] Knowing and even reciting the bible does not make one religious, and reading the bible can often have the opposite effect. The road to atheism is littered with bibles that have been read cover to cover.[13] Allen's knowledge of the bible led him to pen one of the first freethought books in America, *Reason: The Only Oracle of Man* (1785). (According to Herndon, Lincoln wrote a similar book, "in which he made an argument against Christianity, striving to prove that the Bible was not inspired, and therefore not God's revelation, and that Jesus Christ was not the son of God." Others dispute this and, according to Herndon's account, a friend burned the manuscript to secure Lincoln's political future.[14])

Even quoting the bible is not necessarily an indication of the writer's beliefs about that book. Thomas Paine quoted extensively from the bible in *Common Sense* because he was writing to a people who were familiar with biblical stories, like 1 Samuel 8. Paine made a biblical argument for revolution. But I'm an atheist and I regularly quote the bible to argue against government prayer. In Matthew 6:5, Jesus condemns public prayer as hypocrisy: "And when you pray, do not be like the hypocrites, for they love to pray standing in the synagogues and on the street corners to be seen." As an atheist, I use the bible to convince believers not to abuse their public office to promote their personal religion, pointing to the words of their own savior in his Sermon on the Mount. Like Paine and Lincoln, I write to my audience.

Influencing the English language and American culture is not the same as influencing the founding of the American laws and government—our nation. Yet Christian nationalists still claim that the bible is the basis of America. One Christian nationalist went so far as to declare, on the 2017 National Day of Prayer, that "You'll find almost verbatim wording in many clauses of the Constitution to passages in the Bible. It's a one-to-one correlation on the wording."[15] That is demonstrably false. Other Christian nationalist assertions are just as absurd. For instance, they claim that the concept of three separate branches of government contained in Articles I (legislative), II (executive), and III (judicial) of the Constitution came from Isaiah 33:22: "For the LORD is our judge, the LORD is our ruler, the LORD is our king; he will save us."[16] This verse concludes with passages that lay out "the Lord's plans to reveal worldwide sovereignty,"[17] so it is not about a tripartite separation of powers, but about destroying all governments in favor of concentrating power in one being, Yahweh. There is no separation of powers without a separation of people holding those powers.[18] For Jefferson, "concentrating [powers] in the same hands is precisely the definition of despotic government."[19] Madison thought that such a concentration was "the very definition of tyranny."[20] The biblical vision of government supported in Isaiah is exactly what the Constitution ended.

Those two points aside, we *know* that the modern idea of separation of powers did not come from the bible. It came from Montesquieu, who never mentioned or referred to the bible in his discussion of three separate branches of government.[21] *The Federalist* number 47 is entirely devoted to explaining "this invaluable precept in the science of politics."[22] In it, Madison wrote that "no political truth is certainly of greater intrinsic value, or is stamped with the authority of more enlightened patrons of liberty." He added, "The oracle who is always consulted and cited on this subject is the celebrated Montesquieu." Judeo-Christian principles have nothing to do with separation of powers.

Occasionally a similarly implausible argument—that the holy trinity is the basis for our three branches of government—is put forth, evidently because both are made up of three parts. This is especially absurd given that some founders treated the trinity with contempt. In writing about it, Jefferson said, "Ridicule is the only weapon which can be used against unintelligible propositions" and called the trinity the "mere Abracadabra of mountebanks calling themselves the Priests of Jesus."[23] John Adams wrote to Jefferson, "Had you and I been forty days with Moses on Mount Sinai, and been admitted to behold the divine Shekinah [the manifestation of this god dwelling among man], and there told that one was three and three one, we might not have had courage to deny it, but we could not have believed it."[24]

The principles underlying Judeo-Christianity and America conflict on other points. Christianity's view and treatment of its founding documents is at odds with the American view and treatment of its founding documents. God's law is unchangeable. American law is not. The Constitution is not perfect. The framers knew this, and none left the Convention having secured everything they wanted. In his closing address to the Convention, Franklin consented "to this Constitution because I expect no better, and because I am not sure, that it is not the best."[25] Adams, writing a few years later as vice president, was more specific: "The Constitution is but an experiment, and must and will be altered."[26]

These were not men acting with the certainty of religious conviction. They were thoughtful, reasonable men aware that they, and other delegates, were governed partly by passion and self-interest. And so, certain mostly of their own fallibility, they crafted a provision to

Scene at the Signing of the Constitution of the United States,
Howard Chandler Christie's famous 1940 painting of the founders
at Independence Hall on September 17, 1787.

alter—to amend—the Constitution. They would take advantage of Article V almost immediately, to write and pass the first ten amendments, the Bill of Rights. The Constitution has been altered twenty-seven times and nearly always improved. The glaring exception to this steady improvement was partly due to religious groups, such as the Women's Christian Temperance Union, which advocated for the Eighteenth Amendment, Prohibition, and which was repealed by the Twenty-first Amendment.

The framers were wise enough to recognize—as their near-contemporary Alexander Pope put it—that "to err is human,"[27] but the bible is divine and infallible, according to many in the Judeo-Christian traditions. "All scripture is inspired by God," wrote Paul to Timothy.[28] John Wesley, who founded Methodism, called the bible "infallibly true."[29] Catholics believe the bible is "without error," as do many evangelical Christians.[30] The bible has been edited, rewritten, excised, supplemented, translated, retranslated, and mistranslated so many times that claims of immutability are laughable. Yet about thirty percent of Americans, many of them Christian nationalists, believe the bible is the literal, inerrant word of their god.[31]

IF THE BIBLE AND ITS PRINCIPLES influenced America's founding, surely the founders quoted from it regularly? It must have been repeatedly referenced during their important founding debates, such as the Constitutional Convention and state ratifying conventions? And not just for cultural and linguistic stories, but for its theology, thought, and principles, right?

Not so. Some writers during the founding era cited the bible when discussing politics, but they were almost always preachers citing it during their sermons. But it was almost never referenced during important political debates. University of Houston professor Donald Lutz tallied how often writers in the founding era quoted European political thinkers and the bible.[32] Lutz analyzed 15,000 pamphlets, newspaper articles, and books, but not all were relevant to the political principles that influenced the founding. When Lutz included printed sermons—a common form of literature at the time—in the sample, total citations to the bible, a decent proxy for influence, ranked highly.

Unsurprisingly, the sermons cited the bible more than eight times on average.[33] And if you listen to the Christian nationalists, the analysis ends there, with the bible as the "single-most-cited source."[34] But that included every scrap of literature, whether it dealt with politics or not. When Lutz examined only the political writings, the writing relevant to the discussion here (about 2,200 documents), the citations to the bible disappeared. The authors cited the bible about 0.3 times on average, or made about one biblical reference in every three or four works.[35]

Lutz points out something even more striking: the bible was hardly cited in the constitutional debates. In 528 writings published during the formative years of the American Constitution (1787–88), there were thirty-three citations to the bible, or about one in every sixteen publications.[36] Lutz concluded that when looking for biblical influence in the framing of our founding document, "the Bible's prominence disappears, which is not surprising since the debate centered upon specific institutions about which the Bible has little to say."[37] But there is something still more striking. When Lutz separated the Federalists (those arguing *for* the Constitution and a central, federal government) from the Anti-Federalists (those arguing *against* the Constitution), he discovered that the Federalists *never* cited the bible—not once. Put simply, those who argued for and supported the Constitution were not influenced by the bible.[38]

Lutz looked at published writings. But what about unpublished writings—for instance, what about citations to the bible during the Constitutional Convention, which was conducted mostly by voice and the proceedings of which the delegates voted to keep secret? At the Constitutional Convention the bible was briefly mentioned once, by Franklin, during a debate over a proposed property requirement for public office, in what was simply a case of Franklin using religion, again, to attain his political ends.[39]

This lack of influence makes sense because Christian nationalists have never convincingly answered a basic question: How, precisely, did the bible influence American political thought and America's founding? The question is even more pressing knowing that the founders did not cite the bible when writing and debating the Constitution. It is assumed that our government was founded on biblical principles, on Judeo-Christian principles. Because this answer is assumed, few bother to explain which specific Judeo-Christian principles and ideas were so influential to America's founding. Instead, we get vague assertions from men like Tim LaHaye, a Christian nationalist author and co-author of the popular Left Behind series, who lauds "the Christian consensus of our Founding Fathers and the Biblical principles of law that have provided the freedoms we've enjoyed for over two hundred years."[40] These partial answers rely on emotion and desire, not on history or fact, and therefore fail to truly answer anything.

So let's look for the answers ourselves, by comparing the Judeo-Christian principles in the bible—the Golden Rule, obedience, biblical crime and punishment, original sin, vicarious redemption, religious faith, and monarchy—with the tenets of the American Constitution, laws, and government. American principles and Judeo-Christian principles are so irreconcilable that we can fairly say: Judeo-Christianity is un-American.

An Argument Anticipated

Before we look at those principles, let's address the inevitable complaint that I am cherry-picking quotes from the bible that support my argument.

First, occasionally context may be disregarded. Is there a context in which harming innocent children is an appropriate punishment for a parent's misdeeds, as the second commandment requires? Even attempting such an argument proves the point that everything, no matter how immoral, is permissible with divine sanction.

Second, such a complaint would be tangential at best. The themes of this section of the book—vicarious redemption of our sins through the sacrifice of Jesus, hell, and obedience—are indisputably strong themes in the bible and are central to the Judeo-Christianity conceived by Christian nationalists. As such, they are not cherry-picked.

Finally, the argument that the bible also has passages that contradict those cited in this book proves the point that Judeo-Christian principles, as found in the bible, are not a good guide for nation-building. If the bible takes both sides of an argument, it cannot be said that either side is a principle of that document. If the bible says "children should eat peas" and also "children should not eat peas," it takes no lucid stance on pea-eating. That the bible has opposing messages simply shows that some other moral compass or reasoned analysis is working to help us decide whether or not pea-eating is appropriate. Our country is based on clear principles that are attained by reason, not on a text that repeatedly contradicts itself.

7

Christian Arrogance and the Golden Rule

"The Golden Rule would have been just as good
if it had first been whispered by the Devil."
— **Robert Ingersoll**, "The Great Infidels," 1881[1]

Christian nationalists make many claims, but perhaps the most arrogant is that America is a Christian nation because we were founded on the Golden Rule.[2] For argument's sake, let's assume that this is true. The assumption doesn't improve the Christian nationalist's position, because the Golden Rule is not Christian.

Moral behavior can often be boiled down to something like the Golden Rule. The Jewish formulation of the rule first appears in Leviticus: "You shall not hate in your heart anyone of your kin; you shall reprove your neighbor, or you will incur guilt yourself. You shall not take vengeance or bear a grudge against any of your people, but you shall love your neighbor as yourself: I am the LORD."[3] As we'll see with the Ten Commandments (see page 212), the term "neighbor" limits the application of this rule to one's fellow believers. Here, "your kin," "your people," and "your neighbor" are used synonymously. So this version of the rule is not universal and applies only to others who worship the same god—not to heretics. Consequently, it is morally flawed, less deserving of examination, and unfit for reverence.

Jesus may have issued his Golden Rule as interpreted by the Good Samaritan parable to correct this lamentable defect,[4] but he was definitely not the first to do so. The Golden Rule exists in nearly every society and also appears, in one form or another, in many religions, including "Hinduism, Buddhism, Taoism, Zoroastrianism, and the rest of the world's major religions," according to one ethicist.[5] Not only is the Golden Rule more widespread than Christianity, but it predates Christianity by hundreds and even thousands of years:

1. "Now this is the command: Do to the doer to cause that he do."
   ~Ancient Egypt (c. 2040–1650 BCE)[6]

2. "Don't do yourself what you disapprove of in others."
   ~Pittacus of Mytilene, Ancient Greece (c. 640–568 BCE)[7]

3. "Never do ourselves what we blame others for doing."
   ~Thales of Miletus, Ancient Greece (c. 624–545 BCE)[8]

4. "To those who are good (to me), I am good; and to those who are not good (to me), I am also good; and thus (all) get to be good."
   ~Laozi, China (sixth century BCE)[9]

5. "Do not impose on others what you do not desire others to impose upon you."
   ~Confucius, China (551–479 BCE)[10]

6. "What I disapprove of in the actions of my neighbor, that—as best I can—I will not do."
   ~Herodotus, Ancient Greece (fifth century BCE)[11]

7. "If people regarded other people's families in the same way that they regard their own, who then would incite their own family to attack that of another? For one would do for others as one would do for oneself."
   ~Mozi, China (c. 470–391 BCE)[12]

8. "Do not do to others the things that anger you when you experience them from others."
   ~Isocrates, Ancient Greece (c. 436–338 BCE)[13]

9. "We ought not to retaliate or render evil for evil to anyone, whatever evil we may have suffered from him."
   ~Plato/Socrates (fifth–fourth century BCE)[14]

10. "One should never do that to another which one regards as injurious to one's own self. This, in brief, is the rule of Righteousness."
    ~Hindu *Mahabharata* (c. fourth century BCE)[15]

11. Justice is an agreement "neither to harm nor be harmed."
    ~Epicurus, Ancient Greece (341–270 BCE)[16]

12. "What is hateful to you, do not do to your fellow: this is the whole Torah; the rest is the explanation; go and learn."
    ~Hillel (c. 110 BCE–10 CE)[17]

13. "Do to others as you would have them do to you."
    ~Jesus (c. 30 CE)[18]

The timespan between that early Egyptian formulation and the later Christian version is about the same as that between Jesus's life and today. Of course, philosophers can argue about differences in the rule itself. Is the positive formulation (treat others as you'd like to be treated) superior to the negative formulation (don't do to others what you wouldn't want done to yourself)? Is the rule defective, as Kant thought, and is his categorical imperative better? But such arguments are irrelevant here. It is enough to show that the Jewish tradition did not apply the rule universally and that many other versions predated the Judeo-Christian formulations. The dates in the list opposite and above suggest that, if anything, Judaism and Christianity probably borrowed the rule from Ancient Greece.

The Golden Rule is not a Judeo-Christian principle. It is a universal human principle. This "interchangeability of perspectives" is the "foundation of morality" and can be seen in just as many secular, ethical traditions as religious traditions, according to Harvard neuroscientist Steven Pinker.[19] The ethicist Peter Singer put it a bit differently: "The major ethical traditions all accept, in some form or other, a version of the Golden Rule that encourages equal consideration of interests."[20] Therefore, Judeo-Christianity's "Golden Rule" cannot be said to have had any unique impact on the nation's founding—especially given that influential founders such as John Adams knew it was not unique to Christianity. One reflective Sunday, Adams wrote in his diary that Christianity included the rule but did not invent it: "One great advantage of the Christian religion is, that it brings the great principle of the law of nature and nations,—Love your neighbor as yourself, and do to others as you would that others should do to you,—to the knowledge, belief, and veneration of the whole people."[21]

According to Adams, the Golden Rule is *not* a Christian principle: it is a universal principle, a "principle of the law of nature and nations." Christianity was one vehicle to disperse this universal idea, not its origin.

Faith affects a Christian nationalist's self-perception. It is often argued that Christians are humble and that atheists and scientists are arrogant. But this is backward. Atheists, scientists, and other rational citizens—and religious citizens in their nonreligious thinking—claim to have answers supported by evidence, not by faith. Christianity claims to know ultimate truths about the universe with absolute certainty because of faith, not evidence. Faith, almost by definition, is conceit.

Empathy, compassion, guilt, forgiveness, morality, and responsibility cannot be claimed as the monopoly of one religion. They are, to borrow from Christopher Hitchens, part of our "elementary human solidarity." Arguing that the Golden Rule influenced America's founding does nothing to prove that we are a Christian nation, but it does help show the arrogance of Christian nationalism.

8

Biblical Obedience or American Freedom?

"Inquiry is Human; Blind Obedience Brutal.
Truth never loses by the one, but often suffers by the other."
—**William Penn**, *Some Fruits of Solitude*, 1682[1]

"It is verily a great thing to live in obedience,
to be under authority, and not to be at our own disposal.
Far safer is it to live in subjection."
—**Thomas à Kempis**, *The Imitation of Christ*[2]

The founding documents of the United States revere and protect freedom above all else. The bible worships and demands the opposite: obedience, submission, and servility. And it secures that obedience through fear. Fear and obey god. The principles of the two traditions diverge.

People on both sides of the American Revolution understood the American drive for freedom. The British statesman Edmund Burke, in a 1775 speech advocating reconciliation with the colonies, said that "a love of freedom is the predominating feature which marks and distinguishes the [character of the Americans]. . . . This fierce spirit of liberty is stronger in the English colonies probably than in any other people of the earth."[3] William Pitt echoed that sentiment in a 1777 speech to the House of Lords, asserting, "You may ravage—you cannot conquer; it is impossible; you cannot conquer the Americans."[4]

On the other side of the conflict, Thomas Paine wrote in *Common Sense* that a government is in the business of "securing freedom and property to all men, and above all things, the free exercise of religion, according to the dictates of conscience."[5] Paine and Burke famously disagreed, but not about America's yearning for freedom. Our Constitution concurs. One of its purposes is to "secure the Blessings of Liberty." The Fifth and Fourteenth Amendments declare that no citizen can be "deprived of life, liberty, or property, without due process of law" by federal or state governments respectively. The First Amendment protects the freedoms of speech, press, and association and the free exercise of religion by ensuring a secular government. The Second Amendment mentions bearing arms in relation to a militia because the framers thought a militia was necessary to ensure a "free state." Freedom was always a goal. Without the freedoms protected by our Constitution and its mandate to separate the government from religion, citizens would not have a genuine choice in religion or belief. If most Americans are religious, they are free to be only because there is no government-endorsed religion that devours religious freedom. Christian nationalists are *required* by their bible to believe in eternal punishment and Noah's ark; they are *free* to believe such things because of our Constitution.

Judeo-Christianity is not concerned with freedom or liberty—quite the opposite. The bible is rife with obedience and servility. Perhaps the most familiar example of biblically mandated obedience is the story in which the all-powerful god commands Abraham to murder his son, Isaac, as a sacrifice, a "burnt offering."[6] The sacrifice of Isaac was "a test of true devotion," as one scholar has noted.[7] Abraham takes Isaac into the wild, gathers wood, builds the pyre, binds his son's hands and feet, and places him on the pyre.[8] As Abraham raises the knife to plunge it into his own child, the biblical god stops the murder, "for now I know that you fear God, since you have not withheld your son, your only son, from me."[9] God was testing Abraham's obedience, ensuring that he was sufficiently scared to obey. This fearful obedience is rewarded: "Because you have done this, and have not withheld your son, your only son, I will indeed bless you, and I will make your offspring as numerous as the stars of heaven . . . because you have obeyed my voice."[10] God requires fear and unquestioning obedience to the point of killing your children.

That story alone, and the frequency with which it is preached and referenced, should be enough to show the bible's fetish for fear-based obedience. But there's so much more. Lot's wife is turned into a pillar of salt for breaking a "no peeking" rule.[11] The first few of the Ten Commandments are all about serving and obeying this petulant god: I am your god, have no other, etc. Believers must "*fear* the LORD your God, to walk in all his ways, to love him, to *serve* the LORD your God with all your heart and with all your soul."[12] Paul wrote that we should be "obedient slaves" to his god, for "obedience . . . leads to righteousness."[13] And there will supposedly come a time when Jesus, "with his mighty angels in flaming fire," will inflict "vengeance on . . . *those who do not obey* the gospel of our Lord Jesus."[14] If Christianity is about anything, it is about obedience to god. That's why the original sin is not genocide, murder, or rape, but eating a piece of fruit after being told not to.

As we've seen, the bible's demand for slavish obedience prohibits rebellions of the very type that freed the American colonies from Great Britain: "If you are willing and obedient, you will eat the good things of the land; but if you resist and rebel, you will be devoured by the sword, for the mouth of the LORD has spoken."[15]

There are many more passages in the bible that not only revere but also require servility, especially in the New Testament:

- "Slaves, obey your earthly masters with fear and trembling." ~Ephesians 6:5–9.
- "But I do as the Father has commanded me, so that the world may know that I love the Father." ~John 14:31.
- "Taking every thought captive to the obedience of Christ." ~2 Corinthians 10:5
- "He became to all who obey Him the source of salvation." ~Hebrews 5:9.
- "That you may obey Jesus Christ and to be sprinkled with his blood." ~1 Peter 1:2.
- "As obedient children . . . be holy." ~1 Peter 1:14.
- "We must obey God rather than men." ~Acts 5:29.

- "Through the obedience of the One, the many will be made righteous." ~Romans 5:19.
- "If you love me, you will keep my commandments." ~John 14:15.

Is it any wonder that slaveholders in the American South found support in the bible? Or that they wanted to convert their slaves to an obedience-inducing religion like Christianity?

PERHAPS THE ONLY BIBLICAL COUNTEREXAMPLE to such servility is the Exodus flight from Egypt. However, there is virtually no archaeological, historical, linguistic, or other evidence that suggests this was an actual event.[16] Even if it were true, treating the story as a fight for freedom, as Christians have done for centuries, ignores the bulk of the bible and the story's lesson.

The full Exodus story is about fear and obedience, not freedom. God tells Moses, "Obey my voice and keep my covenant, [and] you shall be my treasured possession out of all the peoples."[17] Moses tells his people, "All that the Lord has spoken we will do, and we will be obedient."[18] The Exodus flight trades one god, Pharaoh, for another god who demands such servile fealty that it can hardly be called freedom.[19]

God even bars Moses from the Promised Land at the end of the Exodus tale because he disobeyed. Wandering in the desert, water quickly became an issue for the nomads. Yahweh instructed Moses to assemble the congregation and command a certain rock to produce water for the complaining multitude. The refugees gathered, and Moses did two things to anger his god. First, he asked them, "Shall *we* bring water out of this rock?" Then, instead of speaking to command the rock, Moses tapped the rock with his wooden rod. For this heresy—tapping, instead of commanding—"the LORD said to Moses . . . 'you shall not bring this assembly into the land that I have given them.'"[20] That's it. For tapping a rock with his magic wand instead of saying the magic words and possibly for saying "we" instead of "he" (i.e., Yahweh), Moses was barred from the Promised Land. The moral of this story is not freedom: it is obedience to arbitrary authority. Even were it an example of freedom in the bible, the story provides no evidence to support the claim that it influenced America's founding.

In the bible story, Yahweh bestowed freedom on the Israelites, but, as Franklin Roosevelt said, "In the truest sense, freedom cannot be bestowed; it must be achieved."[21] Freedom under the yoke of absolute power does not exist, even if it were a benevolent power. "No country can be called free which is governed by an absolute power," observed Thomas Paine.[22] Blind obedience to and fear of an omnipotent being is tyranny, not freedom. At its core, Judeo-Christianity's insistence on obedience and fear conflicts with America's essential value.

9

Crime and Punishment: Biblical Vengeance or American Justice?

"Never avenge yourselves, but leave room for the wrath of God;
for it is written, 'Vengeance is mine, I will repay, says the Lord.'"

—Romans 12:19

"Punishments I know are necessary, and I would provide them,
strict and inflexible, but proportioned to the crime.
Death might be inflicted for murder and perhaps for treason
if you would take out of the description of treason all
crimes which are not such in their nature."

—Thomas Jefferson,
in a letter to Edmund Pendleton, August 26, 1776[1]

One of the starkest conflicts between biblical and American principles is how each treats the guilty. The Eighth Amendment provides that "Excessive bail shall not be required, nor excessive fines imposed, nor cruel and unusual punishments inflicted." Yes, legislators are "tough on crime," and America executes more prisoners than any other first-world country, landing on a list with China, Iran, Saudi Arabia, Iraq, and Pakistan for most citizens executed.[2] But that is nothing compared to the bible, which overflows with barbaric, violent punishment and blood. Outside of the religious context, it would not be entirely fair to compare a modern justice system with the punishment norms of a tribe of Bronze Age herdsmen. Interpreting history using modern values, known as presentism, is frowned upon by historians. Our society is less primitive than the one that produced the bible, so how can we fairly judge history by the morality of today? Perhaps we shouldn't; but the history is not the issue. The issue is biblical religion and morality. Christian nationalists are claiming not only that archaic standards influenced the thought and actions of the founders many centuries later, but also that Judeo-Christianity is the final authority on an absolute, universal morality. Therefore, we should judge Judeo-Christianity and its moral claims by the highest moral code of any time. Stephen Fry made this point nicely: "What is the point of the Catholic church if it says 'oh, well we couldn't know better because nobody else did.' *Then what are you for?*"[3] "Presentism" is beside the point when dealing with a theology that claims to be timeless, absolute, and perfect.

The framers of the Constitution understood that social norms shift and accounted for those shifts using flexible language such as "cruel and unusual," which defines a category of prohibited punishment in the Eighth Amendment. The "words of the Amendment are not precise, and . . . their scope is not static. The Amendment must draw its meaning from the evolving standards of decency that mark the progress of a maturing society," according to the Supreme Court.[4] By building a standard that can mature, the founders recognized that morality and society inevitably progress. The evolving standard is itself antithetical to the Judeo-Christian idea that morality was perfected millennia ago. Indeed, the shifting standard indicts religion's moral absolutes. The god-given inflexibility of biblical punishments is fundamentally opposed to the progressive standard in the Eighth Amendment.

Judeo-Christianity's claim to the moral high ground makes it perfectly fair to point out its atrocities—for instance, that the bible advocates burning people to death as punishment:[5]

- "When the daughter of a priest profanes herself through prostitution, she profanes her father; she shall be burned to death." ~Leviticus 21:9.
- [The Lord said to Joshua] "And the one who is taken as having the devoted things shall be burned with fire, together with all that he has, for having transgressed the covenant of the LORD, and for having done an outrageous thing in Israel. . . . And all Israel stoned

him to death; they burned them with fire, cast stones on them."
~Joshua 7:10, 7:15, 7:25. "Devoted things" were the people and
possessions of Canaan which the Lord commanded the Israelites
to destroy, as in "devoted to the Lord for destruction." ~Joshua 6:17.

The first example treats a daughter's actions as a crime against her
father. In the second, an entire family is burned for not giving a bit of
gold and silver to Yahweh's treasury after the sack of Jericho.

The New Testament also advocates this brutal punishment. In
John 15:6, Jesus says, "Whoever does not abide in me is thrown away
like a branch and withers; such branches are gathered, thrown into
the fire, and burned." So promiscuous women, sabbath-breakers,
idol-worshippers, Jews, and non-Christians should be gathered and
burned. Those who do not willingly kill and steal at their god's command should be stoned, burned, and stoned again.

Death by stoning—a punishment still used by extremist groups
and in some parts of the Muslim world, typically as a sentence for
adultery—is also mandated in the bible. Unlike modern execution
methods, stoning requires the entire community to take part, ensuring
all are responsible. This biblical punishment is imposed for relatively
minor crimes. The tribe of Israel was required to bludgeon their family
and friends with rocks for the following infractions—some as trivial as
picking up a stick on the sabbath:

1. **Working—specifically, collecting sticks—on the sabbath.**
   Numbers 15:32–36. "The Israelites . . . found a man gathering
   sticks on the sabbath day. Those who found him gathering sticks
   brought him to Moses, Aaron, and to the whole congregation.
   They put him in custody, because it was not clear what should be
   done to him. Then the Lord said to Moses, 'The man shall be put
   to death; all the congregation shall stone him outside the camp.'
   The whole congregation brought him outside the camp and
   stoned him to death."

2. **Blasphemy.** Leviticus 24:16. "One who blasphemes the name
   of the Lord shall be put to death; the whole congregation shall
   stone the blasphemer. Aliens as well as citizens, when they

blaspheme the Name, shall be put to death." **Notice that god's law differentiates between members of the tribe—neighbors or "citizens"—and aliens. Here, they receive the same punishment, but elsewhere, as we'll see, they are treated very differently.**

The penalty is reiterated in 1 Kings 21:10: "Seat two scoundrels opposite him, and have them bring a charge against him, saying, 'You have cursed God and the king.' Then take him out, and stone him to death."

3. **Suggesting another religion or god.** Deuteronomy 13:5–10. "If anyone secretly entices you—even if it is your brother, your father's son or your mother's son, or your own son or daughter, or the wife you embrace, or your most intimate friend—saying, 'Let us go and worship other gods,' . . . you must not yield to or heed any such persons. Show them no pity or compassion and do not shield them. But you shall surely kill them; your own hand shall be first against them to execute them, and afterwards the hand of all the people. Stone them to death for trying to turn you away from the Lord your God."

4. **Being a stubborn child.** Deuteronomy 21:18–21. "If someone has a stubborn and rebellious son who will not obey his father and mother . . . then his father and his mother shall take hold of him and bring him out to the elders of his town at the gate of that place. They shall say to the elders of his town, 'This son of ours is stubborn and rebellious. He will not obey us. He is a glutton and a drunkard.' Then all the men of the town shall stone him to death."

5. **Being a medium or wizard.** Look out, Harry Potter. Leviticus 20:27. "A man or a woman who is a medium or a wizard shall be put to death; they shall be stoned to death, their blood is upon them."

6. **Having premarital sex—if you are a woman.** Deuteronomy 22:20–21. "[If] evidence of the young woman's virginity was not found, then they shall bring the young woman out to the entrance of her father's house and the men of her town shall stone her to death, because she committed a disgraceful act in Israel by prostituting herself in her father's house." Incidentally, if a man falsely accuses his new wife of premarital promiscuity, he is only fined.[6]

7. **A woman failing to cry out for help when she is raped.**
   Deuteronomy 22:23–24. "If there is a young woman, a virgin already engaged to be married, and a man meets her in the town and lies with her, you shall bring both of them to the gate of that town and stone them to death, the young woman because she did not cry for help in the town and the man because he violated his neighbor's wife."

Numbers one through four are crimes against god—a supposedly all-powerful god. Number five is punished because it is a threat to god's priests, who couldn't have magicians stealing some of the awe that is due to their god. The final two crimes are threats to the patriarchy, so the women must be killed.

Worshipping another god, suggesting that someone worship another god, and even proselytizing are protected by the Constitution. But they are capital crimes under biblical principles—as are the other so-called crimes for which the bible commands death: breaking the sabbath, blasphemy, promiscuity, obstinacy, being raped, and witchcraft—a crime with a unique history on the North American continent. It's hard to quantify the misery caused by the biblical command "you shall not permit a witch to live."[7] Mark Twain tried:

> The Church, after doing its duty in but a lazy and indolent way for eight hundred years, gathered up its halters, thumbscrews, and firebrands, and set about its holy work in earnest. She worked hard at it night and day during nine centuries and imprisoned, tortured, hanged, and burned whole hordes and armies of witches, and washed the Christian world clean with their foul blood. Then it was discovered that there was no such thing as witches, and never had been. One does not know whether to laugh or to cry.[8]

Churches have since abandoned burning and stoning those accused of witchcraft. But Christian churches today still terrify parishioners and children with the prospect of being burned alive for eternity: hell.[9] While almost every culture and religion has an afterlife, Jesus was the first to preach about it as a place of eternal punishment. The place of torment is mentioned 162 times in the New Testament and not once in the Old Testament.[10] The Hebrew bible mentions an unseen world of the dead, Sheol. But Sheol has little in common with Jesus's hell. It was not a place of punishment, but a silent shadow world. Literary heroes of the Hebrew bible such as Jacob,[11] David,[12] and even Jesus[13] supposedly visited Sheol. Job longed to get there.[14] Hell, on the other hand, is most certainly a place of punishment. According to the Book of Mark, Jesus taught that it is better to cut off your hand or foot or put out your eye than risk being "thrown into hell, where their worm never dies, and the fire is never quenched."[15] We are told to "fear him who can destroy both body and soul in hell."[16] The Christian bible describes hell as a "furnace of fire";[17] a place where the unworthy "will burn with unquenchable fire";[18] "the eternal fire" and "the hell of fire";[19] "the eternal fire prepared for the devil and his angels";[20] "eternal punishment"[21] where everyone is "salted with fire";[22] a "place of torment" where residents are in constant "agony in these flames";[23] "a punishment of eternal fire";[24] and "the lake that burns with fire and sulfur,[25] and "the lake of fire,"[26] where those who worship other gods will "drink the wine of God's wrath, poured unmixed into the cup of his anger, and they will be tormented with fire and sulfur in the presence of the holy angels and in the presence of the Lamb. And the smoke of their torment goes up forever and ever. There is no rest day or night."[27]

Leading Christian writers from the first to the fifth centuries, taking their cues from the bible, were just as unflinching in their descriptions of hell. Ignatius of Antioch thought that the "defiled shall go into unquenchable fire."[28] Irenaeus wrote of "The eternal fire for those who should transgress."[29] Cyprian specifically tied eternal torture to people's innate fear of death, "Let him fear to die, on whom, at his going away from life an eternal flame will lay pains that never cease."[30]

Augustine of Hippo devoted all twenty-seven chapters of the twenty-first book of his *The City of God* (426 CE) to an exposition on eternal torment, deeming it "absurd to suppose that either body or soul will escape pain in the future punishment."[31] After quoting many of the biblical passages cited above, Augustine pointed out that both body and soul are tortured, the body by everlasting fire, and that "in a body thus tormented, the soul also is tortured with a fruitless repentance."[32]

These Christian fathers favor a grisly place, but it is nothing compared to what a truly macabre imagination can do with the heat, torture, and eternity. The colonial preacher Jonathan Edwards (1703–58) sermonized about the "great furnace of wrath, a wide and bottomless pit, full of the fire of wrath, that you are held over in the hand of that God."[33] In a particularly foul metaphor, Edwards likened humans to insects subject to his vicious god: "The God that holds you over the pit of hell, much as one holds a spider, or some loathsome insect, over the fire, abhors you, and is dreadfully provoked; his wrath towards you burns like fire; . . . you are ten thousand times so abominable in his eyes as the most hateful venomous serpent is in ours."

Edwards also spoke admiringly of a future state where he, one of the saved, could watch the damned burn: "When you shall be in this state of suffering, the glorious inhabitants of heaven shall go forth and look on the awful spectacle, that they may see what the wrath and fierceness of the Almighty is, and when they have seen it, they will fall down and adore that great power and majesty."[34] Many Christian thinkers appear to take a perverse pleasure in the idea of hell. Thomas Aquinas wrote that the eternal torture of the unworthy will be "delightful" entertainment for the saints: "In order that the happiness of the saints may be more delightful to them and that they may render more copious thanks to God for it, they are allowed to see perfectly the sufferings of the damned."[35] The third-century Carthaginian author Tertullian was even more joyful at the prospect: "What sight shall wake my wonder, what my laughter, my joy and exultation? as I see all those kings . . . groaning in the depths of darkness! And the magistrates who persecuted the name of Jesus, liquefying in fiercer flames than they kindled in their rage against the Christians!"[36] This hellish delight was alive at America's founding. The Congregationalist minister and president of Yale, Ezra Stiles, smugly recorded Ethan Allen's death in his diary: "Died in Vermont the profane and impious Deist Gen Ethan Allen, Author of the *Oracles of Reason* [sic], a Book replete with scurrilous Reflexions on Revelation.—'And in Hell he lift up his eyes, being in torments,'" quoting Luke 16:23.[37]

This outlook is thriving among today's Christians. While revising this chapter, I received a voicemail at the Freedom From Religion

Foundation office, laced with this selfsame joy: "You all are gonna burn in Hell—goody, goody, goody. . . . I'm a Christian . . . I hope y'all burn in Hell. You deserve it!"[38]

THE EIGHTH AMENDMENT TO THE US CONSTITUTION could have been written with hell in mind: "Excessive bail shall not be required, nor excessive fines imposed, nor cruel and unusual punishments inflicted." The exact scope of "cruel and unusual" has not been fully explored by the Supreme Court, partly because of the standard's inherent changeability.[39] But the court has declared that the "basic concept underlying the Eighth Amendment is nothing less than the dignity of man."[40] Relatively few cases involve this clause, and "in an enlightened democracy such as ours," pointed out the high court, "this is not surprising."[41] The court also noted that the "State has the power to punish, [but] the Amendment stands to assure that this power be exercised within the limits of civilized standards. Fines, imprisonment, and even execution may be imposed depending upon the enormity of the crime, but any technique outside the bounds of these traditional penalties is constitutionally suspect."[42]

Techniques such as crucifixion, which is simply death by torture, exceed those bounds. The Supreme Court has explicitly said so. "If the punishment prescribed for an offense against the laws of the State were manifestly cruel and unusual as burning at the stake, crucifixion, breaking on the wheel, or the like," wrote the court in 1890, "it would be the duty of the courts to adjudge such penalties to be within the constitutional prohibition."[43] Christians venerate the crucifixion; the evidence hangs around their necks and in their churches. Revering another person's torture and murder is disturbing. Although crucifixion is not itself a Judeo-Christian principle, the idea that sins can be forgiven on the sacrifice of another is a Christian principle, one that we'll explore in the next chapter.

Other cruel and unusual punishments, according to the court, include physical penalties, such as fifteen years of "hard and painful labor" in irons for falsifying records.[44] So is nonphysical punishment such as denationalization for deserting an army post[45] or "deliberate indifference to serious medical needs of prisoners."[46] Even being jailed with a five-pack-a-day smoker is cruel and unusual.[47] One would think that if being locked up with a smoker is cruel, the "everlasting sulphur" in hell is too.

The eternity of hell alone would raise serious issues under any standard of cruel or unusual punishment. Unlike the hell in Dante's *Inferno*, the bible does not mention varying levels. Hell is one-size-fits-all, and the punishment is eternal. That sinners are punished eternally for a finite crime is arguably hell's greatest offense to justice; yet this did not concern St. Augustine. He scorned "those tender-hearted Christians who decline to believe that any, or that all of those whom the infallibly just Judge may pronounce worthy of the punishment of hell, shall suffer eternally, and who suppose that they shall be delivered after a fixed term of punishment, longer or shorter according to the amount of each man's sin."[48] Aquinas made this same point, though in a slightly different manner: "The higher the person against whom it is committed, the graver the sin—it is more criminal to strike a head of

Fifteenth-century Italian engraving depicting Satan and demons torturing sinners in hell.

state than a private citizen—and God is of infinite greatness. Therefore an infinite punishment is deserved for a sin committed against Him."[49] In Christianity, the punishment does not fit the crime. Every crime rates the same, eternal punishment.

Some modern liberal Christians simply describe hell as an eternal separation from Jesus and ignore the persistent, graphic descriptions offered by their forebears and the bible. This interpretation is based on a single quote from Second Thessalonians. On Judgment Day, "those who do not obey the gospel of our Lord Jesus . . . will suffer the punishment of eternal destruction, separated from the presence of the Lord and from the glory of his might."[50] But this separation "from the presence" is an *addition to* the torture, not a substitute for it. Even liberally construed, this interpretation does not end the conflict with the Eighth Amendment. Creative interpretation might limit the agony of the hellbound, but not the infinity of the punishment. Christopher Hitchens convincingly compared Christianity to a "celestial North Korea," and he was careful to add that "at least you can fucking die and leave North Korea. Does the Koran or the Bible offer you that liberty? No. The tyranny, the misery, the utter ownership of your entire personality, the smashing of your individuality only begins at the point of death. This is evil. This is a wicked preachment." No matter what the crime, hell is forever. An infinite punishment for a finite crime is antithetical to the Eighth Amendment.[51]

Thomas Paine was correct when he wrote, "Of all the tyrannies that afflict mankind, tyranny in religion is the worst. Every other species of tyranny is limited to the world we live in, but this attempts a stride beyond the grave and seeks to pursue us into eternity."[52] The eternal torture created by Jesus, and its unmitigated application for any and every crime, is cruel and unusual.

10

Redemption and Original Sin or Personal Responsibility and the Presumption of Innocence?

"I am told of a human sacrifice that took place two thousand
years ago, without my wishing it and in circumstances so ghastly
that, had I been present and in possession of any influence,
I would have been duty-bound to try and stop it. In consequence
of this murder, my own manifold sins are forgiven me, and I
may hope to enjoy everlasting life. . . . In order to gain the benefit
of this wondrous offer, I have to accept that I am *responsible*
for the flogging and mocking and crucifixion, in which
I had no say and no part. . . . Furthermore, I am required to
believe that the agony was *necessary* in order to compensate for
an earlier crime in which I also had no part, the sin of Adam."

—Christopher Hitchens, *God Is Not Great*, 2007[1]

The American justice system and government, and perhaps our entire society, rest on the principle that people are personally responsible for their actions. We depend on the ability to hold people accountable. The founders were explicit about the need for personal responsibility in the new constitutional system they had created.[2] In criminal law, banking and lending, voting, paying taxes, civil law, insurance, and more, personal responsibility is a prerequisite.

Religion tends to lessen one's sense of personal responsibility and, in some instances, can even be an indicator that a person intends to avoid all such responsibility. Data backs this up. In one study, researchers looked at keywords people used when applying for loans. An applicant who mentioned their god—as in, "I swear to God I'll pay you back"—was 2.2 times more likely to default on the loan, making it "among the single highest indicators that someone would not pay back."[3]

The entire Christian religion is based on a singular claim that violates the principle of personal responsibility so critical to our systems: that Jesus died for your sins. Christianity's rejection of personal responsibility is actually twofold. First, a person is guilty of original sin simply because they were born. To believe this, you must accept not only that all humans descended from two originals that a god created for his garden, but also that all human beings are culpable for the actions of those two forebears, whose disobedience was prompted by a talking snake and was committed millennia ago. Guilt without action is rare under our law, but it is *the* law in much of Christianity. Second, the sacrifice of Jesus means that one's sins are forgiven. This is vicarious redemption through human sacrifice—Jesus as a sacrificial scapegoat. Each idea is repugnant to American principles in its own way. Original sin confers guilt without regard for personal actions, while vicarious redemption absolves that guilt through the torture and murder of another human.

Although vicarious redemption through Jesus's sacrifice is central only to Christianity, vicarious redemption is common within Judeo-Christianity. The sacrifice of Jesus culminates a long tradition of human sacrifice. The Israelite general Jephthah sacrifices his daughter to the biblical god for granting him victory in battle,[4] and that same god tells Moses to "take all the chiefs of the people, and impale them in the sun before the LORD, in order that the fierce anger of the LORD may turn away from Israel."[5]

Biblical animal sacrifice is even more common than human sacrifice. The Hebrew bible has an astonishing variety of commands for animal sacrifice, detailed down to the minutiae. Animals that are to be slaughtered and burned to appease the vengeful god are often required to be unblemished.[6] Everyone remembers that Noah brought two of each animal on his ark, but the bible also says that he brought an additional seven pairs of each animal that were "clean." He brought these animals successfully through the yearlong flood and then, when the waters subsided, built an altar and killed the clean animals as a sacrifice to his god.[7] Jesus, himself a sacrificial offering, was called "the lamb of god" and was depicted in art as "a lamb without defect or blemish" for centuries.[8] His supposedly sinless nature was equivalent to the unblemished animals.

The modern reader may think such sacrifices are limited to primitive times and places, but they are still practiced today, including by members of some Ultra-Orthodox Jewish sects who, on Yom Kippur, the Day of Atonement, practice *kapparot*.[9] Participants grab a chicken by the wings and swing it around their heads three times to transfer their sins to the bird while chanting, "This be my substitute, my vicarious offering, my atonement."[10] The chickens are then slaughtered (an estimated 50,000 chickens are killed annually for *kapparot* in Brooklyn alone).[11] Muslims undertaking the Hajj during Eid al-Adha, the Feast of Sacrifice, sacrifice lambs, goats, or cows as a symbolic reenactment of Abraham's sacrifice of a ram in place of Isaac.

Vicarious redemption supposedly expunges some cosmic criminal record, but is the very definition of two wrongs not making a right.

The Sacrifice of Isaac by Caravaggio, 1603.

The biblical ambition to abolish personal responsibility is not limited to vicarious redemption through human and animal sacrifice, though. The biblical god regularly punishes innocent people, including children who are penalized for their parent's mistakes (we'll see this in the Second Commandment too, in chapter 15), as well as entire groups of people who are punished for the minor infractions of one person in the group:

- Genesis 6:7, 6:13, 6:17; 7:4, 7:21–23—God kills everything and everyone except Noah, Noah's family, and a pair of each animal because he regrets making humans.

- Genesis 22:2–12—God commands a father to kill his son as a test. Neither has done anything wrong; god just wants to make sure Abraham is so scared of him that he will kill Isaac, his child.

- Genesis 34:25—Jacob's sons "took their swords and came against the city unawares, and killed all the males." To avenge the rape of their sister they kill the rapists—and every other male.

- Exodus 11:4–6; 11:29–30—God kills firstborn children unless there is lamb's blood on the family's doorframe. Morality, innocence, and age are irrelevant.

- Exodus 20:5, 34:7, Numbers 14:18, Deuteronomy. 5:9—God promises to punish children for their parents' crimes, to the third and fourth generation, in each verse.

- Exodus 22:20—If you sacrifice to another god you shall be *devoted to destruction*. This entails eradicating the offender's family, according to Levitcus 27:28–29.

- Exodus 23:23—Six races of people are wiped out because they happen to live in Canaan, a land that god promised to the Israelites. "When my angel goes in front of you, and brings you to the Amorites, the Hittites, the Perizzites, the Canaanites, the Hivites, and the Jebusites, and I blot them out."

- Levitcus 26:29—"You shall eat the flesh of your sons, and you shall eat the flesh of your daughters." Making guilty parents cannibalize their innocent children and killing the innocent to punish the guilty in the process.

- Numbers 9:13—Failing to keep Passover gets your family exterminated.
- Numbers 14:33—"Your children . . . shall suffer for your faithlessness."
- Numbers 16:20–35—"Their wives, their children, and their little ones . . . the earth opened its mouth and swallowed them up, along with their households—everyone who belonged to Korah."
- Numbers 25:7–8, 25:16–18—After a Jewish man "brought a Midianite woman into his family," Aaron's grandson, Phinehas, took a spear "and pierced the two of them, the Israelite and the woman, through the belly." For this murder, Phinehas is commended by his god, who then orders destruction of the Midianites for being Midianites.
- Deuteronomy 28:41—"You shall have sons and daughters, but they shall not remain yours, for they shall go into captivity."
- Deuteronomy 28:53—"You will eat the fruit of your womb, the flesh of your own sons and daughters."
- Deuteronomy 28:59—"The LORD will overwhelm both you and your offspring with severe and lasting afflictions and grievous lasting maladies."

And this list only includes examples from the Pentateuch, the first five biblical books.

Eighteenth-century English politician and philosopher Henry St. John, the Viscount Bolingbroke, heavily influenced the founders, including both Jefferson and Adams (who read his works through five times).[12] Bolingbroke observed that if vicarious "redemption" is "the main and fundamental article of the Christian faith," then the "fall of man is the foundation of this fundamental article."[13] The combination of these doctrines, he noted, "is, in all its circumstances, absolutely irreconcilable to every idea we can frame of wisdom, justness, and goodness, to say nothing of the dignity of the Supreme Being."[14] And it is irreconcilable to American principles.

The American justice system rejects a presumption of guilt in favor of its opposite, the presumption of innocence. Unlike the biblical god's law, our laws protect the innocent.[15] Discussing this principle in 1895, the Supreme Court related a tale from the annals of Roman law:

> Numerius contented himself with denying his guilt, and there was not sufficient proof against him. His adversary, Delphidius, "a passionate man," seeing that the failure of the accusation was inevitable, could not restrain himself, and exclaimed, "Oh, illustrious Caesar! if it is sufficient to deny, what hereafter will become of the guilty?" to which Julian replied, "If it suffices to accuse, what will become of the innocent?"[16]

Christians effectively answered Julian's riposte several centuries later when Pope Innocent IV issued a bull in 1252, *Ad extirpanda*, allowing the Inquisition to torture to extract confessions from the accused.[17] "The principle that there is a presumption of innocence in favor of the accused is the undoubted law, axiomatic and elementary, and its enforcement lies at the foundation of the administration of our criminal law," said the Supreme Court more than one hundred years ago.[18] Benjamin Franklin thought it "better for a hundred guilty persons to escape than for one innocent person to suffer."[19] Franklin may have discussed the principle with Voltaire when the two met in Paris in 1778. Years earlier, the French philosopher had written, "It is better to run the risk of sparing the guilty than to condemn the innocent."[20] America's justice system demands proof of guilt to avoid punishing innocents; the Judeo-Christian god intentionally harms innocents to punish the guilty.

Some have tried to argue that presuming innocence is in fact biblical. The chain of logic[21] is tenuous and difficult to trace, but if followed it leads to a single quote from Deuteronomy 17:2–5, which reads:

> If there is found among you . . . a man or woman who . . . serve[s] other gods and worship[s] them . . . and if it is reported to you or you hear of it, and you make a thorough inquiry, and the charge is proved true . . . then you shall bring out to your gates that man or that woman who has committed this crime and you shall stone the man or woman to death.

This is a command to kill everyone of another religion. The "thorough inquiry" requirement is not a presumption of innocence, nor is it all that original. The deficit in this passage is especially obvious when weighed against every biblical example of punishing innocent people. The children killed for and by god—Egypt's firstborn, Jephthah's unnamed daughter, Eli's descendants, Achon's family, the thousands of babies and children who died in Noah's flood—were all innocent; they did "not yet know right from wrong," as the bible says.[22] But the biblical god slaughtered them just the same. The bible kills too many innocents to be the wellspring of this important concept; it shuns the axiom on nearly every page.

SEPARATION OF POWERS CAME FROM MONTESQUIEU, not Isaiah. The bible venerates principles such as obedience and fear, not freedom, as the Constitution does. Biblical justice is so severe and vicious that it would, if implemented, violate the Constitution. Hell, a central tenet of Christianity, conflicts with the Constitution on at least two major counts: both as a place of torture and as an eternal punishment. Original sin, another essential Christian principle, transgresses the core presumption of American justice. And vicarious redemption, the defining Christian principle, repudiates personal responsibility, upon which all American law, society, and government rest. It doesn't look as if the bible positively influenced the American founding. But perhaps the Christian nationalist means to argue that it was actually religious faith and not biblical or religious principles per se that were influential?

11

The American Experiment: Religious Faith or Reason?

"We remember before our God and Father your work
produced by faith, your labor prompted by love, and
your endurance inspired by hope in our Lord Jesus Christ."

—1 Thessalonians 1:3 NIV

"It will never be pretended that any persons employed
in that service had interviews with the gods, or were in any
degree under the inspiration of heaven, more than those at work
upon ships or houses, or laboring in merchandize or agriculture;
it will forever be acknowledged that these governments were
contrived merely by the use of reason and the senses."

—John Adams, "A Defence of the Constitutions of
Government of the United States of America,"1787[1]

What about faith? Was America founded on the Christian faith? The bible says that faith can move mountains. Jesus tells his disciples, "If you have faith the size of a mustard seed, you will say to this mountain, 'Move from here to there,' and it will move; and nothing will be impossible for you."[2] He repeats this a few chapters later, with an additional benefit: not only can faith move mountains, it can also kill a harmless shrub. Jesus smites a fig tree for not producing fruit, though he knew figs were not in season, and then tells his followers, "If you have faith and do not doubt, not only will you do what has been done to the fig tree, but even if you say to this mountain, 'Be lifted up and thrown into the sea,' it will be done."[3]

Notice the dodge: the impossible becomes possible *if* you have enough faith. Since the impossible is, by definition, impossible, the believer's faith is always wanting. If the stubborn mountain refuses to move, it is because the follower had doubts, a weak faith. The quantity or strength of one's faith is irrelevant because one can never have enough. Faith enough to fill a mountain would not move a mustard seed. The impossibility binds the believer to the religion, forcing them to seek ever greater faith.

If the Christian nationalists are to be believed, America was founded on faith. Though some, such as Michael Novak, at least admit that a government cannot be built on faith alone, "Reason and faith are the two wings by which the American eagle took flight."[4] On the contrary, faith, at least when mixed with government, is antithetical to American principles.

But first, let's get our vocabulary straight. The word "faith" is used here as it is by modern Christians, to signify religious faith. It is not used as a synonym for trust, confidence, a wish, a deeply held non-religious belief, or hope. Nor is it used to signify an evidence-based belief such as "having faith" that flipping a switch will turn on a light or "having faith" that a spouse will not stray. Both of those beliefs are based on evidence. The light goes on 99.9 percent of the time; your spouse loves you and shows it. We don't have religious faith that the light will turn on—we have a reasonable expectation based on evidence, a mouthful that often gets shortened to "having faith." The bible conflates religious faith with hope in a favorite passage of many believers: "Faith is the substance of things hoped for, the evidence of things not seen."[5] This is right in one sense: religious faith is not an evidence-based belief. It is a belief in spite of the evidence. Religious faith is, as Professor Peter Boghossian observes, "pretending to know things you don't know."[6]

Religious faith is useless and even harmful when one is trying to build a country and government. Imagine a delegate at the Constitutional Convention arguing for five branches of government instead of three. To support the claim, he cites his personal religious faith: "because my God said so." He would have been laughed out of Independence Hall. Cornell historian and political scientist Clinton Rossiter observed that "science and its philosophical corollaries were perhaps the most important intellectual force shaping the destiny of eighteenth-century America."[7]

It is hardly credible to argue that Judeo-Christianity, and especially Protestantism, is responsible for the founders' use of reason when Martin Luther, the founder of Protestantism, called reason "the Devil's greatest whore."[8] Many Christian beliefs, including the resurrection and the virgin birth, require the believer to suspend, not apply, reason. Hence, Martin Luther's argument that "reason in no way contributes to faith . . . reason is the greatest enemy that faith has: it never comes to the aid of spiritual things, but—more frequently than not—struggles against the divine Word, treating with contempt all that emanates from God."[9]

American law and our Constitution were not passed down from on high. Some of the greatest minds of the day reasoned, debated, and compromised for months, years even, to agree on the laws that would guide the new nation. Our Constitution is the product of human thought and perseverance, not faith.

Jefferson rejected a faith-based government and any government attempt to declare articles of faith: "The Newtonian principles of gravitation is now more firmly established, on the basis of reason, than it would be were the government to step in, and to make it an article of necessary faith. Reason and experiment have been indulged, and error has fled before them. It is error alone which needs the support of government. Truth can stand by itself."[10] Reason and experiment dispel error; faith propagates it. The founders relied on the former. John Adams said of the "formation of the American governments" that it should "never be pretended that any persons employed in that service had interviews with the gods"; rather, those governments "were contrived merely by the use of reason and the senses."[11]

The framers indulged experiment when building America because many were scientists, though they may not have identified themselves using that word. Franklin's scientific chops are perhaps best known. He tamed electricity; he invented the lightning rod, the Franklin wood-burning stove, and bifocals—to name a few of his most popular innovations. He also mapped the Gulf Stream, designed swim fins, invented the glass armonica, and experimented with an early odometer as a colonial postmaster.[12]

Jefferson viewed all of Monticello as an experiment.[13] He installed several of his architectural inventions, such as an improved dumb-waiter, a revolving clothes rack in his closet, and a ventilation system. Jefferson improved the plow with a lower-resistance moldboard, and he invented a wheel cipher, a swivel chair, and a spherical sundial.[14] He also launched Lewis and Clark on what might have been America's first expedition with scientific goals.

Washington kept meticulous agricultural logs and continually experimented with better planting methods, new crops, and different rotations.[15] He invented a drill plow to help seed his fields along with a threshing barn, a sixteen-sided brick barn to help sift and sort grain.[16] He also inoculated the Continental Army against smallpox (variolation, an earlier, less reliable inoculation method was used at the time). This was the first army-wide immunization in military history, and it dropped mortality rates in infected soldiers from more than 30 percent to below 1 percent.[17]

James Madison's scientific curiosity led him to invent a walking stick with a microscope inside it to better view nature close up on his country strolls.[18] He wanted a telescope walking stick too, and designed a chair with a writing desk attached to the arm, something seen for decades in schools.[19]

Alexander Hamilton created American credit in the global economy—we probably owe more to his inventive ideas than other founder. His reports, such as *First Report on the Public Credit*, *Report on a National Bank*, *Report on Manufactures*, and *Report on the Establishment of a Mint*, laid the foundation for American economic supremacy.[20]

Thomas Paine invented a smokeless candle, and designed an iron bridge that Jefferson was excited about because it "promises to be cheaper by a great deal than stone, and to admit of a much greater arch."[21]

In 1780, John Adams founded the American Academy of Arts and Sciences in Boston, along with John Hancock and a few other scientifically minded revolutionaries.[22] Many founders—Washington, Adams, Jefferson, Hamilton, Madison, Paine, and others—joined the American Philosophical Society, which Franklin founded in 1743 as America's oldest scientific society.[23]

The founders even put science in the Constitution. The sole purpose behind patents and copyrights, which the Constitution protects, is to "promote the Progress of Science and useful Arts."[24]

They may not have been scientists in the modern sense, but the founders deserve the title, and not just for their contributions to agriculture, architecture, physics, engineering, and other fields. To the founders, politics and government were sciences. When convincing Americans to ratify the new federal constitution, Alexander Hamilton wrote about "the science of politics" and how it, in their age, "like most sciences has received great improvement."[25] James Madison read and studied "the most oracular Authors on the Science of Government,"[26] as did his mentor and friend, Jefferson.[27] For Adams, politics was not just science; it was *the* science—"the divine science of politics."[28] Why? Because "politics . . . is the science of human happiness."[29] Political science sought to make people happy, not to repress, terrorize, and misuse them. Its divinity was a product of this world and not in any way supernatural. Adams also penned the era's most memorable line about the purpose of political science and nation-building:

> The Science of Government it is my Duty to study, more than all other Sciences: the Art of Legislation and Administration and Negotiation, ought to take Place, indeed to exclude in a manner all other Arts. I must study Politicks and War that my sons may have liberty to study Mathematicks and Philosophy. My sons ought to study Mathematicks and Philosophy, Geography, natural History, Naval Architecture, navigation, Commerce and Agriculture, in order to give their Children a right to study Painting, Poetry, Musick, Architecture, Statuary, Tapestry and Porcelaine.[30]

The founders were not supplicants seeking to interpret divine revelation; they were political scientists, using reason, experience, and history to build a nation. During the Constitutional Convention, they debated which theory of government would work best for the United States, and then put that theory to the test in the "American experiment," as Madison dubbed it.[31]

That's how scientists determine whether their ideas are correct: they experiment. They actively try to disprove their own hypotheses by testing them. In 1786, Benjamin Franklin was asked about America's progress in improving its governments. He responded, "We are, I think, in the right Road of Improvement, for we are making Experiments. I do not oppose all that seems wrong, for the Multitude are more effectually set right by Experience, than kept from going wrong by Reasoning with them."[32] The Constitutional Convention met the next year and would be a tour de force of reasoning, political science, experience, and enlightened thought; all were debated and compromised. Religion was left out, both out of the convention—the delegates rejected a motion for daily prayers, finding them "unnecessary"[33]—and out of the Constitution, which mentioned religion only to prohibit religious tests for public office. (The First Amendment was added later and it too excludes religion, keeping religion out of government and vice versa; see pages 173–74).

Many founders shared Franklin's view of the Constitution: it was an experiment. Adams regularly spoke of constitutions as experiments[34] and wanted to see "rising in America an empire of liberty."[35] At least one of his correspondents thought it impossible. Adams retorted, "If I should agree with you in this, I would still say, let us try the experiment."[36] During his first inaugural, when Adams explained that though he "first saw the Constitution of the United States in a foreign country," he had "read it with great satisfaction, as a result of good heads, prompted by good hearts; as an experiment better adapted to the genius, character, situation, and relations of this nation and country than any which had ever been proposed or suggested."[37]

Jefferson, who was also abroad during the Constitutional Convention, echoed Adams's sentiment in his own first inaugural: "Would the honest patriot, in the full tide of successful experiment, abandon a government which has so far kept us free?"[38]

Madison called the Constitution "the great political experiment in the hands of the American people."[39] The *Federalist Papers*, many of which he authored, talk of political "experiments" forty-five times, mostly to refer to testing theories of republican government.[40] James Madison and George Mason each skillfully summarized the unique phenomenon of American minds crafting the American political experiment. Madison, perhaps the most brilliant political theorist at the Convention, said, "The first question that offers itself is, whether the general form and aspect of the government be strictly republican. It is evident that no other form would be reconcilable with the genius of the people of America; with the fundamental principles of the Revolution; or with that honorable determination which animates every votary of freedom, to rest all our political experiments on the capacity of mankind for self-government."[41] Madison covered all the important bases: freedom, self-government, the genius of the people, and political experiments. Faith was absent.

George Mason wrote a letter to his son the first week the Constitutional Convention met. Quorum had been declared less than a week before and Edmund Randolph had introduced the Virginia Plan just three days prior. The letter shows Mason's remarkable grasp of the magnitude of the framers' task and, more importantly, of how it would be accomplished. The war for independence and drafting state constitutions "were nothing compared to the great business now before us; there was then a certain degree of enthusiasm, which inspired and supported the mind."[42] It was not difficult to drum up popular support for a war; people need only be scared and roused. "But," Mason continued, "to view, through the calm, sedate medium of reason the influence which the establishment now proposed may have upon the happiness or misery of millions yet unborn, is an object of such magnitude, as absorbs, and in a manner suspends the operations of the human understanding."[43] Nation-building must be done through calm, sedate reason. It absorbs the "operations of human understanding" while simultaneously filling one with awe. There is no place for faith in such an operation. Faith did not have a seat at the birth of our Constitution. Reason reigned.

12

A Monarchy and "the morrow" or
a Republic and "our posterity"

"I will establish his kingdom forever if he continues
resolute in keeping my commandments."

—1 Chronicles 28:7

"A republic, if you can keep it."

—Benjamin Franklin, at the end of the
Constitutional Convention, 1787[1]

From George Mason's letter to his son, we know that he and his
fellow delegates were not creating a nation for the moment,
but for posterity, for "the millions yet unborn" (see page 151).
They were building a country for us. Had Mason's letter not survived,
the Constitution's Preamble would still provide evidence of the framers' goals. At least one of these purposes—"to secure the blessings of
liberty to ourselves and our posterity"—conflicts with the tenets of
Judeo-Christianity. The Constitution is meant to build a better country for the future, ensuring prosperity and freedom for our children,
grandchildren, and great-grandchildren down through the generations.
James Wilson wanted his fellow delegates at the Constitutional Convention to "consider that we are providing a Constitution for future
generations and not merely for the circumstances of the moment."[2]
They were "laying the foundation of a building, which is to last for
ages, and in which millions are interested."[3] Madison wanted the
nation to "last for ages" too—he said so twice.[4] Fellow delegate John
Rutledge echoed the sentiment: "As we are laying the foundation for

a great empire, we ought to take a permanent view of the subject and not look at the present moment only."[5] Even the Declaration of Independence tells us that people who exercise their right to "throw off" despotic government have a responsibility to "provide new Guards for their future security." The founders were building a government to help future generations secure liberty and happiness in this world.

Jesus's biblical message is not about building a future in this world, and certainly not for future generations. Christianity is about ensuring one's own place for eternity, others be damned—literally. Jesus demanded that his followers "take no thought for the morrow." And though his justification relied on god's care for the "lilies of the field" and the "fowls of the air," we can assume Jesus meant what he said.[6] For him, tomorrow was not important because the end of the world was supposedly imminent. Jesus would die and his second coming would bring judgment for all and determine their place in eternity. Judgment Day would come in the next thirty or so years, before Jesus's generation had died. At least, that's what the bible claims Jesus said: "Truly I tell you, this generation will not pass away"[7] and "There be some standing here, which shall not taste of death, till they see the Son of man coming in his kingdom."[8] When Jesus tells his disciples to spread news of the coming end, he tells them, "You will not have gone through all the towns of Israel before the Son of Man comes."[9] Jesus thought he'd be back before his friends had died. (In the thirteenth century, a bizarre story about a "Wandering Jew"—a fictional, immortal Jew and a contemporary of Jesus, doomed to walk the earth until the second coming—was invented, likely to give credence to Jesus's erroneous predictions.)

Early Christians believed Jesus's promise,[10] and preachers have been terrifying their congregations with predictions of impending Armageddon for 2,000 years. To this day, 41 percent of Americans think Jesus is returning to earth sometime in the next forty years—presumably bringing Armageddon with him.[11] That is a remarkably stubborn belief, given that every Christian who has ever held this belief has been wrong.

The true Christian should not be concerned with the paltry cares of this world, but with the next. Had the framers taken Jesus at his word, they never would have built a country for the future. The English philosopher Anthony Ashley Cooper, 3rd Earl of Shaftesbury, discussed this well-known problem:

> Private friendship and zeal for the public and our country are purely voluntary in a Christian. . . . He is not so tied to the affairs of this life, nor is he obliged to enter into such engagements with this lower world as are of no help to him in acquiring a better. His conversation is in heaven. Nor has he occasion for such supernumerary cares or embarrassments here on earth as may obstruct his way thither or retard him in the careful task of working out his own salvation.[12]

In Harper's Lee's classic American novel, *To Kill a Mockingbird*, the protagonist, Scout, learns that a "Bible in the hand of one man is worse than a whisky bottle. . . . There are just some kind of men who—who're so busy worrying about the next world they've never learned to live in this one."[13] It's difficult to see how, or even why, Christianity would contribute to a government founded to secure a future for "ourselves and our posterity" when Christian dogma specifically declares that there is no such future.

If Jesus had been concerned with building a government and society, what would it have looked like? The bible mentions government quite a bit, but the bible's governments do not resemble the government the founders created. Biblical regimes look more like the government from which the colonies declared independence in July 1776.

The governments the bible espouses and those it has bred are theocratic monarchies. The bible is brimming with monarchy. Two books of the bible are titled "Kings." Many of the bible's heroes are kings, such as King Saul, King David, and King Solomon. The bible tells readers to "keep the king's command,"[14] and the entire collection is concerned with god's kingdom: including, in the Old Testament, the "kingdom of the Lord" and "a great King above all gods," and in the New Testament, "the kingdom of God" and "thy kingdom come." God himself promises on several occasions to assign kings to rule over his followers.[15] And not just kings, but "a king whom the Lord your God will choose."[16] Jesus himself "is the blessed and only Sovereign, the King of kings and Lord of lords."[17]

The biggest of these monarchies is the New Testament "Kingdom of God," which, as with most biblical monarchies, is hereditary. The father has a son whose kingdom is coming. The bible says, "He . . . will be called the Son of the Most High, and the Lord God will give to him the throne of his ancestor David."[18] It also says that Jesus will only "[hand] over the kingdom to God the Father, after he has destroyed every ruler and every authority and power."[19]

There is no whiff of representative government in the bible. And when given a chance, the Israelites actually request a king, not a democracy or a republic.[20] The closest the bible gets to discussing representative government—and it's not close—is in the noncanonical books of the Maccabees, which partly describe that eponymous tribe's revolt against Hellenizing cultural influences.[21]

Unlike the Maccabees, America's founders did not reject the Grecian culture that birthed democracy. Quite the opposite: they rejected the bible and looked to ancient Greek city-states and pre-Christian Rome when drafting our Constitution. Jefferson wrote in his *Notes on the State of Virginia* that rather than "putting the Bible and Testament into the hands of the children, at an age when their judgments are not sufficiently matured for religious enquiries, their memories may here be stored with the most useful facts from Grecian, Roman, European and American history."[22] Jefferson had been writing about the youth, but the framers at the Constitutional Convention heeded his advice. Greek thinkers such as Isocrates, Aristotle, and Solon had far more to offer than biblical monarchists. The Greeks actually thought and wrote about other forms of government, not just divinely sanctioned monarchies. Isocrates thought that "the constitution is the soul of the state."[23] Although the bible speaks often of souls, it never mentions constitutions.[24] Aristotle more concisely noted that "the constitution *is* the state."[25] Both men, along with many other Greek writers, spoke extensively about government and constitutions.

John Adams had been ruminating about the structure of government and how to build it since at least 1765, when he wrote "A Dissertation on the Canon and the Feudal Law." He did not find inspiration in the bible: "Let us study the law of nature; search into the spirit of the British constitution; read the histories of ancient ages; contemplate the great examples of Greece and Rome; set before us the conduct of our own British ancestors, who have defended for us the inherent rights of mankind against foreign and domestic tyrants and usurpers, against arbitrary kings and cruel priests, in short, against the gates of earth and hell."[26] Although Adams studied civil and ecclesiastical government, he failed to mention Christianity when discussing historical examples, going from England to the ancients, to Greece and Rome.[27]

The American commitment to classical, not Christian, principles is contained in the very name of the government chosen. Constitutional Convention delegate James McHenry of Maryland recorded a wonderful anecdote about a lady who asked Benjamin Franklin at the close of the Constitutional Convention, "Well Doctor, what have we got, a republic or a monarchy?"[28] Franklin's response was the legendary "A republic, if you can keep it." A republic—*res publica*—is literally "a public thing," a thing of the people. Not something divine, not something handed down from on high, and not something that could be maintained without effort—but a thing "of the people, by the people, for the people," as Lincoln so beautifully phrased it.[29]

When James Madison studied government, his primary examples were Greek and Roman. The *Federalist Papers*, written by Madison, Alexander Hamilton, and John Jay, mention the "early ages of Christianity" once, and only to criticize it as part of the feudal system.[30] But the papers contain numerous references to Sparta, Carthage, Rome, the Achaean League, Thebes, Crete, Athens, and other federations.[31] The framers studied these governments and their histories and lawgivers (whether real or legendary), including Minos, Theseus, Draco, Solon, Lycurgus, Romulus, Numa, and Tullus Hostilius.[32]

The classical influence on the American founding was recognized at the time by those outside of the Convention and by later religious thinkers. Just after the Constitution was adopted, Harvard president Joseph Willard received a letter from Thomas Brand Hollis, a pro-revolutionary Englishman, about reviving the Olympic games in America because "having acted on Greek principles, [America] should have Greek exercises."[33]

Thomas Cuming Hall, an early twentieth-century theologian and professor of Christian ethics, complained bitterly about the American founding completely ignoring the bible. He wrote at length about the records of the Constitutional Convention:[34]

> The whole atmosphere of the entire literature is secular. . . . The fact that the Old Testament is never even alluded to as an authority by the principal authors of the Constitution should give some pulpit rhetoric pause. . . . Where a hundred years before every case, whether civil, political or criminal, was decided by a reference to the Old or New Testament . . . in *The Federalist* the Bible and Christianity, as well as the clergy, are passed over as having no bearing upon the political issues being discussed. . . . The eighteenth-century conception of Greco-Roman Paganism has completely supplanted Puritanic Judaism.

Hall, who held degrees from Princeton and Union Theological Seminary, was right. The founders studied the classics extensively, and they were familiar with Judeo-Christian principles, but they relied on the former and shunned the latter at the Constitutional Convention. One would expect to see the opposite if Christian nationalists are correct. The founders did not ignore the centuries when religion ruled—they simply forswore the doctrines that permitted religion to reign. Perhaps this was because, as atheist author Ruth Hurmence Green put it, "There was a time when religion ruled the world. It is known as the Dark Ages."[35]

PART III

THE TEN COMMANDMENTS v. THE CONSTITUTION

"Some Christian lawyers—some eminent and stupid judges—
have said and still say, that the Ten Commandments are the
foundation of all law. Nothing could be more absurd . . . all that
man has accomplished for the benefit of man since the close of
the Dark Ages—has been done in spite of the Old Testament."

—Robert G. Ingersoll, *About the Holy Bible: A Lecture*, 1894[1]

"Where human laws do not tie men's hands from wickedness,
religion too seldom does; and the most certain security which
we have against violence, is the security of the laws."

—John Trenchard and Thomas Gordon, *Cato's Letters*, 1721[2]

"Men never do evil so completely and cheerfully as when
they do it from religious conviction."

—Blaise Pascal, *Pensées*, 1670[3]

13

Which Ten?

"All pay heed, the Lord, the Lord Jehovah, has given unto you
these Fifteen [drops one of three stone tablets] . . . oy.
Ten! Ten Commandments for all to obey."

—Mel Brooks as Moses in *History of the World: Part I*, 1981[4]

"Which one of the Ten Commandments that's out there
on the lawn of the Texas capitol bothers you so much? I mean,
which one of those is bad public policy? Which one of those
is so onerous to how we as a people function?"

—US Secretary of Energy **Rick Perry**[5]

Before reading any further, go get a bible and open it to the Ten
Commandments. Go on, I'll wait.

This is not such a simple task. The Ten Commandments,
also known as the Decalogue—supposedly the most moral law known
to humanity and supposedly authored by the biblical god himself—
are not easy to find. They're not at the beginning of the bible. God
didn't give the rules to Eve and Adam, even after their fall. Nor did he
give them to Noah after exterminating all human and animal life save
Noah's crew. And Noah needed a bit of moral guidance. Noah's son,
Ham, accidentally walks in on him, drunk, naked, and passed out.
Refusing to take responsibility for his frat boy behavior, Noah curses an
innocent child, Canaan, Ham's son and Noah's own grandson, to a life
of slavery for Ham's "crime" of seeing him naked. [6] This was the only
man the Jewish god thought moral enough to save from a worldwide
flood. Yahweh did not see fit to give out the laws, his most moral laws if
Christian nationalists are to be believed, until much further along the

biblical storyline. The first set—there are four—doesn't appear until halfway through the second book of the bible, Exodus.

H. L. Mencken reportedly once quipped, "Say what you will about the Ten Commandments, you must always come back to the pleasant fact that there are only ten of them."[7] If this wit does indeed belong to Mencken, so does the error. There are not Ten Commandments, but four different sets of Ten Commandments (see comparison tables of four sets on pages 164–65).

The first set was given to Moses on Mount Sinai in chapter 20 of Exodus and later written on stone tablets.[8] These are the ten that Heston, DeMille & Co made famous. This set is probably what most people think of as *the* ten. According to the story, after three months wandering in a desert wilderness with little to eat or drink other than manna from heaven and water that they could squeeze from rocks, the vagabonds make camp at the base of Mount Sinai. Exhausted, starving, and dehydrated, Moses climbs to the top of the 7,500-foot-tall mountain and hears a voice he attributes to a god.[9] Is it any wonder? Three months of marching under the hot desert sun and then scaling a mountain—it would almost be odd if he hadn't been hearing disembodied voices.

Moses descended the mount to present his people with their god's perfect law[10] only to find them worshipping a golden calf, an idol. Moses was so furious that his followers would break one of the commandments—a commandment on which they had not yet been instructed—that he smashed the stone tablets.[11] The only physical evidence that a divine being had visited this world was in his hands. The most priceless object in all history and possibly proof that god exists, yet the religious leader destroyed it . . . before any of his followers got a chance to examine or even read it. This is suspicious, reckless—and a convenient dodge. Joseph Smith used a similar ploy when dictating the Book of Mormon. Smith claimed he discovered two golden plates etched with reformed Egyptian hieroglyphics. An angel led him to the plates but also decreed that Smith could not show the plates to anyone. He translated the story on the plates using a hat and a magic seeing stone. Smith returned the plates to the angel after his translation was complete. All the priceless physical evidence of divine existence was destroyed or returned to the divine plane. Moses's destructive temper tantrum in Exodus 32:19 is even more suspect if one reads 32:7–8, in which Yahweh tells Moses to go back down the mountain because his people have "acted perversely" and "cast for themselves an image of a calf." Moses knew beforehand that they were worshipping an idol, and still he destroyed the tablets.

Not content with simply destroying god's word, Moses ordered the slaughter of 3,000 of his "brothers," "friends," and "neighbors" for worshipping an idol. Moses commanded the priestly clan, the Levites, to "Put your sword on your side, each of you! Go back and forth from gate to gate throughout the camp, and each of you kill your brother, your friend, and your neighbor."[12] They succeeded: "the sons of Levi did as Moses commanded, and about three thousand of the people fell on that day."[13] The synonymous language Moses used in pronouncing the death sentence, "your brother, your friend, and your neighbor,"[14] and the language the Exodus author uses to describe those killed, "three thousand of *the people* fell on that day," is instructive for interpreting the commandments, as we shall see.

Post-slaughter, Yahweh orders Moses to fashion new tablets and gives him the second set of ten commandments in chapter 34 of Exodus.[15] God kicks off this set by vowing to sweep all the current residents from the land he promised to Moses, thereby sealing his moral laws with genocide.[16] God said: "I will drive out before you the Amorites, the Canaanites, the Hittites, the Perizzites, the Hivites, and the Jebusites."[17]

In this second set and as payment for his role as genocidal patron, Yahweh lays claim to all the firstborn of Israel, although he spares the firstborn human sons: "All that first opens the womb is mine, all your male livestock, the firstborn of cow and sheep. The firstborn of a donkey you shall redeem with a lamb, or if you will not redeem it you shall break its neck. All the firstborn of your sons you shall redeem."[18] "Redeem" in this context means substituting one sacrificial victim for another, such as a goat for a human (see also chapter 10). (What does it say about a god who repeatedly orders his followers to kill their sons, only to occasionally retract the death sentence at the last moment? Abraham and Isaac, this commandment, and the later sacrifice of Jesus—filicide is common in the bible. God himself says that these sacrifices are meant to horrify his subjects: "I defiled them through their very gifts, in their offering up all their firstborn, in order that I might horrify them, so that they might know that I am the Lord," according to Ezekiel 20:26).

Decalogue version 2.0 includes the prohibition on casting idols and the mandate to keep the sabbath,[19] but the similarities to the first set end there. God's final commandment of the second batch is to "not boil a kid in its mother's milk."[20] This refers to a baby goat, not a human child. Though, given the preceding filial-sacrificial language and the sacrifice of a son in the New Testament, one can be forgiven for thinking otherwise.

The differences between the first two sets of commandments, the Exodus sets, are particularly vexing for believers in the bible's infallibility because Yahweh says they should be identical, yet they are not. God says that he meant to write the same thing: "The LORD said to Moses, 'Cut two tablets of stone like the former ones, and I will write on the tablets the words that were on the former tablets, which you broke.'"[21] But regarding these most moral, important laws—the biblical god could not keep his rules straight.

The third set, issued in chapter 5 of Deuteronomy, is basically the same as the first.[22] In the biblical narrative, the third set is really just Moses retelling the story of how he received the first set. But even the retelling is flawed because the sabbath commandments of the third and first sets don't match.

The fourth set issued later in Deuteronomy is markedly different from the others, but it meets the criteria: they are commandments from Moses set in stone tablets. According to Moses, his followers must "keep the entire commandment that I am commanding you today" and "set up large stones. . . . Write on them all the words of this law" and "set up these stones, about which I am commanding you today" when they reach the promised land.[23] This final set is not a list of prohibitions or injunctions; rather, it is a list of people who are cursed, "cursed be" the so-and-sos. Among the cursed are those who make idols or fail to honor their parents,[24] but otherwise this bears little resemblance to the other sets. Much of the cursing is directed at sexual behavior.[25]

Four Sets of the Ten Commandments in the Bible[26]

[Note: Language is underlined in the second, third, and fourth sets to facilitate comparison with the first set. Some verses were combined into paragraphs to conserve space.]

FIRST SET
Exodus 20:2–17

2 I am the LORD your God, who brought you out of the land of Egypt, out of the house of slavery;

3 you shall have no other gods before me. 4 You shall not make for yourself an idol, whether in the form of anything that is in heaven above, or that is on the earth beneath, or that is in the water under the earth. 5 You shall not bow down to them or worship them; for I the LORD your God am a jealous God, punishing children for the iniquity of parents, to the third and the fourth generation of those who reject me, 6 but showing steadfast love to the thousandth generation of those who love me and keep my commandments.

7 You shall not make wrongful use of the name of the LORD your God, for the LORD will not acquit anyone who misuses his name.

8 Remember the sabbath day, and keep it holy. 9 Six days you shall labor and do all your work. 10 But the seventh day is a sabbath to the LORD your God; you shall not do any work—you, your son or your daughter, your male or female slave, your livestock, or the alien resident in your towns. 11 For in six days the LORD made heaven and earth, the sea, and all that is in them, but rested the seventh day; therefore the LORD blessed the sabbath day and consecrated it.

12 Honor your father and your mother, so that your days may be long in the land that the LORD your God is giving you.

13 You shall not murder.
14 You shall not commit adultery.
15 You shall not steal.
16 You shall not bear false witness against your neighbor.

17 You shall not covet your neighbor's house; you shall not covet your neighbor's wife, or male or female slave, or ox, or donkey, or anything that belongs to your neighbor.

SECOND SET
Exodus 34:11–28

11 Observe what I command you today. See, I will drive out before you the Amorites, the Canaanites, the Hittites, the Perizzites, the Hivites, and the Jebusites.

12 Take care not to make a covenant with the inhabitants of the land to which you are going, or it will become a snare among you. 13 You shall tear down their altars, break their pillars, and cut down their sacred poles 14 (for you shall worship no other god, because the LORD, whose name is Jealous, is a jealous God). 15 You shall not make a covenant with the inhabitants of the land, for when they prostitute themselves to their gods and sacrifice to their gods, someone among them will invite you, and you will eat of the sacrifice. 16 And you will take wives from among their daughters for your sons, and their daughters who prostitute themselves to their gods will make your sons also prostitute themselves to their gods.

17 You shall not make cast idols. 18 You shall keep the festival of unleavened bread. Seven days you shall eat unleavened bread, as I commanded you, at the time appointed in the month of Abib; for in the month of Abib you came out from Egypt. 19 All that first opens the womb is mine, all your male livestock, the firstborn of cow and sheep. 20 The firstborn of a donkey you shall redeem with a lamb, or if you will not redeem it you shall break its neck. All the firstborn of your sons you shall redeem.

21 Six days you shall work, but on the seventh day you shall rest; even in plowing time and in harvest time you shall rest. 22 You shall observe the festival of weeks, the first fruits of wheat harvest, and the festival of ingathering at the turn of the year. 23 Three times in the year all your males shall appear before the LORD God, the God of Israel. 24 For I will cast out nations before you, and enlarge your borders; no one shall covet your land when you go up to appear before the LORD your God three times in the year. 25 You shall not offer the blood of my sacrifice with leaven, and the sacrifice of the festival of the passover shall not be left until the morning. 26 The best of the first fruits of your ground you shall bring to the house of the LORD your God. You shall not boil a kid in its mother's milk. 27 The LORD said to Moses: Write these words; in accordance with these words I have made a covenant with you and with Israel.

28 He was there with the LORD forty days and forty nights; he neither ate bread nor drank water. And he wrote on the tablets the words of the covenant, **the ten commandments**.*

[*This is the first time "the ten commandments" is referred to; later in Deuteronomy 4:13 and 10:4, the reference to tablets is again made. Given that the first set was destroyed, those later references probably refer to this set of commandments and not to those that are now so popular.]

THIRD SET
Deuteronomy 5:6–21

6 I am the LORD your God, who brought you out of the land of Egypt, out of the house of slavery; 7 you shall have no other gods before me.

8 You shall not make for yourself an idol, whether in the form of anything that is in heaven above, or that is on the earth beneath, or that is in the water under the earth. 9 You shall not bow down to them or worship them; for I the LORD your God am a jealous God, punishing children for the iniquity of parents, to the third and fourth generation of those who reject me, 10 but showing steadfast love to the thousandth generation of those who love me and keep my commandments.

11 You shall not make wrongful use of the name of the LORD your God, for the LORD will not acquit anyone who misuses his name.

12 Observe the sabbath day and keep it holy, as the LORD your God commanded you. 13 Six days you shall labor and do all your work. 14 But the seventh day is a sabbath to the LORD your God; you shall not do any work—you, or your son or your daughter, or your male or female slave, or your ox or your donkey, or any of your livestock, or the resident alien in your towns, so that your male and female slave may rest as well as you. 15 Remember that you were a slave in the land of Egypt, and the LORD your God brought you out from there with a mighty hand and an outstretched arm; therefore the LORD your God commanded you to keep the sabbath day.

16 Honor your father and your mother, as the LORD your God commanded you, so that your days may be long and that it may go well with you in the land that the LORD your God is giving you.

17 You shall not murder.
18 Neither shall you commit adultery.
19 Neither shall you steal.
20 Neither shall you bear false witness against your neighbor.
21 Neither shall you covet your neighbor's wife. Neither shall you desire your neighbor's house, or field, or male or female slave, or ox, or donkey, or anything that belongs to your neighbor.

FOURTH SET
Deuteronomy 27:1–2, 27:15–26

1 Then Moses and the elders of Israel charged all the people as follows: Keep the entire commandment that I am commanding you today. 2 On the day that you cross over the Jordan into the land that the LORD your God is giving you, you shall set up large stones and cover them with plaster.

15 "Cursed be anyone who makes an idol or casts an image, anything abhorrent to the LORD, the work of an artisan, and sets it up in secret." All the people shall respond, saying, "Amen!"

16 "Cursed be anyone who dishonors father or mother." All the people shall say, "Amen!"

17 "Cursed be anyone who moves a neighbor's boundary marker." All the people shall say, "Amen!" 18 "Cursed be anyone who misleads a blind person on the road." All the people shall say, "Amen!" 19 "Cursed be anyone who deprives the alien, the orphan, and the widow of justice." All the people shall say, "Amen!"

20 "Cursed be anyone who lies with his father's wife, because he has violated his father's rights." All the people shall say, "Amen!" 21 "Cursed be anyone who lies with any animal." All the people shall say, "Amen!" 22 "Cursed be anyone who lies with his sister, whether the daughter of his father or the daughter of his mother." All the people shall say, "Amen!" 23 "Cursed be anyone who lies with his mother-in-law." All the people shall say, "Amen!"

24 "Cursed be anyone who strikes down a neighbor in secret." All the people shall say, "Amen!" 25 "Cursed be anyone who takes a bribe to shed innocent blood." All the people shall say, "Amen!" 26 "Cursed be anyone who does not uphold the words of this law by observing them." All the people shall say, "Amen!"

So which ten influenced our founding? The second set, a pact sealed with genocide and requiring the sacrifice, but redeeming, of all first-born males? The final set, cursing anyone "who lies with his mother-in-law"?[27] Is it the first set of Ten Commandments, which is not even called the "Ten Commandments" in the bible, but actually called the "Ten Words" or "Ten Sayings"?[28] (The English shorthand phrase for the commandments, the Decalogue, comes from the literal Greek translation: *deca* or "ten," and *logue* from *logos*, meaning "word.") The first time the phrase "Ten Commandments" appears in the text, it refers to the second set, the set that ends with the kid-mother's-milk cooking prohibition.

These intra-biblical differences are not the only conflicts among the Ten Commandments that confuse the "which Ten" question. There are dozens of different English translations of bibles and thousands of translations into other languages that render the commandments differently, all of which were translated, often several times, from ancient languages. The *inter*-biblical differences are often more consequential than they first seem. For instance, the New Revised Standard Version reads: "You shall not make wrongful use of the name of the LORD your God,"[29] while the King James Version reads: "Thou shalt not take the name of the LORD thy God in vain;"[30] The NRSV prohibits "idols,"[31] while the KJV prohibits "graven images."[32] The KJV says, "Thou shalt not kill,"[33] while other translations prohibit "murder."[34] These are not minor differences. The difference between prohibiting murder and prohibiting killing is the difference between outlawing the intentional, premeditated taking of a life and outlawing even killing done in self-defense, in war, or to protect your child. Religious sects also interpret the commandment prohibiting art differently. Some think it prohibits "idols," some think it prohibits "graven images," some think it prohibits all religious art. These differing interpretations split Christendom in the eighth and ninth centuries during the Byzantine Iconoclasm or Iconoclastic controversy.[35] Religious artwork was destroyed because it violated the commandment, and both sides of the controversy had their martyrs, all due to the interpretation of this "minor" discrepancy.

Seemingly small differences are magnified because religion claims to possess ultimate truth on the basis of faith alone. Any deviation from an absolute truth is significant. And deviations cannot be reasoned away because believing the "truth" requires faith or, as Catholic Canon Law puts it, "a religious submission of the intellect and will."[36] Certainty without reason breeds absurdity. An eighteenth-century Christian group in Russia thought Jesus was not the Redeemer, Iskupitel', but the Castrator, Oskopitel', and that God commanded they castrate themselves, *plotites*, rather than be fruitful, *plodites*.[37] Group members acted accordingly and cut off their genitals.[38] The idea that Jesus was born of a virgin is a transliterative mistake that cannot be admitted because of religious certitude. The original Hebrew text labels Mary *alma*, Hebrew for "young woman."[39] This was mistranslated into Greek as *parthenos*, "virgin," even though there is a different Hebrew word for virgin.[40]

Minor variations are further magnified by believers' righteous superiority and the violence expended—or, as James Madison put it, the "torrents of blood" that have been spilled— trying to eliminate religious differences.[41] Thomas Jefferson once asked whether these minor points of division could ever be eliminated and uniformity attained. He thought not: "Millions of innocent men, women, and children, since the introduction of Christianity, have been burnt, tortured, fined, imprisoned; yet we have not advanced one inch towards uniformity." The religious coercion made "one half the world fools, and the other half hypocrites" and "support[ed] roguery and error all over the earth."[42]

IN ADDITION TO INTER- AND INTRA-BIBLICAL DISPARITIES, there are sectarian disparities. The various Jewish and Christian denominations have unique interpretations about which directive belongs to which commandment. The chart on page 168 is a simplified summary of these theological differences.[43]

Again, the numbering of the commandments may seem insignificant to modern readers, but Christianity warred with itself over this during the idol/graven image controversy.[44] The Catholic Church, so fond of its statuary, art, and gold-leafed finery, buries the prohibition on graven images and expands the coveting prohibition into two commandments.

Commandment	Most Jewish Traditions	Eastern Orthodox, Anglican, Most Protestant	Roman Catholic
1	I am the Lord thy God	I am Lord thy God and No other gods	I am Lord, No other gods or graven images
2	No other gods and No Idols	No Idols	Use of name of Lord
3	Use of name of Lord	Use of name of Lord	Sabbath
4	Sabbath	Sabbath	Honor your Parents
5	Honor your Parents	Honor your Parents	Do not Kill
6	Do not Kill	Do not Kill	No Adultery
7	No Adultery	No Adultery	No Theft
8	No Theft	No Theft	Do not Bear False Witness
9	Do not Bear False Witness	Do not Bear False Witness	Do not Covet Neighbor's Wife
10	Do not Covet	Do not Covet	Do not Covet Neighbor's Property

The variety and intensity of these differences—intra-biblical, inter-biblical, and inter-religious—complicate the claimed influence on America's founding. So does the plethora of commands in the bible.

Mosaic Law actually encompasses some 613 commandments found in the first five books of the Hebrew bible: Genesis, Exodus, Leviticus, Numbers, and Deuteronomy. These 613 rules, known as the *mitzvot*, are as important in Judaism as the Ten Commandments. There is no biblical or theological reason to think that the Ten Commandments are special.

Of course, one might argue that the *real* ten are obviously those rules Yahweh handed to Moses, a literal gift from god. But if that makes them special, why did Moses destroy those god-given tablets? Furthermore, within the book of Exodus, there are actually four full chapters of laws that could be part of the first set of commandments. God speaks to Moses on Mount Sinai almost continuously from Exodus 20 to Exodus 31, before finally carving the commandments into stone tablets in 31:18. Nothing sets off the first ten commands as more important than the rules god dictates in the eleven remaining chapters. As just noted, there are even four other *books* of laws, all of which must be followed. We are told read the law and "learn to fear the Lord his God, diligently observing all the words of this law and these statutes."[45] *All* 613, not just ten. (Note again that obedience to god is based on fear.) These biblical books are clear: "If you do not diligently observe all the words of this law that are written in this book, fearing this glorious and awesome name, the Lord your God, then the Lord will overwhelm both you and your offspring with severe and lasting afflictions and grievous and lasting maladies."[46] We must "take to heart all the words [and] give them as a command to your children, so that they may diligently observe all the words of this law."[47]

These 613 commandments include orders against erecting pillars in public places,[48] communing with ghosts or spirits,[49] performing magic,[50] getting tattoos,[51] and mating different species or planting different crops in the same field or wearing fabrics woven from two different materials.[52] Not all the 613 *mitzvot* are so benign or risible. Some are undeniably divorced from anything that could be considered an American principle, such as the prohibitions on mixing fabrics and trimming facial hair; others are downright barbaric.[53] We can forgo an examination of all 613 rules as a small charity to both the Christian nationalist and the reader. However, these brutal laws are fair game for two reasons. First, Christian nationalists are careful to say that we are founded on *Judeo*-Christian principles, not Christian principles, and the *mitzvot* come from the Hebrew Bible (Old Testament). Second, even if Christian nationalists claim that only Christian principles were influential, Jesus himself said that he came to uphold all 613 rules: "Do not think that I have come to abolish the law or the prophets; I have come not to abolish but to fulfill. For truly I tell you, until heaven and earth pass away, *not one letter, not one stroke of a letter, will pass from the law*."[54] This is not some passing reference; Jesus said it during the Sermon on the Mount.

Despite no valid biblical, theological, or logical reason to hold the Ten Commandments special, our inquiry into the possible influence of Mosaic Law on America's founding will be limited to them because that is what the Christian nationalists themselves emphasize. The Texas School Board altered its curriculum in 2014 to include Moses in American History because of his supposed influence on the Constitution.[55] The Ten Commandments appear, often illegally, in government buildings, schools, and courthouses around the country. They appear at the Texas Capitol in Austin and on the robes of a judge in Alabama.[56] They dot government property courtesy of Cecil B. DeMille, who promoted his movie with granite monuments and some help from the Fraternal Order of Eagles. When Bloomfield, New Mexico, lost a court battle over a Ten Commandments monument displayed in front of City Hall, Mayor Scott Eckstein was "surprised (by the decision) and had never really considered the judge ruling against it because it's a historical document just like the Declaration of Independence and the Bill of Rights."[57] The city's reliance on bad history cost the taxpayers $700,000.[58] The commandments are ubiquitous not just because of Hollywood promoters, but because they are argued to be the basis of American law and morality.[59]

They are not. Every one of the ten would be considered unconstitutional in our system—every single one, including the commandments against killing and thievery. The Ten Commandments conflict with our American principles so completely that they alone of the 613 amply prove that our nation is not founded on Mosaic Law.

The question remains: *Which* Ten Commandments were so influential on American law? Christian nationalists refuse to answer. The argument that America was founded on the Ten Commandments is actually an argument that America was founded on one of four discrepant sets of ten rules selected—without reason—from more than 600 other rules, which were in turn plucked from one of many divergent English translations, which was selected from any one of hundreds of different Judeo-Christian sectarian interpretations of the bible. When properly worded, the assertion is unconvincing.

It is possible, indeed probable, that Christian nationalists are ignorant about the imprecision of their religion's ten paramount rules. Supreme Court Justice Antonin Scalia admitted as much in a case involving a Ten Commandments monument on government land: "I doubt that most religious adherents are even aware that there are competing versions [of the Ten Commandments] with doctrinal consequences (I certainly was not)."[60] And if the country's leading originalist, a Catholic who believed in the literal existence of the devil, didn't know which set influenced America's founding, how would the average Christian nationalist?

Many Americans' knowledge of the Ten Commandments comes from Cecil B. DeMille and Charlton Heston and their Hollywood epic. DeMille often felt accused "of gingering up the Bible with large infusions of sex and violence."[61] He said of these allegations, "I can only wonder if my accusers have ever read certain parts of the Bible. If they have, they must have read them through that stained-glass telescope which centuries of tradition and form have put between us and the men and women of flesh and blood who lived and wrote the Bible."[62] Despite this insight, DeMille could not shatter Americans' stained-glass view. DeMille's influence sadly means that most Americans, like Justice Scalia, are ignorant about the commandments. It also means that the first set of ten, which appear so prominently in DeMille's epic, is likely what most Americans think of when they think of the Decalogue. And although Protestants are no longer a majority of citizens, most religious Americans are Protestant; so for the purposes of this book, let's use the Protestant interpretation of the first set to answer, in the next eight chapters, the apparently unanswerable question: which Ten?[63]

14

The Threat Display:
The First Commandment

I. "I am the LORD your God, who brought you
out of the land of Egypt, out of the house of slavery;
you shall have no other gods before me."

—Exodus 20:2–3

"Principal Errors of Our Time . . . #15. Every man
is free to embrace and profess that religion which,
guided by the light of reason, he shall consider true."

—Pope Pius IX, *Syllabus of Errors* encyclical, 1864[1]

"Whilst we assert for ourselves a freedom to embrace, to profess
and to observe the Religion which we believe to be of divine origin,
we cannot deny an equal freedom to those whose minds
have not yet yielded to the evidence which has convinced us."

—James Madison, "Memorial and Remonstrance
against Religious Assessments," 1785[2]

Male gorillas slap their puffed-out chests to show off their size and strength. So does Yahweh in his first commandment. This insecure self-declaration of superiority must be important to Yahweh, given its primacy. William Jennings Bryan, three-time presidential candidate and champion of creationism during the Scopes "Monkey Trial," wrote that the first commandment's placement "indicate[s] that it is the most important of the ten, and the same conclusion is reached if we compare it with the other nine."[3]

It would be difficult to write a law that conflicts more with America's founding document, the Constitution, than this rule: "I am the Lord your God . . . you shall have no other gods before me." First, our Constitution protects every citizen's freedom to worship as they choose, chiefly by requiring and guaranteeing a secular government. Second, the people, not god, are supreme. The Constitution's first words are more poetic and quite obviously more reflective of American principles: "We the People."

The First Amendment is one of humanity's greatest political and legal triumphs. Every fiber of that legal commandment stands opposed to the Judeo-Christian god's Ten Commandments. The First Amendment was originally proposed as several different amendments that were consolidated. The six rights enshrined in the First Amendment—secular government, religious freedom, free speech, free press, free assembly, and a right to petition the government—can be summed up as the freedom of thought. It reads:

> Congress shall make no law respecting an establishment of religion, or prohibiting the free exercise thereof; or abridging the freedom of the speech, or of the press; or the right of the people to peaceably assemble, and to petition the Government for a redress of grievances.[4]

The first two clauses protect your right to think for yourself about life's most important questions; the third, fourth, and fifth protect your right to speak and even publish those thoughts without fear of censure, and to gather with others to discuss them; the sixth protects your right to ask the government to listen to those ideas. Of the six clauses, the first two are arguably the most important, for without the ability to think freely about life's questions, little would be added to the discourse protected by the other rights.

Of those first two clauses—the Establishment Clause ("Congress shall make no law respecting an establishment of religion") and the Free Exercise Clause ("or prohibiting the free exercise thereof")—the first is more important. The freedom *of* religion cannot exist without a government that is free *from* religion (nor can the freedom of religion exist without the freedom to choose no religion at all). True religious freedom depends on a secular government.

If the Establishment Clause were faithfully upheld, there might be no need for the Free Exercise Clause because, as one Supreme Court justice put it, when the Constitution says "make no law respecting an establishment of religion," "'no' means no."[5] Unfortunately, a representative secular government is vulnerable to violations of this stricture because people occupy government offices, and when most people are religious, officeholders are religious, too. As history and the work of the Freedom From Religion Foundation show, people often abuse civil power in the name of their personal religion. Majority religions consistently torment minority religions when they have the power to do so. John Locke, a major influence on the founders, wrote of this phenomenon: "Where they [religions] have not the Power to carry on Persecution, and to become Masters, there they desire to live upon fair Terms, and preach up Toleration."[6] But when "they begin to feel themselves the stronger, then presently Peace and Charity are to be laid aside."[7]

Sixteenth-century Protestant reformer John Calvin often wrote in favor of toleration while he was powerless. Yet when he attained power, Calvin burned Spanish theologian Michael Servetus at the stake for his views on baptism and the trinity, "question[s] that neither of them knew anything about," as Robert Ingersoll put it. "In the minority, Calvin advocated toleration—in the majority, he practised murder."[8] The Catholic Church tyrannized Europe while it had control. As the civil authority or alongside the civil authority, it burned, tortured, imprisoned, blackmailed, and murdered to ensure conformity. But as the minority in the United States, the Catholic colonists fought for a secular government. Daniel Carroll, a Constitutional Convention delegate from heavily Catholic Maryland and one of two Catholics present at that convention,[9] later argued for the amendment to ensure a secular government and protect religious worship because "the rights of conscience are, in their nature, of peculiar delicacy, and will little bear the gentlest touch of governmental hand."[10]

John Adams noticed this historical trend,[11] as did James Madison, the Father of the Constitution and the Father of the Bill of Rights. Madison penned the greatest defense of religious freedom and secular government in 1785 to oppose a three-cent tax that would support Christian ministers. His "Memorial and Remonstrance against Religious Assessments" examined what churches with civil power—ecclesiastical establishments—had wrought. "In some instances they have been seen to erect a spiritual tyranny on the ruins of the Civil authority; in many instances they have been seen upholding the thrones of political tyranny: in no instance have they been seen the guardians of the liberties of the people," wrote Madison. "Rulers who wished to subvert the public liberty, may have found an established Clergy convenient aux-

Engraving of James Madison from c. 1828, after a painting by Gilbert Stuart.

iliaries." He concluded, "A just Government instituted to secure & perpetuate it needs them not."[12]

The other framers were familiar with this history, which is partly why most concluded, as Carroll did, that religious freedom is dependent on the government not taking sides on any religious issue, however gently or lightly. They therefore chose, in Jefferson's words—words later adopted by the Supreme Court to explain the principle underlying the religion clauses—to build "a wall of separation between Church & State."[13]

THE FIRST COMMANDMENT is fundamentally at odds with the US Constitution in another respect—the source of power. The Constitution sites power in the people. The Ten Commandments' authority rests on the claim that they are the words of a god—even though the first commandment's prose and feral threat, the "other gods" it refers to, and even the "god" himself, all suggest a man-made, not divine, author.

The claim of divine authority is shaky even according to the bible's own story. Moses was the sole witness to a god actually giving the commandments and may have been a tad delirious (see page 161). Rather suspiciously, he had the priests set a perimeter around the mountain to ensure that no other person could see, or not see, his god.[14] So even assuming the bible reports these events accurately—a rather large assumption—the divine authorship claim rests squarely on Moses's word. This is Thomas Paine's point in the *Age of Reason*: "When Moses told the children of Israel that he received the two tables of the commandments from the hands of God, they were not obliged to believe him, because they had no other authority for it than his telling them so; and I have no other authority for it than some historian telling me so."[15] Yet the authority of all the commandments rests tenuously on the claim that this particular god—one of many acknowledged in this very commandment—is supreme.

Those other gods cast even more doubt on the commandments' claim to divine authorship and authority. Christopher Hitchens pointed out that the commandment "carries the intriguing implication that there perhaps *are* some other gods but not equally deserving of respect or awe."[16] The *Jewish Encyclopedia* says that the early Hebrews were "monolatrous rather than monotheistic; they considered Yhwh to be the *one* God and *their* God, but not the one and only God."[17] Yahweh was "the national God of Israel as Chemosh was the god of Moab and Milkom the god of Ammon."[18] That there was "no other God in Israel . . . did not affect the reality of the gods of other nations."[19] Whether or not the bible admits that there are other gods and that the Israelites believed in them without worshipping them—and even if one particular god did write the Ten Commandments—is beside the point. The first commandment still conflicts with American principles.

In the United States, the people are supreme, not god. Article VI of the Constitution reads: "This Constitution . . . *shall be the supreme Law* of the Land."[20] The Supreme Court has specifically decided that religious belief cannot take precedence over the Constitution: "To permit this would be to make the professed doctrines of religious belief superior to the law of the land, and in effect to permit every citizen to become a law unto himself. Government could exist only in name under such circumstances."[21] Religious belief is a personal right individuals possess, not the source of governmental power.

The people are not one source of power and god another; "the people are the only legitimate fountain of power," wrote Madison.[22] Madison was echoing Hamilton's statement in *The Federalist* number 22: "The fabric of American empire ought to rest on the solid basis of THE CONSENT OF THE PEOPLE. The streams of national power ought to flow immediately from that pure, original fountain of all legitimate authority."[23] Benjamin Franklin thought that "in free Governments the rulers are the servants, and the people their superiors." He believed this so strongly that he claimed that leaving public office and rejoining the ranks of the people was a promotion: "For the former therefore to return among the latter was not to *degrade* but to *promote* them."[24] Writing of the Constitution, our fifth president, James Monroe, explained that "the people, the highest authority known to our system, from whom all our institutions spring and on whom they depend, formed it."[25]

Not only are the people supreme, but America is "founded on the natural authority of the people alone without a pretence of miracle or mystery,"[26] as John Adams put it. The people are solely responsible for the Constitution. Remember, while defending American ideals during the Revolutionary War, Adams cautioned that it should "never be pretended that any persons employed in that service had interviews with the gods."[27]

The conspicuous absence of a god from the Constitution, and the rather heavy emphasis the founders gave to its first three words—"We the People"— embody its conflict with the first commandment. The framers "formed our Constitution without any acknowledgment of God," as Yale president Timothy Dwight later complained.[28] As the framers excluded god from the document, the document excludes religion from government—its only references to religion are exclusionary:

- Prohibiting a religious test for public office.[29]
- Prohibiting governmental interference with religious worship.[30]
- Prohibiting religious interference with government.[31]

That's it. Nothing is said about Jesus, Yahweh, or any other god, or any of the sets of Ten Commandments.[32]

The First Amendment enshrines rights that are necessary for a functioning democracy. It allows free thought and free communication, and it allows citizens to interact freely with their government. The free exchange of ideas fosters a thriving democracy. Constitutional scholar Geoffrey Stone perfectly captured the First Amendment's importance to self-governance when he wrote:

> To meet the responsibilities of democracy, individuals must have access to a broad spectrum of opinions, ideas, and information. For the government to censor public debate because *it* thinks a particular speaker unwise or ill informed would usurp the authority of citizens to make their own judgments about such matters and thus undermine the very essence of self-government . . . . The First Amendment promotes the emergence of character traits that are essential to a well-functioning democracy, including tolerance, skepticism, personal responsibility, curiosity, distrust of authority, and independence of mind.[33]

The first commandment stands directly opposed to these freedoms. About one hundred years after the Constitution was proposed and ratified, Pope Leo XIII used the first commandment to declare it "unlawful to demand, to defend, or to grant unconditional freedom of thought, of speech, or writing, or of worship, as if these were so many rights given by nature to man."[34] Leo had the gall to title this order *On the Nature of Human Liberty*. The shackling of the human mind sanctioned by Leo's encyclical is sought by most religions and would destroy the freedoms of the First Amendment. The Judeo-Christian first commandment and the US First Amendment fundamentally conflict. They are irreconcilable.

15

Punishing the Innocent:
The Second Commandment

II. "You shall not make for yourself an idol [alternate translation:
"any graven image"[1]], whether in the form of anything that is in
heaven above, or that is on the earth beneath, or that is in the
water under the earth. You shall not bow down to them or worship
them; for I the LORD your God am a jealous God, punishing children
for the iniquity of parents, to the third and the fourth generation of
those who reject me, but showing steadfast love to the thousandth
generation of those who love me and keep my commandments."

—Exodus 20:4–6

"A curse from the Lord righteously falls not only on the
head of the guilty individual, but also on all his lineage."

—John Calvin, Institutes of the Christian Religion, 1559[2]

"We are to look upon it as more beneficial, that many guilty persons
should escape unpunished, than one innocent person should suffer."

—John Adams, opening statement defending British
soldiers accused of murder in the Boston Massacre, 1770[3]

We mortals must read any divine command in its entirety.
The second commandment is a tad verbose, but if we
simply skim the order or read one of the modern para-
phrases that appear on monuments around the country—such as the
abridged language on the monument that sits outside the Texas capitol
in Austin, "Thou shalt not make to thyself any graven images"—we

will miss the appalling punishment "the LORD your God" doles out to innocent children.

This commandment conflicts with the American principles embedded in the First Amendment in several ways. The First Amendment guarantees freedom of speech, the press, and worship.[4] It protects one's ability to worship any idol one chooses, be it a saint, as the Catholics do, or a sandal, as in Monty Python's *Life of Brian*. It also protects the right to reject worship. The amendment protects not only worship, but also many forms of expression, including religious or even blasphemous imagery.[5] The second commandment, on the other hand, prohibits more than just *religious* imagery. The text prohibits images of anything in heaven, on earth, or in the water. That covers most of the known world. In short, it ends art. The commandment prohibits a basic, universal human impulse: to create something that reflects and thereby enhances the beauty of life. The freedom to make and display images of Jesus, a freedom most Christians cannot resist exercising, is protected by our Constitution but prohibited by this commandment. It is specious to argue that a command punishing the very rights protected by the Constitution could have influenced it in some way.

The second commandment did not influence our nation's founding, but it did shape history. It has robbed historians, archaeologists, anthropologists, and humanity of many riches and wonders. The underlying sentiment—my god is the right god and your beliefs are wrong—appears in each of the first four commandments. This attitude led the Taliban to blow up the monumental sixth-century Buddhas of Bamiyan in Afghanistan in March 2001.[6] Judeo-Christianity behaved similarly when it held absolute power. Waves of idol destruction in the name of one god or another have swept the world. These destructions are distinctly un-American, but quintessentially Judeo-Christian. After all, God commanded Moses to slay three thousand of his friends, brothers, and neighbors, for violating this stricture. The early Christian theologian Origen interpreted the commandment to mean that "it is not possible at the same time to know God and to address prayers to images."[7] Celsus and Tacitus, two non-Christian historians living during the first two centuries of Christianity, both note that Christianity opposed imagery of its god[8]—much like Islam today.

Beginning with Emperor Leo III in 726 until about 843 CE, the Byzantine Empire tore itself apart over idols.⁹ Iconoclasts demanded the destruction of idols and art, and the controversy is the reason different sects number commandments differently.¹⁰ Idolatry eventually beat iconoclasm, and the Eastern Orthodox Church still celebrates this glorious victory on the Feast of Orthodoxy, the first Sunday of Great Lent. Before Byzantine Iconoclasm or the Iconoclastic controversy, as it became known, the Byzantine Church dictated precisely how Jesus should be represented in art. For the first few hundred years, Jesus was typically represented as a lamb—the sacrificial lamb, killed to satisfy the bloodlust of his dad. The Quinisext Council of Constantinople in 692 CE, authorized the crucifix (not the cross) as *the* symbol of Christianity: "Hereafter instead of the lamb, the human figure of Christ shall be set up on the images."¹¹ This heavy-handed patronage would continue through the Renaissance, when the church dictated to the world's most brilliant artists how they ought to ply their brushes and chisels. During that explosion of art, John Calvin wrote that "all the idols of the world are cursed, and deserve execration."¹²

A sixth-century mosaic of Jesus as the lamb of god in the Euphrasian Basilica in Poreč, Croatia.

Failure to keep this commandment is the root of all evil, according to the Wisdom of Solomon. If you don't recognize the name of this biblical book, it may be because not all sects include it in their bibles. Early Christians and church leaders thought the book holy and, according to scholars, it was "certainly used as Scripture by such early third-century writers as Tertullian, Clement of Alexandria, and Pseudo-Hippolytus."¹³ The book is also included in the Vulgate, the Latin translation of the bible.¹⁴ The Wisdom of Solomon sums up the religious worldview nicely:

All is a raging riot of blood and murder, theft and deceit, corruption, faithlessness, tumult, perjury, confusion over what is good, forgetfulness of favors, defiling of souls, sexual perversion, disorder in marriages, adultery, and debauchery. For the worship of idols not to be named is the beginning and cause and end of every evil.[15]

Also, "the idea of making idols was the beginning of fornication, and the invention of them was the corruption of life."[16] That's monotheism in a nutshell: the world is terrible and full of evil and perversion because people are worshiping idols and/or the wrong god.

As the Nazis were stealing and destroying the art of Europe, Franklin Roosevelt dedicated the National Gallery of Art in Washington, DC, in 1941. The objects in the gallery are "not only works of art . . . they are the symbols of the human spirit, symbols of the world the freedom of the human spirit has made . . . a world against which armies now are raised and countries overrun and men imprisoned and their work destroyed."[17] To accept the art on behalf of the people was "to assert the belief of the people of this democratic Nation in a *human spirit* which now is everywhere endangered and which, in many countries where it first found form and meaning, has been rooted out and broken and destroyed. To accept this work today is to assert the purpose of the people of America that *the freedom of the human spirit and human mind* which has produced the world's great art and all its science—shall not be utterly destroyed."[18]

Art is freedom: freedom of expression, freedom of thought, freedom to explore what it means to be human. Religion cannot thrive in the face of such freedom, so it seeks to muzzle or control it. As the Wisdom of Solomon explains, artists' creations are "ungodly" works that mirror what is supposedly god's creation and are therefore "a hidden trap for humankind."[19]

FREEDOM OF EXPRESSION AND FIRST AMENDMENT CONFLICTS are the least of the problems embodied in the second commandment. The initial command is simple: do not make idols or images. However, the rationale Yahweh gives for obeying the command is coercion of the worst kind. God promises to punish children, grandchildren, and great-grandchildren for their parents' mistakes. God's most moral law promises to deliberately punish innocent children.

This vicarious punishment conflicts with principles underlying American justice. In Article III, the Constitution explicitly forbids punishing children for the crimes of their parents, even for crimes as serious as treason: "No Attainder of Treason shall work Corruption of Blood, or Forfeiture except during the Life of the Person attainted."[20] This means that "even if all of one's antecedents had been convicted of treason, the Constitution forbids its penalties to be visited upon him."[21] James Madison explained that the entire point of this limitation was to restrain Congress "from extending the consequences of guilt beyond the person of its author."[22] In 1833, Justice Joseph Story described the problem the clause was meant to solve: "By corruption of blood all inheritable qualities are destroyed; so, that an attainted person can neither inherit lands, nor other hereditaments from his ancestors, nor retain those, he is already in possession of, nor transmit them to any heir. And this destruction of all inheritable qualities is so complete, that it obstructs all descents to his posterity." Story summed up this terrible punishment in biblical terms: "Thus the innocent are made the victims of a guilt, in which they did not, and perhaps could not, participate; and the sin is visited upon remote generations."[23]

In his powerful dissent in the *Korematsu* case, which upheld the internment of Japanese Americans without due process during World War II, Justice Robert Jackson wrote that "if any fundamental assumption underlies our system, it is that guilt is personal and not inheritable."[24] Justice Frank Murphy made the same point in his dissent: "Under our system of law individual guilt is the sole basis for deprivation of rights."[25] This is true; under American principles, the sins of the father cannot be visited upon the son or daughter. Yet the biblical god's principles command precisely that.

This constitutional command is not limited to treason or the Constitution; it forms the bedrock of criminal justice in America and in any other civilized nation: punish only the guilty.

Punishing the innocent is not a Ten Commandments quirk; it's a biblical constant. God handed down this barbaric commandment shortly after he slaughtered the firstborn of Egypt, both infants and octogenarians alike. Repudiations of personal responsibility such as punishing innocents (including genocide), vicarious redemption, and vicarious condemnation are rife in both the Hebrew and the Christian bibles. Jesus dying for our sins is the most prominent example. He was innocent, but somehow his punishment absolves others of wrong-doing. The second commandment is no different than putting a gun to an innocent child's head in an effort to force action from the child's parents. It is terrorism by an all-powerful being.

Seventeenth-century Flemish engraving depicting Lot (in the doorway with the angels) before the mob in Sodom.

Liberal believers occasionally try to explain away their god's lust for innocent blood with a story from Genesis 18:23–32. God wants to kill all of Sodom, but Abraham argues with Yahweh, saying that he cannot punish both "the righteous" and "the wicked." Some Christians point to this as evidence that those Yahweh kills are not actually innocent. But the term "righteous" here does not mean "innocent" or even "good;" it means something closer to "believing in Yahweh." The next chapter tells the story of Lot's rescue from Sodom, the same town Abraham and his god are arguing about,[26] and it becomes evident that "righteous" is not synonymous with moral, upstanding, or innocent. Lot is the only "righteous" man in the town,[27] so Abraham's god sends two angels to rescue Lot before the city is destroyed. A gang of men come to Lot's door to rape the angels.

Lot, the "righteous" man, offers up his two virgin daughters to the mob instead. Sacrificing your daughters to an angry mob hardly qualifies as moral, but Lot is "righteous" in the sense that he believes in the "right" god. In this god's eyes, actions do not determine guilt—beliefs do, an idea that resurfaces in the final five commandments. Abraham's argument with god is irrelevant; it saves people, but not because they are innocent or moral. In any event, this passage would not show that the biblical god possesses a discerning morality, but only that Abraham, a human, knew it was wrong to kill innocent people and the omniscient deity did not.

From punishing innocent children to prohibiting art to banning freedom of religion, the second commandment is an anti-liberty dictate that thoroughly conflicts with America's founding principles.

16

Suppressed Speech:
The Third Commandment

III. "You shall not make wrongful use of the name of the LORD
your God, for the LORD will not acquit anyone who misuses his
name." [or "Thou shalt not take the name of the LORD
thy God in vain; for the LORD will not hold him guiltless
that taketh his name in vain." (KJV)]

—Exodus 20:7

"If thought corrupts language, language can also corrupt thought."

—George Orwell, "Politics and the English Language,"
Horizon, April 1946[1]

"Call him Voldemort, Harry. Always use the proper name for things.
Fear of a name increases fear of the thing itself."

—Albus Dumbledore in J. K. Rowling's
Harry Potter and the Sorcerer's Stone, 1999[2]

Yahweh apparently took the third commandment pretty seriously, for he refused to even tell the Israelites his name: "I appeared to Abraham, Isaac, and Jacob as God Almighty, but by my name 'The LORD' [YHWH] I did not make myself known to them."[3] In the more careful translations of the bible, when the word LORD is written in small capitals it is not a generic title, but a substitute translators developed to refer specifically to the Hebrew god, Yahweh. Yahweh was represented by four Hebrew letters, *YHWH*. This was known as the tetragrammaton, from the Greek for "having four letters." But given the taboo on using the name, the word "LORD" in small caps was substituted.

The Israelites took this commandment as seriously as their god. According to the bible, they stoned a half-Israelite to death for blaspheming during a fistfight.[4] Under Jewish law, Jews could blaspheme heathen deities, but, as that incident shows, heathens blaspheming the Jewish god were guilty of a capital crime.[5] According to Jesus, breaking this commandment is the one unforgivable sin in the bible: "People will be forgiven for their sins and whatever blasphemies they utter; but whoever blasphemes against the Holy Spirit can never have forgiveness, but is guilty of an eternal sin."[6] And if a parent were to violate this command, Yahweh would kill their newborn child, as he did to David and Bathsheba.[7]

Thomas Aquinas could not decide whether blasphemy was worse than murder. His indecision is hard to understand, because blasphemy is directed at an unassailable, omnipotent god, while murder harms a fellow human being in the most egregious way possible. In his *Summa Theologica*, Aquinas wrote:

> If we compare murder and blasphemy as regards the objects of those sins, it is clear that blasphemy, which is a sin committed directly against God, is more grave than murder, which is a sin against one's neighbor. On the other hand, if we compare them in respect of the harm wrought by them, murder is the graver sin, for murder does more harm to one's neighbor, than blasphemy does to God. Since, however, the gravity of a sin depends on the intention of the evil will, rather than on the effect of the deed . . . it follows that, as the blasphemer intends to do harm to God's honor, absolutely speaking, he sins more grievously than the murderer.[8]

Punishing crimes against the regime more harshly than crimes against other people is typical in totalitarian systems.

But are we sure that blasphemy is really the issue here? For a god, Yahweh's legislation is remarkably imprecise. "Misusing" or "taking a name in vain" is so vague as to mean nothing yet somehow prohibits everything. In the United States, sloppy legal drafting is grounds for declaring a law unconstitutional. If citizens cannot know what is prohibited by a law, they cannot be expected to obey the law, and it can be struck down as too vague. Then again, vague laws that permit many interpretations are also typical in totalitarian regimes. This is actually one reason the founders carefully defined treason as a crime within the Constitution itself. "If the description of treason be vague and indeterminate under any government; this alone will be a sufficient cause why that government should degenerate into tyranny," James Wilson explained to a grand jury in 1791.[9] Treason, or any other crime, if poorly defined, "furnishes an opportunity to unprincipled courtiers, and to demagogues equally unprincipled, to harass the independent citizen, and the faithful subject, by treasons, and by prosecutions for treasons, constructive, capricious, and oppressive," added Wilson in a law lecture that same year. [10]

Some uncertainty in the law is unavoidable because language expresses the law. In an oblique jab at biblical literalism, James Madison pointed out in *Federalist* number 37 that even "when the Almighty himself condescends to address mankind in their own language, his meaning, luminous as it must be, is rendered dim and doubtful, by the cloudy medium through which it is communicated."[11] God's meaning is certainly dim and doubtful in the third commandment, so what does it actually mean? Ambrose Bierce thought it was not an issue of language, but of timing: "Take not God's name in vain; select a time when it will have effect."[12] A perfectly valid interpretation. Is this really just an issue of language? Suppose I say, "God damn it" or mutter "Jesus Christ" in anger. Would I be violating this commandment? Saying "God damn it" is asking god to damn something, so it has a purpose— the request is not in vain. And who says I was asking Yahweh to do the damning? Maybe I was asking it of Zeus or Thor.

Is "Jesus Christ" uttered as an imprecation even using god's name? The name Jesus Christ is made up of an English word followed by a Greek title. "Jesus" is the English translation of a Latin translation of a Greek translation of a Hebrew name. If Jesus did exist, he would have had a Hebrew name: Yeshua. Yeshua is closer to our Joshua than to Jesus and was a remarkably common name at the time of Jesus's supposed virgin birth. The Hebrew Yeshua was translated into Greek, and then into the Latin Iesus, then into English: Jesus. Appended to that thrice-translated name is the title Christ, which comes from the Greek *christos*, meaning "anointed," i.e., someone daubed with oil. *Christos* is a translation of the Hebrew *mashiach*. Christ is not a name, but a title. It'd be better to translate the whole phrase into English: Jesus Messiah. Or, better yet, revert to the original Hebrew—as Jesus was Jewish—and call him Yeshua mashiach ben-Yossef (Jesus, the anointed one, the son of Joseph).

If saying "Jesus Christ" doesn't violate the commandment, what about saying "oh my god," or texting "OMG"? What about ubiquitous Jesus bumper stickers and T-shirts? And, given that there is no god to answer prayers, aren't all appeals to heaven in vain? To paraphrase Joseph Lewis, one of the greatest atheist activists of the last century: Thou shalt not take the name of the LORD thy God in vain? Thou canst not use the name of God in any other way.[13]

The due process clauses of the Fifth and Fourteenth Amendments require laws to "give adequate guidance to those who would be law-abiding, to advise defendants of the nature of the offense with which they are charged, or to guide courts in trying those who are accused."[14] Legislation violates these amendments if it fails to do so. Laws prohibiting loafing, wandering, or strolling, for instance, may be meant to curb loitering but are too vague to explain what they actually prohibit and are often struck down.[15]

As a law, the third commandment would raise more questions than it answers: What constitutes a wrongful use of the name? Does it have to be the actual name, or will any mention of god suffice? What if you wrongfully use the name of somebody else's god? What does it mean to use a name in vain? Any law so vague would violate the US Constitution.

If the third commandment prohibits blasphemy, which is not at all clear, then it must be conceded that this commandment had some repressive and embarrassing influences on laws in the United States and abroad, both before and after the founding. (This is one of several negative Judeo-Christian principles that *have* influenced America since the founding by *impeding* progress.) Nearly thirty-five years after the First Amendment was adopted, John Adams wrote to Thomas Jefferson questioning the American commitment to liberty because of blasphemy laws:

We think ourselves possessed, or, at least, we boast that we are so, of Liberty of conscience on all subjects, and of the right of free inquiry and private judgment in all cases, and yet how far are we from these exalted privileges in fact! There exists, I believe, through-out the whole Christian world, a law which makes it blasphemy to deny or to doubt the divine inspiration of all the books of the Old and New Testaments, from Genesis to Revelations. In most countries of Europe it is punished by fire at the stake, or the rack, or the wheel. In England itself it is punished by boring through the tongue with a red-hot poker. In America it is not much better; even in our Massachusetts. . . . Now, what free inquiry, when a writer must surely encounter the risk of fine or imprisonment for adducing any argument for investigation into the divine authority of those books? . . . I think such laws a great embarrassment, great obstructions to the improvement of the human mind. Books that cannot bear examination, certainly ought not to be established as divine inspiration by penal laws.[16]

Adams was certainly correct that blasphemy laws are embarrass-ments; they are obstructions to the human mind that stifle free inquiry. They retard progress and destroy societal well-being. Afghanistan, Egypt, Iran, Kuwait, Pakistan, and Yemen are some of the countries that actively enforce and brutally punish blasphemy today, including with whipping and execution.[17] Raif Badawi was jailed in Saudi Arabia in June 2012 for "insulting Islam" and was sentenced to 10 years and 1,000 lashes. His wife, Ensaf Haidar, and children fled to Canada, and his attorney was arrested. The first 50 lashes meted out received international outcry, but, as of this writing, Badawi remains in jail and under threat of another 950 strokes for peacefully speaking his mind.[18] All these nations suffer under the iron hand of religion. But criticism of religion is the true beginning of freedom. Criticizing the system that claims to punish you for your thoughts is the first step against totalitarianism.

Adams wrote the above condemnation in a letter to Jefferson, who had particular reason to loathe these statutes. Had they been enforced, Jefferson himself could have been prosecuted for taking a razor to the

New Testament and cutting out all the supernatural nonsense: the virgin birth, the resurrection, the miracles. The man who drafted the Virginia Statute on Religious Freedom, on which his friend James Madison based our First Amendment, did not think such laws in keeping with liberty. In an 1814 letter, Jefferson attacked blasphemy laws:

> I am really mortified to be told that, in the United States of America, a fact like this can become a subject of inquiry, and of criminal inquiry too, as an offence against religion; that a question about the sale of a book can be carried before the civil magistrate. Is this then our freedom of religion? and are we to have a censor whose imprimatur shall say what books may be sold, and what we may buy? And who is thus to dogmatize religious opinions for our citizens? Whose foot is to be the measure to which ours are all to be cut or stretched? Is a priest to be our inquisitor, or shall a layman, simple as ourselves, set up his reason as the rule for what we are to read, and what we must believe? It is an insult to our citizens to question whether they are rational beings or not, and blasphemy against religion to suppose it cannot stand the test of truth and reason.[19]

American principles dictated a diversion from laws like the third commandment, laws that had been tried early in our history but were found too oppressive. This commandment runs afoul of the First Amendment several times over, violating the two religion clauses and the speech and press clauses. "It is not the business of government in our nation to suppress real or imagined attacks upon a particular religious doctrine," said the Supreme Court in 1952.[20] The Supreme Court has also noted that laws prohibiting "sacrilegious" speech "raise substantial questions under the First Amendment's guaranty of separate church and state with freedom of worship for all."[21] Given this history and the constitutional conflicts, any influence this commandment had was not positive. At best, it was a lighthouse that warned the founders away from regulating speech in the name of god.

Robert Ingersoll mounted an eloquent attack on an archaic New Jersey blasphemy law in May 1877, defending Charles B. Reynolds, who had been charged under the law before a packed courtroom in

Morristown.[22] (In 2018, Morristown and Morris County were the site of another watershed religious freedom case. The county was giving away millions of taxpayers' dollars to churches so that they could repair their buildings and the active congregations could continue to worship. I litigated the case to the New Jersey Supreme Court, which agreed, unanimously, that this violated the state constitution: citizens cannot be taxed to support religious worship.[23])

Reynolds had been a preacher, an itinerant Seventh-day Adventist. The ex-reverend moved from preaching about the Saturday sabbath in a tent to lecturing on freethought in that tent.[24] He aroused local ire with his freethinking and was eventually arrested and charged. Ingersoll attacked the law as counter to American principles. Blasphemy laws suppress "intellectual liberty" and "without that, we are poor miserable serfs and slaves," he argued. Like Adams, Ingersoll observed that "the ignorant bigots of this world have been trying for thousands of years to rule the minds of men by brute force. They have endeavored to improve the mind by torturing the flesh—to spread religion with the sword and torch."[25]

Charcoal portrait of Robert Green Ingersoll, c. 1875.

The history of the New Jersey blasphemy law Ingersoll challenged is particularly interesting. It was passed before the Constitution was written and was not enforced until the 1877 case Ingersoll waded heroically into. Ingersoll expounded on the law's sad history; it "was passed hundreds of years ago, by men who believed it was right to burn heretics and tie Quakers at the end of a cart, men and even modest women—stripped naked—and lash them from town to town. . . . [The statute] has slept all this time . . . there never has been a prosecution in this state for blasphemy." New Jersey and its "people became civilized—but that law was on the statute book. It simply remained. . . . Nobody savage enough to waken it. And it slept on, and New Jersey has flourished."[26]

Ingersoll thought the rationale underlying the law was ridiculous:

Did anybody ever dream of passing a law to protect Shakespeare from being laughed at? Did anybody ever think of such a thing? Did anybody ever want any legislative enactment to keep people from holding Robert Burns in contempt? The songs of Burns will be sung as long as there is love in the human heart. Do we need to protect him from ridicule by a statute? Does he need assistance from New Jersey? Is any statute needed to keep Euclid from being laughed at in this neighborhood? And is it possible that a work written by an infinite being has to be protected by a legislature? Is it possible that a book cannot be written by a God so that it will not excite the laughter of the human race?[27]

The jury found Reynolds guilty of breaking a law that made it a crime to "wilfully blaspheme the holy name of God, by denying, cursing, or contumeliously reproaching His being . . . or by cursing or contumeliously reproaching Jesus Christ, or the Holy Ghost, or the Christian religion, or the holy word of God."[28] The fine and costs amounted to about $75, which Ingersoll himself paid, a small price to expose and mortally cripple American blasphemy laws.[29]

Blasphemy laws and religious restrictions on speech are un-American. This commandment stands opposed to all that makes our country great. The American who values the Constitution and the liberties it protects will stand with Adams, Jefferson, and Madison, and, as Ingersoll stated, "deny the right of any man, of any number of men, of any church, of any State, to put a padlock on the lips—to make the tongue a convict [and] passionately deny the right of the Herod of authority to kill the children of the brain."[30]

17

Forced Rest: The Fourth Commandment

IV. "Remember the sabbath day, and keep it holy. Six days
you shall labor and do all your work. But the seventh day is
a sabbath to the LORD your God; you shall not do any work—you,
your son or your daughter, your male or female slave,
your livestock, or the alien resident in your towns. For in six
days the LORD made heaven and earth, the sea, and all that
is in them, but rested the seventh day; therefore the
LORD blessed the sabbath day and consecrated it."

—Exodus 20:8–11

"The word Sabbath, means rest, that is, cessation from labour,
but the stupid Blue Laws of Connecticut make a labour of rest,
for they oblige a person to sit still from sunrise to sunset on a
Sabbath day, which is hard work. Fanaticism made those laws,
and hypocrisy pretends to reverence them, for where
such laws prevail hypocrisy will prevail also."

—Thomas Paine, "Of the Sabbath Day in Connecticut," 1804[1]

The rationale for the sabbath rule is slightly ridiculous: it celebrates lazy omnipotence. If one is all-powerful, there is no such
thing as toil; all is rest. Yahweh would not need six days to do
anything—he'd need only the briefest moment. Nor would he need to
rest. It would have been far better to declare a day of rest to spend with
family and friends in relaxation from the rigorous week, rather than
invent a lazy god.

Ridiculous justifications aside, at first blush this stricture would appear to have influenced America's foundations. Perhaps so. It may be necessary to concede some influence here, but the rule was not influential in the way Christian nationalists suppose or accept. Sabbath, or, more accurately, Sunday closing laws, are part of American culture and laws, though the concept is not central to the foundations of our country. But to determine its influence, we must first understand the rule.

The biblical penalty for sabbath-breaking is death.[2] The Israelites stoned a man to death for gathering kindling on the sabbath.[3] At least a part of this rule is meant to encourage, or perhaps coerce, worship. If everyone has the same day off, nobody has an excuse for missing church. This need to coerce attendance at worship services undercuts the favorite argument that humans are religious beings. David Tappan, a Congregationalist reverend and Harvard theologian, gave a sermon in Boston on Election Day, 1792, explaining that preachers need the sabbath to control their flock: "Many of us [preachers] are connected with societies, which are chiefly composed of the labouring and more illiterate class; that these peculiarly need the privileges of a weekly sabbath and public religious instruction; and that many of them require very plain, and very pungent applications, in order to enlighten their ignorance, to rouse their stupidity, or to check their vicious career."[4] The sabbath exists not because people need a day to worship, but because clerics need to continually reassert their role in the lives of the credulous. If there were, as oversimplified Blaise Pascal quotations suggest, a god-shaped hole or vacuum in humans, there would be no need to mandate church attendance.[5]

But the American colonies, which were part of Great Britain, and their established churches, passed sabbath laws to do just that: coerce attendance. British colonists in Virginia passed the first in 1610:[6]

> Every man and woman shall repair in the morning to the divine service and sermons preached upon the Sabbath day, and in the afternoon to divine service, and catechising, upon pain for the first fault to lose their provision and the allowance for the whole week following; for the second, to lose the said allowance and also be whipt; and for the third to suffer death.

This law is not about rest. It is about imposing religious conformity; about forcing people to worship and believe in a certain god.
Nothing could be more fundamentally opposed to our First Amendment and founding principles than such a law. This is why the Supreme
Court, although it has upheld Sunday closing laws in some instances,
has struck down any religious aspects of or religious rationale for those
laws. American Sunday closing laws have been around since the founding but are upheld in court for strictly secular reasons.[7] A law like
the fourth commandment would be struck down by American courts.
So too, would the aforementioned 1610 law, especially after Virginia
adopted the Virginia Statute on Religious Freedom in 1785, which
Thomas Jefferson authored. That marvelous text, upon which our First
Amendment is based, directly refutes such laws:

> That the impious presumption of legislators and rulers, civil as well
> as ecclesiastical, who, being themselves but fallible and uninspired
> men have assumed dominion over the faith of others, setting up
> their own opinions and modes of thinking as the only true and
> infallible, and as such endeavouring to impose them on others,
> hath established and maintained false religions over the greatest
> part of the world and through all time.[8]

The Supreme Court has catalogued "the evolution of Sunday
Closing Laws from wholly religious sanctions to legislation concerned
with the establishment of a day of community tranquility, respite and
recreation, a day when the atmosphere is one of calm and relaxation
rather than one of commercialism, as it is during the other six days
of the week."[9] Even this rationale rings a bit false in America's highly
commercialized society. But as early as 1885, the Supreme Court recognized that Sunday closings were not about the sabbath:

> Laws setting aside Sunday as a day of rest are upheld not from any
> right of the government to legislate for the promotion of religious
> observances, but from its right to protect all persons from the phys-
> ical and moral debasement which comes from uninterrupted labor.
> Such laws have always been deemed beneficent and merciful laws,

especially to the poor and dependent, to the laborers in our factories and workshops, and in the heated rooms of our cities, and their validity has been sustained by the highest courts of the states.[10]

As the United States Post Office expanded alongside the nation in the early nineteenth century, a debate erupted over the then regular delivery of mail on Sundays. The practice was halted, and a congressional committee issued a report on the controversy on January 19, 1829, that specifically stated that religious reasons did not and constitutionally could not motivate stopping Sunday delivery. The report explained that "some respite is required from the ordinary vocations of life, is an established principle, sanctioned by the usages of all nations, whether Christian or pagan. One day in seven has also been determined upon as the proportion of time; and, in conformity with the wishes of the great majority of citizens of this country, the first day of the week, commonly called Sunday, has been set apart to that object."[11] Thus, it was not for religious reasons that the government chose Sunday to close the postal department, but a matter of convenience.

The report continued, "The proper object of government is to protect all persons in the enjoyment of their religious as well as civil rights, and not to determine for any whether they shall esteem one day above another, or esteem all days alike holy. We are aware that a variety of sentiment exists among the good citizens of this nation on the subject of the Sabbath day; and our Government is designed for the protection of one, as much as for another." The report then chastised the religious zealots seeking to shut down the government on Sundays:

> The transportation of the mail on the first day of the week, it is believed, does not interfere with the rights of conscience. The petitioners for its discontinuance [that is, the Christians petitioning Congress to stop the delivery of mail on Sundays] appear to be actuated from a religious zeal, which may be commendable if confined to its proper sphere; but they assume a position better suited to an ecclesiastical than a civil institution. . . . Should Congress, in their legislative capacity, adopt the sentiment, it would establish the principle that the Legislature is a proper tribunal to determine

what are the laws of God. It would involve a legislative decision in a religious controversy. . . . Among all the religious persecutions with which almost every page of modern history is stained, no victim ever suffered but for the violation of what government denominated the law of God. To prevent a similar train of evils in this country, the constitution has wisely withheld from our government the power of defending the divine law.

This ringing statement was followed by an even stronger defense of the separation of state and church:

Extensive religious combinations to effect a political object are, in the opinion of the [congressional] committee, always dangerous. . . . All religious despotism commences by combination and influence; and when that influence begins to operate upon the political institutions of a country, the civil power soon bends under it; and the catastrophe of other nations furnishes an awful warning of the consequence.

So despite their history, not all Sunday closing laws were adopted for religious reasons. And, as the Supreme Court has explained, any Sunday closing law would violate "the Establishment Clause if it can be demonstrated that its purpose . . . is to use the State's coercive power to aid religion."[12]

As with the second commandment punishing innocent children to the third and fourth generations, reading the entire fourth commandment reveals a darker side (again, which is typically omitted on Ten Commandments monuments). The fourth commandment recognizes that human beings can be property: "You shall not do any work—you, your son or your daughter, your male or female slave, your livestock . . ." Surely any god's ultimate collection of moral precepts should include an injunction against slavery, not a recognition of it? This is the influence Christian nationalists are unwilling to admit. Judeo-Christianity contributed significantly to our country's long and shameful history of slavery.

Speaking of his former master, Frederick Douglass wrote, "His religion hindered him from breaking the Sabbath, but not from breaking my skin on any other day than Sunday. He had more respect for the day than for the man for whom the day was mercifully given; for while he would cut and slash my body during the week, he would on Sunday teach me the value of my soul, and the way of life and salvation by Jesus Christ."[13] Christianity, the bible, and, despite Douglass's musing, Jesus, all affirm the legality and morality of slavery. This divine sanction influenced America's founding. Both Christianity and our Constitution discuss slavery as an institution, the details of dealing with that institution, and did not prohibit it. In short, both implicitly recognized the viability of one human owning another.

The Hebrew bible is rife with slavery. Exodus and Leviticus lay out the laws for beating, selling, buying, and raping one's slaves. Slaves who worshipped the Hebrew god were treated more leniently, some even being set free after six years.[14] Religious apologists and some bible translations claim that the word "slave" actually means servant. Ownership distinguishes a servant from a slave. Slaves are owned, servants are not. While the bible sometimes distinguishes between servants and slaves, in Leviticus 25:39–46 for instance ("If any who are dependent on you become so impoverished that they sell themselves to you, you shall not make them serve as slaves. They shall remain with you as hired or bound laborers"), *The Jewish Encyclopedia* says, "The Hebrew word 'ebed' really means 'slave'; but the English Bible renders it 'servant.'"[15] Hebrew slaves owned by other Israelites had a higher status—e.g., they were freed after a set time—but they were still owned, still *ebed*, and, therefore, still slaves. Hebrew girls were eligible to be sold as *ebed*— sold into sexual slavery—and were never to go free, so long as their father sold them and they "pleased" their new master:

> When a man sells his daughter as a slave . . . If she does not please her master, who designated her for himself, then he shall let her be redeemed.[16]

Just to be clear, "who designated her for himself" means the buyer can rape the young girl. The law is not concerned for the girl unless "she does not please her master," in which case she may be returned like a defective product. If there is any lingering doubt about the sexual nature of this deal, it's cleared up in the subsequent verses, which treat wives and female slaves as synonymous:

> If he designates her for his son, he shall deal with her as with a daughter. If he takes another wife to himself, he shall not diminish the food, clothing, or marital rights of the first wife. And if he does not do these three things for her, she shall go out without debt, without payment of money.[17]

Jesus endorses slavery too. He tells his disciples a story involving the appropriate force with which to beat a slave: "That slave who knew what his master wanted, but did not prepare himself or do what was wanted, will receive a severe beating. But the one who did not know and did what deserved a beating will receive a light beating."[18] Had Jesus been antislavery, this would have been a good time to mention it.

Saint Paul expanded his savior's immoral teachings: "Slaves, obey your earthly masters with fear and trembling, in singleness of heart, as you obey Christ . . . . Render service with enthusiasm."[19]

The American justification for slavery was inextricably tied to Christianity and the bible. We'll see more of this later (see chapters 17 and 24). For now, it is enough to know that our Constitution is not free from what Thomas Jefferson, himself a slaveowner, called that "hideous blot." Just like the Ten Commandments, it legitimized slavery.

> Article I, Section 2: Representatives and direct Taxes shall be apportioned among the several States which may be included within this Union, according to their respective Numbers, which shall be determined by adding to the whole Number of free Persons, including those bound to Service for a Term of Years, and excluding Indians not taxed, three fifths of all other Persons.

> Article I, Section 9: The Migration or Importation of such Persons as any of the States now existing shall think proper to admit, shall not be prohibited by the Congress prior to the Year one thousand

eight hundred and eight, but a Tax or duty may be imposed on such Importation, not exceeding ten dollars for each Person.

Article IV, Section 2: No Person held to Service or Labour in one State, under the Laws thereof, escaping into another, shall, in Consequence of any Law or Regulation therein, be discharged from such Service or Labour, but shall be delivered up on Claim of the Party to whom such Service or Labour may be due.

Article 1, Section 9, the clause protecting the slave trade until 1808, illustrates how the framers viewed the slavery problem. The southern states would not give up their slaves. They would sooner refuse to join the union. The founders thought the union more important for the moment, so they postponed the slavery fight. The failure to stand for the principle of universal equality led to the Civil War seventy-five years later. Madison thought the twenty-year waiting period protecting the slave trade until 1808 "more dishonorable to the National character than to say nothing about it in the Constitution."[20] But abolition was not a goal of the 1787 Constitution; uniting the colonies into one nation—the United States—was. During a particularly tense moment at the Virginia Ratifying Convention, when some were threatening secession over the possibility of abolition, Edmund Randolph delivered a speech noting the difference:

> Where is the part [of the Constitution] that has a tendency to the abolition of slavery? Is it the clause which says that "the migration or importation of such persons as any of the states now existing shall think proper to admit shall not be prohibited by Congress prior to the year 1808"? This is an exception from the power of regulating commerce, and the restriction is only to continue till 1808. Then Congress can, by the exercise of that power, prevent future importations; but does it affect the existing state of slavery? Were it right here to mention what passed in convention on the occasion, I might tell you that the southern states, even South Carolina herself, conceived this property to be secure by these words. I believe, whatever we may think here, that there was not a member of the Virginia delegation who had the smallest suspicion of the abolition of slavery.[21]

Randolph was right: the Constitution did not prohibit slavery. It would prohibit slavery later, but that would require a war and constitutional amendments. Our Constitution was not perfect when it was written, nor is it perfect now. The first African American Supreme Court Justice, Thurgood Marshall, thought that the government the framers "devised was defective from the start, requiring several amendments, a civil war, and momentous social transformation to attain the system of constitutional government, and its respect for the individual freedoms and human rights, we hold as fundamental today."[22] The framers recognized that they were fallible and were embarking on a great social experiment. The framers knew the document would be flawed—the inevitable result of political compromises—and would require alteration over time, so they provided procedures for future changes. Americans tend to forget that the amendments they so often cite actually *amended* the Constitution. The Thirteenth, Fourteenth, and Fifteenth amendments ended slavery as an institution, while slavery's supporters continued to cite the holy, unalterable, infallible word of god.

THE SABBATH COMMANDMENT ITSELF is a reminder to believers that they are, as Paul wrote, owned, not free. The sabbath is not meant for people to rest; it is to remind them whom they serve. The fourth commandment in the third set of Ten Commandments (see pages 164–65), very like the first, reminds readers that they were once slaves to an earthly master and are now slaves to a more powerful one: "Remember that you were a slave in the land of Egypt, and the LORD your God brought you out from there with a mighty hand and an outstretched arm; therefore the LORD your God commanded you to keep the Sabbath day."[23] Ownership simply transferred from Pharaoh to Yahweh.

One final point on this commandment: Yahweh differentiates Israelites from other "alien residents," listing non-Israelites after livestock: "you, your son or your daughter, your male or female slave, your livestock, or the alien resident in your towns."[24] He makes a point of saying that, although non-Israelites are lesser and treated as such in most of his laws, even they should not be made to work on the sabbath. As we'll see, differential treatment for Israelites and non-Israelites plays a crucial role in interpreting commandments six through ten.

18

On Family Honor:
The Fifth Commandment

V. "Honor your father and your mother, so that your days
may be long in the land that the LORD your God is giving you."

—Exodus 20:12

"All three monotheisms, just to take the most salient example,
praise Abraham for being willing to hear voices and then
to take his son Isaac for a long and rather mad and
gloomy walk. And then the caprice by which his murderous
hand is finally stayed is written down as divine mercy."

—Christopher Hitchens, *God Is Not Great*, 2007[1]

There is little serious argument that this particular commandment influenced the American founding. Culture, yes. But few
assert with any real conviction that parental reverence built this
nation. Since we'll touch on Christian family values later, there are only
a few points to note here.

Interestingly, this is the "only commandment that comes with an
inducement instead of an implied threat," as Christopher Hitchens
observed.[2] The reward is not only long life, but long life on the land
you were given—the Promised Land. The rule has "the slight suggestion of being respectful to Father and Mother in order to come into an
inheritance."[3] Whether Hitchens is correct that this is an inducement
for inheritance or whether it is a veiled threat that this god may take
away the Promised Land, the rule is tainted. Remember, "the land
that the LORD your God is giving you" is given with the promise of

genocide, according to the second set of Ten Commandments (see pages 164–65). That gruesome promise is kept in subsequent books of the bible, such as Joshua.

The fifth commandment requires respect simply because of a family connection. Intellectual honesty requires that only those worthy of respect receive it. The "biological fact of fatherhood or motherhood does not in and of itself warrant honor," observed Freedom From Religion Foundation cofounder Anne Gaylor.[4] Not all parents are worthy of honor or respect. Recall that Noah cursed his own grandson because he, Noah, passed out drunk and naked. We already met Lot of Sodom, the person the Judeo-Christian god considered the sole bastion of morality in that doomed town, who offered up his daughters to be raped by a mob.[5]

This horror is indefensible, and one ought to think twice before accepting moral advice from anyone who defends these actions. But things got worse for Lot's unnamed daughters. Both "became pregnant by their father."[6] The bible blames this on the young, nameless girls, claiming that they plotted together and, to preserve the family line, got their dad drunk and raped him without his knowledge. Yes, really. Which is more likely: that a male author of a book of the bible blames women for a crime committed by a male assailant, or that two young girls who had been offered up for gang-rape by their father and who had lost their mother seduced their drunken, unconscious father? The latter is too absurd to be believed. But there is plenty of biblical precedent for the former—Eve, to name one. God clearly believes Lot worthy of honor; he sent his angels to save him. But must his victims honor him? Must these girls really honor the man who would give them to a gang of rapists and later rape them himself—the more plausible explanation for their paternal impregnation?

Because not every parent is worthy of respect, this commandment is, to use a legal term, overinclusive: it's a law that protects people it should not. But curiously, it is also underinclusive, failing to protect people it should. Since the code already mandates blind respect, it could easily be improved by extending the requirement to honor to all one's family, or better yet, one's fellow human beings. However, if blind respect is to be mandatory, perhaps the best formulation would require that every human deserves the chance to earn respect. One might justifiably end a moral code there and have done better than the Judeo-Christian god.

If the true purpose of this commandment is not to spread familial bliss, as seems evident by its shortcomings, what might it be? There are three possibilities: (1) ensuring obedience, (2) supporting priests, and (3) supporting the clan. All three purposes work to perpetuate the religion that issued the mandate. This commandment is not about honor and respect; it is about obedience and power. Gaylor labeled it "an extension of the authoritarian rationale behind the first four" commandments.[7] The idea is simple: honor your god-fearing parents if you want a reward. And since parents will worship the biblical god with no other gods before him, this commandment helps ensure the worship of the "correct" deity. "Take to heart all the words [and] give them as a command to your children, so that they may diligently observe all the words of this law," preached Moses.[8] Paul echoes this in the New Testament, commanding all fathers to bring their children "up in the discipline and instruction of the Lord."[9] This commandment teaches obedience at an early age and comingles household obedience with obedience to god.

The blurring of the familial and religious duties also supports the priestly caste. Protestant reformer Martin Luther applied this commandment to priests, whom he labels "spiritual fathers." He writes, "Since they [the priests] are fathers they are entitled to their honor, even above all others. . . . Those who would be Christians are under obligation in the sight of God to esteem them worthy of double honor who minister to their souls, that they deal well with them and provide for them."[10] He goes on to say that Christians should bankroll priests, even if they are starving, for they will be rewarded in heaven for doing so. Televangelists preaching the "prosperity gospel"—essentially a divine lottery with a healthy dose of guilt and coercion in which followers donate or "vow" money, pray, and are supposedly rewarded with wealth—echo this. Said one televangelist: "Vowing is one of the best ways to stretch your faith—but only when your vow goes beyond your natural resources or abilities. I don't need much faith to vow $100 if I have $2,000 in a savings account. But, if I don't even have a savings account and can barely pay my bills, then a $100 vow will stretch my faith indeed. For I will have to seek God and focus on Him to supply the seed to pay that vow."[11] Better you go hungry than your priestly, telegenic "father."

The command also has a clannish element. The Jewish religion is built on patriarchs—Abraham, Moses, David, Solomon—the fathers of their people. They in turn ensured that their people worshipped *the* father, Yahweh.[12] Jesus took worship of the father to new heights,[13] even instructing his followers to "call no one your father on earth, for you have one Father—the one in heaven."[14] This pipeline to the gods, controlled by a single patriarch, eventually led to the divine right of kings. Even the most woeful student of United States history knows that America's founding generation spurned kings.

Gaylor was correct to describe this commandment as the authoritarian culmination of the previous orders. That authoritarianism—the veneration of authority—may have helped elect Donald Trump. With his immodesty, lack of liturgical and scriptural knowledge, and "unchristian behavior," Trump seemed like an improbable choice for American evangelicals. Yet 81 percent of white evangelicals supported him, more than supported Mitt Romney, John McCain, or George W. Bush.[15] Trump promised these voters plenty, but previous candidates had promised more and fared worse among them. They have demonstrated a strong distaste for female leaders.[16] While that might account for evangelicals not voting for Hillary Clinton, it does not fully account for them flocking to Trump in greater numbers than they did for past candidates.

Trump's dictatorial tendencies and mendacity, negative attributes for many voters, poised him perfectly to manipulate the evangelical mind. Like the biblical god evangelicals worship, Trump is a thin-skinned authoritarian with totalitarian tendencies. He craves love and punishes any disloyalty or slight. Evangelicals have been taught to worship and adore that type of being above all others. This strain of religion cultivates a veneration for extreme authority. Studies bear this out: religious fundamentalism and a tendency to submit to authoritarianism are highly correlated.[17] Trump acted like the character evangelicals worship and benefited from their ingrained adulation. Evangelicals were simply seeing in Trump a character they'd been taught to revere. As if to prove the point, Ann Coulter called Trump her "Emperor God."[18]

Coulter's failed attempt at humor, which came before she turned on Trump in early 2018 for signing a $1.3 trillion spending bill, contains an uncomfortable grain of truth. With the evangelicals' ready heart comes an overly receptive mind, a blind faith in the righteousness of the strongman authority. If he says something, it is true. It becomes an article of faith, not an issue of fact or evidence or reality. "You shouldn't be in the totalitarianism business if you can't exploit a ready-made reservoir of credulity and servility," observed Christopher Hitchens.[19] Hitchens was speaking about Stalin and the highly religious, and therefore credulous, population on whom Stalin imposed his will, but the analogy is apt. Evangelicals believe in virgins giving birth, talking snakes, and all manner of obvious falsehoods. The religious mind is primed to accept lies. Presented with an extraordinary claim, it does not demand extraordinary evidence, but instead engages faith to overcome skepticism. Their religion has taught evangelicals to accept, rather than to question. Trump's constant waterfall of outright lies landed on amenable minds. His support was greater among regular churchgoers than among lukewarm believers.[20] The greater the faith, the more subordinate healthy skepticism becomes. So the biblical fetish for totalitarians may have helped America elect its first.

The US Constitution honors individual rights over naked authority. The fifth commandment is about perpetuating religion, ensuring obedience, and venerating authority. It had no influence on America's founding.

19

Unoriginal and Tribal: The Sixth, Eighth, and Ninth Commandments

VI. "You shall not murder." [or "Thou shalt not kill." (KJV)]

VIII. "You shall not steal."

IX. "You shall not bear false witness against your neighbor."

—Deuteronomy 5:17, Exodus 20:13, 15, 16

"Just think about Irish history, the Middle East, the Crusades,
the Inquisition, our own abortion-doctor killings and, yes,
the World Trade Center to see how seriously religious people
take Thou Shalt Not Kill. Apparently, to religious folks—especially
the truly devout—murder is negotiable. *It just depends on
who's doing the killing and who's getting killed.*"

—George Carlin, *When Will Jesus Bring the Pork Chops?*, 2004[1]

Virtually all that can be said of commandments six, eight, and nine can be said of commandment seven, the adultery commandment. All four are similar in structure, language, concision, and application. According to scholars, several of the oldest and "most significant"[2] manuscripts of the Decalogue actually list the adultery commandment before the murder commandment.[3] This ordering is echoed in the King James Version of the New Testament in several places, including in Jesus's own words to his apostles: "Thou knowest the commandments, Do not commit adultery, Do not kill, Do not steal . . . "[4] However, the adultery ban's influence on America's founding requires additional discussion, so it will be treated separately in the next chapter.

It is not until halfway through god's most moral precepts that we begin to see, if not influence, at least some resemblance to American law and government. That these few commandments resemble some of our laws does not necessarily mean that they influenced those laws or the founding of this country. Prohibitions on theft, perjury, and murder are vital—so much so that every successful society agrees with them.[5] These biblical commands fail to prove America's Judeo-Christian foundations because they are not uniquely or originally Judeo-Christian and, as formulated in these commandments, they are not as moral as people suppose.

First, these principles are not exclusive or original to Judeo-Christianity. They are universal principles that all humans understand and arrive at regardless of their participation in the Judeo-Christian religion.[6] This includes cultures and religions that predate Judaism and even holds true within Judaism itself, as Christopher Hitchens pointed out:

> My mother's Jewish ancestors are told that until they got to Sinai, they'd been dragging themselves around the desert under the impression that adultery, murder, theft, and perjury were all fine, and they get to Mount Sinai only to be told it's not kosher after all.[7]

Interestingly, the biblical god does not base his rules on their universal moral qualities. Instead, the Ten Commandments "unmistakably rest even the universally accepted prohibitions (as against murder, theft, etc.) on the sanction of the divinity proclaimed at the beginning of the text," as the Supreme Court noted in a ruling against governmental displays of the Ten Commandments.[8] This puts the commandments on shaky ground, as we've seen it is, at best, only Moses's word that vouches for the divine origins of the tablets. Formulations of these rules in other cultures are actually based on morality, not on the tenuous authority of a divine character. Which are better: rules that exist because they are valuable precepts for humanity, or rules that exist because a dictator decreed them?

Other, earlier legal codes in the region of the Levant contained similar prohibitions, as did other religions.[9] Although Christians often talk of Jesus's humility and their desire to emulate him, it is monstrously arrogant to claim that a universal human principle belongs to one religion, especially a relatively young religion. This belief marries that arrogance to ignorance—ignorance of other cultures, countries, religions, and ideas.

Second, America's statutory versions of these universal principles apply to everyone; the biblical god's commandments do not. Judeo-Christianity limits the application of these principles to other believers, destroying their universality. George Carlin's quip on page 208, "It just depends on who's doing the killing and who's getting killed," is accurate. The god of the bible allows murder if the victim believes in a different god. The biblical commandments protect only other believers. You may not murder, steal from, or bear false witness against *other members of our group*. This is why the first five commandments deal with god's supremacy and how he should be worshipped, so that believers can recognize each other, the people to whom the final commandments apply. The in-group application of the final commands is why rather obvious rules against murder, stealing, and lying are not listed first.

The commandments in their original Hebrew support this in-group interpretation. They were set down when the art of writing was in its infancy, and were later translated from Hebrew texts that do not have commas, periods, capital letters, or breaks for paragraphs.[10] Translators and editors made the grammatical and punctuation decisions we see today long after the originals were written.

This may seem trivial, but punctuation, capitals, and breaks clarify writing. Unpunctuated or poorly punctuated writing, like the original commandments, can easily confuse the writer's message. Examples abound, including this popular one:

A woman without her man is nothing

Add some varying punctuation to this and you can get two contradictory meanings:

A woman, without her man, is nothing.

A woman: without her, man is nothing.

Had this been a biblical sentence in need of punctuation, it's not difficult to guess which punctuation early bible scribes, men writing the laws of a patriarchal religion, would have chosen. Punctuation can even save lives:

Let's eat, Grandpa!

Let's eat Grandpa![11]

Had the voice Moses heard in the wilderness—a voice he heard after starving for weeks during a forced desert march—bothered to invent punctuation for the Hebrews, thousands of lives might have been saved over the millennia. Here's how commandments six through nine read, without the added punctuation:

you shall not murder you shall not commit adultery you shall not
steal you shall not bear false witness against your neighbor

The preferred modern interpretation breaks this into four separate sentences, with the neighbor clause ("your neighbor") modifying only the lying prohibition. Another viable interpretation, one that makes more sense given the surrounding books of the bible, is:

You shall not murder, you shall not commit adultery, you shall not
steal, you shall not bear false witness against, your neighbor.

The alteration is subtle, but it completely changes the meaning. In the former interpretation, all the prohibitions except lying are absolute—one can lie, just not to his neighbor. In the latter interpretation, "neighbor" limits all the prohibited acts: You can kill, steal, cheat, or lie, so long as the victim is not your neighbor.

Here's a parallel example, something a first-grade teacher might tell a student. Again, punctuation changes the meaning:

> Do not cross the street. Do not talk to strangers. Do not go trick-or-treating without your parents.

> Do not cross the street, do not talk to strangers, do not go trick-or-treating, without your parents.

In the first example, the child cannot ever cross the street. The child can never talk to strangers. But the child can go trick-or-treating, so long as her parents are present. The punctuation gives the sentence an incorrect meaning—of course the child may cross the street and talk to strangers with her parents; otherwise she'd never go anywhere or meet anyone. In the second example, punctuation clarifies the message: she can do any of the three activities so long as her parents are present.

The more accurate *interpretation* of these four commandments might be: do not kill your neighbor or commit adultery with your neighbor or steal from your neighbor or bear false witness against your neighbor.[12] Under this interpretation, which not all scholars agree with, the prohibitions are not applied equally; they are applied only to one's neighbor. So it is permissible to kill and steal, so long as you don't kill your neighbor or steal from your neighbor. There are different rules for people, depending on their status as a neighbor.

I've hinted at this interpretation several times already, and it makes learning who one's neighbor is all the more important—which is why the first five commandments help identify neighbors before explaining that you should not kill them. Do you worship my god? Only my god? Do you curse my god or do you respect him? Do you worship and rest when my god says to? Do you obey your parents and priest who tell you to worship my god? If so, you're my neighbor and it's important that I not kill you.

Our modern, broadminded interpretation of "neighbor" encompasses all humans, but that was not the meaning for Moses and his tribe.[13] Immediately after receiving the first set of commandments,

Moses descends from the mount to find his followers violating the idol-worship prohibition. Enraged, Moses destroys the only physical evidence that a god exists and relays a command from Yahweh to his priests to "kill your brother, your friend, and your neighbor." Moses uses those terms synonymously. The murders are acceptable to Moses and Yahweh because these neighbors have betrayed their god and worshipped an idol, essentially forfeiting their status as neighbors by breaking one of those commandments meant to identify those to whom the latter commandments apply.

Leviticus 19:18 provides another contemporaneous contextual definition of the word "neighbor:" "You shall not take vengeance or bear a grudge against *any of your people*, but you shall love your *neighbor* as yourself."[14] Two verses earlier is another example: "You shall not go around as a slanderer among *your people*, and you shall not stand against the *blood of your neighbor*."[15] God also tells the Israelites that they should occasionally expunge debts "held against a neighbor, not exacting it of *a neighbor who is a member of the community*."[16] Of course, you can still recover debts from "foreigners."[17]

Thus, according to the biblical text itself, "neighbor" refers only to your fellow believers.[18]

The in-group interpretation of these commandments makes even more sense given the events that follow the covenant. Shortly after receiving the commandments, the Israelites go on a killing spree. According to the bible, they commit genocide after genocide—more than seventy all told.[19] "Thou shalt not kill" is a contradiction that cannot be reconciled with the genocides the Israelites inflict on the inhabitants of the region, unless their killings are not murder because the victims did not worship Yahweh. All the groups of people they destroyed were people who did not worship their god. The Israelites did not violate the divine prohibition on murder because that commandment applied only to other Israelites.

This interpretation also makes more sense given the sheer levels of brutality and violence in the bible. There is so much bloodshed that it's almost as if there are no limits on murder at all. In *The Better Angels of Our Nature*, Pinker makes the point so beautifully that it is worth reproducing in whole:

The Bible depicts a world that, seen through modern eyes, is staggering in its savagery. People enslave, rape, and murder members of their immediate families. Warlords slaughter civilians indiscriminately, including the children. Women are bought, sold, and plundered like sex toys. And Yahweh tortures and massacres people by the hundreds of thousands for trivial disobedience or for no reason at all. These atrocities are neither isolated nor obscure. They implicate all the major characters of the Old Testament, the ones that Sunday-school children draw with crayons. And they fall into a continuous plotline that stretches for millennia, from Adam and Eve through Noah, the patriarchs, Moses, Joshua, the judges, Saul, David, Solomon, and beyond. According to the biblical scholar Raymund Schwager, the Hebrew Bible "contains over six hundred passages that explicitly talk about nations, kings, or individuals attacking, destroying, and killing others. . . . Aside from the approximately one thousand verses in which Yahweh himself appears as the direct executioner of violent punishments, and the many texts in which the Lord delivers the criminal to the punisher's sword, in over one hundred other passages Yahweh expressly gives the command to kill people." Matthew White, a self-described atrocitologist who keeps a database with the estimated death tolls of history's major wars, massacres, and genocides, counts about 1.2 million deaths from mass killing that are specifically enumerated in the Bible. (He excludes the half million casualties in the war between Judah and Israel described in 2 Chronicles 13 because he considers the body count historically implausible.) The victims of the Noachian flood would add another 20 million or so to the total.[20]

The Sanhedrin, the high religious court, interpreted these rules in this exclusive, in-group manner before Jesus entered the scene. According to this court, an Israelite was not guilty of murder unless he killed another Israelite.[21] Even if he *intended* to kill a non-Israelite ("heathen"), the act was not murder.[22] *The Jewish Encyclopedia* is explicit on this point, explaining that under some laws, "the Gentile . . . is not a neighbor."[23]

Far from the universal human meaning bestowed upon it by modern believers, "neighbor" means your clan, your tribe, your brother believer—and no one else. The basis of Judeo-Christian morality and ethics is the clan. The tribe is more important than morality; people who are different are lesser. Those who exercise their freedom of religion to worship differently will be treated as nonhumans. Does that sound like an American principle?

Christian apologists seek to paint Jesus as redefining "neighbor" to include all humans. But the bible tells a different story.

When Jesus sent out his twelve apostles to convince people that he was god, he didn't send them out to everyone: "Do not go among the Gentiles or enter any town of the Samaritans. Go rather to the lost sheep of Israel."[24] Not exactly an equal opportunity preacher. When Jesus gives his new commandment to "love one another," he does not extend it beyond brother believers.[25] He says "one another," and he is commanding only his closest followers, the twelve apostles. He gives them that command so that "everyone will know that you are my disciples, if you have love for one another."[26] This is not an expansion of loving your neighbor into other religions—it is just a command that Jesus's closest followers love each other. If you were to say at your next office meeting, to twelve coworkers or subordinates, "be nice to each other," no one would reasonably think you were addressing the statement to anyone outside that room. So why treat Jesus's words differently? One book attributed to John the Evangelist reiterates the believer-must-love-believer point several times.[27] The author even specifically says that believers only need to love other believers:

> Whoever says, "I am in the light," while hating a brother or sister, is still in the darkness. Whoever loves a brother or sister lives in the light, and in such a person there is no cause for stumbling. But whoever hates another believer is in the darkness, walks in the darkness, and does not know the way to go.[28]

Other authorities, some ancient, leave out the word "sister."[29] Either way, the command to love can only be read as an in-group command. The next chapter of 1 John specifically interprets the "love your neighbor" commandment to mean "brothers" (again, other authorities leave out the "sisters"):"

For this is the message you have heard from the beginning, that we should love *one another*. We must not be like Cain who was from the evil one and murdered his *brother*. . . . Do not be astonished, *brothers and sisters*, that the world hates you. We know that we have passed from death to life because we love *one another*. . . . All who *hate a brother or sister* are murderers, . . . and we ought to lay down our lives *for one another*. How does God's love abide in anyone who has the world's goods and *sees a brother or sister* in need and yet refuses help?[30]

"The world" is other people and believers are not commanded to love them—only "one another" and their "brothers and sisters."

The books of both Matthew and Mark tell of a woman, a non-Israelite, with a sick daughter. She asks Jesus to cure the child. Jesus ignores her and his disciples urge him to send her away, but she persists. Finally, Jesus chides the woman, saying, "It is not fair to take the children's food and throw it to the dogs." In other words, miracles are for my people, my neighbors, my children—not for dogs who worship other gods. It is not until after she has professed her faith in him, until after she calls Jesus "master" and "Lord" for the third time, that he relents, noting, "Woman, great is your faith!" Jesus deigns to save the innocent, sick child only because the mother converts and declares her obedience to and belief in him.[31]

The closest Jesus gets to a command for universal love is in his Sermon on the Mount. He says to "love your enemies"[32] and lays out his version of the Golden Rule (Matthew 7:1–5, in which "neighbor" has been interpreted as "brother"). Immediately after explaining his Golden Rule, Jesus says, in verse 6, "Do not give what is holy to dogs; and do not throw your pearls before swine, or they will trample them under foot and turn and maul you." This is not a tolerant, expansive message or ministry; it is elitist and insular. In the final chapter of the last book of the bible, the literary acid trip that is the Book of Revelation, Jesus points out that his followers will be in the kingdom of heaven, while "outside are the dogs and sorcerers and fornicators and murderers and idolaters, and everyone who loves and practices falsehood."[33] Also according to Revelation, before Jesus returns, he'll send plagues, including locusts. But the locusts will harm "only those people who do not have the seal of God on their foreheads. They were allowed to torture them for five months, but not to kill them."[34] Once again, believers, followers, and coreligionists are saved. Insects torture everyone else for five months.

There is also the small matter of hell, the place of eternal torment for all who do not believe that Jesus is god.[35] Love your enemies indeed. If you are of the correct religion, you get eternal bliss; if not, eternal torment (see chapter 9).

Even the seemingly open-minded, inclusive passages of the New Testament betray tribalism. Standing alone, this sentiment penned by the apostle Paul sounds broad and inclusive: "There is no longer Jew or Greek, there is no longer slave or free, there is no longer male and female; for all of you are one in Christ Jesus."[36] But in context, this is more like the slogan of the Orwellian farm: "All animals are equal, but some animals are more equal than others." Paul's version might read "Everyone is equal, so long as you are a Christian,"[37] for that is the true sentiment behind the passage:

> *For in Christ Jesus you* are all children of God through faith. *As many of you as were baptized into Christ* have *clothed yourselves with Christ.* There is no longer Jew or Greek, there is no longer slave or free, there is no longer male and female; for all of you are one in Christ Jesus. And *if you belong to Christ,* then you are Abraham's offspring, heirs according to the promise.[38]

The modern attempt to portray Jesus as a bastion of equality instead of an elitist was valuable to the civil rights movement but is belied by American history. During the civil rights movement, Jesus was also used to argue *for* segregation. On May 23, 1954—the Sunday after the Supreme Court decided *Brown v. Board of Education*, integrating the nation's schools—Reverend Carey Daniel of the First Baptist Church of West Dallas delivered a sermon titled "God: The Original Segregationist."[39] When he published it in pamphlet form, it sold over a million copies.[40] Like Daniel, Mississippi Presbyterian minister Guy Gillespie's "A Christian View on Segregation" was influential, was widely distributed, and made the same arguments, drawing on the bible for support.[41] Bob Jones, the evangelist and founder of an eponymous religious school, infamously declared that segregation was scriptural in his 1960 Easter sermon: "If you are against segregation and against racial separation, then you are against God."[42] At the height of the Montgomery bus boycott, the Montgomery City Council issued a statement saying that it "will forever stand like a rock against racial equality, intermarriage, and mixing of the races in schools" and rooted its intransigence in religion:"There must continue the separation of the races under God's creation and plan."[43]

The City of Montgomery, Carey, Gillespie, Jones, and their brethren drew support from both the Old and the New Testaments. Reverend T. Robert Ingram of St. Thomas' Episcopal Church of Houston thought segregation "was simply applied Christianity," according to one scholar.[44] "The most complete and devastating discriminatory practices that can ever be exercised," wrote Ingram, "are those of Jesus Christ."[45] In a pamphlet entitled "Jesus: Master-Segregationist," Lawrence Neff, a Methodist minister in Atlanta, noted that Jesus sent out his disciples with instructions to avoid Gentiles and Samaritans and to preach only to Jews.[46] Neff had support in the New Testament, as we've just seen. In his second letter to the Corinthians, Paul quotes the Hebrew bible and reminds Christians to "be separate from them [unbelievers], says the Lord, and touch nothing unclean."[47]

Even Alabama governor George Wallace, in his 1963 inaugural speech—which is also known as the "Segregation Now, Segregation Forever" speech—called on the Christian god and Jesus Christ. Fearful of integration, Wallace attacked the federal government as the instrument that would destroy segregation. He argued that "we are become government-fearing people . . . not God-fearing people. We find we have replaced faith with fear . . . and though we may give lip service to the Almighty . . . in reality, government has become our god. . . . The politician is to change their status from servant of the people to master of the people . . . to play at being God . . . without faith in God . . . and without the wisdom of God. It is a system that is the very opposite of Christ for it feeds and encourages everything degenerate and base in our people as it assumes the responsibilities that we ourselves should assume." He then drew "the line in the dust and toss[ed] the gauntlet before the feet of tyranny" and uttered the notorious line: "I say . . . segregation today . . . segregation tomorrow . . . segregation forever."[48]

Trump supporters are often driven by a longing for this bygone era, when religion supported their racism and they could claim to be superior to others simply by looking at the color of their skin, not the content of their character.[49] Christian nationalism is inextricably tied up in the bigotry and longing for a restoration to a racist golden age. Remember, it was not economic anxiety or even racism that was the best predictor of a 2016 Trump voter—it was Christian nationalism. It's easy for Christian nationalists to sweep aside anything that might be construed as sentiments about treating strangers and foreigners as if they were natives, as in Leviticus 19:33–34, because most of the bible, including the New Testament, backs up *their* scriptural interpretation.

The *Washington Post* profiled a small-town congregation hearing a series of sermons on the Ten Commandments in Alabama in July 2018. The *Post* recounted an exchange between two congregants. These "followers of Donald Trump" are the everyday Christian nationalists that carried Trump into office, and they implicitly understand this us-versus-them interpretation of their book:

> Love thy neighbor . . . meant "love thy American neighbor." Welcome the stranger . . . meant the "legal immigrant stranger." "The Bible says, 'If you do this to the least of these, you do it to me,'" Sheila said, quoting Jesus. "But the least of these are Americans, not the ones crossing the border."[50]

In the minds of these Christian nationalists, Trump "woke a sleeping Christian nation" that is threatened by "unpapered people," and the bible justifies bigotry against such people. After all, slavery was never "as bad as people said it was. 'Slaves were valued. . . . They got housing. They got fed. They got medical care.'"[51] The us-versus-them tenet of Christian nationalism is not only central to Trumpian rhetoric but is also being promoted at the highest levels of power in a bible study conducted for the President's cabinet, for US Senators, and for US

Representatives. This bible study is the reason former attorney general Jeff Sessions cited Romans 13 to justify separating children from their parents at America's southern border.[52]

US laws incorporate prohibitions that are reflected in at least three of the Ten Commandments: murder, theft, and lying (e.g. fraud, perjury). However, unlike the Decalogue and Christian nationalism with its insularity, our laws apply to everyone and do not rest on divine claims but on an agreement of "We the People."[53] More importantly, these universal principles are not unique to Judeo-Christianity, so they fail to support the myth that America is founded on Judeo-Christian principles. It cannot be denied that our country was founded to favor a similarly small group of people: white men. True, white men of various religions were welcomed, but that is still a narrow group. But the ideal that America is attempting to live up to is the nonbiblical principle inscribed on the Supreme Court in Washington, DC: "Equal Justice Under Law." Whereas the immutable, imperfect law of the Judeo-Christian god will forever discriminate against people who don't believe in the "right" god, American law comes ever closer to attaining the equality ideal. God's law holds that some people are more equal than others. American law has expanded to include men of other races, then women, and so on, until now we are finally beginning to treat people of different sexual orientation equally under the law. We have not fully realized the ideal, but at least our founders gave us room and a process to grow. Progress is possible under our founding documents, while the bible will forever enshrine an ancient and outdated morality. Nothing in these commandments supports the Christian nationalist argument.

20

Perverting Sex and Love:
The Seventh Commandment

VII. "You shall not commit adultery."

—Exodus 20:14

"Sex, sin, and the Devil were early linked."

—Arthur Miller, *The Crucible*, 1953[1]

"Adultery is the highest invasion of property."

—Regina v. Mawgridge, Queen's Bench, 1706[2]

L aws regulating sex tend toward the ridiculous. Indiana and Wyoming enacted sodomy laws in the late nineteenth century to punish anyone who "entices, allures, instigates or aids any person under the age of twenty-one years to commit masturbation or self-pollution."[3] To this day, Maryland outlaws oral sex as an "unnatural or perverted sexual practice."[4] And in Michigan, adultery is still a crime.[5] This country has a long history of regulating and prohibiting sex. More often than not, it is a history not just of ridiculousness, but of racism, sexism, and discrimination, all actively pushed by Christian churches. The history is still being written. The vice president of the United States, Mike Pence, once called for criminalizing adultery, bemoaning the modern "discomfort with a law against adultery." He, for one, did not think it an "antiquated sin," but believed that "the Seventh Commandment contained in the Ten Commandments is still a big deal."[6] Pence is not alone—he's just not in the right century. Once upon a time, adultery was a crime and a cause for civil action in the

United States. The trial that gripped the nation in the 1870s—there's always one—was newspaper editor Theodore Tilton's lawsuit against his mentor and pastor, the famous abolitionist minister who preached about "God's love," Reverend Henry Ward Beecher, for "criminal conversation." Basically, Tilton sued Beecher in civil court for $100,000 for committing adultery with his wife.[7]

Whether this history of legislating sex is essential to the American founding is unclear, but the Judeo-Christian influence on legislating sexual mores is undeniable and, as this chapter concedes, can be legitimately claimed by Christian nationalists. But upon that history, shame, not a country, should be built, and therefore this commandment demands special attention, even though, like the sixth, eighth, and ninth commandments, it applies only to one's co-religionists.

The biblical prohibition on adultery is narrow; it is certainly not as broad as most read it today. Biblically speaking, the prohibition did not pertain to all believers: it applied only to married women. The married woman and her sexual partner were both considered adulterers. But if her husband slept around, or even took another wife, as Abraham, Jacob, Solomon, David, Gideon, and Moses all did, he was not an adulterer. According to *The Jewish Encyclopedia*, adultery is "sexual intercourse of a married woman with any man other than her husband. The crime can be committed only by and with a married woman; for the unlawful intercourse of a married man with an unmarried woman is not technically Adultery in the Jewish law."[8] The encyclopedia clarifies that a husband can have sex with women other than his wife without breaking god's commands: "The ancient Jewish law, as well as other systems of law which grew out of a patriarchal state of society, does not recognize the husband's infidelity to his marriage vows as a crime."[9] A man was an adulterer when he slept with another man's wife.[10] Essentially, adultery was a crime against a husband. Because husbands owned their wives.[11]

This raises the question of why a god that passed a prohibition on adultery designed to prevent married women from straying would have chosen a married woman to bear his son, but that is not for me to answer. It may even be fair to say that Christianity is founded on adultery. Joseph and Mary were "betrothed" with solemn espousals when "she was found to be with child," a child that was not Joseph's.[12] As two scholars on the role of women in the ancient world, Mitchell Carroll and the Reverend Alfred Brittain, have noted, that betrothal and those espousals are "as sacred as . . . marriage. . . . The woman was not allowed to withdraw from the contract, and the man could not fail to fulfill his promise unless he gave her a formal bill of divorcement for cause, as in the case of marriage; the laws relating to adultery were also applicable."[13] If that is true, the whole of Christianity may be predicated on Mary's adultery.

Of course, the bible, and therefore Judeo-Christianity's, obsession—and that word is used with all its unhealthy connotations—with sex is not limited to adultery. The adultery commandment is just a symptom of that broader preoccupation. The bible demands that we "Shun fornication! Every sin that a person commits is outside the body; but the fornicator sins against the body itself."[14] It also prohibits homosexuality,[15] cross-dressing,[16] sex while or with a partner who is menstruating,[17] masturbation,[18] lying about your virginity (but only if you're female),[19] being raped,[20] and bestiality (an excellent prohibition with a punishment that demands the death of yet another innocent victim: both human and animal are killed.)[21]

Many of the sex regulations are as sexist as they are absurd. The bible declares that menstruating women are unclean,[22] but allows polygamy.[23] Fathers may sell their daughter into sexual slavery, but only to another Israelite.[24] Soldiers may sexually enslave any female virgins after they've killed the virgins' men.[25] Men can get away with rape, if they pay the victim's family 50 shekels and marry the victim.[26] There are many prohibitions against having sex with family members, but men have a duty to impregnate the wives of their dead brothers.[27] Biblical heroes even trade in flesh. David purchased a wife by giving his future father-in-law, King Saul, one hundred foreskins of the king's enemies.[28]

The bible authors also demand—as part of the covenant with god—that all males have a part of their genitals removed:

> This is my covenant, which you shall keep, between me and you and your offspring after you: Every male among you shall be circumcised. You shall circumcise the flesh of your foreskins, and it

shall be a sign of the covenant between me and you. Throughout your generations every male among you shall be circumcised when he is eight days old, including the slave[s]. . . . Any uncircumcised male who is not circumcised in the flesh of his foreskin shall be cut off from his people; he has broken my covenant."[29]

"Cut off from his people" in this instance is both an unfortunate pun and a regular biblical punishment that meant killing or banishing the person. Other books of the bible reiterate the divine covenant's demand for an ounce of flesh.[30] Even the New Testament advocates it; Paul circumcises Timothy.[31]

The Christian bible tries to halt the biblical sex craze by endorsing celibacy.[32] Recognizing that "sexual immorality" is unlikely to stop, Paul concedes that people may get married, even though it would be better if they remained unmarried and celibate, like him. The bible treats marriage as a safety valve, necessary because people are not pious enough to abstain.

There might actually be a twisted sort of logic to religious leaders imposing these rules on followers. Perhaps the true rationale behind the sexual commandments and Christianity's unnatural enthusiasm for celibacy is not to curb immorality, but rather to guard the primacy of one's relationship with the religion. Jesus has to be more important than anything else, including your husband, wife, or lover. He said so himself: "I have come to set a man against his father, and a daughter against her mother."[33] His followers' love and attention must be directed toward Jesus first. Family can have what is left over.

Destroying relationships that elevate loyalty to one another above loyalty to the leader is typical in totalitarian systems. In Orwell's *Nineteen Eighty-Four*, Winston and Julia betray each other and repudiate their love while being tortured by the Ministry of Love (a title that some apply to Jesus's ministry). Of all the agencies operated by Big Brother, the "Ministry of Love was the really frightening one."[34] Its goal "was not merely to prevent men and women from forming loyalties which it might not be able to control. Its real, undeclared purpose was to remove all pleasure from the sexual act."[35] Sex is a threat to the leader:

All marriages between Party members had to be approved . . . and—though the principle was never clearly stated—permission was always refused if the couple concerned gave the impression of being physically attracted to one another. The only recognized purpose of marriage was to beget children. . . . Sexual intercourse was to be looked on as a slightly disgusting minor operation, like having an enema. There were even organizations such as the Junior Anti-Sex League, which advocated complete celibacy for both sexes.[36]

Sterilizing sex and degrading that lovely and loving act to the lowest form of uncontrolled reproduction should ring familiar bells for Christians, particularly those raised in more conservative churches. Sex, when done properly, fosters and improves loving relationships, creating loyalty outside of the church. Judeo-Christianity's and Big Brother's goals are chillingly similar: "trying to kill the sex instinct, or, if it could not be killed, then to distort it and dirty it"[37] to ensure loyalty to the leader, not to one another.

The Catholic Church uses the same rationale to control its priests. According to Catholic law, Canon 277, "Clerics are . . . bound to celibacy which is a special gift of God by which sacred ministers can *adhere more easily to Christ with an undivided heart* and are able to dedicate themselves more freely to the service of God and humanity."[38] An "undivided heart" is preferred because the church and its god do not want followers to love anyone in this world above the church. Allowing them to do so weakens the church. Clerical celibacy dates back to at least 300 CE, when, according to the Catholic Church, it decided that "all clerics who exercise a ministry . . . must abstain from relations with their wives and must not beget children; those who do are to be removed from the clerical state."[39]

Jesus himself lays down the most vile and controlling sexual law by making it impossible to obey the adultery commandment: "But I say to you that everyone who looks at a woman with lust has already committed adultery with her in his heart."[40] This commandment then, at least as interpreted by Jesus, is meant to make believers feel guilty and, in doing so, builds their spiritual debt. Lusty, guilty sinners are bound more tightly to the person who can expiate their sin, Jesus, and later to his deputies, the priestly caste, every time they even think of having sex. That perpetual guilt binds people to their church and is the basis of thoughtcrime, which appears undisguised in the final commandment (see chapter 21).

THIS SAD LEGAL CATALOG, with all its totalitarian leanings, has infected American law. Judeo-Christianity presumes the power, intelligence, and feasibility of legislating the bedroom behavior of two consenting adults, and this arrogance has been responsible for immense pain and discrimination throughout American history.

Until 1967, penalties for miscegenation—mixed-race sex, relationships, or marriages—were common, and had been since the colonial period.[41] Hugh Davis, in 1630, received the earliest recorded punishment in the colonies for "lying with a negro." Davis was "soundly whipped before an assembly of Negroes and others for abusing himself to the dishonor of God and the shame of Christians by defiling his body in lying with a negro; which fault he is to acknowledge next Sabbath Day."[42] Notice that this crime had no victim; rather, it was a crime against "God" and against other Christians who were not involved or harmed.

The unconstitutional anti-miscegenation law that the Supreme Court struck down in 1967 in the famous *Loving v. Virginia* case was similarly based on religion, as the trial judge explained: "Almighty God created the races white, black, yellow, malay and red, and he placed them on separate continents. . . . The fact that he separated the races shows that he did not intend for the races to mix."[43]

Another example of Judeo-Christianity's sexual legislation is America's history of discrimination against homosexuals. The District of Columbia Court of Appeals wrote in 1976, "There is no dispute that religious forces motivated the original laws proscribing sodomitic acts."[44] When the Supreme Court initially upheld laws criminalizing sodomy in 1986 in *Bowers v. Hardwick*, Chief Justice Warren Burger wrote that "decisions of individuals relating to homosexual conduct have been subject to state intervention throughout the history of Western civilization. Condemnation of those practices is firmly rooted in Judeo–Christian moral and ethical standards."[45] When the court overturned these prohibitions in 2003, it disagreed with the *Bowers* outcome but did not dispute the religious nature of such prohibitions. The majority confirmed that "the condemnation [of homosexuality] has been shaped by religious belief"[46] and cited a historiography article that argued:

> The primary historical justification for penalizing crimes against nature reaches back to the early Christian era and the Middle Ages. Following the lead of Saint Paul, early church fathers synthesized ideas from Christianity's Jewish heritage and Roman context to create a regime whereby sex and pleasures of the body were considered presumptively suspect—morally valuable only when engaged in for procreative purposes within marriage.[47]

The *Bowers* Court's reliance on Judeo-Christian principles was historically accurate, but legally wrong. American courts cannot uphold laws for religious reasons; nor can our government legislate religion. The government must have valid secular reasons for its legislation. When overturning *Bowers*, the Court wrote, "The issue is whether the majority may use the power of the State to enforce [religious beliefs] on the whole society through operation of the criminal law."[48] The Court concluded that *Bowers* "was not correct when it was decided, and it is not correct today. It ought not to remain binding precedent. *Bowers v. Hardwick* should be and now is overruled."[49]

Judeo-Christian principles reared up in the push to criminalize sodomy, but also in the attempt to ban gay marriage. When the Supreme Court overturned the Defense of Marriage Act in 2013, it noted that the House of Representatives intended DOMA to express "both moral disapproval of homosexuality, and a moral conviction that heterosexuality better comports with traditional (especially Judeo–Christian) morality,"[50] a sentiment correctly struck from our laws.

What goes on in the bedroom of two consenting adults is no business of the state. When the state does intrude, it is often with a law based on Judeo-Christian principles, like those embodied in the seventh commandment. The influence of these principles cannot be denied. But such laws are a shameful part of America's past, and the sooner we purge that venomous influence, the better.

In a way, even this influence proves the larger point of this book. Judeo-Christianity's influence leads to unconstitutional laws that courts are forced to strike down because Judeo-Christian principles conflict with the higher principles of our Constitution. Justice Harry Blackmun, in his powerful dissent in *Bowers*, made this same point:

> The assertion that "traditional Judeo-Christian values proscribe" [sodomy] cannot provide an adequate justification for [the law]. That certain, but by no means all, religious groups condemn the behavior at issue gives the State no license to impose their judgments on the entire citizenry. The legitimacy of secular legislation depends instead on whether the State can advance some justification for its law beyond its conformity to religious doctrine. . . . Thus, far from buttressing his case, petitioner's invocation of Leviticus, Romans, St. Thomas Aquinas, and sodomy's heretical status during the Middle Ages undermines his suggestion that [the law] represents a legitimate use of secular coercive power. A State can no more punish private behavior because of religious intolerance than it can punish such behavior because of racial animus.[51]

The American government cannot punish citizens for violating religious laws, and all citizens are freer and our society better for this. Judeo-Christian principles have corrupted our laws, but the greater constitutional principles are finally rooting out and eliminating their poisonous effects.

21

Misogyny, Slavery, Thoughtcrime, and Anti-Capitalism: The Tenth Commandment

X. "You shall not covet your neighbor's house; you shall not covet your neighbor's wife, or male or female slave, or ox, or donkey, or anything that belongs to your neighbor."

—Exodus 20:17

"The enacting clauses past without a single alteration, and I flatter myself have in this country extinguished forever the ambitious hope of making laws for the human mind."

—James Madison to Thomas Jefferson, on the Virginia Statute for Religious Freedom, 1786[1]

The final commandment is triply disturbing. First, the Judeo-Christian god allows, for the second time in his ten moral precepts, slavery. Second, he recognizes that a wife "belongs to" her husband; women are chattel, like the slave, ox, or donkey. Third, he criminalizes thought. Thoughtcrime is the defining feature of totalitarian regimes.[2] Slavery is discussed in detail in regard to the fourth commandment (see chapter 17), and we will touch on it again in chapter 24. But the tenth commandment's treatment of women and criminalization of thought must be addressed. The former is one way in which Judeo-Christianity can legitimately claim to have influenced America's founding, and the other is opposed to the most basic freedom the Constitution protects.

Remember the Ladies

Abigail Adams portrait, 1880, after a painting by Gilbert Stuart.

"I long to hear that you have declared an independancy—and by the way in the new Code of Laws which I suppose it will be necessary for you to make I desire you would Remember the Ladies, and be more generous and favourable to them than your ancestors. Do not put such unlimited power into the hands of the Husbands. Remember all Men would be tyrants if they could."

—ABIGAIL ADAMS, in a letter to John Adams, 1776[3]

Judeo-Christian principles have had a devastating impact on women— half the country's population—and the tenth commandment exemplifies the problem. The bible treats women like property, not people.

"Man enjoys the great advantage of having a God endorse the codes he writes; and since man exercises a sovereign authority over woman, it is especially fortunate that this authority has been vested in him by the Supreme Being," wrote Simone de Beauvoir. "For the Jews, Mohammedans, and the Christians, among others, man is master by divine right; the fear of God, therefore, will repress any impulse toward revolt in the downtrodden female."[4] The bible supports Beauvoir's powerful words; reread the fourth commandment: "But the seventh day is a sabbath to the LORD your God; you shall not do any work— you, your son or your daughter, your male or female slave, your livestock, or the alien resident in your towns."[5] Wives are the only people not explicitly prohibited from working. Slaves, sons, daughters—all get a day off, but not wives.

Wives are to "submit" to their husbands,[6] and to "learn in silence with full submission,"[7] according to the New Testament. Mosaic law treats women as lesser, allowing an unsatisfied husband to divorce his wife on a whim, but not the reverse.[8] God fashions woman as an afterthought from an unnecessary appendage of man.[9] As we saw in the last chapter, the bible's sexual rules, including the adultery commandment, favor men and beat down women.

The bible repeatedly subjugates women, but treating women as chattel was not simply a sign of the times. Other contemporaneous cultures in the region were often less misogynistic. Archaeologist and priest Roland de Vaux wrote, "The social and legal position of an Israelite wife was . . . inferior to the position a wife occupied in the great countries round about. In Egypt the wife was often the head of the family, with all the rights such a position entailed. In Babylon she could acquire property, take legal action, be a party to contracts."[10] But in Judeo-Christianity, the "degraded status of women,"[11] to borrow a phrase from Elizabeth Cady Stanton, was complete. According to de Vaux, the biblical verb "to marry a wife" has the root meaning "to become master."[12] Perhaps this is why, in Genesis, Rachel and Leah complain to their new husband/master Jacob that their father "sold us, and he has been using up the money given for us."[13] While the woman lived at home she was the property of her father, until he sold her or married her off, at which point she became the property of her husband.

God even forces women to bear children as a punishment, not as the gift of bringing forth life (since he claims credit for that too):

> To the woman [the Lord God] said, "I will greatly increase your pangs in childbearing; in pain you shall bring forth children, yet your desire shall be for your husband, and he shall rule over you.[14]

"Barren" women, not sterile men, are the problem for nearly every biblical couple that has trouble conceiving. Sarai (later Sarah), Rebekah, Rachel, Manoah's unnamed wife, Hannah, and Elisabeth were "barren," yet somehow mothered children.[15] The bible claims that these births were miraculous. Manoah's wife tells a story about getting pregnant with her son, Samson, immediately after "a man of God" whose "appearance was like that of an angel" visited her.[16] Is it more likely that the husbands were sterile or inattentive lovers who treated their wives like property instead of partners and that the women sought solace elsewhere, or that the laws of nature were suspended? Either way, the bible refuses to credit women for bringing life into this world. And when a "barren" woman does conceive, Yahweh the patriarch gets the credit. Men get the credit; women get the blame. The biblical narrative itself reflects this. Manoah's wife is one of many biblical women, like Jephthah's daughter, Lot's daughters, and the wives on Noah's ark, whom we know of only by reference to her male relations.

Childbirth is not just viewed as god's punishment—it is considered unclean. Women must be purified afterward.[17] Women are unclean when they menstruate.[18] Everything an unclean woman touches is unclean.[19] In this childish understanding of the world, the bible essentially tells us that women have cooties. The menstruating woman must sacrifice two turtledoves or two pigeons to her god before he will cure this terrible affliction.

Although sons are "holy to the Lord," daughters are not.[20] This disparity is embodied in the morning blessings recited by many Orthodox Jews. Men and women begin with the same two verses:

> Blessed are You, HASHEM, King of the Universe, for not having made me a gentile.
> Blessed are You, HASHEM, King of the Universe, for not having made me a slave.

Then the prayers diverge. The women say: "Blessed are You, HASHEM, King of the Universe, for having made me according to His will." The men, on the other hand say, "Blessed are You, HASHEM, King of the Universe, for *not having made me a woman*."[21]

And let's not forget: all the pain, evil, and suffering in this world is Eve's fault. True, the biblical god actually created that pain, evil, and suffering, but Eve had the temerity to exercise the curiosity that god gave her, so she gets the blame.

The Catholic Church so feared women and has such warped senses of morality and sexuality that, to comply with Paul's order for women to be silent in church,[22] it castrated young boys. In 1589, Pope Sixtus V issued a papal bull, *Cum pro nostro pastorali munere*, which enrolled *castrati* in the choir of Saint Peter's.[23] Castrati, young boys whose testicles were removed or destroyed (by severing the testicles from the spermatic cord)[24] were needed because women could not be a part of the liturgy. Since some songs in the liturgy required high voices and women were to remain silent, the religious solution was to castrate boys.

Most of American history reflects the religious subjugation of women. The founders did not, as Abigail Adams asked, "remember the ladies." Under a legal doctrine known as coverture, American women had no legal existence separate from their husbands.[25] Courts denied that married women were individuals capable of lives independent of their husbands. Marriage was a contract between one man and the man who previously owned his wife, usually her father. It was not a loving agreement between two equals to stand together against the world. It was ownership. A woman's being given her husband's name is a remnant of this practice. This vision of marriage closely resembles the bible's, in that it is a biblically imposed burden. One noted Cambridge law professor traced coverture's origins back through English law and found that "the notion of conjugal unity has a biblical origin. Genesis, 2:24, is explicit that husband and wife 'shall be one flesh,' and this is repeated in the New Testament (Matthew 19:5–6; Mark 10:8). There can be no doubt that it was this theological metaphor that produced the legal maxim."[26]

The Judeo-Christian belief that women are a form of property significantly affected this country. Because the belief was religious, based on divine law and divine order, it provided an unquestionable justification for oppression. To question woman's place was to question "God's plan." As with slavery, religion might not have been the root cause, but it provided an unassailable moral justification for diminishing half the population. For instance, when Myra Bradwell decided she wanted to practice law, the Illinois Supreme Court told her that, as a woman, she was unfit. This 1872 decision rested partly on the fact "that God designed the sexes to occupy different spheres of action, and that it belonged to men to make, apply, and execute the laws." When it upheld the Illinois Supreme Court's decision, the US Supreme Court quoted this "axiomatic truth."[27] Concurring in that decision, Justice Joseph Bradley added, "The family organization, which is founded in the divine ordinance . . . is repugnant to the idea of a woman adopting a distinct and independent career from that of her husband. . . . The paramount destiny and mission of woman are to fulfill the noble and benign offices of wife and mother. This is the law of the Creator."[28] Notice the choice of language: "axiomatic truth," "divine ordinance," "paramount destiny," and "law of the Creator." What mortal can challenge this celestial order, even if it is nonsensical? Presiding over the case was Chief Justice Salmon P. Chase, whom we will encounter again in chapter 24 because, earlier in his career when he was treasury secretary and the nation was in the midst of the Civil War, he etched a message of faith in his god onto American coins. Chase's court was correct to point out that Judeo-Christianity makes women second-class citizens, but wrong to suggest that that station is right.

The bible has been a millstone around the neck of women for millennia. The women fighting for suffrage and equality had to challenge religion. The suffragists had to battle against bible verses, like those above, which subjugate women. Suffragist leaders, like Elizabeth Cady Stanton and Lucretia Mott, revised the bible to make it more accurate and fair. *The Women's Bible* was born. In an article candidly titled "The Degraded Status of Women in the Bible," Elizabeth Cady Stanton wrote:

> The Bible and the church, they have been the greatest block in the way of her development. The vantage ground woman holds to-day is due to all the forces of civilization, to science, discovery, invention, rationalism, the religion of humanity chanted in the golden rule round the globe centuries before the Christian religion was known. It is not to Bibles, prayer books, catechisms, liturgies, the canon law and church creeds and organizations, that woman owes one step in her progress, for all these alike have been hostile, and still are, to her freedom and development.[29]

Women gained ground in spite of religion, not because of it. Stanton "endeavored to dissipate these religious superstitions from the minds of women, and base their faith on science and reason, where I found for myself at last that peace and comfort I could never find in the Bible and the church."[30] She scoffed at the idea that Jesus's New Testament was any better than the old: "No symbols or metaphors can twist honor or dignity out of such sentiments. Here [in the New Testament], in plain English, woman's position is as degraded as in the Old Testament."[31]

Other women's rights advocates criticized Judeo-Christianity and its influence on law. The National Woman Suffrage Association, which Susan B. Anthony and Elizabeth Cady Stanton organized, declared: "We deny that dogma of the centuries, incorporated in the codes of all nations—that woman was made for man—her best interests, in all cases, to be sacrificed to his will."[32]

The pair of men who entered the White House in 2017 cling to a benighted view of women, criticizing working wives and working mothers. In a 1994 interview, Donald Trump said he thought women should stay in the home because working is unattractive: "Putting a wife to work is a very dangerous thing" because a woman's "softness disappear[s]" and because "when I come home and dinner's not ready, I go through the roof."[33] This is language the Christian nationalist no doubt appreciates and concurs with. For Mike Pence, his beliefs about the role of women surface in his oft-expressed defense of "traditional marriage" and his assertion that "marriage was ordained by God."[34] Pence once shamed working mothers who made their children "day-care kids" to fulfill the siren's song of pop culture "that you can have it all, career, kids and a two-car garage." Using daycare—which is to say leaving the home to work—would "stunt" the child's emotional growth and make the child "less affectionate toward his mother," according to Pence's unsupported beliefs.[35] Other lawmakers are more explicit. Representative Stevan Pearce of New Mexico cited the bible to argue that "the wife is to voluntarily submit" to her husband. This wasn't an off the cuff remark—he actually wrote it in his 2013 memoir, *Just Fly the Plane, Stupid*, continuing, "The wife's submission is . . . self-imposed as a matter of obedience to the Lord and of love for her husband."[36] Mike Huckabee, a Republican hanger-on, failed presidential candidate, and once governor of Arkansas, signed a statement of faith that a wife must "submit herself graciously to the servant leadership of her husband."[37] During the 2008 primary debates, Huckabee was asked about this statement of faith, which ran as a full-page ad in *USA Today*, and he reaffirmed his commitment to the subjugating principle: "I certainly am going to practice it unashamedly, whether I'm a president or whether I'm not a president."[38]

The theory of female servitude is written into the Ten Commandments. Thousands of years of slow moral progress had done little to erode it, and any gain was not sufficient for the nation's founders to treat women as equals. They did not take Abigail Adams's sage advice to be more "generous and favorable" to the ladies. Judeo-Christianity was instrumental in this failure and continues to fuel battles against the civil and reproductive rights of American women to this day.

Thoughtcrime

> "Power is in tearing human minds to pieces and putting
> them together again in new shapes of your own choosing."
> —GEORGE ORWELL, *Nineteen Eighty-Four*, 1949 [39]

The nucleus of the tenth commandment is "shall not covet," which prohibits specific thoughts. But the First Amendment protects—absolutely—the freedom of thought.[40] The right to believe whatever one chooses is the only unlimited right under the Constitution.[41] This Judeo-Christian principle does the opposite, seeking to stifle thought and enforce ideological uniformity.

Religion must maintain a closed information system to perpetuate itself.[42] Religious dogma cannot withstand the facts, scrutiny, or doubt that come with exploration, discovery, and expanded horizons. Religion is often too inflexible to incorporate new information, like human evolution or a heliocentric solar system, so it demands that followers shut out reality. Judeo-Christianity's attempt to keep the information loop closed is evident in the demands the biblical god makes in the Ten Commandments: no other gods before me, do not disrespect even my name, stop work for a full day to worship me, heed your parents because they will tell you to worship me, killing is acceptable if the victim is not someone who worships me, and finally, a decree to suppress certain thoughts. The very concept of the Judeo-Christian god encapsulates thoughtcrime. He is, as Christopher Hitchens so memorably phrased it, "an unalterable, unchallengeable, tyrannical authority who can convict you of thoughtcrime while you are asleep, who can subject you—who must, indeed, subject you—to a total surveillance around the clock every waking and sleeping minute of your life . . . before you're born and, even worse and where the real fun begins, after you're dead. A celestial North Korea. Who wants this to be true? Who but a slave desires such a ghastly fate?"[43]

This commandment is but one of Judeo-Christianity's attempts at outlawing thoughts. Paul himself wrote, "We take every thought captive to obey Christ,"[44] and many sects, Christian or otherwise, have built-in safeguards to exclude new information and the outside world: persecuting outsiders, shunning doubters, encouraging intrafaith marriage and punishing interfaith marriages, punishing apostates (sometimes with death), homeschooling or religious schooling, gathering together to shout down the doubts on at least a weekly basis, approving some texts and burning others. The engines of this closed information system are what make religious dogma and its adherents inflexible and regressive—acting as a "taillight" instead of a "headlight," as Martin Luther King Jr. put it on several occasions.[45]

Thoughtcrime is another device to close that information system. Catholic canon law governs the Catholic Church and mandates beliefs for Catholics worldwide. Arguably the most important precept for people claiming to be Catholic is also the most repellant. The law requires a total submission of the intellect: "A religious submission of the intellect and will must be given to a doctrine which the Supreme Pontiff or the college of bishops declares concerning faith or morals . . . Therefore, the Christian faithful are to take care to avoid those things which do not agree with it."[46] This is canon law: *the* law of *the* Church and, as far as Catholics are concerned, the law of their god.

John Adams considered canon law nothing short of mind control, finding it "the most refined, sublime, extensive, and astonishing constitution of policy that ever was conceived by the mind of man."[47] The anti-human, totalitarian sentiment in this canon lies at the heart of all religions, but one rarely sees it stated so baldly as here: "a religious submission of the intellect and will."

The Catholic Church's power players convened the Council of Trent in the mid-1500s to determine how to impose their will for the next few centuries. The Council analyzed the coveting commandment and declared that thoughtcrimes "are more dangerous, than those which are committed outwardly."[48] Failing to engage in groupthink was worse than committing murder. Banking on the perpetual guilt these crimes ensure, the Council required that "all mortal sins, even those of thought" be confessed to the priests.[49]

Criminalizing thought intensifies the power of the church, because laws against thought cannot possibly be followed. Jesus himself promulgated two rather devious thoughtcrimes, both of which humans have little hope of obeying. First, an impossible prohibition on sexual thoughts. Looking "at a woman with lust"[50] is adultery. He forbids even the briefest sexual thought flitting across the mind. This criminalizes the most basic of all human impulses, the sexual impulse. Second, Jesus sermonized on the Mount, "You have heard that it was said to those of ancient times, 'You shall not murder'; and 'whoever murders shall be liable to judgment.' But I say to you that if you are angry with a brother or sister, you will be liable to judgment."[51] Anger is a crime on par with murder.

Feeling randy? Angry? Then you're guilty. With Jesus, humans are guilty for being human.

The noted twentieth-century American legal philosopher Lon Fuller explained that one way to write an ineffectual law is to have it ask the impossible, unless the goal is perpetual guilt: "On the face of it a law commanding the impossible seems such an absurdity that one is tempted to suppose no sane lawmaker, not even the most evil dictator, would have any reason to enact such a law. . . . Such a law can serve what [John] Lilburne called 'a lawless unlimited power' by its very absurdity; its brutal pointlessness may let the subject know that there is nothing that may not be demanded of him and that he should keep himself ready to jump in any direction."[52] Christopher Hitchens put it more simply when he observed, "The essential principle of totalitarianism is to make laws that are impossible to obey."[53]

This strategy allows those in power a pretense to eliminate anyone at any time, because they are surely guilty of something. Judeo-Christianity, and particularly Catholicism with its confession and priestly absolution, relies on thoughtcrime to ensure perpetual guilt.

Then the guilty—everyone—must turn to the Church for forgiveness and absolution.

The coveting prohibition is fundamentally opposed to the Constitution and antithetical to our criminal laws. The only influence it may have had is as an exemplar of how laws should *not* be written. The founders strove to protect the freedom of thought. In his 1802 letter that memorialized the "wall of separation between Church & State," Thomas Jefferson wrote, "The legitimate powers of government reach actions only, & not opinions."[54] The Supreme Court has explicitly ruled that "the First Amendment protects against the prosecution of thought crime."[55] No truly civilized society will punish for thoughts alone.[56] This is perhaps the precept at the heart of the American experiment: our thoughts are free.

The freedom of thought is the only absolute right protected under our Constitution. Every other right is limited in some respect. You have free speech, but can't threaten others. The press is free, but the media can't publish willful lies that destroy someone's reputation. We have the freedom of assembly, but we cannot trespass on someone's property to exercise that right. There may be a right to bear arms, but we can't take those guns on planes or into courthouses. Even the free exercise of religion is limited. Every freedom we have is limited, except for the freedom of thought.

Our country has not always fulfilled this ideal, particularly during times of war and national fear. Amid the Red Scare of the 1950s, the Supreme Court upheld an anti-communist oath that labor unions forced on their leaders. In his magnificent partial dissent, Justice Robert Jackson noted that, if uniformity of thought were valid and enforceable, our country could not have revolted against Great Britain: "The idea that a Constitution should protect individual nonconformity is essentially American . . . our Constitution excludes . . . governments from the realm of opinions and ideas, beliefs and doubts, heresy and orthodoxy, political, religious or scientific."[57] Using the language of religion, Jackson warned of the "evangelists and zealots of many different political, economic and religious persuasions whose fanatical conviction is that all thought is divinely classified into two kinds— that which is their own and that which is false and dangerous. . . .

All ideological struggles, religious or political, are primarily battles for dominance over the minds of people."[58] In short, American principles rebel against this fundamental religious principle.

In another dissent penned twenty years earlier, Supreme Court Justice Oliver Wendell Holmes wrote, "If there is any principle of the Constitution that more imperatively calls for attachment than any other it is the principle of free thought—not free thought for those who agree with us but freedom for the thought that we hate."[59]

The United States may not always live up to the ideal, but it is written into our Constitution. Justice Jackson again: "Our Constitution relies on our electorate's complete ideological freedom to nourish independent and responsible intelligence and preserve our democracy from that submissiveness, timidity and herd-mindedness of the masses which would foster a tyranny of mediocrity. The priceless heritage of our society is the unrestricted constitutional right of each member to think as he will. Thought control is a copyright of totalitarianism, and we have no claim to it."[60] Judeo-Christianity attempts just such a claim; I refer you again to Catholic Canon law, "a religious submission of the intellect and will."[61]

The particular thought the tenth commandment prohibits—covetousness—is itself a problem for the Christian nationalist. Even Americans with no historical or legal training should recognize that coveting is the basis of American capitalism and our consumer society. Both would fail without the desire to get what we don't have. Coveting created America. Without it, no European settlers would have come to America. Coveting is human. This particular Judeo-Christian prohibition is both anti-American and anti-human.

22

The Ten Commandments: A Religious, Not a Moral Code

"Religion is an insult to human dignity. Without it you would have good people doing good things and evil people doing evil things. But for good people to do evil things, that takes religion."

— **Steven Weinberg**, speech, Conference on Cosmic Design, Washington, DC, 1999[1]

"As a historian, I confess to a certain amusement when I hear the Judeo-Christian tradition praised as the source of our concern for human rights. In fact, the great religious ages were notable for their indifference to human rights in the contemporary sense. They were notorious not only for acquiescence in poverty, inequality, exploitation and oppression but for enthusiastic justifications of slavery, persecution, abandonment of small children, torture, genocide."

— **Arthur Schlesinger Jr.**, "The Opening of the American Mind," *New York Times*, 1989[2]

Nearly all of the Ten Commandments conflict with America's ideals in one way or another. America values the freedom of worship, expression, and thought, while the Ten Commandments attempt to destroy each. America has abandoned or is still trying to escape the parts of the Ten Commandments that can rightly be said to have influenced it: legalized slavery, codified sexism and suppression of the sexual impulse, and inequality among races and religions under the law. These are not the influences the Christian nationalists wish to claim, but they are all that history justifies. The American ideal is equality, though it is often unmet and progress can be slow. Judeo-Christianity's ideal is elitism—being part of a favored class singled out for special treatment.

The Christian nationalist might still argue that, although the Ten Commandments did not specifically influence the founding, the morality featured in those commandments did.[3] Or they may claim that the morality implicit in our nation's foundations is impossible without religion and the Ten Commandments. Given the "morality" of the commandments the previous chapters exposed, this argument should be a nonstarter; but perhaps the Christian nationalist is tempted by its vagueness. The alleged moral and ethical superiority of the Ten Commandments is important to the Christian Nation myth and, like the myth, is inaccurate. The Ten Commandments are not a moral code; they are a religious code. That distinction, often lost, is crucial. A moral code is a set of principles that help us analyze and reach moral solutions in the innumerable dilemmas life presents. A religious code is a set of rules based on divine authority—its only "morality" is to obey, to follow. Those who obey are treated favorably; others are killed, excommunicated, banished, or otherwise removed from favored status. Ignatius Loyola stated this quite plainly for the followers of his monkish order. Virtue was to be secondary to obedience, and the intellect—one's understanding—ought to be sacrificed to god: "Obedience is nothing less than a holocaust. . . . By obedience one puts aside all that one is, one dispossesses oneself of all that one has, in order to be possessed and governed" by god through his superiors in the order.[4] At a more basic level, the confusion arises, particularly in America, because many people assume that religion and morality are the same thing.

The idea that religion is the source of morality is a fallacious assumption that underlies the claim that religion and the Decalogue influenced American foundations. Religion gets its morality from us, not the other way around.

One need only look to the Ten Commandments monuments that dot our public lands to see that they are not moral, to see that we give religion its morality. Humans have edited and abridged these monuments to "improve" the Word of God, to make it more moral. If you live in Denver or Austin, or near another Ten Commandments monument on public land, go and examine it. See if the full text of each commandment is carved into the stone. See if slavery is recognized, if women are considered chattel, and if the supposed pinnacle of morality punishes innocent children to the third and fourth generations. If the Ten Commandments were truly moral, there would be no need to edit these displays to fit today's standards. Morality evolves. These edited monuments undercut the very claim they were set up to make. They are monuments to a lie.

The Ten Commandments Monument on the Texas
State Capitol grounds in Austin, Texas.

FOR THE PERSON WHO BELIEVES A GOD IS ON HIS SIDE, not only is everything possible, but everything is also justifiable. Dostoevsky famously observed that "if God does not exist, everything is permitted."[5] But that's backwards. Everything is permitted if a god commands it: subjugating women, prohibiting two consenting adults from happily marrying, or flying planeloads of innocent people into buildings full of innocent people.

Summoning the intellectual honesty and fortitude to distinguish between religion and morality is difficult for many, particularly those who have been told all their lives that religion *is* morality. The point can be made if we ask ourselves—and honestly answer—a few simple questions: what would you do if one of your family members asked you to go to a different religion's church or temple? What would you do if your child discussed her lack of religion with you, attempting to convince you she was right? More than one-third of the younger generation is nonreligious[6] and 21 percent are atheist or agnostic,[7] and those numbers are increasing, so there is a good possibility this will happen to some readers. What would you do if your best friend asked you to come to mass or the high holidays or morning prayers just so you could better understand their beliefs?

What would you do?

Probably not kill them. If you have any moral sense, you would not even consider murdering that family member, child, or friend. The mere hint that you might kill a friend or family member for exploring other beliefs ought to be viscerally repugnant.

Yet the bible commands you to kill anyone who would "entice" you to worship any god other than the Judeo-Christian god—especially your family members.[8] There is no worming out of this order. No matter who it is, you must kill them, "even if it is your brother, your father's son or your mother's son, or your own son or daughter, or the wife you embrace, or your most intimate friend."[9] The death sentence is inflexible: "You must not yield to or heed any such persons. Show them no pity or compassion and do not shield them. But you shall surely kill them."[10] More grotesquely still, "your own hand shall be first against them to execute them."[11]

This is one of Judeo-Christianity's laws. That we find it abhorrent proves the point: your moral judgment is your own. It is independent from the bible and religion. If religion or the bible dictated our morality, we would not have the moral judgment to condemn this command as murder. If religion or the bible dictated your morality, the commandment to kill your family and friends who explore other faiths would be your morality. But it is not. Most believers are more moral than their god. Most disagree with the Judeo-Christian principles that inform their god's law. This revelation should alarm us because it means that preachers claiming to know god's moral law are simply giving their personal moral judgment a divine sanction. They ascribe their morality to a supernatural being instead of to themselves. They are claiming that their judgment is divine.

The biblical authors did the same. Biblical morality is archaic because it reflects the primitive morality of its authors, who wrote at a time when life was brutal and short. Life was cheap, and so was their morality. There was no perfect god writing down laws with moral deficits so obvious that today's second-graders could improve them. There are hundreds, perhaps thousands, of bible passages that conflict with modern moral judgment. Passages advocating genocide, murder, rape, slavery, subjugation of women and races—we've seen many in these last few chapters.[12] That enlightened citizens ignore these passages shows that their morality is independent of religion. The founding fathers were more civilized than the bible's authors, with much higher moral standards, but even they fell short of today's standards.

AN HONEST EXAMINATION OF BIBLICAL FAMILY VALUES can also help illuminate the distinction between religion and morality. The Hebrew bible shows a distinct lack of familial warmth. The first half of the first book, Genesis, contains, among other things, fratricide,[13] polygamy,[14] incest,[15] pimping one's wife to a king,[16] and a father offering his daughters up to gang rape and then later impregnating them himself.[17]

"Christian family values" are little better. During the "great commission"—when Jesus commands his apostles to spread his word—he stressed the destruction of the family:

> I have not come to bring peace, but a sword. For I have come to set a man against his father, and a daughter against her mother, and a daughter-in-law against her mother-in-law; and one's foes will be members of one's own household. Whoever loves father or mother more than me is not worthy of me; and whoever loves son or daughter more than me is not worthy of me.[18]

Luke confirms the message.[19] This alone casts suspicion on Christianity's value to healthy families. Jesus did not want to share his followers with their families. Divided loyalty weakened his influence. In one tale from the Book of Matthew, Jesus would not even allow a follower to attend his father's funeral, saying "Follow me, and let the dead bury their own dead."[20] Jesus was no exemplar of family values himself. He rudely chastised and spurned his mom,[21] thought his dad was a god, never married, never had children, seems to have ignored his brothers and sisters,[22] and, if he practiced what his church preaches, remained a virgin until his death.[23]

Jesus died a victim of Judeo-Christianity's filicidal tendencies. His alleged father has him tortured and murdered by the state out of some perverse love: "For God so loved the world that he gave his only son."[24] The first epistle of John, 1 John 4:7–21, exalts this sacrifice and betrays the writer's ignorance of the true meaning of love, although he uses the word nearly thirty times in the passage. In his attempt to explain that which he does not know, he bastardizes love into an exaltation of child sacrifice:

> Beloved, let us love one another, because love is from God; everyone who loves is born of God and knows God. Whoever does not love does not know God, for God is love. God's love was revealed among us in this way: God sent his only Son into the world so that we might live through him. In this is love, not that we loved God but that he loved us and sent his Son to be the atoning sacrifice for our sins. Beloved, since God loved us so much, we also ought to love one another. No one has ever seen God; if we love one another, God lives in us, and his love is perfected in us.

The rest of the passage is just as mind-numbing and meaningless. It is a string of words that sound powerful together but mean nothing ("deepities," as philosopher Daniel Dennett calls them).[25] Nonsense like this cheapens real love.

Love does not permit child sacrifice; yet it is common in the bible. God demands that Abraham murder his son Isaac,[26] and the Israelite general Jephthah's battle plan to defeat the Ammonites consisted of sacrificing his daughter (see page 139).[27] Interestingly, Yahweh saves Isaac, Abraham's only child and a boy, yet requires Jephthah to sacrifice his only child, a girl, unnamed as so many female characters are (including Noah's wife and the wives of his three sons, even though, according to the bible, they must be mothers to the whole human race). This contrast offers further insight into the value of women in the Judeo-Christian family.

In the United States today, religiously motivated child murder is not a mainstream Christian family value; it has died out, but not altogether. In fact, devout parents can still get away with child murder in some states. In Virginia, West Virginia, Iowa, Ohio, Mississippi, Arkansas, Washington, and Idaho, laws for negligent homicide, manslaughter, and capital murder have religious exemptions.[28] This means that if a child is sick the parent can pray instead of seeking real help. Insulin might save the diabetic child, but parents can substitute prayer. They can pray until their child dies. And not suffer any consequences. Many other states, nearly forty, have religious exemptions to child abuse and neglect laws. These faith-healing exemptions are new; most date only to the mid-1970s.[29] American common law (law made in the courts through precedent in the absence of explicit legislation or statutes) rejected the attempts to claim religion as a defense for killing one's child.[30]

Religions are taking advantage of these exemptions. There are cemeteries in Idaho filled with children born to a mother and father who consider themselves "Followers of Christ," a sect that, like Christian Scientists, considers "professional medicine an engine of the devil."[31] Over about a decade, children born to parents in the Followers of Christ had an infant mortality rate that was ten times greater than that of Idaho as a whole.[32] Advocates from groups such as Child Healthcare Is a Legal Duty estimate that nearly 200 children have died since states began passing these exemptions in the 1970s.[33] Faith healing? Faith does not heal these children—it kills them. The sheriff in one Idaho county who's been working for years to overturn this exemption pointed out that Idaho law treats livestock better than children: "If it was cattle being treated like this, no medical care, in distress, if you saw that from the street, we'd have a search warrant and we'd be kicking down doors."[34] Despite immense and mounting pressure, Republicans in the Idaho legislature refused to repeal this religious exemption every time it has been proposed. Idaho aside, states have been slowly but surely repealing these murderous exemptions.

We are witnessing the gradual death of another Christian family value that is still influential, though waning: homophobic discrimination. Nationally, there are as many as 2.4 million homeless American youth, 20 to 40 percent of whom are LGBTQ, despite comprising only 3 to 5 percent of the total youth population.[35] The two most common reasons for homelessness in LGBTQ youth are: (1) family rejection on the basis of sexual orientation and gender, and (2) being evicted from family homes as a result of coming out.[36] In these situations the family either rejects the child, making it unbearable for them to stay, or deliberately disowns the child, kicking them out. LGBTQ youth who are rejected by their families are eight times more likely to attempt suicide than those who are accepted.[37] Ann Coulter, a mouthpiece for Christian nationalism, approves these Christian family values: "Last Thursday was national 'coming out' day. This Monday is national 'disown your son' day," she wrote.[38] Religion perverts love.

Without doubt, there are plenty of Christians who exercise positive family values such as understanding, acceptance, and love, but they are not acting like Christians. For instance, Senator Rob Portman (R-OH) consistently opposed gay rights and even sponsored the hateful Defense of Marriage Act. His son came out as a homosexual in 2011. In 2013, Portman announced his support for marriage equality. Portman tried to ground his turnaround on the bible.[39] But his new position conflicts with biblical values. He placed his family above the bible and Jesus's words. Christians do this all the time. *But they are not acting like Christians.* They are exercising their own moral judgment and coming to better, more ethical conclusions than their savior.

Herein lies a major problem with the Judeo-Christian principles argument. Society has traditionally labeled anything good, virtuous, or kind as "Christian." When people are misbehaving, a father disowning his gay daughter for instance, people may say, "That's not very Christian." But it *is* very Christian—it's just that the tenets of Christianity are immoral. Ann Coulter's horrible comment is perfectly Christian, and also immoral. Choosing to follow the teachings of the Hebrew bible (and remember, Jesus came to fulfill the law of the Hebrew bible) over loving your family is precisely what Jesus commanded. What would Jesus do with a gay son? At the very least, kick him out of his house. Parents who do so are exercising Christian values—they're just bad values. They are doing what Jesus would do, what Jesus commanded they do: choosing him over their family. Judeo-Christianity is anti-family.

RELIGION IS NOT MORALITY. Of course, religion will reflect the morality of the time and place of its origin. Such morality is often archaic, as the Ten Commandments illustrate. The Ten Commandments and the rest of the mosaic laws are not a moral code—they are a religious code. They enforce religious conformity, not morality. The most important question for determining whether a commandment has been broken is: do you believe in the right god? If so, you can get away with murder, so long as the victim believes in the wrong god. These commandments are so fundamentally at odds with our laws, with our morality, with our principles that one is almost forced to choose: are you a Christian or an American? Your answer to that question, which, if incorrect, the biblical god punishes with death, is protected under our Constitution. The separation of state and church and our First Amendment protect your right to be an American Christian. Christians can choose to personally follow the Ten Commandments' totalitarian tendencies because their rights are protected by the Constitution. The Constitution puts checks and limits on what would otherwise be unbridled, tyrannical power, while the Ten Commandments demand worship and obedience of just such a power. The Constitution protects us by limiting power and defining our rights. God's commandments limit our rights and impose power on us. The Ten Commandments punish crimes against an all-powerful god. The Constitution proclaims that our rights cannot be infringed, no matter how powerful the ruler.

The Ten Commandments did not positively influence the foundations of the United States. America would survive without them—indeed, it survives in spite of them—because the United States is founded on ideals that are far more important, impressive, and timeless than anything Judeo-Christianity can offer.

PART IV

AMERICAN VERBIAGE

"In civilized society most educated people are not
even aware of the extent to which these relics of
savage ignorance survive at their doors."

—Sir James Frazer, *Psyche's Task: A Discourse Concerning
the Influence of Superstition on the Growth of Institutions*, 1913[1]

23

Argument by Idiom

"It is much easier to alarm people than to inform them."

—**William R. Davie**, delegate to the Constitutional Convention,
in a letter to James Iredell, during the run-up to
North Carolina's ratifying convention, 1788[2]

George Washington stood tall, his six-plus feet impressive as he recited the presidential oath on April 30, 1789, in New York City, concluding with a promise that he would, to the best of his ability, "preserve, protect, and defend the Constitution." Period. The oath and Washington's recitation both end there. The words "so help me God" do not appear in the oath prescribed in Article 2, §1 of the Constitution. Our godless Constitution does not ask presidents to seek a god's help or call down a god's wrath on oath breakers. There is no evidence that even hints at Washington adding these words, nor is such an addition in keeping with his character.

Contemporary accounts of the inauguration don't mention the phrase. The French foreign minister, the Comte de Moustier, contemporaneously recorded the ceremony as he stood next to George Washington.[3] De Moustier's account does not include the godly language, a moment that surely would have been remarkable because the phrase is not in the Constitution. Tobias Lear was Washington's personal secretary for his final fifteen years. Lear's detailed diary entry does not shy away from mentioning the religious aspects of the day, but fails to mention any religious appendage to the oath:

> He immediately descended from his seat, and advanced through the middle door of the Hall to the balcony. The others passed through the doors on each side. The oath was administered in

public by Chancellor Livingston; and, the moment the chancellor proclaimed him President of the United States, the air was rent by repeated shouts and huzzas,—'*God bless our Washington! Long live our beloved President!*'[4]

Senator William Maclay's firsthand account mentions the oath, but makes no mention of adding a phrase.[5] Nor does the *Senate Journal*.[6] No newspaper accounts of the day mention the words "so help me God." Yet many assume and assert that Washington added the appeal for divine assistance.

The misconception has even snared experts like editors for the US Senate Historical Office. One editor mistakenly claimed that presidents dating back to Washington's inauguration had said "so help me God."[7] Now she agrees that Chester A. Arthur was first to alter the oath: "When I made the video, it was common wisdom that [Washington] said it and I did not check it. After investigating this, I would say there is no eyewitness documentation that he did—or did not—say this."[8]

Most serious historians now agree that the addition of "so help me God" did not begin with Washington. Peter R. Henriques, George Mason University professor of history emeritus and author of *Realistic Visionary: A Portrait of George Washington*, has written extensively on this subject, concluding: "There is absolutely no extant contemporary evidence that President Washington altered the language of the oath."[9] Nobody knows Washington's words better than Edward G. Lengel, editor of the George Washington papers and of over sixty volumes of Washington's documents. Lengel concluded that "any attempt to prove that Washington added the words 'so help me God' requires mental gymnastics of the sort that would do credit to the finest artist of the flying trapeze."[10]

Not only is there no evidence that Washington said the phrase, but other evidence refutes the claim. First, when Washington spoke of a god, he did not typically use the word "god." In his inauguration speech, given just after his oath, he used phrases like "Almighty Being who rules the Universe," "Great Author," "benign parent," and "invisible hand," making it unlikely he used "so help me God" over more characteristic language. (See also pages 27–30.)

Second, Washington followed etiquette scrupulously. He compiled 110 rules on the subject in his *Rules of Civility & Decent Behavior in Company and Conversation*. Washington presided over the debates at the Constitutional Convention for four long months and followed the ratification debate in Virginia closely from Mount Vernon. He knew perfectly well the precise wording of the oath that was laid out in Article II, Section 1 and that the Constitution prohibited religious tests for public office in Article VI, Section 3. Vice President–elect John Adams and the Senate spent that entire morning debating the protocol of the inauguration ceremony, down to the minutiae. "Gentlemen, I wish for the direction of the Senate. The President will, I suppose, wish to address Congress," said Adams, who then kicked off the hairsplitting by asking, "How shall I behave? How shall I receive it? Shall I be standing or sitting?"[11] It may seem absurd, but these were actually important questions for a newly formed republican nation, one that had just thrown off a monarch, to consider. Settling on etiquette that was suitably republican for federal ceremonies was a point of national honor and would help forge a national identity.

Washington meticulously followed this protocol during every aspect of the inauguration. It's impossible to think that, in the very act of promising to uphold the Constitution whose shaping he had overseen, word by word, he would then violate its terms by amending the carefully chosen language in the oath—especially when the document lays out procedures for amendments in Article V. Rule #82 in his *Rules of Civility* reads, "Undertake not what you cannot perform but be careful to keep your promise."[12] Washington's word was important; he wouldn't swear to "preserve, protect, and defend" a document only to amend and thereby contravene it moments later.

Third, though some oaths of the era included the phrase "so help me God," secular oaths were very much in *en vogue* at that moment. Three days before Washington's inauguration, on April 27, 1789, the House of Representatives passed their first bill, a godless oath of office.[13] The Senate passed its version, also godless, five days after the inaugural, on May 5.[14] (See page 89.)

Thus, not only is there a total absence of evidence suggesting that Washington *did* use the words, but his own actions and character suggest that he would *not* have used the words. So where did this myth come from? Apparently, we have Washington Irving, the creator of so much early American folklore, including *The Legend of Sleepy Hollow* and *Rip Van Winkle*, to thank for this myth too. The earliest claims appear nearly seventy years after the event, in Rufus Griswold's *The Republican Court; or, American Society in the Days of Washington* (1856) and in Washington Irving's *Life of Washington* (1857). Both accounts rely on Washington Irving's childhood recollection—he was six years old at the time—as their source.[15] According to Griswold, the six-year-old Irving viewed the balcony inauguration "from the corner of New street and Wall street."[16]

That a short child could hear and remember for half a century the final words of this oath—which no present and much closer adults recording the moment did—through an "innumerable throng" of adults, over a distance of more than 200 feet, uttered by a notoriously soft-spoken man, without the aid of modern technology, is simply not to be believed. You can stand on the corner of New and Wall Streets today, as I did while writing this chapter. The experiment is not perfect because the current Federal Hall, with its iconic steps, was built in 1842. (The original Federal Hall building, where the inauguration took place, was razed in 1812.) Washington took his oath on a balcony with no access from the street. But stand on that corner and try to peer through the streams of pedestrians to the tourists taking photos on the steps of Federal Hall. Try to hear what they are saying. Now imagine that you're a six-year-old swamped in a massive throng in which you stand, at best, waist high, trying to hear Washington's murmured words, and then trying to accurately recall the words you could not hear fifty years later. The claim is simply absurd.

No evidence suggests that any early president—John Adams, Thomas Jefferson, James Madison, James Monroe, John Quincy Adams—added pious words to the oath. The first reliable, contemporaneous account of a president adding these words comes nearly a century after the founding, at Chester A. Arthur's public inauguration in 1881.[17] Arthur was assuming what had become a dangerous office, taking the oath after James Garfield was assassinated, the second president gunned down in sixteen years. This public oath was actually

Arthur's second presidential oath. He had already taken the official oath and assumed the office of president two days earlier, immediately on Garfield's death. In that private ceremony, he did not edit the oath. The second oath, the one with the religious language, was a public reenactment done for show.[18] It was more strategic piety.

Like Arthur, Woodrow Wilson took two oaths: a private oath on March 4, 1917, and a public oath the next day. "Private" may be the wrong word to describe the first oath. Wilson took that first oath in the Capitol at noon, and it was private only in the sense that is was not open to the public, though some government officials and legislators attended. This was the last truly nonpublic oath; every subsequent oath taken without the pomp of a full inauguration ceremony was recorded. All the evidence suggests that Wilson *did not* add the phrase to the oath in the private ceremony, though he *did* add it in the public ceremony.[19]

The inflection point for presidents adding the words seems to have been the United States teetering on the brink of the First World War. In fact, up through Wilson's private 1917 oath, the phrase was used in, at most, only two of forty oaths, about 5 percent of the time.[20] Beginning with Wilson's public 1917 oath, it was used in thirty-four of thirty-five oaths, about 97 percent of the time.[21] Of the first three times the words were added, the president had already assumed office in two (Arthur 1881, Wilson 1917), and the oath to which they added the words was purely ceremonial.

Wilson's motivations for deviating from constitutionally pre-scribed language during that second, public oath are not entirely clear, but he may have been relying on Washington Irving's tale about George Washington's oath. He was certainly familiar with the tale. Wilson wasn't always a politician. He was an academic first, and in 1896, he authored a poorly regarded biography of Washington. A historian, pro-fessor, and Wilson biographer has criticized the short work as "rest[ing] on slender research," using a "saccharine, flowery style" atypical of Wilson's writing, and being generally of a "low caliber."[22] In that romanticized biography, Wilson wrote that, at the conclusion of his oath, Washington "said 'So help me God!' in tones no man could mis-take."[23] Thus, the modern tradition of presidents adding a god to the oath can be tied directly to the Washington Irving myth about George

Washington through Woodrow Wilson, the president largely responsible for that modern trend. Myths are powerful, regardless of their truth.

Before the "so help me God" fad took hold of presidential oaths, Wilson's 1917 inauguration was one of the few wartime inaugurations up to that point in US history, along with Madison's in 1813 and Lincoln's in 1865. Rather like the early 1860s and 1950s, this was a time of national fear and strife. A similar fear existed when Chester Arthur took his public oath in 1881, though it may have been stronger in the run-up to America entering World War I. Less than five weeks after Wilson took this pair of oaths, the US would join World War I. On the very day he took the first oath, senators had been filibustering to prevent conferring additional war powers on Wilson. Two months earlier, Germany had resumed unrestricted submarine warfare, and the US responded by severing diplomatic relations.[24] Just days before the oaths were uttered, the Zimmerman telegram, in which Germany proposed a military alliance with Mexico that would allow Mexico to reconquer Texas, New Mexico, and Arizona, came to light and was confirmed as genuine by Germany.[25]

It is easy to characterize both Arthur's and Wilson's godly addition to the oath as turning to religion at times of personal fear and stress, especially given that Wilson was the son of a reverend, and so pious—he frowned on dancing and found the idea of balls frivolous—that he canceled all the inaugural balls in 1913. But that claim is undercut because both men did not turn to a deity for assistance when taking the private oath—the oath that actually made them president. Instead, they snuck religion into the secular oath only in the public ceremony.

The "turning to religion" argument is even harder to make for America's three other holy epigrams. To a greater extent than "so help me God," these appear to have been foisted on Americans at times of national peril when their attention was turned toward more important matters, when dissent was dangerous, and when religion was a convenient political distraction.

AT THE FREEDOM FROM RELIGION FOUNDATION OFFICES, we often get phone calls from upset individuals wishing to register their intense disapproval of our fight to uphold the Constitution. As you would expect from someone who takes the time to call an organization with which they disagree, these individuals are less than polite. Words my publisher won't print are constantly hurled at our wonderful staff, along with the occasional argument. Almost without fail, that argument takes one of three forms. First, "we're America, in God we trust!" Second, "we're one nation under God," often followed by a less-than-cordial invitation to move to Iran. Finally, if they wish to disguise their passive-aggressiveness as taking the high road, they either say they are praying for us (managing to make it sound as though they are spitting on us instead) or they get presidential and say, "God bless America."

Though it is hard to credit, people regularly invoke these slogans to prove that America is a Christian nation, and even a nation founded on Christian principles.[26] It's argument by idiom. A little bit of research reveals that none of these phrases dates to the founding era. "In God we trust" was first added to American coinage in 1863, during the height of the Civil War, seventy-five years after the Constitutional Convention. It was added to paper currency in 1955 and became the national motto in 1956. "Under God" was added to the Pledge of Allegiance in 1954. The first president to close a speech with "God bless America" was Richard Nixon, in a mendacious presidential message about Watergate.

"In God we Trust," "one nation under God," "God bless America." These tidbits are not historical so much as they are rhetorical. Their tardiness precludes arguments that they somehow prove the founding ideology, but it is worth analyzing how the verbiage entered the American vernacular because doing so reveals something interesting about Christian nationalism. Christian nationalists take advantage of times of fear and use them to impose their god on everyone. When doing so, they often destroy earlier unifying messages with their new, divisive message. Since the first years of our founding, citizens' rights have been jeopardized and curtailed by war. Or rather, our rights are curtailed, perhaps even willingly given up, because of the fear of war. During the Quasi-War in 1798, Congress passed the Sedition Act "in an atmosphere of fear, suspicion, and intrigue" that Thomas Jefferson dubbed the Reign of Witches.[27] Understandably, no one today points to the ignominious Sedition Act to prove that our nation was founded on the government's ability to punish speech critical of the government. Government censorship of speech is anathema to our founding principles, despite the Sedition Act's passage and enforcement a mere seven years after the First Amendment was ratified. It is merely a sad, short-lived example of fear trumping our founding principles.

But Christian nationalists ignore this logic and recite these religious idioms, each more delinquent relative to the founding than the next, to bolster their argument. In each instance, the truant language entered the American vernacular during times of fear and national crisis—during a war in one case, and in another case, at a time when witch hunters were looking for nonconformists and non-Christians while big business was peddling religion to repeal regulations. In the final instance, the intent was to cover the most notorious presidential crimes ever committed.[28]

24

"In God We Trust": The Belligerent Motto

"A man by the name of Pollock was once superintendent
of the mint at Philadelphia. He was almost insane about having
God in the Constitution. Failing in that, he got the inscription on
our money, 'In God we Trust.' As our silver dollar is now, in fact,
worth only eighty-five cents, it is claimed that the inscription
means that we trust in God for the other fifteen cents."

—**Robert Ingersoll**, interview with *Secular Review*, 1884[1]

"We used to trust in God. I think it was in 1863 that
some genius suggested that it be put upon the gold and
silver coins which circulated among the rich. They didn't
put it on the nickels and coppers because they didn't
think the poor folks had any trust in God."

—**Mark Twain**, "Education and Citizenship," May 14, 1908, speech[2]

Three men are ultimately responsible for getting "God" on American currency: a preacher, a secretary, and a man seeking to amend the Constitution to promote his personal deity. It reads like a bad joke, but the truth is more sad than funny.[3]

The men's work spanned from late 1861 until 1864, but the final wording—"in God we trust"—was decided on in 1863, when the Civil War was at its height. That year began with Lincoln's Emancipation Proclamation, which went into effect on January 1. Conscriptions followed soon after, as did the battles of Chancellorsville, Vicksburg, Chattanooga, and the two bloodiest of the war, Gettysburg and Chickamauga. Brothers were killing brothers; families and the country were being torn apart. The war would eventually kill some 750,000 Americans, more than 2 percent of the population—which would be equivalent to almost eight million Americans in 2019.[4] Walt Whitman, who worked at a military hospital in Washington, DC, during the war, perhaps best captured the horror of the time:

> The dead in this war . . . the dead, the dead, the dead—*our* dead—or South or North, ours all, . . . our young men once so handsome and so joyous, taken from us—the son from the mother, the husband from the wife, the dear friend from the dear friend . . . the infinite dead—the land entire saturated, perfumed with their impalpable ashes' exhalation. . . . . And everywhere among these countless graves . . . we see, and ages yet may see, on monuments and gravestones, singly or in masses, to thousands or tens of thousands, the significant word UNKNOWN.[5]

Not only did the war take the son from the mother, but it was also fought in America's front yards, not some foreign, faraway battlefield. It affected every citizen. Eighteen sixty-three was a year of great and terrible fear.

The United States may be the only country that needed civil war to end slavery; not coincidentally, it was also becoming an increasingly religious country at the time.[6] To a larger extent than is usually discussed, the Civil War was a religious war. "I am for peace under any plan or able readjustment the people will make," wrote former Illinois governor and US representative John Reynolds in a December 17, 1862, letter to an Ohio newspaper, "but, in the name of God, no more bloodshed to gratify a religious fanaticism."[7] Reynolds's wish was unfulfilled. The war dragged on for another two and a half years. Reynolds attack on "religious fanaticism" was written against the war, but also against abolition; but his point about religious fanaticism fueling the war is accurate.

Religion commandeered both sides of the slavery issue. Lincoln made this point in his Second Inaugural: "Both [sides] read the same Bible, and pray to the same God; and each invokes His aid against the other."[8] The bloodshed might have been stemmed were it not for the unmovable certainty religion breeds in the faithful. We might say today that abolitionists motivated by religion were correct to be certain on such an obvious issue, but their brethren south of the Mason-Dixon Line were just as certain, and they had the stronger side of the biblical argument. As William Lloyd Garrison, a leading abolitionist, put it, "In this country, the Bible has been used to support slavery and capital punishment; while in the old countries, it has been quoted to sustain all manner of tyranny and persecution. All reforms are anti-Bible."[9] This is not to say that religion caused slavery, but it did justify slavery and allow others to justify it. The bible gave slavery a divine sanction (see chapter 17). Diametrically opposed certitude on an issue like slavery, held without evidence or reason but instead on religious faith, is a blueprint for conflict.

David Goldfield makes a similar point in his book *America Aflame*. America's "political system could not contain the passions stoked by the infusion of evangelical Christianity into the political process."[10] Evangelical Christianity invaded and polarized the political debate in the decades leading up to the Civil War, limiting the potential political solutions.[11] It turned the democratic process, which relies on compromise, into a battle over sacrosanct issues of faith. Religion did exactly what the framers feared: it poisoned the political system. Incidentally, this fear was not confined to the founders; nor is it an issue the left and right need disagree on. The father of the modern conservative movement, Barry Goldwater, recognized and feared the inflexibility of religion in politics in 1994 when he famously insisted, "If and when these preachers get control of the [Republican] party, and they're sure trying to do so, it's going to be a terrible damn problem. Frankly, these people frighten me. Politics and governing demand compromise. But these Christians believe they are acting in the name of God, so they can't and won't compromise."[12]

Goldfield dates the launch of religion's political invasion to the 1844 presidential race between Democrat James K. Polk and Whig Henry Clay, and James Birney of the Liberty Party: "From then on, political parties paraded their religious bona fides and attacked opponents as infidels. The campaigns themselves came to resemble religious revivals as much as political exercises. Religion was not only an issue itself, it permeated other issues of the day, especially slavery."[13] The country's first major religious political party, the Liberty Party, founded in 1839, gained prominence then and used spiritual blackmail to win votes by telling citizens to "vote the Liberty ticket as a religious duty."[14] The party hosted revival-like conventions and was, according to one of its leaders, "unlike any other [party] in history" because "it was founded on moral principles—on the Bible, originating a contest not only against slavery but against atheistic politics from which Divine law was excluded."[15] Religion had been largely absent from politics and government up to that point. The Liberty Party bemoaned "the common law of political life" that "religion has nothing to do with politics."[16] But that separation, so assiduously cultivated by the founders, was obliterated during the buildup of tensions that were released in the Civil War. According to Goldfield, "Churches became party gathering places; ministers stumped for the party's candidates and even served as poll watchers."[17] Religion became a political weapon.

More than a decade before the war, Daniel Webster, who served as secretary of state, US senator, and US representative, warned Congress about the passion religion creates when it mixes with politics. Examining the history of slavery, he also warned Congress about the historical justifications for slavery, including those found in Judeo-Christianity. "There was slavery among the Jews—the theocratic government of that people made no injunction against it," Webster explained, adding later, "and I suppose there is to be found no injunction against that relation between man and man in the teachings by the Gospel of Jesus Christ, or by any of his Apostles."[18] Webster then warned against mixing religion and politics: "When a question of this kind takes hold of the religious sentiments of mankind, and comes to be discussed in religious assemblies of the clergy and laity, there is always to be expected, or always to be feared, a great deal of excitement. It is in the nature of man, manifested by his whole history, that religious disputes are apt to become warm, and men's strength of conviction is proportionate to their views of the magnitude of the questions."[19] Webster found it curious that believers failed to realize how unconvincing religious arguments are to everyone else: "They do not remember that the doctrines and miracles of Jesus Christ have, in eighteen hundred years, converted only a small portion of the human race; and among the nations that are converted to Christianity, they forget how many vices and crimes, public and private, still prevail, and that many of them—public crimes especially, which are offences against the Christian religion—pass without exciting particular regret or indignation."[20]

Of course, we are correct today to treat slavery as an intolerable violation of human rights, one on which no compromise is possible. The North was morally justified to fight a war to free the slaves if that was necessary. But had there not been a divine justification for slavery to begin with, the institution might have failed without a war. Religion on both sides solidified arguments, many untenable, as articles of faith. That was Webster's point. And that was the point of Lincoln's religious language in his second inaugural.

Northerners used the bible to justify their position and some, in the throes of the misnamed Second Great Awakening, thought that reforming their society by abolishing slavery would even bring on "the Second Coming of Jesus Christ," according to Goldfield.[21] But the South, though morally wrong, had the stronger religious argument for its position and was therefore far less likely to do away with slavery because of religious pleading or moral reasoning. After all, God was on their side. The Confederate States of America motto said so: *Deo vindice*, "God will vindicate" or "With God our protector [or avenger]."[22] The motto meant to call upon the "Christian God."[23]

The South believed in the righteousness, in the religious sense, of its cause. "To evangelical Christians," explains Goldfield, the secession and formation of the Confederate States of America "represented a rebirth, just as they had been reborn in Christ."[24] After secession, the South rushed to inject religion into politics wherever possible, such as in its motto. The confederacy essentially copied the 1787 US Constitution's preamble but added the one thing the confederacy thought most important, a clause "invoking the favor and guidance of Almighty God."[25] Jefferson Davis, president of the Confederacy, thought that slavery "was established by decree of Almighty God. . . . It is sanctioned in the Bible, in both Testaments, from Genesis to Revelation. . . . It has existed in all ages, has been found among the people of the highest civilization, and in nations of the highest proficiency in the arts."[26] He might have added that Abraham, the patriarch of Judaism, Christianity, and Islam, owned slaves. At the "behest" of his barren wife, Sarah, Abraham impregnated her slave Hagar, and married her as well.[27]

Jefferson Davis and Daniel Webster were right: the bible supported the southern slaveholders, not the northern abolitionists.[28] The point was even made in the House of Representatives during the first US Congress. Two months before his death, Benjamin Franklin petitioned Congress to abolish slavery. Franklin was in an abolition society that included Thomas Paine, other founders, and Quakers. Representative James Jackson of Georgia attacked the petition, at least partly because the bible allows slavery: "If they [the petitioners] were to consult that book, which claims our regard, they will find that slavery is not only allowed, but commended. Their Saviour, who possessed more benevolence and commiseration than they pretend to, has allowed of it."[29] Representative William Smith of South Carolina also favored slavery on religious grounds, as "the professors of its [Christianity's] mild doctrines never preached against it."[30]

Slavery is sanctified and permitted in the bible. Jesus even discusses the proper force with which to beat one's slaves in Luke 12:45–49, a passage the Southern states often used to justify slavery.[31]

Another major argument for slavery was not just biblical sanction, but that Christianity civilized "the Negro race" by bringing them to Jesus. Slavery created Christians. Reverend Frederick A. Ross, author of *Slavery Ordained of God* (1857), wrote that "harmony among Christians . . . [which] can be preserved only by the view . . . *that slavery is of God,* and to continue for the good of the slave, the good of the master, the good of the whole American family, until another and better destiny may be unfolded."[32] William C. Daniel of Georgia, "a gentleman having the talent, education and comprehensive view to do justice to so grave a subject," spoke extensively to a southern agricultural congress on the civilizing benefit to the slave in 1854.[33] Daniel thought "the operation of slavery generally throughout Christendom" had been to civilize the slaves.[34] He preached that southern agriculture's goals should include "cultivat[ing] the aptitudes of the negro race for civilization, and consequently Christianity."[35] Freedom would come eventually, but not "by imposing upon them the duties and penalties of civilization before they have cast off the features of their African barbarism."[36] This civilization gospel rationalized slavery and imposed a duty on slave owners to use the "subjection" to prepare the "African race" for "civilization, and consequently Christianity."[37]

Slaveholders believed themselves to be executing the Christian duty to "love our neighbors" by civilizing their slaves, by bringing them out of "the barbarisms and idolatries of paganism," as Daniel put it.[38] By exposing "the African race" to "the humanizing influence of Christianity" through their bonds, the slavers believed they were doing the slaves a favor—they were saving Africans by enslaving them.[39] The slave owners justified enslaving an entire race using the perceived superiority of Christianity.

If slavery was a divine trust, abolition was also atheistic. The month before South Carolina seceded, Reverend Benjamin Palmer of the First Presbyterian Church in New Orleans delivered a Thanksgiving sermon on the division seizing the country: "Last of all, in this great struggle, we defend the cause of God and religion. The abolition spirit is undeniably atheistic . . . . Among a people so generally religious as the American, a disguise must be worn; but it is the same old threadbare disguise of the advocacy of human rights. . . . This spirit of atheism, which knows no God who tolerates evil, no Bible which sanctions law, and no conscience that can be bound by oaths and covenants, has selected us for its victims, and slavery for its issue."[40] To be pro-slavery was to be pro-bible; abolitionists were atheists and anti-biblical.

Today, many might doubt these religious rationales for slavery, believing the church to have been the major force for abolition, or above reproach. Religion played an important role in the abolition movement, but it played a bigger role on the other side of the argument. While speaking to an audience in London in 1846, Frederick Douglass encountered a vocal doubter as to the culpability of churches. The report of that encounter, noting the crowd reaction in parentheses, survives:[41]

Mr. DOUGLASS.—Why, as I said in another place, to a smaller audience the other day, in answer to the question, "Mr. Douglass, are there not Methodist churches, Baptist churches, Congregational churches, Episcopal churches, Roman Catholic churches, Presbyterian churches in the United States, and in the southern states of America, and do they not have revivals of religion, accessions to their ranks from day to day, and will you tell me that these men are not followers of the meek and lowly Saviour?" Most unhesitatingly I do. Revivals in religion, and revivals in the slave trade, go hand in hand together. (Cheers.) The church and the slave prison stand next to each other; the groans and cries of the heartbroken slave are often drowned in the pious devotions of his religious master. (Hear, hear.) The church-going bell and the auctioneer's bell chime in with each other; the pulpit and the auctioneer's block stand in the same neighbourhood; while the blood-stained gold goes to support the pulpit, the pulpit covers the infernal business with the garb of Christianity. We have men sold to build churches, women sold to support missionaries, and babies sold to buy Bibles and communion services for the churches. (Loud cheers.)

A Voice.—It is not true.

Mr. DOUGLASS.—Not true! is it not? (Immense cheers.) Hear the following advertisement:—"Field Negroes, by Thomas Gadsden." I read now from *The American Churches, the Bulwarks of American Slavery*; by an American, or by J. G. Birney. This has been before the public in this country and the United States for the last six years; not a fact nor a statement in it has been called in question. (Cheers.) The following is taken from the *Charleston Courier* of Feb. 12, 1835:—"Field Negroes, by Thomas Gadsden. On Tuesday, the 17th inst., will be sold at the north of the Exchange, at 10 o'clock, a prime gang of ten negroes, accustomed to the culture of cotton and provisions, belonging to the Independent Church, in Christ Church parish." (Loud cheers.) I could read other testimony on this point, but is it necessary? (Cries of "No," and "One more.")

Some Christian sects advocated abolition—the Quakers before almost everyone else—but most took a while to come around. Christianity's switch to pro-abolition may have been driven by secular forces. "On a profound moral dilemma like slavery, one might expect people to derive their views from their religion," writes Professor Mark Smith. While counter-examples can be found, "the more common pattern over hundreds of years shows the tail wagging the dog," that is, secularism drove religion to abolition.[42] Smith has pointed out that "Christian resistance" to slavery "was nowhere to be found" when the colonies instituted slavery in the 1600s and that the "timing of Northern emancipation suggests that secular rather than religious forces were the primary causes."[43] Secular forces drove religious sects to reexamine their collective consciences or, as Smith puts it, "Religious advocacy trailed behind the path secular ideas had already laid."[44] Even if secular culture did not primarily liberalize religion, it is clear that religion justified slavery for centuries and that the chief moral justifications for American slavery were religious.

Again, Christianity may not have caused slavery. Slavery predates Christianity and factors other than religion, such as economics, play a role. But in America, Christianity and the bible justified slavery and allowed otherwise moral people to assuage their consciences by telling themselves that they were acting in accord with their god's law. That divine sanction was critical. "To do evil a human being must first of all believe that what he's doing is good, or else that it's a well-considered act in conformity with natural law," wrote Aleksandr Solzhenitsyn.[45] Whatever factors caused slavery, Christianity helped make its patent immorality palatable to believers. Both sides had religious arguments to buttress their position. The idea that "God is on our side" breeds a certainty that no logic, reason, or fact can shake. Thomas Jefferson was right to "tremble" for his country after poetically reflecting that god's "justice cannot sleep for ever"[46] (see page 83). Religious fervor brought god's war to America, and we bled for it.

As THE WAR PROGRESSED, the piety on both sides began to subside. "The randomness of death regardless of piety and the general horror of war transformed the soldiers' faith," according to Goldfield.[47] Herman Melville captured the general disillusionment with the war in his haunting poem *Shiloh, a requiem (April 1862)*, which tells of a church filled with dead and dying soldiers from both sides uttering their "natural prayers." Melville asks, "What like a bullet can undeceive"?[48]

The realities of war shattered the deception of faith. As commanders have for millennia, Civil War generals and preachers stoked soldiers' piety, recognizing religion's usefulness in convincing men and boys to march to their death without fear because god is on their side. Margaret Mitchell commented on this phenomenon in *Gone with the Wind.* Rhett Butler dryly asks, "If the people who started wars didn't make them sacred, who would be foolish enough to fight?"[49]

The soldiers recorded their disenchantment. Major Abner Small of the 16th Maine Volunteers attended his brigade chaplains' service before the Battle of Chancellorsville (the fourth bloodiest battle of the war, also fought in 1863). The chaplains "besought us all to stand firm, to be brave; God being our shield, we had nothing to fear," recalled Small. But when a Confederate bombardment hit camp during the service, "the explosions of shells, the screams of the horses, and the shouted commands of officers were almost drowned out by the yells and laughter of the men as the brave chaplains, hatless and bookless, their coat-tails streaming in the wind, fled madly to the rear over stoned walls and hedges and ditches, followed by [the soldiers'] gleefully shouted counsel: 'Stand firm, put your trust in the Lord!'"[50]

Confederate captain Alexander Hunter observed that "devotional exercises languished, except in a few favored localities. It is hard to retain religion on an empty stomach; a famine-stricken man gains consolation from no creed."[51] Soldiers "had gone through so much that many of them honestly thought, as one ragged sinner profanely put it, 'they had such a hell of a time in this country that the good Lord would not see them damned in the next.'"[52] Soldiers began to throw away their bibles, over the chaplain's protests, because "Bibles and blisters didn't go well together," said Hunter.[53]

Open contempt of ministers followed. Massachusetts soldier Theodore Lyman, General Meade's aide-de-camp, recorded his views on one chaplain: "He was like all of the class, patriotic, one-sided, attributing to the Southerners every fiendish passion; in support of which he had accumulated all the horrible accounts of treatment of prisoners, slaves, etc., etc., and had worked himself into a great state."[54]

Colonel Richard Hinton wrote an account of his recovery in the Union's Armory Square Hospital in Washington, DC, for the

Cincinnati Commercial. He had plenty of visitors, who packed his meager personal space "full of tracts and testaments." "Every Sunday," about six preachers "would come into my ward and preach and pray and sing to us, while we were swearing to ourselves all the time and wishing the blamed old fools would go away." Hinton preferred the visits from the freethinking Walt Whitman; the "old heathen" whose "funny stories, and his pipes and tobacco were worth more than all the preachers and tracts in Christendom."[55]

The ebb of religion in the ranks as the conflict dragged on is well documented by the soldiers themselves. Before the disillusioning bullets extinguished the pious fervor, the Christian god was placed on American coinage.

At the end of 1861, Mark Watkinson—the preacher in our tale of Christian nationalism—wrote a letter to the secretary of the Treasury, Salmon Chase, proposing godly language for American coinage.[56] Watkinson raised what he believed was a "seriously overlooked" issue—"the recognition of the Almighty God in some form in our coins." Watkinson did not know Salmon Chase personally, but presumptuously began his letter, "You are probably a Christian." After noting that they were both members of that club, Watkinson moved to fear-mongering, asking, "What if our Republic were now shattered beyond reconstruction?" If that were to happen, Watkinson argued, posterity would look at America's coinage and "rightly reason from our past that we were a heathen nation." Watkinson proposed removing that heathen, "the Goddess of Liberty," and putting on a new motto, words such as "God, liberty, law." With the sense of entitlement typical of a religious majoritarian, Watkinson claimed that "no possible citizen could object" to such language. The change, Watkinson concluded, "would relieve us from the ignominy of heathenism. This would place us openly under the divine protection we have *personally* claimed. From my heart I have felt our national shame in disowning God as not the least of our present national disasters. To you first I address a subject that must be agitated."[57]

As a self-styled "Minister of the Gospel,"[58] Watkinson had time to consider such minutiae and how he could best impose his religion on a population distracted by a bloody war. Other preachers, such as the Reverend Henry A. Boardman of Philadelphia, joined his fight.[59] What better way to spread their version of the Good Word than by putting it on currency everyone has to use? In fact, that was one reason Congress added the phrase to paper currency during the Red Scare of the 1950s, to spread the gospel "behind the Iron Curtain," as one congressman put it.[60] In a 1907 congressional debate on the phrase— after Teddy Roosevelt refused to include it on $10 and $20 gold coins because doing so was irreverent and bordering on sacrilege[61]—Rep. Ollie James declared:

> we are . . . sending to foreign countries and to distant people our missionaries to preach the religions of Jesus Christ, and . . . when this gold . . . is held in the hands of those who do not know of the existence of the Saviour of the world, we can say: "Here are the dollars of the greatest nation on earth, one that does not put its trust in floating navies or in marching armies, but places its trust in God."[62]

US currency would effectively become a Christian missionary, and it began with this preacher and secretary.

Chase took Watkinson's suggestion seriously and wrote the director of the Mint, James Pollock, discussing how a nation becomes strong enough to win a war: "No nation can be strong except in the strength of God, or safe except in His defense. The trust of our people in God should be declared on our national coins."[63]

Pollock must have been overjoyed to read Chase's suggestion. He would go on to be the vice president of the National Convention to Secure the Religious Amendment of the Constitution of the United States—a group dedicated to injecting god into America's godless Constitution (as the South had done in its constitution).[64] Similar efforts had failed repeatedly since almost immediately after the Constitution was first proposed. Failing to impose his religion by amending one government instrument did not stop him from using his government office to do so.

Pollock believed that because the United States is "a Christian Nation . . . the time for the introduction of this or a similar motto, is propitious and appropriate. 'Tis an hour of National peril and danger—

an hour when man's strength is weakness—when our strength and our nation's salvation, must be in the God of Battles."[65] Pollock could not have been more explicit about desiring to take advantage of the nation's fear. He went so far as to declare the war lucky, "propitious." Fear is a friend to those who would violate inalienable rights, including the right to a secular government.

On December 9, 1863, Secretary Chase approved the final language: "In God We Trust."[66] Congress made the change official a few months later when it passed a new coinage bill, though it did not actually vote on the new language—it simply gave the Mint director, Pollock, the power to fix the shape, motto, and devices of the coins, with the approval of the Treasury secretary.[67]

So, at the advice of a proselytizing preacher, two government officials—one with a religious agenda so all-consuming he was trying to amend the Constitution to honor his god—deliberately used the time of "national peril and danger," when people were too busy dying for the Constitution to protect it from a rear-guard assault, to promote their personal religion. Even if this addition were not decades after the founding, it's hard to see how three men betraying a founding principle—keeping state and church separate—is itself a founding principle. Watkinson, Pollock, and Chase took advantage of a fearful, distracted nation and abused their government offices to impose their personal religious beliefs on all citizens.

THERE IS A PERVERSE IRONY IN THREE MEN choosing to promote the world's most divisive force, religion, when fighting a war to preserve a national union. To choose something so quintessentially divisive to replace a unifying sentiment in the middle of a war that actually sundered the nation shows hubris typical of religious privilege. The three imagined that the fate of our nation hinged not on reunification or full equality for black Americans, but on placing a reference to the Christian god on coins, which, luckily, could be done, given the nation's fear. One would think that this idea would not appeal to those who think highly of their god: "Those great philosophers who formed the Constitution had a higher idea of the perfection of that INFINITE MIND which governs all worlds than to suppose they could add to

his honor or glory, or that He would be pleased with such low famil-
iarity or vulgar flattery."[68] That author, writing in 1788, was discussing
objections to the godlessness of the American Constitution during the
ratification debates, but the point is apt.

The founding generation adopted very different language for US
coinage. The Continental Congress, on April 21, 1787, just before
the Constitutional Convention met, resolved to create a new copper
cent.[69] On July 6, they selected a design by Benjamin Franklin. On one
side it was inscribed "FUGIO. MIND YOUR BUSINESS" with a sun
and sundial. *Fugio* ("I fly") and the sundial together mean *time flies*.[70]
The other side contained a unifying message: thirteen interlocking
rings around the perimeter, one for each state, made a chain. Within
the chain was a smaller circle with the words "UNITED STATES"
circumscribed. Within that circle were the words "WE ARE ONE."[71]

These two designs appeared on earlier paper Continental currency,
dating to February 1776, before the Declaration of Independence. These
paper notes, fractional bills as they are known, had the same thirteen
interlocking rings forming a strong chain and the inner circle with "We
are one."[72] Ben Franklin designed this early unifying theme, something
he had a talent for, if his "Join, or Die" snake print is any indication.[73]

The US Congress, following Alexander Hamilton's advice, established the US Mint in 1792. It decreed that coins should have "an
impression emblematic of liberty" and the word "Liberty" on one
side and an eagle with "United States of America" on the other side.[74]

Front and back of 1787 Franklin-designed copper coin.

Another early coin was inscribed "Liberty: Parent of Science & Industry." The only deity that used to appear on US coins was the metaphorical goddess Liberty.

The original maxim that appeared on many American coins and still appears on US currency also had unifying language: *E pluribus unum* or "from many, one."[75] On the day the Second Continental Congress officially adopted the Declaration of Independence, it also appointed the same three men responsible for the Declaration—Jefferson, Franklin, and John Adams—to a committee to recommend the Great Seal, which would appear on American currency.[76] (Ben Franklin actually proposed a national seal featuring imagery from the Exodus myth, as did Jefferson, but the proposals, like Franklin's proposal for prayer at the Constitutional Convention, were rejected.[77] Those rejections, perhaps because of their religious nature (though that is unclear), say more about the propriety of a secular republic adopting religious imagery than about the initial proposals. Many variations and new committees dealt with the issue for more than eight years, but those three drafters, with help from French émigré Pierre Eugene du Simitiere, decided on the unifying motto *E pluribus unum*.[78] The three fearmongers of the 1860s sought to undo the work of these great men. The original idea expresses the belief that people or states with differences can come together to form a great country. The religious motto expresses an inherently divisive religious belief and applies to only a portion of the population. That language would not only trump the unifying sentiment on our coins, but also officially become America's national motto during another time of great fear—the Red Scare of the 1950s.

An 1856 interpretation of the early Great Seal design of 1776, with the the unifying motto *E pluribus unum*.

25

"One nation under God": The Divisive Motto

"We can deny our heritage and our history, but we cannot
escape responsibility for the result. There is no way for a citizen
of a republic to abdicate his responsibilities. . . . [McCarthy]
didn't create this situation of fear; he merely exploited it—and
rather successfully. Cassius was right. 'The fault, dear Brutus,
is not in our stars, but in ourselves.'"

—**Edward R. Murrow**, *See It Now*, 1954[1]

"In the context of the Pledge, the statement that the United States is a
nation 'under God' is an endorsement of religion. It is a profession of
a religious belief, namely, a belief in monotheism. The recitation that
ours is a nation 'under God' is not a mere acknowledgment that many
Americans believe in a deity. . . . To recite the Pledge is not to describe
the United States; instead, it is to swear allegiance to the values for
which the flag stands: unity, indivisibility, liberty, justice, and—since
1954—monotheism. The text of the official Pledge, codified in federal law,
impermissibly takes a position with respect to the purely religious question
of the existence and identity of God."

—**US Court of Appeals for the Ninth Circuit**, 2002[2]

A t the Freedom From Religion Foundation, we work to keep
state and church separate. So when an FFRF member from a
small town in Florida complained about prayers being held
before every town meeting, I wrote to the mayor explaining that those
prayers were legally problematic and alienated many citizens. The may-
or's response is reproduced without alteration here:

Mr. Seidel,

Thank you for your email, as a nation founded under god I am surprised by it. Our invocations are generic and no one is forced to participate much like the pledge of allegiance. One Nation under God by the way

Under the freedom of information act and Florida's government in the sunshine laws please forward me copies of the complaints you have received or identify those that have complained. I am sure this information is readily available.

In case you are not familiar with Florida law any complaint made is public record and available for public review.

Thank you.

The mayor was confused about more than punctuation and the Florida Sunshine Law, which applies only to government entities, not to nonprofits headquartered in another state. He invoked "under God" twice, even incorrectly claiming that America is "a nation founded under god." This confusion is commonplace, particularly in the Christian nationalism movement, and originates in the 1950s, when ad men told America to buy religion.

AN OSTENSIBLE PARADOX OF STATE-CHURCH SEPARATION is that citizens living under secular governments tend to be more religious than citizens in countries with established churches. England, with the Anglican Church and a religiously apathetic populace, and the United States, with a rabidly devout (though shrinking) majority, typify this paradox. But it's not actually a paradox. This is precisely what we would expect to see if religion is like any other product for sale. In a country with an established church, that church has a monopoly. With no competitors and taxes supporting the church, the priests grow fat and indolent, and feel entitled to a flock. They can be successful without effort. In countries with secular governments and protections for the freedom of worship, the religious marketplace is a jungle. If a church gets lazy or a preacher feels entitled, their flock can easily worship across the street. As a result, preachers in America are better salesmen. They have to be. The jungle-like market ensures that the religions that are the best at attracting and keeping members survive. Adam Smith, writing in 1776, actually predicted this, as did James Madison in 1819, who used the idea of a thriving religious marketplace to help sell state-church separation.[3]

In America's wild marketplace, religion must be at least partly about marketing. It should come as no surprise that during the golden age of American marketing—the Mad Men era—religion was quite literally sold to the country. In his book *One Nation Under God: How Corporate America Invented Christian America*, Princeton historian Kevin Kruse convincingly shows that the wave of public piety in America, which peaked in the 1950s, was the result of a coordinated corporate strategy. The campaign was launched during the 1930s and 1940s as a response to Franklin Roosevelt's New Deal and the regulation it prompted.[4]

Businesses and industrialists, including DuPont, Firestone, US Steel, and many more, sought to undermine the New Deal regulations they viewed as overly burdensome and to erode the power of the newly influential labor unions.[5] The corporations' existing lobby groups, such as the National Association of Manufacturers and the American Liberty League, were too transparent. Most Americans understood that these groups were just extensions of the companies and dismissed them for what they were, "a collection of tycoons looking out for their own self interest."[6]

Undeterred, the corporations and industrialists turned to religious individuals, groups, and messages that were more sophisticated and less transparent. They began financing preachers who proclaimed messages such as: "Every Christian should oppose the totalitarian trends of the New Deal."[7] One of the more prominent corporate evangelists, James Fifield, sought to enlist seventy thousand ministers "in the revolt against Roosevelt" by arguing that the New Deal undermined Christianity.[8] The clergy who joined Spiritual Mobilization, as it was called, argued with a religious fervor. Their message could not be countered with logic because it was based on faith. They claimed that freedoms are given by their god, that "Christianity and capitalism [are] inextricably intertwined," that the "New Dealers were the ones violating the Ten Commandments," and, most familiarly, that this is a nation "under God."[9]

The high-water mark for the religious messaging was the Religion in American Life campaign conducted by the Ad Council in partnership with America's best admen and advertising agencies. RIAL professed two goals: "(1) to accent the importance of all religious institutions as the basis of American life" and "(2) to urge all Americans to attend the church or synagogue of their choice."[10] The Ad Council ran 2,200 RIAL ads in newspapers in 1949 and steadily increased that number each year, to nearly 10,000 ads in 1956.[11] Magazine, radio, television, billboards, posters in transportation hubs, and ad cards all told Americans that "free civilization rests upon a basis of religious faith."[12] Truman even recorded a radio address for the campaign, and in it, botched history that the previous chapter of this book sought to straighten out: "When the United States was established, its coins bore witness to the American faith in a benevolent deity. The motto then was 'In God We Trust.' That is still our motto and we, as a people, still place our firm trust in God."[13] The RIAL message, though inaccurate, was "inescapable," according to Kruse.[14]

It should be no surprise that an inescapable message, created by the biggest and best ad agencies and relentlessly promoted by the Ad Council, had an impact. Church attendance increased, and so did piety in politics.[15] The ubiquity of that message, pushed on a frightened population, also brought on the unprecedented invasion of religion into American government. A. Roy Eckardt, an Oxford and Lehigh University religion professor and Methodist minister, wrote about this "new look in American piety" for *Christian Century* magazine in 1954, observing that "the new piety has successfully invaded the halls of government."[16]

As president, Dwight Eisenhower nationalized a tepid Christianity, not only meeting with preachers regularly (Billy Graham in particular), but also becoming the first president to be baptized in office—two weeks after being sworn in. In another presidential first, at his 1953 inauguration, Eisenhower wrote and read his own prayer for his inaugural speech.[17] The lead float in his inaugural parade was dubbed "God's Float." It featured churches and the slogans "In God We Trust" and "Freedom of Worship."[18] This inaugural piety set the tone for Eisenhower's entire administration. He opened each cabinet meeting with a prayer. Halfway through one meeting, Ike apparently realized he'd forgotten the opening prayer. "Oh, God dammit, we forgot the silent prayer," swore the pious politician.[19] During a signing ceremony in the Oval Office, he and Vice President Richard Nixon even officially declared that the United States government was based on biblical principles.[20]

Some found Eisenhower's showy religion, displayed so late in life and immediately after assuming political office, hypocritical. Professor and journalist William Lee Miller observed, "President Eisenhower, like many Americans, is a very fervent believer in a very vague religion."[21] Miller was right. The newfound piety of Eisenhower and many Americans was both shallow and ignorant. In 1951, 53 percent of Americans could not name even *one* of the gospels.[22] America's religious literacy has not improved; in 2010 about 49 percent could not name one gospel.[23] This is precisely the result we'd expect to see from a group of citizens who were deliberately being marketed a vague religion. Despite this vast ignorance of Christianity's basic tenets, religion invaded the halls of government.

Between 1952 and 1956, as RIAL and the anti–New Deal religion peaked, Congress saddled Americans with most of the political piety so familiar today. The timeline is telling:

- 1952 – **National Day of Prayer.** Billy Graham says it would be "thrilling" and "glorious" to "see the leaders of our country kneeling before almighty God in prayer" and to use those leaders to bring the nation to Jesus.[24] On the Capitol steps, Graham calls for a National Day of Prayer.[25] Congress quickly agrees.[26]

- 1953 – **The National Prayer Breakfast** is held for the first time, and President Eisenhower attends.[27] This was integral to the anti–New Deal, corporate religion.[28]

- 1953 – Congressmen propose **18 separate resolutions to add "under God"** to the pledge on April 20.[29]

- 1953–54 – **Flanders Amendment proposed.** This constitutional amendment, which was attempted during the Civil War by the then director of the Mint James Pollock, of "In God We Trust" infamy (see page 271), would have added the Christian god to the godless American Constitution: "This nation devoutly recognizes the authority and law of Jesus Christ, Saviour and Ruler of Nations, through whom are bestowed the blessings of Almighty God." The Senate Judiciary Committee holds hearings on the amendment.[30] It fails, again.

- 1954 – "In God We Trust" is placed on a US postage stamp for the first time.[31]

- 1954 – Installing a **prayer room in the US Capitol** is proposed, and the resolution passes.[32] The Congressional Prayer Room, built in 1955, features a stained-glass window depicting the lie that Washington prayed in the snow at Valley Forge.

- 1954 – Congress adds "**under God**" to the Pledge of Allegiance.[33]

- 1955 – Eisenhower signs a bill placing "**In God We Trust**" on US paper currency.[34] The first bills printed with the phrase appear in 1957.[35]

- 1956 – "**In God We Trust**" is officially adopted as the US national motto.[36]

- 1956 – Cecil B. DeMille's *The Ten Commandments* movie is released, and, as part of the publicity push, granite Ten Commandments monuments are gradually erected on government property around the country. This tactic was also integral to the anti–New Deal spiritual mobilization.[37]

If any constitutional test were actually applied to these government endorsements of religion, they'd be struck down under the First Amendment. Instead, courts have either dodged the constitutional question or argued that religion has faded from the transgressions. In the case of the National Day of Prayer, the only court to examine the merits of the constitutional question held that the day and the underlying federal statute were unconstitutional (a case the Freedom From Religion Foundation litigated).[38] On appeal, the Seventh Circuit in 2011 said that proclaiming a day on which citizens should pray does not injure any citizen and that the law cannot be challenged unless it injures someone. With this catch-22, the court then concluded, "If this means that no one has standing [to bring the lawsuit], that does not change the outcome . . . even if the upshot is that no one can sue."[39] No one has standing to challenge the law, according to the court. We have a right to a secular government, but the court will not let citizens enforce it.

After the successful challenge to "under God" in the Pledge quoted at the beginning of this chapter, the Supreme Court overturned that decision by the Ninth Circuit because the father suing did not have custody over his daughter and therefore, as in the National Day of Prayer case, he had no ability to bring the case—no standing.[40] Still, three justices took the time to say that they would have upheld "under God" and signaled that another challenge would be a bad idea. For support, the three justices pointed to "George Washington's first inauguration on April 30, 1789," because he "repeated the oath, adding, 'So help me God.'"[41] They also pointed to Lincoln's second inaugural address and "In God We Trust."[42]

The courts have upheld "under God" and even the motto because those patently religious phrases are no longer religious: "any religious freight the words may have been meant to carry originally has long since been lost." Put another way, these have "lost through rote repetition any significant religious content."[43] In a government where state and church are walled off from one another, federal courts have basically declared that entrusting this world to god is not religious. Imagine for a moment if the courts had declared that John 3:16 or praying the rosary had "no theological or ritualistic" importance because it had been so often repeated. What American Christian would let a court declare that his or her god is not religious or that trusting in this god is not a religious declaration?

Christianity benefits when the federal courts declare that "In God We Trust" is not religious, and Christian nationalists are willing to turn a blind eye when the government desecrates their religion so long as it also allows them to promote their religion with the government. The words "In God We Trust" cut into coins or engraved on a government building are not only relics from our fearful past, but also monuments to religious hypocrisy.

INJECTING A DEITY INTO THE PLEDGE OF ALLEGIANCE has proved central to the Christian nationalist narrative and identity. As with "In God We Trust," the phrase's history tells us more about Christian nationalism than about America's founding, especially given the timing. As with "In God We Trust," a unifying national maxim was made divisive. In this instance, rather than seeking to replace the unifying motto, the religious proponents drove a sectarian wedge into it. Prior to the change, the pledge glorified "one nation, indivisible,"[44] an important theme for a nation that was still recovering from the Civil War when Francis Bellamy wrote the pledge in 1892. In a fitting precursor to American companies actively selling religion to undermine governmental regulation, Bellamy was hired to write the pledge by a children's magazine, the *Youth's Companion*, for their campaign to sell flags to schools to help boost subscriptions.[45] Bellamy would go on to become a New York ad man, even penning a book called *Effective Magazine Advertising*. But when he wrote the pledge, Bellamy was a Baptist minister and thought the pledge complete without references to his personal god.[46] Some six decades later, the Catholic fraternal order, the Knights of Columbus, disagreed. It conceived of a pious pledge and pushed Congress to include the nod to their god in the early 1950s. The Knights found a champion for their crusade in Michigan representative Louis C. Rabaut, himself a devout Catholic—three of his daughters were nuns and one of his sons was a Jesuit priest.[47] More than sixty years later, "One nation, indivisible" became "one nation, under God, indivisible." This change places religion, history's most belligerent, contentious force, smack in the middle of the unifying sentiment. It literally divides the indivisible with religion.

Dividing the indivisible might be ironic if not for the method used: the politics of fear.[48] Since Jesus became the original ad man for hell, Christianity has been comfortable using fear to intimidate and to force conformity. Historian J. Ronald Oakley has referred to the first half of the 1950s as "The Age of Fear and Suspicion."[49] Nuclear war and communism were the main fears. The atomic bomb was designed to be an American monopoly that would guarantee the nation's safety for the foreseeable future. When President Truman announced in September 1949 that the Russians had unexpectedly developed the bomb too, fear spread. Then Mao and the Communists seized power in China, also in 1949. In 1950, North Korea invaded South Korea, dragging the United States into another conflict halfway around the globe; Congress overrode Truman's veto to pass the McCarran Internal Security Act, which forced communists and communist groups to declare themselves; the Rosenbergs were arrested for spying; Truman was nearly assassinated; and Senator Joseph McCarthy made a speech in Wheeling, West Virginia, claiming to have a list naming either 57 or 205—it's unclear— communists in the State Department.[50] By 1953, McCarthy's rhetoric and stature and increased, Stalin's death had destabilized a nuclear superpower, and the Russians had successfully detonated their first hydrogen bomb, the largest weapon ever detonated. By 1954, the McCarthy hearings were in full swing.

The fear-ridden climate in the United States was similar to that in Nazi Germany during Hitler's rise to power, according to at least one journalist who lived through both. William Shirer, a war correspondent stationed in Germany during Hitler's ascension and author of the definitive book on the subject, the 1960 bestseller *The Rise and Fall of the Third Reich: A History of Nazi Germany*, returned home to America to find "an atmosphere . . . of suspicion, intolerance, and fear. . . I had seen these poisons grow into ugly witch hunting and worse in totalitarian lands abroad, but I was not prepared to find them taking root in our own splendid democracy."[51]

Another reporter, John Hunter from the *Capital Times* in Madison, Wisconsin, attempted an interesting social experiment to measure the fear. On July 4, 1951, Hunter asked passersby to sign a petition comprising the first six amendments to the Constitution; the Fifteenth Amendment, which guarantees the right to vote regardless of race; and the preamble to the Declaration of Independence ("We hold these truths . . ."). People were so scared and suspicious that of the 112 people Hunter asked, only one agreed to sign.[52] Most declined because they thought the ideas contained in those excerpts were too communist, un-American, or subversive. Twenty actually accused Hunter of being a communist. Responses included: "That might be from the Russian Declaration of Independence, but you can't tell me that it is ours," and "You can't get me to sign that—I'm trying to get a loyalty clearance for a government job."[53] Other newspapers around the country repeated the experiment, with similar results.[54] Reactions like these, remarked Chief Justice Earl Warren in 1955, "cause[d] some thoughtful people to ask the question whether ratification of the Bill of Rights could be obtained today if we were faced squarely with the issue."[55]

Religion preys on fear. With the ground prepared by Madison Avenue advertising, it was easy for religious leaders to capitalize on the national fear of communism and nuclear death. If mutually assured destruction was truly assured, Christians would be happy in the afterlife with Jesus, while the godless communists would burn twice. As one author put it, "Americans, being Christians, believed in life after death and [were] self-confident that if even the world itself were destroyed in a righteous cause, they would go to their heavenly reward. Communists, by contrast, were atheists, held out no hope of life after death, and would be correspondingly less willing to escalate a confrontation all the way to nuclear exchange."[56] Senator McCarthy warned people "that this is the era of the Armageddon—that final all-out battle between light and darkness foretold in the Bible."[57] In the best of times, clergymen love to preach about the world ending. With nuclear Armageddon a real possibility and so many advertisements telling them to go to church, preachers were winning terrified converts.

Soon, the words "American" and "Christian" became synonymous, realizing one of the goals of the Religion in American Life campaign and laying the groundwork for the Christian nationalist identity. Many religious leaders complimented this deliberate strategy. Fred Schwarz, a doctor and evangelical preacher, with encouragement from Billy Graham and the other corporate preachers, united evangelism and anti-communism in the Christian Anti-Communist Crusade.[58] Schwarz's "opposition to Communism was not based upon economics or politics, but upon its false doctrines about God and man."[59] Graham echoed the propaganda, warning that "a great sinister and anti-Christian movement masterminded by Satan has declared war upon the Christian God."[60] Another clergyman, John Courtney Murray, wrote that it is "almost impossible to set limits to the danger of Communism as a spiritual menace."[61] Religious stars such as Fulton Sheen, Oral Roberts, Billy James Hargis, and Norman Vincent Peale all achieved new prominence in the early and mid-1950s. They bombarded radio, bookshelves, and particularly television, making people sick with fear and at the same time selling them the cure—the promise of an eternal, fearless future. RIAL added to the barrage. Collectively, they "appealed to millions of Americans who equated Christianity and Americanism and saw the world locked in a life-and-death struggle between godless communism and Christian democracy," as *The Atlantic* observed.[62]

William Shirer's prediction about witch-hunting proved prescient. Conformity was soon valued more highly than civil rights. During this era, Congress passed the Alien Registration or Smith Act of 1940, the McCarran Internal Security Act of 1950, and the Communist Control Act of 1954. All were designed to punish nonconformists. Any thinkers not strictly orthodox—i.e., American, capitalist, and Christian—were suspicious. According to polls, people suspected their neighbors of being communists because they "would not attend church," "talked against God," "didn't believe in the Bible" or were "poisoning the minds of young people . . . with things that are contrary to the Bible."[63] President Truman, a failed businessman with no college degree (the last president elected sans degree and one of only a few since Reconstruction) and probably touchy about that shortcoming, attacked "ivory tower professors."[64] It became fashionable to vilify academics and the intelligentsia.[65] According to Ronald Oakley, "By the time the Great Fear had run its course, six hundred college professors had been dismissed" for being insufficiently orthodox.[66]

This climate essentially made it impossible for citizens to speak out against legislative piety, such as "In God We Trust" and "one nation, under God." The same year that "under God" was added to the pledge, a Presbyterian minister, Reverend George MacPherson Docherty, gave a sermon in Washington, DC, that President Eisenhower attended and took to heart. Docherty "came from Scotland, where we said, 'God save our gracious queen,'"[67] and pressed for adding "under God" to the pledge because "an atheistic American is a contradiction in terms."[68] The Scotsman's mistaken notion that to be American is to be Christian is now central to the Christian nationalist identity, and the stubborn idea that all atheists—or more accurately all non-Christians—were communists, and vice versa effectively silenced opposition to those measures. To be anything but an outspoken Christian was to set oneself up for alienation and even investigation, perhaps before the House Committee on Un-American Activities. Citizens, and particularly politicians, had to play up their Christianity. As the legislative history of the law shows, when Congress amended the pledge, it played upon this fear: "At this moment of our history the principles underlying our American Government and the American way of life are under attack by a system whose philosophy is at direct odds with our own. . . . The inclusion of God in our pledge therefore would . . . serve to deny the atheistic and materialistic concepts of communism with its attendant subservience of the individual."[69]

Between Armageddon, McCarthy, and Madison Avenue advertising, it would have been social or political suicide for citizens or politicians to challenge the religious verbiage Christian nationalists now rely on to argue that the United States was founded on Christian principles.

Eisenhower's own words about the new pledge encapsulate the era: "From this day forward, the millions of our school children will daily proclaim . . . the dedication of our nation and our people to the Almighty. To anyone who truly loves America, nothing could be more inspiring than to contemplate this rededication of our youth, on each school morning, to our country's true meaning."[70] That's it in a nutshell—Eisenhower, Graham, Schwarz, McCarthy, the Knights of Columbus, Madison Avenue, the anti–New Deal businesses, and the rest were *rededicating* this country, not to founding principles, but to a very vague religion. "True Americans" no longer believed in American principles. They believed in being Christian, though most were unsure what that meant in the theological sense.

Even the Supreme Court was not immune to the plague of shallow religious nationalism. In April 1952, the court decided that releasing children from public school classes to receive religious education did not violate the Constitution.[71] The entire rationale underlying religious release time is flawed, as three justices pointed out in three separate dissents. Each explained that religious release time allows churches to piggyback on the machinery of the state and mandatory attendance laws to inculcate religion. For Justice Robert Jackson, the "released time program is founded upon a use of the State's power of coercion, which, for me, determines its unconstitutionality."[72] To Justice Hugo Black, the purpose of religious release time class was clear. It was meant to "help religious sects get attendants presumably too unenthusiastic to go [to religion class] unless moved to do so by the pressure of this state machinery. . . . Any use of such coercive power by the state to help or hinder some religious sects or to prefer all religious sects over nonbelievers or vice versa is just what I think the First Amendment forbids." But the majority agreed with Justice William O. Douglas who, in a gratuitous paragraph, wrote one of the Christian nationalist's favorite lines, which does not mention Christianity: "We are a religious people whose institutions presuppose a Supreme Being."[73] Scholars and Wilson biographers are critical of this anomalous Douglas opinion ("There has always been one Douglas opinion that doesn't fit—the opinion for the Court in" this case).[74] This "presuppose a Supreme Being" line is a curious statement given that our institutions (including the Supreme Court) were established by a godless Constitution that prohibits religious tests for public office and fails to mention a god. But this decision and Douglas's fallacy are products of that fearful time, when even a Supreme Court justice might not wish to be seen as opposing religion, especially if that justice was contemplating, as Douglas may have been, a presidential run that would have begun shortly after or even as the opinion in this case was released.[75] (In 1961, after the fear of the '50s died down, the Supreme Court decided the case that held that Sunday-closing and other laws could only be upheld and justified on secular grounds. Douglas then clarified his remark in a way that speaks against the government's adding religious language to the pledge: "If a religious leaven is to be worked into the affairs of our people, it is to be done by individuals and groups, not by the Government. This necessarily means, first, that the dogma, creed, scruples, or practices of no religious group or sect are to be preferred over those of any others.")[76]

In a pluralistic society, religious fervor cannot endure when coupled to a representative government. People grow tired of the divisiveness that religion spawns. As it did during the Civil War, piety began to wane. In 1957, McCarthy died, and the Supreme Court curbed HUAC's power.[77] The signal moment of the decline might be John F. Kennedy's September 1960 speech to the Greater Houston Ministerial Association, where he famously declared:

I believe in an America where the separation of church and state is absolute—where no Catholic prelate would tell the President (should he be Catholic) how to act, and no Protestant minister would tell his parishioners for whom to vote—where no church or church school is granted any public funds or political preference—and where no man is denied public office merely because his religion differs from the President who might appoint him or the people who might elect him.[78]

Soon after, citizens began to fight for their right to a secular government in court. The Supreme Court obliged, declaring that non-Christians and nonbelievers could not be barred from office (1961), that organized public school prayers were unconstitutional (1962), that bible-readings in public school were unconstitutional (1963), and that public schools could not prohibit the teaching of evolution (1967).[79] Though the fervor and fear died, future generations were saddled with the religious verbiage from that age of fear and suspicion. The ratchet had turned a few more stops, the noose had tightened.

These epigrams have survived even though the religion they proclaim divides us. Fear is part of the reason they've survived, but there is another factor. For the average American during the 1950s, afraid of facing societal backlash, the question may simply have been: Which god or which religion? Today, the question is not *which* god or religion, but: Should I accept *any* god or religion? Increasingly, the answer is no. America is seeing a surge in atheism. A 2018 survey found that 21 percent of Americans born after 1999 are atheist or agnostic.[80] Another 14 percent have no religious affiliation.[81] These Americans do not trust in a god; they do not consider themselves or their nation to be under a god. Evangelical Christians, right-wing Catholics, orthodox Jews, and other hardline believers often find themselves in bed together, defending these idioms against secular Americans trying to uphold the Constitution. The advance of atheism and the rise of the "nones" have oddly unified religion, forcing believers to circle the wagons for a common defense of phrases that were imposed on a fearful nation. But such a legacy cannot last. For these phrases, the end is near.

26

"God bless America":
The Diversionary Motto

"Politicians say it at the end of every speech as if
it were some sort of verbal tick that they can't get rid of. . . .
They should admit that 'God Bless America' is really just some
sort of an empty slogan, with no real meaning except for
something vague like 'good luck.' 'Good luck, America,
you're on your own,' which is a little bit closer to the truth."

—George Carlin, *It's Bad for Ya*, 2008[1]

"God bless America. Let's try to save some of it."

—Edward Abbey, *Postcards from Ed: Dispatches and
Salvos from an American Iconoclast*, 2006[2]

Richard Nixon, Eisenhower's vice president, tried to revive the popular piety of the 1950s when he became president in 1969. He was attempting, as one Catholic lay theologian put it, to resurrect the "corpse of civic religion."[3] The presidential tradition of troubling deaf heaven with bootless cries by closing presidential remarks with the phrase "God bless America" dates to Nixon and is rooted in one of the worst scandals to mar the presidency. Nixon used religion to distract Americans from Watergate.

On April 30, 1973, Nixon announced that three White House staffers—Chief of Staff H. R. Haldeman, Deputy Attorney General Richard Kleindienst, and Chief Domestic Advisor John Ehrlichman—had resigned and that White House Counsel John Dean had been fired. It was Nixon's first address to the nation about "the Watergate

289

affair." Nixon spoke to the nation from his "heart" and found occasion to mention "Christmas"—in April—and "God-given rights."[4] The address marks the first of many times a US President concluded an address with an appeal for supernatural support: "I ask for your prayers to help me in everything that I do throughout the days of my presidency. God bless America and God bless each and every one of you."[5] The four staffers were later convicted of, among other crimes, conspiracy, obstruction of justice, and perjury. Nixon had resigned within eighteen months.

That wasn't the only time Nixon used religion and this phrase in particular to distract from his wrongdoing. Eleven months later, Nixon's popularity had plummeted, his desperation soared, and his impeachment loomed larger, so he set off on a tour to win over southern members of the House committee in charge of that impeachment. His first stop was the Grand Ole Opry in Nashville, where he closed the evening by playing "God Bless America" on the piano.[6] (Trump set off a national debate when he tweeted about bible classes in public schools just days after his close associate Roger Stone was arrested and the day before Stone's initial court appearance.[7])

Watergate, like the Civil War and Red Scare, was a moment of national turmoil. This time however, piety was being used to distract the masses and, as is so often the case, to cloak a criminal in the mantle of religion. The next two presidents, Gerald Ford and Jimmy Carter, abjured the phrase "God Bless America," perhaps seeing it for what it was or associating it with Nixon. But Ronald Reagan saw a powerful political weapon and used it to curry favor with the voters and, presumably, his deity. Reagan revived Nixon's Watergate distractor and did so early, when he accepted the Republican nomination for president in 1980:

> I'll confess that I've been a little afraid to suggest what I'm going to suggest—I'm more afraid not to—that we begin our crusade joined together in a moment of silent prayer.
>
> [*about ten seconds of silence*]
>
> God bless America.[8]

Reagan's supplications are now standard practice for every president. With this speech, Reagan inaugurated a modern strain of Christian nationalism.

David Domke and Kevin Coe point out in *The God Strategy* (2008) that this phrase is a political expedient. As with the Continental Congress's appointment of Reverend Jacob Duché to say a prayer during the American Revolution (see pages 94–96), this phrase is strategic piety. Domke and Coe examined every major presidential address, starting with Franklin Roosevelt's 1933 inauguration through 2007, and noticed that although pre-Reagan presidents occasionally requested divine favor, most did so less than 30 percent of the time. After Reagan rediscovered religion's power as a political weapon, those numbers jumped. Reagan "ended 90 percent of his major addresses by requesting divine guidance. George H. W. Bush also did so in 90 percent of his speeches, and Bill Clinton and George W. Bush followed suit 89 percent and 84 percent of the time, respectively."[9] Religion became the weapon in a rhetorical arms race, with each president needing to match the piety of his predecessors. The ratchet had tightened on presidential rhetoric.

Religion is a cheap shorthand for tribal allegiance, but it also has the power to distract from important issues that actually affect governance. Nixon asked people to pray for him and ended with "God bless America" to remind the nation that he was religious and therefore moral, and either innocent or deserving of forgiveness. It was an emotional ploy, but his final note would ring in American history.

When religion is used as a political weapon, it becomes weakened and tainted. And this is the flip side of the state-church separation coin. The separation of state and church is also meant to allow religion to remain free of the taint of this world, of the day-to-day political power struggle. This is why Madison wrote that "religion and government will both exist in greater purity, the less they are mixed together."[10] Nixon, Reagan, and many of today's politicians have tainted religion by using it as a political tool. Indeed, Madison's writing is a prescient warning about Donald Trump.

Like Eisenhower's, Trump's personal religion seemed to appear alongside his political ambitions. During the campaign, it became clear that he was not familiar with the bible, as the "two Corinthians" gaffe and his inability to name a favorite bible passage show.[11] Whenever he spoke of religion he seemed uncomfortable and, above all, insincere. Trump was simply exploiting religion, casting it about like a net to snare voters, and, as we saw in the discussion of religion's role in leading to the Civil War, to immunize his policies from criticism. In Trump's case, we actually have Trump admitting to "using" religious leaders, especially black religious leaders. In a tape released by his former attorney Michael Cohen, Trump asks Cohen, "Can we use him any more? . . . Are we using him?"[12] Trump was referring to two African American pastors who helped legitimize Trump's campaign and whom he and Cohen seemed to have difficulty distinguishing from one another. Trump's exploitation and say-anything tactics are what Madison meant when he warned that injecting religion into politics is an "unhallowed perversion of the means of salvation."[13]

Nixon, Reagan, and Trump's abuse of religion for political gain signals to every other politician that lying about religion is perfectly acceptable. Lawrence O'Donnell wrote some dialogue in *The West Wing* that captures this point perfectly: "And I want to warn everyone in the press and all the voters out there: if you demand expressions of religious faith from politicians, you are just begging to be lied to. . . . And it will be the easiest lie they ever had to tell to get your votes."[14] Voters are not just asking to be lied to—they are demanding it. This is a voter-imposed religious test, an auto-da-fé for public office. Religious voters are willingly handing over the tools of their own manipulation, and they may come to regret it. Typically, the majority religion is content to let itself be corrupted by politics, so long as it is in the majority. But as soon as it becomes a minority it seeks to buttress the wall of separation. Christianity is declining in this country, so it will be interesting to see whether American Christians come to realize the value of state-church separation as they lose their majority.

THE MARRING OF AMERICAN CURRENCY, the religious revision of the pledge, and the diversionary religious blessing of America are not evidence that we are a Christian nation or founded on Christian principles. They are catchphrases. They are slogans Christian nationalists can remember even when they can't name a single gospel or right protected by the First Amendment.[15] Small groups of fanatics exploited times of fear and superstition to force their religion upon all citizens and violate our founding principles in the process. These shibboleths exemplify how religious entitlement, which every religious majority enjoys, has eroded the Bill of Rights. If we truly care about America's founding principles and about keeping religious freedom, these phrases ought to be excised from our laws, currency, pledges, and government.

Conclusion

Take alarm: this is the first experiment on our liberties

"It is proper to take alarm at the first experiment on our liberties.
We hold this prudent jealousy to be the first duty of Citizens,
and one of the noblest characteristics of the late Revolution.
The free men of America did not wait till usurped power had
strengthened itself by exercise, and entangled the question in
precedents. They saw all the consequences in the principle,
and they avoided the consequences by denying the principle.
We revere this lesson too much soon to forget it."

— **James Madison,** "Memorial and Remonstrance
against Religious Assessments" (1785)[1]

I write these final words on a beautiful spring morning, a Sunday, sitting in the last pew at the St. Dennis Catholic church in Madison, Wisconsin. An elderly relative, visiting for a week and unable to drive, insisted on attending mass. I gave her a ride and now sit working in the back. (I did not last long. After about four or five paragraphs, I abandoned the nearly empty service for the company of my faithful dog and a long walk in a nearby dog park—to me, a far better way to spend a beautiful Sunday morning.)

The last mass I witnessed was during a full Catholic wedding. The priest mentioned the happy couple about sixty times—a respectable number, given that we had gathered together to celebrate them. But the priest was also able to mention his church and god more than 235 times.[2] This four-to-one ratio of church over couple has held at the two other Catholic weddings I've attended. The Catholic Church is co-opting the prestige of more illustrious events, people, and moments for itself. Two people dedicate their lives to each other, and religion injects itself in the middle. Christian nationalism excels at this type of piracy and imposition. It attempts, like the Catholic priest at those weddings, to bask in unwarranted glory. It seeks to co-opt undeserved greatness, accolades, and credit. It claims a nation dedicated to the freedom of and from religion, for one particular religion. It insists that a nation with a godless Constitution is dedicated to one particular god. A religion that demands fearful, unwavering obedience takes credit for a rebellion and revolution in self-government. It declares that that revolution was the brainchild of a few Christians rather than of a group of unorthodox thinkers testing Enlightenment principles. It even claims universal human morality as its own invention.

Christian nationalism also contends that the United States of America is exceptional because the nation was chosen by a god, not because the founders' enlightened experiment was successful. Christian nationalists sometimes misconstrue a 1983 *Newsweek* quote: "Historians are discovering that the Bible, perhaps even more than the Constitution, is our founding document."[3] Ken Woodward and David Gates's full quote is more interesting, and, as one would imagine, more reflective of reality: "Now historians are discovering that the Bible, perhaps even more than the Constitution, is our founding document: the source of a powerful myth of the United States as a special, sacred nation, a people called by God to establish a model society, a beacon to the world."[4] Biblical America is indeed a myth, a powerful one.

The sad irony of the myths of the Christian nation, biblical America, and Judeo-Christian principles is that they are born out of a misplaced zeal to revive or extend American exceptionalism. Trump and his Christian nationalist brethren want a *return* to a Christian nation; they want to "make America great *again*." But religion did not make the United States, let alone make it great. "We the People" make America exceptional.

Religion is the millstone around the neck of American exceptionalism because religious faith denies experience and observation to preserve a belief.[5] It is for this reason that it is unlikely to contribute to progress,[6] though it will take credit for what science, rationality, experience, and observation have accomplished. America succeeded as an experiment because it was based on reason. If we abandon reason in favor of faith—or if our elected leaders commit this sin—we are asking to regress. Not to some golden age, but to a time "when religion ruled the world . . . called the Dark Ages,"[7] to again borrow from Ruth Green.

Many specifics of Christian nationalism are not covered in this book, including some of its favorite minutiae.[8] It is unnecessary to debunk every mined quote or disingenuous misrepresentation, because the foundational claim of the Christian nationalist identity—that Judeo-Christian principles influenced American principles—must be discarded. Christian principles conflict with American principles.

In the end, the Christian nationalists try to prove too much. Ben Franklin cautioned, "When a religion is good, I conceive that it will support itself; and when it cannot support itself, and God does not take care to support it, so that its professors are obliged to call for the help of the civil power, it is a sign, I apprehend, of its being a bad one."[9] By seeking to graft his religion on to the structure of the American government, the Christian nationalist is simply showing his religion to be "a bad one." Not only bad, but also, according to Thomas Jefferson, erroneous, for "it is error alone which needs the support of government. Truth can stand by itself."[10] Christian nationalism, by its very existence, admits the weakness of Christianity's truth claims, the frailty of a morality based on supernatural authority, and the shortcomings of an antiquated book. As with the Catholic wedding, Christian nationalists' attempt to co-opt the power and prestige of the American Enlightenment for their own ends says far more about their insecurity and the genuine blindness of their faith than it does about America's founding.

THE PAGEANTRY OF THE CATHOLIC MASS has distracted me from writing, as it has presumably distracted the congregation from an otherwise noticeable lack of substance—remember, faith is "the evidence of things not seen." As if to compensate for this shortfall, the Catholic Church has built a ceremony to engage all the senses. Incense for the nose. Song and chanting for the ears. For touch, uncomfortable wood between bouts of rising and kneeling. For the eyes, soaring ceilings, stained glass, and long, flowing robes colorfully and ornately embroidered. And of course, wine and wafers or, depending on one's level of credulity, blood and human flesh, for the tongue. It is hard to ignore these expensive distractions, but if we could, we might pare religions down to what is valuable. If we could ignore the differences in nomenclature and liturgy and costume and literature—we might find a few universal truths, such as the golden rule. Provided, of course, that we excise the tribalism along with the pageantry. This is not because all religion is correct or because all religion worships the same god under different guises, but because all religion is man-made. There are some universal human principles that the human authors of religion can't help but put into their religion. Don't steal, kill, or lie; treat others as you'd like to be treated; help those who can't help themselves. But these are not religious principles. These are universal human principles, and we must jettison the religious from the humane. Humans need saving, but they need to be saved from religion.

As America nears the tipping point in which Christianity's power and privilege are reduced to equality, the Christian nation myths will be trumpeted with renewed vigor. Christian nationalists will not go gently into the obsolescence for which they are bound; they have grown accustomed to religious privilege. They are used to imposing their beliefs on unsuspecting schoolchildren, to politicians paying lip service to their deity, to their warped idea of "religious freedom" exempting them from universally applicable laws. But that time is ending. The end of Christian privilege is near.

As the myths debunked in this book are professed with more desperation, we must be prepared to refute them factually and vocally. This book provides the first half of that recipe. You are responsible for the rest. Outspoken resistance is, as Madison might say, the "first duty of citizens."[11] Christian nationalists have successfully persuaded too many Americans to abandon our heritage, to spurn our secular foundations in favor of their myth. It is time to reclaim that heritage and refute these myths. We need to remind Americans that our Constitution demands an absolute separation between church and state, as John Kennedy said. We must raise hell when the wall of separation between state and church is breached. We must, as Madison warned, take "alarm at the first experiment on our liberties."[12]

Acknowledgments

This book required serious help, and I owe many my thanks. Most importantly, to my family, especially Elizabeth, Oliver, and Simon, thank you for your love and support. Elizabeth taught me to write well, read countless drafts, offered unflinching criticism, and was exceedingly patient and supportive. I love you. To Mom and Wally, Dad and Liz, Jessie and Sean, and Aunt Missy for their love and support. And to friends for the same, you know who you are.

To Dan Barker and Annie Laurie Gaylor for welcoming me at FFRF, supporting this book at every turn, and to Dan for his kind preface. To my FFRF family, especially the amazing legal team, for listening to me drone on about history.

To Susan Jacoby for encouraging me to think bigger with my manuscript and for providing supportive guidance and a thoughtful foreword. **To Katherine and Matthew Stewart** for mentoring a struggling writer. **To Jerry DeWitt** for his big heart. **To Joe Cunningham** for reading the first-ever draft and offering insight that only a 90-year-old veteran can.

To Ryan Jayne and **Colin McNamara**, two diligent, careful lawyers who checked every citation and collected bourbon bounties for mistakes found and holes poked.

To Mark Chancey for his guidance on biblical texts and history; **Kevin Kruse** for his advice and for reviewing a few chapters; **Ed Brayton** for reading an early draft; **Warren Throckmorton**, who has vanquished several Christian nationalists and who kindly gave time and insights; and **Amanda Knief**, who helped with a thorny research question.

To Jane Dystel, who took me in; **Sterling Publishing** for taking a chance; and **Barbara Berger**, whose editing, professionalism, and judgment improved this book significantly.

To those who preferred not to be or aren't named. You know who you are. Thank you.

As with nearly all authors, I owe a debt to many better thinkers and writers. To Christopher Hitchens, whose *Vanity Fair* article revising the Ten Commandments inspired part of this book. He took the time to do a writer he'd never met a favor. I miss his pen.

Notes

Text and punctuation for the Declaration of Independence, the Constitution, and the Bill of Rights is based on the National Archives official transcripts: http://www.archives.gov/exhibits/charters/declaration_transcript.html (emphasis added in each reference). The Draft of the Declaration of Independence is available on the Library of Congress (LOC) website: http://www.loc.gov/exhibits/treasures/trt001.html and http://www.loc.gov/exhibits/creating-the-united-states/interactives/declaration-of-independence/equal/index.html.

For the American Presidency Project (APP), by John Woolley and Gerhard Peters, see https://www.presidency.ucsb.edu/ and search by name, document or speech, and date.

For the Federalist Papers, see http://avalon.law.yale.edu/subject_menus/fed.asp.

For letters cited in Founders Online at the National Archives (FO-NA), see https://founders.archives.gov/ (Search by letter title and date).

Epigraph

1 James Madison to Edward Everett, March 19, 1823, http://www.loc.gov/resource/mjm.20_0368_0370/, in Gaillard Hunt, ed., *The Writings of James Madison, Comprising His Public Papers and His Private Correspondence* . . . (New York: G. P. Putnam's Sons, 1900), vol. 9, 128–29. All 9 vol. at https://perma.cc/ZVW6-KYUW

2 George Orwell, "The Prevention of Literature," *Polemic*, no. 2, January 1946.

Introduction • Prelude to an Argument

3 Peter Raby, *The Cambridge Companion to Oscar Wilde* (Cambridge, UK: Cambridge Univ. Press, 1997), 101.

4 This was available on Judge James Taylor's website, http://www.judgejamestaylor.com/foundationsdisplay.html, which is now defunct. However, it can still be seen here: https://perma.cc/WBV4-DFMC.

5 See Taylor's website, *supra*.

6 Jeff Bobo, "Hawkins judge faces $3 million sexual harassment, wrongful dismissal lawsuit," *Times News*, January 14, 2011. The former staff received restitution in the criminal case against Taylor; see next note.

7 Bobo, "Former judge Taylor pleads to Hawkins charges, won't get off probation until 2028," *Times News*, October 12, 2012. See the formal charges against Taylor at *In re: The Honorable James Taylor General Sessions Judge, Hawkins County, Tenn.*, at the Tenn. Court of the Judiciary, filed January 24, 2012, file no. 11-4731, docket no. M2011-00706-CJ-CJ-CJ, in Tenn. Appellate Court, Nashville, https://perma.cc/Z9Y8-XX8G.

8 For a history of the evolution of the phrase "Judeo-Christian values," see Douglas Hartmann, Xuefeng Zhang, and William Wischstadt "One (Multicultural) Nation Under God? Changing Uses and Meanings of the Term 'Judeo-Christian' in the American Media," *Journal of Media and Religion* 4, no. 4 (2005): 207–34.

9 Kenneth Woodward, "Losing Our Moral Umbrella," *Newsweek*, December 6, 1992.

10 Jnanada Prakashan, ed., *World Encyclopaedia of Interfaith Studies: Religious Pluralism*, vol. 2 (New Delhi, India: Jnanada Prakashan, in assoc. with Global Open Univ., Nagaland, 2009), 388, quote from Rabbi Eliezer Berkovits.

11 Mark Silk, "Notes on the Judeo-Christian Tradition in America," *American Quarterly* 36, no. 1 (Spring 1984): 65–85, at 69.

12 Patrick Henry, "'And I Don't Care What It Is': The Tradition-History of a Civil Religion Proof-Text," *Journal of the American Academy of Religion* 49, no. 1 (March 1981): 35–47.

13 Lloyd E. Ambrosius, *Woodrow Wilson and the American Diplomatic Tradition: The Treaty Fight in Perspective* (Cambridge, UK: Cambridge Univ. Press, 1987), 12.

14 Michael T. Benson, *Harry S. Truman and the Founding of Israel* (Westport, CT: Praeger, 1997), 34.

15 Robert Davi, "'War on Christmas' Part of Secular Battle vs. Judeo-Christian Values," *Breitbart*, December 24, 2013, http://www.breitbart.com/big-hollywood/2013/12/24/davi-die-hard-christmas/.

16 Judeo-Christian Voter Guide, see, e.g., https://perma.cc/P3EQ-TTUN.

17 See Pew Research Center, U.S. Religious Landscape Study, 2014, https://perma.cc/QAM2-QD56.

18 "Our Mission," American Family Assoc., February 14, 2017, https://www.afa.net/who-we-are/our-mission/.

19 Christian Voter Guide, can be accessed via archive.org and compared with similar dates from the Judeo-Christian voter guide website, http://www.christianvoterguide.com/.

20 "Mission Statement," Family Research Council, http://www.frc.org/mission-statement.

21 Peter Montgomery, "Tony Perkins Attacks DAR Moves toward Religious Inclusion," Right Wing Watch online, January 4, 2013, www.RightWingWatch.org/post/tony-perkins-attacks-dar-moves-toward-religious-inclusion/.

22 John McCain, "Constitution Established a Christian Nation," interview by Beliefnet.com, 2007, https://perma.cc/B8WL-CK3P.

23 See, e.g., Michelle Goldberg, *Kingdom Coming: The Rise of Christian Nationalism* (New York: W. W. Norton, 2007); and Goldberg, "What Is Christian Nationalism?" *Huffington Post*, May 14, 2006: "Christian nationalists believe in a revisionist history, which holds that the founders were devout Christians who never intended to create a secular republic; separation of church and state . . . is a fraud perpetrated by God-hating subversives." http://www.huffingtonpost.com/michelle-goldberg/what-is-christian-nationa_b_20989.html.

24 See, e.g., John Eidsmoe, *Christianity and the Constitution: The Faith of Our Founding Fathers* (Grand Rapids, MI: Baker Book House, 1987) (arguing that the Constitution is grounded in biblical principles); Alf J. Mapp Jr., *The Faiths of Our Fathers: What America's Founders Really Believed* (Lanham, MD: Rowman & Littlefield, 2003); Michael Novak, *On Two Wings: Humble Faith and Common Sense at the American Founding* (San Francisco: Encounter Books, 2002), 5–47.

25 McCreary County, Kentucky v. American Civil Liberties Union of Kentucky, 545 U.S. 844, 876 (2005).

26 Andrew L. Whitehead, Samuel L. Perry, and Joseph O. Baker, "Make America Christian Again: Christian Nationalism and Voting for Donald Trump in the 2016 Presidential Election," *Sociology of Religion* 79, no. 2 (May 19, 2018): 147–71, https://doi.org/10.1093/socrel/srx070. | 27 Ibid., 148, 157.

28 The researchers summed up their study for the *Washington Post*. See Andrew L. Whitehead, Joseph O. Baker and Samuel L. Perry, "Despite Porn Stars and Playboy Models, White Evangelicals Aren't Rejecting Trump. This is Why," *Washington Post*, March 26, 2018. | 29 Ibid.

30 Whitehead, Perry, Baker, "Make America Christian Again, 147–71, at 165.

31 Congressional Prayer Caucus Foundation website, "Project Blitz," https://perma.cc/45MJ-LUJL.

32 Congressional Prayer Caucus Foundation, "Report and Analysis on Religious Freedom Measures Impacting Prayer and Faith in America (2017): Legislation, Proclamations, Talking Points, Notes, Fact Sheets," PDF 4, https://drive.google.com/file/d/0BwfCh32HsC3UYmV0NUp5cXZjT28/view.

33 Ibid., 9. | 34 Ibid., 5. | 35 Ibid., 10. | 36 Ibid., 15. | 37 Ibid., 5–6, 23. | 38 Ibid., 27–30, 33.

39 Frederick Clarkson, "'Project Blitz' Seeks to Do for Christian Nationalism what ALEC Does for Big Business," *Religion Dispatches*, April 27, 2018, https://perma.cc/YJ5H-TN6G.

40 Alan Dershowitz, *Blasphemy: How the Religious Right Is Hijacking Our Declaration of Independence* (Hoboken, NJ: John Wiley & Sons, 2007), 83.

41 Jerry Falwell, *Listen, America!* (New York: Bantam Books, 1981), 29. See also Randall Terry's (formerly of Operation Rescue) speech in Bob Caylor, "Terry Preaches Theocratic Rule 'No More Mr. Nice Christian' Is the Pro-Life Activist's Theme for the '90s," *News-Sentinel* (Fort Wayne, IN), August 16, 1993, 1A. Terry wanted listeners "to let a wave of hatred wash over you. . . . Our goal is a Christian nation. We have a biblical duty, we are called by God, to conquer this country. . . . Theocracy means God rules."

42 Jimmy Swaggart, *Questions & Answers* (Baton Rouge, LA: Swaggart Ministries, 1985), 268.

43 Michael W. Chapman, "Rev. Graham: 'This Country Was Built on Christian Principles' Not Islam," CNSNews. com (January 20, 2015). Franklin Graham has also claimed that "America is being stripped of its biblical heritage and God-inspired foundations" and that "secularism came and it infiltrated and it infected our government." Franklin Graham, January 12, 2016, remarks at the "Decision America Tour" stop in Tallahassee, FL, see https://www.youtube.com/watch?v=DP3PIn5tyUs. This first was a line from his father according to Franklin Graham, *Through My Father's Eyes* (Nashville: Thomas Nelson, 2018), 266.

44 Marc J. Ambinder, "Vast, Right-Wing Cabal? Meet the Most Powerful Conservative Group You've Never Heard Of," ABCNews.com, May 2, 2002, https://perma.cc/A3Q7-HJLG.

45 David Kirkpatrick, "The 2004 Campaign: The Conservatives; Club of the Most Powerful Gathers in Strictest Privacy," *New York Times*, August 28, 2004.

46 Council for National Policy, 2014 directory, https://www.splcenter.org/sites/default/files/cnp_redacted_final.pdf.

47 Ibid.

48 Donald Trump, interview by Steven Strang, *Strang Report* podcast, August 11, 2016, Orlando, FL, at about 15:30, https://perma.cc/86R8-NGCD. See also Miranda Blue, "Christian Values, Things 'So Different From What Our Country Used to Be,'" Right Wing Watch online, August 24, 2016, https://perma.cc/YQV6-6GFJ.

49 See, e.g., Donald Trump, speech at Faith and Freedom Coalition's Road to Majority Conference, June 8, 2017. Omni Shoreham Hotel, Washington, DC, https://perma.cc/54JL-G29P; and Donald Trump, remarks at the Conservative Political Action Conference, February 23, 2018, Gaylord National Resort and Convention Center, Fort Washington, MD, https://www.c-span.org/video/?441592-1/president-trump-pushes-concealed-carry-teachers-cpac-speech; Donald Trump, Commencement Address, May 13, 2017, Liberty Univ., Lynchburg, VA, http://time.com/4778240/donald-trump-liberty-university-speech-transcript/.

50 See Trump, Commencement Address, May 13, 2017; and Trump, speech at Faith and Freedom Coalition's Road to Majority Conference, June 8, 2017.

51 Marco Rubio, remarks during a town hall meeting Q&A, January 18, 2016, Waverly Country Club Waverly, Iowa. Video at https://youtu.be/gkP9RqPA2PQ.

52 Ted Cruz, interview by Dan Bash, *New Day*, CNN, February 2, 2016, quote at 07:05:04, transcript at http://transcripts.cnn.com/TRANSCRIPTS/1602/02/nday.04.html.

53 Nick Gass, "Cruz Vows to Fight Trump on Abortion Plank in RNC Platform," *Politico*, May 27, 2018, https://www.politico.com/story/2016/05/ted-cruz-trump-abortion-fight-223654.

54 John Kasich, remarks at the National Press Club, November 17, 2015, Washington, DC.

55 John Kasich, interview by Peter Alexander, NBC News online, November 17, 2015, http://www.nbcnews.com/feature/short-take/video/kasich-wants-new-agency-to-promote-values-568695875609.

56 Rick Perry, remarks at the Thanksgiving Family Forum, November 19, 2011, First Federated Church, Des Moines, IA, https://www.youtube.com/watch?v=aY8Zw5NzUXQ at 57:35.

57 Rick Perry, remarks for the 40 Days to Save America conference call, September 18, 2012, http://www.rightwingwatch.org/content/perry-christian-warriors-spiritual-warfare-satan-separation-church-state.

58 Arlette Saenz, "Rick Santorum Disagrees with Pastor's Statement about Non-Christians," ABC News online,

March 19, 2012, https://perma.cc/9B5F-8NJF. | 59 Ibid.

60 Michele Bachmann, remarks at the Thanksgiving Family Forum, November 19, 2011, First Federated Church, Des Moines, IA,), https://www.youtube.com/watch?v=aY8Zw5NzUXQ at 1:01:00.

61 Mitt Romney, Presidential Candidates Debates, "Republican Candidates Debate in Jacksonville, Florida," January 26, 2012. Online at APP.

62 Doug Lamborn (R-CO), a member of the Congressional Prayer Caucus, has worked to ensure that nonreligious military men and women do not have the same access to Humanist chaplains as Christian servicemen and women. He believes that "our Nation was founded on Judeo-Christian principles." *Congressional Record* (House), 113th Congress, 1st Sess., vol. 159, no. 162 (November 14, 2013): H7099.

63 *Congressional Record* (House), 111th Congress, 2nd Sess., vol. 156, no. 81 (May 26, 2010): H3865.

64 *Congressional Record* (House), 115th Congress, 1st Sess., vol. 163, no. 209 (December 21, 2017): H10411, see https://perma.cc/5L4C-QEAZ; see also Gomhert's remarks, *Congressional Record* (House), 114th Congress, vol. 162, no. 31 (February 26, 2016): H994.

65 Randy Forbes (R-VA), sermon, October 25, 2015, at Pastor Will Langford's Great Bridge Baptist Church, Chesapeake, VA, https://youtu.be/w9nKqJm1VPE.

66 See David Barton, "Unconfirmed Quotations," January 2000, https://wallbuilders.com/unconfirmed-quotations/. Barton apparently edits this article regularly and it formerly resided at http://www.wallbuilders.com/LIBissuesbooks.asp?id=126, which can be accessed via www.archive.org.

67 See Nate Blakeslee, "King of the Christocrats," *Texas Monthly*, September 2006, https://www.texasmonthly.com/articles/king-of-the-christocrats/.

68 Elise Hu, "Publisher Pulls Controversial Thomas Jefferson Book, Citing Loss of Confidence," NPR, August 9, 2012, https://perma.cc/DBT5-N6VN.

69 Andy Birkey, "Meet David Barton, Bachmann's Constitution Class Teacher," *Minnesota Independent*, November 16, 2010, https://www.tcdailyplanet.net/meet-david-barton-bachmanns-constitution-class-teacher/.

70 Mike Huckabee, Address at the Rediscovering God in America: One Nation Under God Conference, March 24, 2011, Sheraton West Des Moines, West Des Moines, IA, quote at 1:07, https://youtu.be/N1O1dvN8lag.

71 House Resolution 211, 112th Congress (2011). | 72 Ibid.

73 Michael Novak, *God's Country: Taking the Declaration Seriously* (Washington, DC: American Enterprise Institute Press, 2000), 7.

74 Jefferson to Thomas Cooper, February 10, 1814, in Thomas Jefferson, *Writings*, ed. M. D. Peterson (Washington, DC: Library of America, 1984) 1321–29.

75 Anson Phelps Stokes, *Church and State in the United States*, vol. 2 (New York: Harper & Brothers, 1950), 578–79.

76 Andrew Napolitano, as guest host of *The Big Story with John Gibson*, February 7, 2005, on Fox News, transcript at https://www.foxnews.com/story/the-future-of-islam-in-iraq.

77 Bill O'Reilly, interview by Matt Lauer, *The Today Show*, April 10, 2014, on NBC, https://www.today.com/popculture/bill-oreilly-revisits-last-days-jesus-younger-readers-2D79506022.

78 Emma Green, "The Museum That Places the Bible at the Heart of America's Identity," *The Atlantic*, November 26, 2017.

79 Bruce Stokes, "What It Takes to Truly Be 'One of Us,'" Pew Research Center, February 1, 2017, PDF p. 4, https://perma.cc/42LE-HNYP.

80 Mike Pence, acceptance speech at the Republican National Convention, July 20, 2016, Cleveland, OH, www.c-span.org/video/?c4612581/governor-mike-pence-accepts-gop-vice-presidential-nomination.

81 Catherine Lucey and Jill Colvin, "Clinton Says Trump Gives 'Aid, Comfort' to ISIS Recruiters," Associated Press, September 19, 2016 ("We want to make sure we're only admitting people into our country who love our country").

82 Michael D. Shear and Helene Cooper, "Trump Bars Refugees and Citizens of 7 Muslim Countries," *New York Times*, January 27, 2017.

83 Donald Trump, speech at Liberty Univ., Lynchburg, VA, January 18, 2016, https://www.c-span.org/video/?403331-1/donald-trump-remarks-liberty-university. | 84 Ibid.

85 Diana West, "It's Time to Rally Around Donald Trump," *Breitbart*, December 26, 2015.

86 Jenna Johnson, "Trump Calls for 'Total and Complete Shutdown of Muslims Entering the United States,'" *Washington Post*, December 7, 2015.

87 Jeanine Pirro, "Judge Jeanine Pirro: Trump Sends the World a Message in Recognizing Jerusalem as Israel's Capital," Fox News online, May 13, 2018, https://perma.cc/7XQV-PS4A.

88 George Santayana, *The Life of Reason or The Phases of Human Progress*, vol. 1 (New York: Charles Scribner's Sons, 1905), 284.

89 John F. Kennedy, Commencement Address at Yale Univ., June 11, 1962. Online at APP.

90 Madison, "Memorial and Remonstrance against Religious Assessments" (June 20, 1785), in *The Founders' Constitution* online, vol. 5, Amendment I (Religion), doc. 43, http://press-pubs.uchicago.edu/founders/documents/amendI_religions43.html. Citing William T. Hutchinson et al., eds., *The Papers of James Madison* (Chicago: Univ. of Chicago Press, 1962–77 [vols. 1–10]; Charlottesville, VA: Univ. Press of Virginia, 1977 [vols. 11–17]).

91 Treaty of Tripoli, Art. 11, May 26, 1797, *American State Papers*, 18–19, at 19, http://memory.loc.gov/cgi-bin/ampage?collId=llsp&fileName=002/llsp002.db&recNum=23.

92 Bertrand Russell, *An Outline of Intellectual Rubbish: A Hilarious Catalogue of Organized and Individual Stupidity* (Girard, KS: Haldeman-Julius, 1943), 6.

93 When he ran for president in 2008, Senator John McCain, who otherwise has not typified Christian national-

ism, embraced it. In doing so, he perfectly exemplified these two myths and the backpedaling from the first to the second. First, he said, "The Constitution established the United States of America as a Christian nation." After he drew criticism for the comment, he sought refuge in the second myth: "The United States of America was founded on the values of Judeo-Christian values." See Alexander Mooney et al., "Groups Criticize McCain for Calling U.S. 'Christian Nation,'" CNN, October 1, 2007, http://www.cnn.com/2007/POLITICS/10/01/mccain.christian.nation/index.html.

94 Donald Trump, remarks at the Values Voters Summit, October 13, 2017, Omni Shoreham Hotel, Washington, DC, https://www.c-span.org/video/?435728-1/president-trump-addresses-values-voter-summit.

95 Kennedy, Commencement Address at Yale, 1962.

96 Warren G. Harding, Inaugural Address, March 4, 1921, in *Inaugural Addresses of the Presidents of the United States*, vol. 2, Grover Cleveland (1885) to Barack H. Obama (2009), 65 (Carlisle, MA: Applewood Books, 2009).

PART I: THE FOUNDERS, INDEPENDENCE, AND THE COLONIES

1 Joseph J. Ellis, book jacket blurb for Steve Waldman, *Founding Faith: Providence, Politics, and the Birth of Religious Freedom in America* (New York: Random House, 2008).

2 Salman Rushdie, *The Satanic Verses* (New York: Viking, 1988. Citation from paperback ed., New York: Random House, 2008), 97.

Chapter 1 • Custody of the Fathers

3 George Washington, *The Writings of George Washington*, Collected and Edited by Worthington Chauncey Ford, vol. 10 (New York: G. P. Putnam's Sons, 1890), 256.

4 Sylvia Neely, "Mason Locke Weems's *Life of George Washington* and the Myth of Braddock's Defeat," *Virginia Magazine of History and Biography* 107, no. 1 (Winter 1999), citing Mason Locke Weems, "Letter to Matthew Carey," January 12 or 13, 1800, in Emily Ellsworth Ford Skeel, ed., *Mason Locke Weems: His Works and Ways*, vol. 2 (New York: 1929), 126. | 5–6 Ibid.

7 François Furstenberg, "Spinning the Revolution," *New York Times*, July 4, 2006.

8 Ron Chernow, *Washington: A Life* (New York: Penguin, 2010), 813. See also Lawrence C. Wroth, *Parson Weems: A Biographical and Critical Study* (Baltimore: Eichelberger, 1911), 59, 92h; Harold Kellock, *Parson Weems of the Cherry-Tree* (New York: Century, 1928) 57–58; and Skeel, ed., *Mason Locke Weems: His Works and Ways*, vol. 1 (New York: 1929), 259. Weems took his title from the Douay-Rheims translation of Gen. 38 for the story of Onan.

9 Neely, "Mason Locke Weems," 107.

10 Ibid., citing William Alfred Bryan, *George Washington in American Literature, 1775–1865* (New York: Columbia Univ. Press, 1952), 96, noting that Weems was "by far the most popular book on Washington ever written, running to forty editions by the time of Weems's death in 1825 and to eighty by 1932."

11 Edward G. Lengel, *Inventing George Washington: America's Founder in Myth and Memory* (New York: Harper Collins, 2011), 13, 22–23, 76–86. | 12 Ibid., 22–23.

13 Mason Locke Weems, *The Life of George Washington: With Curious Anecdotes, Equally Honourable to Himself, and Exemplary to His Young Countrymen* (1800; repr. Philadelphia: J. B. Lippincott 1858), 198.

14 François Furstenberg, *In the Name of the Father: Washington's Legacy, Slavery, and the Making of a Nation* (New York: Penguin, 2006), 123.

15 William Holmes McGuffey, "Duties of Parents and Teachers," *Transactions of the Fifth Annual Meeting of the Western Literary Institute* (Cincinnati: Western Literary Inst. Exec. Comm., 1836), 129–52, at 138. | 16 Ibid.

17 Lengel, *Inventing George Washington*, 24.

18 Lorett Treese, *Valley Forge: The Making and Remaking of a National Symbol* (Univ. Park, PA: Penn State Press, 1995), 81.

19 Lengel, *Inventing George Washington*, 83. | 20 Ibid., 22. | 21 Ibid., 13.

22 Brooke Allen, *Moral Minority: Our Skeptical Founding Fathers* (Chicago: Ivan R. Dee, 2006), 31; Lengel, *Inventing George Washington*, 13; Chernow, *Washington*, 131; Joseph J. Ellis, *His Excellency: George Washington* (New York: Vintage Books, 2005).

23 Bishop William White to Colonel Mercer, August 15, 1835, in Bird Wilson, *Memoir of the Life of the Right Rev. William White . . .* (Philadelphia: James Kay, Jun. & Brother, 1839), 197–98.

24 Ibid., letter of December 21, 1832, 193–96. See also Peter R. Henriques, *Realistic Visionary: A Portrait of George Washington* (Charlottesville, VA: Univ. of Virginia Press, 2006), 246.

25 Ellis, *His Excellency: George Washington*, 269.

26 See, e.g., Gordon Wood, *The American Revolution: A History* (New York: Modern Library, 2003), 129–30 ("in all his voluminous papers he never mentions Jesus Christ"). There is one possible exception: During the Revolution a group of Delaware chiefs approached Washington to complain about issues they should have addressed to the Continental Congress. They told him that many in their tribe "have embraced Christianity under the Instruction of the Reverend and worthy Mr David Ziesberger whose honest zealous Labours & good Examples have Induced many of them to listen to the Gospel of Jesus Christ, which has been a means of introducing considerable order, Regularity and love of Peace into the Minds of the whole Nation." See *Collections of the State Historical Society of Wisconsin*, ed. Milo M. Quaife, vol. 23 (Madison, WI: State Historical Society of Wisconsin, 1916), 320, 322–23.

27 Chernow, *Washington*, 131–32.

28 W. W. Abbot, "An Uncommon Awareness of Self: The Papers of George Washington," *Prologue: Quarterly of the National Archives* (Spring 1989), 6–19.

29 Abigail Adams to Mary Cranch, January 28, 1800, FO-NA.

30 Furstenberg, *In the Name of the Father*, 123. | **31** Ibid.

32 Chernow, *Washington*, 813.

33 Leading up to the birth of Christian nationalism, some of those involved in the war include: Tim LaHaye, *Faith of Our Founding Fathers: A Comprehensive Study of America's Christian Foundations* (Green Forest, AR: Master Books, 1994), 15 (arguing the need to "wrest control of this nation from the hands of the secularizers and place it back into the hands of those who founded this nation, citizens who had a personal and abiding faith in the God of the Bible"); Jon Meacham, *American Gospel: God, the Founding Fathers, and the Making of a Nation* (New York: Random House, 2006), 18–19, 217–19 (explaining but not making the argument); Frank Lambert, *The Founding Fathers and the Place of Religion in America* (Princeton, NJ: Princeton Univ. Press, 2003), 4–8 (explaining but not making the claim); John Hutson, *The Founders on Religion: A Book of Quotations* (Princeton, NJ: Princeton Univ. Press, 2005), xi–x (also explaining but not arguing); Eidsmoe, *Christianity and the Constitution* (arguing that the faith of the founders shows a relationship between Christianity and the Constitution); Christian Smith, *Christian America?: What Evangelicals Really Want* (Berkeley: Univ. of California Press, 2002), 21–60 (explaining a survey of evangelicals and their beliefs); Michael Novak, "The Influence of Judaism and Christianity on the American Founding," in *Religion and the New Republic: Faith in the Founding of America*, ed. James Hutson (Lanham, MD: Rowman & Littlefield, 2000), 159–86; Gary T. Amos, *Defending the Declaration: How the Bible and Christianity Influenced the Writing of the Declaration of Independence* (Charlottesville, VA: Providence Foundation, 1989); David Barton, *Original Intent: The Courts, the Constitution & Religion* (Aledo, TX: Wallbuilder Press, 2008); Gary DeMar, *America's Christian History: The Untold Story* (Powder Springs, GA: American Visions, 1995); Benjamin Hart, *Faith & Freedom: The Christian Roots of American Liberty* (Dallas: Lewis and Stanley, 1988); Francis A. Schaeffer, *A Christian Manifesto* (Wheaton, IL: Crossway Books, 1982); John W. Whitehead, *The Second American Revolution* (Tyler, MN: TRI Press, 1982).

34 See Chapter 6 and the Donald S. Lutz study cited therein.

35 Jefferson to the Danbury Baptist Assoc., January 1, 1802, in *The Papers of Thomas Jefferson*, vol. 36, December 1, 1801, to March 3, 1802 (Princeton, NJ: Princeton Univ. Press, 2009), 258. https://jeffersonpapers.princeton.edu/selected-documents/danbury-baptist-association-0.

36 US Const. amend. I. | **37** US Const. art VI.

38 Alexander Hamilton, *The Federalist*, no. 69.

39 US Const. art. I.

40 Some mistakenly believe that "Year of our Lord" appears in the US Constitution. I've refuted that elsewhere. Andrew L. Seidel, "Dating God: What Is 'Year of Our Lord' Doing in the U.S. Constitution?" *Constitutional Studies* 3 (2018): 129–51.

41 Robert G. Ingersoll, Lecture titled "Individuality," in *The Works of Robert G. Ingersoll*, vol. 1 (New York: C. P. Farrell, 1901), 201.

42 Seth Lipsky, *The Citizen's Constitution; An Annotated Guide*, n. 251 (New York: Basic Books, 2011), 205.

43 Joseph Story, *Commentaries on the Constitution*, vol. 3, § 1841 (Boston: Hilliard, Gray, 1833) 705. On the other hand, Story also thought that Christianity was part of the common law. Jefferson, who revised and rewrote colonial Virginia's laws and supported his argument with extensive history, refuted this claim in "Whether Christianity is Part of the Common Law," (1764) in *The Works of Thomas Jefferson, Federal Ed.*, vol. 1, ed. Paul Leicester Ford, (New York: G. P. Putnam's Sons, 1904–5), 453–64. Link to all 12 volumes at: https://oll.libertyfund.org/titles/jefferson-the-works-of-thomas-jefferson-12-vols.

44 For the final version of the oath see 1 Stat. 23; for the original version see *Annals of Congress, House of Representatives*, 1st Congress, 1st Sess., 101, entry for Monday, April 6, 1789.

45 Isaac Kramnick and R. Laurence Moore, *The Godless Constitution: The Case Against Religious Correctness*, (New York: W. W. Norton, 1996) 29–31, 43.

46 John Tyler, "Letter to Joseph Simpson, July 10, 1843," reprinted in *William & Mary Quarterly, Historical Magazine* 13, no. 1 (July 1904), 1–3.

47 Garry Wills, *Under God: Religion and American Politics* (New York: Simon & Schuster, 1990), 383.

48 Illinois ex. rel. McCollum v. Board of Education, 333 U.S. 203, 212 (1948) (Frankfurter, J., concurring), quoting Elihu Root.

49 Edward Gibbon, *The Decline and Fall of the Roman Empire*, vol. 1, ed. Oliphant Smeaton, Modern Library Edition (New York: Random House, 1976–88), 25–26. This quote is often misattributed to older sources, including Seneca.

50 Benjamin Rush, "A Plan of a Peace-Office for the United States," in *The Selected Writings of Benjamin Rush*, ed. Dagobert D. Runes (New York: Philosophical Library, 1947), 20.

51 George Washington to the Virginia Baptist General Committee, May 10, 1789, in *George Washington: A Collection*, comp. and ed. by W. B. Allen (Indianapolis: Liberty Fund, 1988), https://perma.cc/6TRG-3JBN.

52 Joseph Prince of the Presbytery of the Eastward to George Washington, October 28, 1789, FO-NA.

53 Washington to the Presbyterian Ministers of Massachusetts and New Hampshire, November 2, 1789, FO-NA.

54–55 Ibid.

56 Hamilton, *Federalist*, no. 69.

57 Ron Chernow, *Alexander Hamilton* (New York: Penguin, 2004), 66.

58 Jefferson to the Danbury Baptist Assoc., January 1, 1802, 258.
59 Virginia Statue for Religious Freedom (1786). This text is taken from J. F. Maclear, *Church and State in the Modern Age: A Documentary History* (Oxford, UK: Oxford Univ. Press, 1995) 63–65, at 64.
60 Madison to Edward Livingston, July 10, 1822, in *The Writings of James Madison*, vol. 9. 100–103.
61 Madison to F. L. Schaeffer, December 3, 1821, in *Letters and Other Writings of James Madison*, vol. 3, (Philadelphia: J. B. Lippencott, 1867), 242–43; see also Robert S. Alley, *James Madison on Religious Liberty* (Amherst, NY: Prometheus Books, 1985), 82.
62 Madison to Baptist Churches in North Carolina, June 3, 1811, in *Letters and Other Writings of James Madison*, vol. 2 (Philadelphia: J. B. Lippencott, 1865), 511–12.
63 Madison to Livingston, July 10, 1822 ("There remains [in some parts of Our country] a strong bias towards the old error, that without some sort of alliance or coalition between Govt. & Religion neither can be duly supported. . . . The danger cannot be too carefully guarded agst.")
64 Madison, "Memorial and Remonstrance," ¶ 7. | 65 Ibid ¶ 8. | 66 Ibid ¶ 5.
67 Bishop William Meade, *Old Churches, Ministers and Families of Virginia*, vol. 2 (1857; repr. Philadelphia: J. B. Lippencott, 1900), 99.
68 Madison to Baptist Churches in North Carolina, June 3, 1811, 511–12.
69 *Annals of Congress. The Debates and Proceedings in the Congress of the United States* (Gales & Seaton, 1834–56), 1:758, August 15, 1789 debate.
70 Jefferson to Danbury Baptist Assoc., January 1, 1802.
71 *McCollom*, 333 U.S. 203, 231 (1948) (Frankfurter, J., concurring).
72 Madison to Livingston, July 10, 1822.

Chapter 2 • "Religion and Morality": Religion for the Masses, Reason for the Founders

1 Arthur Schopenhauer, *Religion: A Dialogue, and Other Essays*, (1891; repr. London: Forgotten Books, 2013) 50.
2 Jefferson to Mrs. Samuel H. Smith Monticello, August 6, 1816, in *The Writings of Thomas Jefferson: Being His Autobiography, Correspondence, Reports . . .*, vol. 7, ed. H. A. Washington (New York: J. C. Riker, 1854), 28.
3 John Adams, "A Defence of the Constitutions of Government of the United States of America, Against the Attack of M. Turgot in His Letter to Dr. Price, Dated the Twenty-second Day of March, 1778" in *The Works of John Adams . . . by his Grandson Charles Francis Adams*, vol. 4 (Boston: Little, Brown, 1856), 293. Link to all 10 volumes at: https://oll.libertyfund.org/titles/adams-the-works-of-john-adams-10-vols.
4 See note 24 below.
5 William Martin, *With God on Our Side: The Rise of the Religious Right in America* (New York: Broadway Books, 2005), 32; "Graham to Enter Politics if Winners Fail to Clean Up," *Statesville Record & Landmark* (Statesville, NC), July 9, 1952.
6 Willard Sterne Randall, *Ethan Allen: His Life and Times* (New York: W. W. Norton, 2011), 357–58, 411.
7 Rendered as "God helps them that help themselves" in the 1736 edition. Benjamin Franklin, *Poor Richard's Almanack* (1736) from Univ. of Kansas, AmDocs: Documents for the Study of American History 1492–Present, http://www.vlib.us/amdocs/texts/prichard36.html.
8 Versions of this quote appear in the Koran, and the same words appear in Algernon Sidney's 1698 *Discourses Concerning Government*, ch. 2, section 23.
9 George Barna, *Boiling Point: How Coming Cultural Shifts Will Change Your Life* (Ventura, CA: Regal repr. ed., 2003), 173.
10 John Jay to Richard Peters, Bedford, New York, March 29, 1811, in *The Correspondence and Public Papers of John Jay*, vol. 4, ed. Henry P. Johnston (New York: G. P. Putnam's Sons, 1890–93), 349.
11 John Adams to Benjamin Rush, July 24, 1789, in Alexander Biddle, *Old Family Letters Copied from the Originals*, series A (Philadelphia: J. B. Lippencott, 1892), 46–7.
12 Abigail Adams to John Adams, April 28, 1783, in *Letters of Mrs. Adams: The Wife of John Adams*, vol. 1, ed. Charles Francis Adams (Boston: C. C. Little and J. Brown, 1840), 177–78. | 13 Ibid.
14 See, e.g., David L. Holmes, *The Faiths of the Founding Fathers* 39–45, 49–51 (Oxford, UK: Oxford Univ. Press, 2006) (deists believed in "human inquiry as well as a self-confident challenge of traditional political, religious, and social ideas," and among them were "Franklin, Washington, Adams, Jefferson, Madison and Monroe"); Allen, *Moral Minority*; Susan Jacoby, *Freethinkers: A History of American Secularism* (New York: Henry Holt, 2004), 4–6.
15 Jefferson to Mrs. Samuel H. Smith Monticello, August 6, 1816, in *Writings of Thomas Jefferson*, vol. 7, 28.
16 Jefferson, February 1, 1800, diary entry in *Works of Thomas Jefferson*, vol. 1, 352.
17 Jefferson to William Short, October 31, 1819, in the first and only footnote, see https://perma.cc/H3LU-DJEZ.
18 Jefferson to Francis Van Der Kemp, April 25, 1816, https://www.loc.gov/item/mtjbib022426/. *The Papers of Thomas Jefferson*, Retirement Series, vol. 9, September 1815 to April 1816, ed. J. Jefferson Looney (Princeton, NJ: Princeton Univ. Press, 2012), 703–4.
19 *The Constitutional Convention of 1787: A Comprehensive Encyclopedia of America's Founding*, vol. 1, ed. John R. Vile (Santa Barbara, CA: ABC-CLIO, 2005), 219.
20 Richard Brookhiser, *Gentleman Revolutionary: Gouverneur Morris, the Rake Who Wrote the Constitution* (New York: Free Press, 2003), 117; Howard Swiggett, *The Extraordinary Mr. Morris* (New York: Doubleday, 1952), 209. See also Swiggett at 179, 181, 183, 218, 220, 238 for more details on their relationship.
21 Morris, November 9, 1789, diary entry, in *A Diary of the French Revolution*, ed. Beatrix Cary Davenport (Boston: Houghton Mifflin, 1939), vol. 1, 293.

22 Gregg Frazer, "Gouverneur Morris and Theistic Rationalism in the Founding Era," in *Faith and the Founders of the American Republic*, ed. Daniel Dreisbach and Mark David Hall (Oxford, UK: Oxford Univ. Press, 2014), 219.

23 John Jay to Robert Morris, St. [San] Ildefonso, September 16, 1780 ("Gouverneur's Leg has been a Tax on my Heart. I am almost tempted to wish he had lost something else."), https://perma.cc/5Z5T-T5RZ.

24 H. Jefferson Powell, *The Moral Tradition of American Constitutionalism: A Theological Interpretation* (Durham, NC: Duke Univ. Press, 1993), 7–8 (noting that Christians are tempted to "treat the American political system as theologically unique, the reflection in the political realm of Christian moral principles"), citing William J. Everett, *God's Federal Republic* (New York: Paulist Press, 1988); Mark David Hall, abstract for "Did America Have a Christian Founding?," Heritage Foundation, June 7, 2011("In short, while America did not have a Christian Founding in the sense of creating a theocracy, its Founding was deeply shaped by Christian moral truths"), https://perma.cc/R5GJ-Z2VP (the founding fathers "firmly believed that God ordained moral standards, that legislation should be made in accordance with these standards); Mark Beliles and Stephen McDowell, *America's Providential History*, 3rd ed. (Charlottesville, VA: Providence Found., 2010), 178 ("'Virtue . . . Learning . . . Piety.' These words are found throughout our official documents and statements of our Founders. Sometimes they are called 'Morality,' 'Knowledge,' and 'Religion,' such as are found in the Northwest Ordinance. 'Religion' meant Christianity. 'Morality' meant Christian character. 'Knowledge' meant a Biblical worldview"); Gary Bauer, "Judeo-Christian Values Make America the Light of the World," Human Events.com, April 24, 2011, http://humanevents.com/2011/04/24/judeochristian-values-make-america-the-light-of-the-world/; Ronald R. Cherry, "The Judeo-Christian Values of America," American Thinker.com, September 15, 2007 ("Judeo-Christian Values have a foundational role in America, beginning with the Declaration of Independence"), http://www.american-thinker.com/articles/2007/09/the_judeochristian_values_of_a.html#ixzz3WxB4CwGv.

25 In the US, 53 percent think it is necessary to believe in God to be moral, though the number drops to 37 percent when surveying only college graduates. Pew Research Center (March 2014), "Worldwide, Many See Belief in God as Essential to Morality Richer Nations Are Exception," https://perma.cc/V9RA-VVBJ.

26 George Washington, Farewell Address, September 19, 1796. Madison worked on an early draft of this speech when Washington was first considering retirement after his first term. Hamilton finished the draft years later.

27 Chernow, *Alexander Hamilton*, 504–8. See also Victor Hugo Paltsits, *Washington's Farewell Address, in Facsimile, with Transliterations of All the Drafts of Washington, Madison, & Hamilton . . .* (New York: New York Public Library, 1935).

28 Chernow, *Alexander Hamilton*, 507.

29 Hamilton, *Draft of Washington's Farewell Address, [July] 1796*. Hamilton's original draft can be found in Paltsits, *Washington's Farewell Address*, 192; George Washington, *The Writings of George Washington*, vol. 13, 308. See also http://www.loc.gov/exhibits/religion/images/vc6575th.jpg.

30 John Adams to Massachusetts Militia, October 11, 1798, FO-NA.

31 John Adams to Jefferson, April 19, 1817, *Works of Thomas Jefferson*, vol. 1, 254. | 32 Ibid.

33 Jefferson, Retirement Library organization tree, http://tjlibraries.monticello.org/transcripts/retirementlibrary/retirementlibrary.html, *The Thomas Jefferson Papers* ser. 7, http://hdl.loc.gov/loc.mss/mtj.mtjbib026579.

34 Jefferson to Matthew Carey, November 11, 1816, in *Works of Thomas Jefferson*, vol. 12, 41–42, at 42.

35 Madison, *Federalist*, no. 10.

36 John Stuart Mill, *Autobiography* (New York: Henry Holt, 1887) 45.

37 Gordon S. Wood, *Revolutionary Characters: What Made the Founders Different* (New York: Penguin, 2007), 221.

38 Ibid., 221–22. | 39 Ibid., 15.

40 Gordon S. Wood, *The Radicalism of the American Revolution* (New York: Alfred A. Knopf, 1992), 27.

41 Ibid., 330.

42 Baruch Spinoza, *Tractatus Theologico-Politicus*, 2nd ed., trans. Samuel Shirley (Indianapolis: Hackett Publishing, 2001), 67.

43 John Locke, "The Reasonableness of Christianity as Delivered in the Scriptures," in *The Works of John Locke in Three Volumes*, vol. 2, ed. Pierre des Maizeaux (London: D. Browne, 1759), 509–86, at 577.

44 Benjamin Franklin, *The Works of Benjamin Franklin, including the Private as well as the Official and Scientific Correspondence, together with the Unmutilated and Correct Version of the Autobiography . . .* , compiled and edited by John Bigelow, vol. 11 (New York: G. P. Putnam's Sons, 1904), 298.

45 Ibid.

46 Charles Louis de Secondat, Baron de Montesquieu, *Spirit of Laws*, bk. 24, ch. 8, in *The Complete Works of M. de Montesquieu*, vol. 2 (London: T. Evans, 1777), 165–66, https://perma.cc/E794-6LAD.

47 Franklin, *Works of Benjamin Franklin*, vol. 11, 298.

48 Phil Zuckerman, "Atheism, Secularity, and Well-Being: How the Findings of Social Science Counter Negative Stereotypes and Assumptions," *Sociology Compass* 3, no. 6 (2009): 949–71, 955.

49 Ibid., 955. | 50 Ibid., 960–61. | 51 Ibid., 955, 961.

52 Michael Gaddis, *There Is No Crime for Those Who Have Christ* (Berkeley: Univ. of California Press, 2005), 1.

53 Steven Weinberg, speech, American Assoc. for the Advancement of Science, Conference on Cosmic Design, Washington, DC, April 1999.

54 Thomas Paine to Camille Jordan, *The Writings of Thomas Paine*, vol. 4 (New York: G. P. Putnam's Sons, 1896), 252.

55 See, e.g., Jonathan Clark, *English Society, 1660–1832* (Cambridge, UK: Cambridge Univ. Press, 2000).

Chapter 3 • Declaring Independence from Judeo-Christianity

1 John Adams to Hezekiah Niles, February 13, 1818, in *Works of John Adams*, vol. 10, 283.

2 Anson Phelps Stokes wrote that the "ideal of the Declaration [of Independence] is of course a definitely Christian one" that is clearly based on "fundamental Christian teachings." Stokes, *Church and State in the United States*, vol. 2 (New York: Harper & Brothers, 1950), 578–79. Former judge Andrew Napolitano thinks that "in America, as we all know from basic high school social studies, we have a Constitution and a Declaration of Independence that embodies Judeo-Christian moral values." *The Big Story with John Gibson*, February 7, 2005, on Fox News. Gary T. Amos and Richard Gardiner *Never Before in History*, ed. William Dembski (Dallas: Haughton, 1998). Amos and Gardiner wrote their "supplemental textbook" because "tens of millions of public school graduates are illiterate regarding our nation's great history and traditions." See www.neverbeforeinhistory.com, which is now owned by the Discovery Inst. Press, the publishing arm of the Seattle-based creationist-promoting Discovery Inst., but which can still be seen at https://perma.cc/4PXQ-HKVH. The authors claim that "if we look closely at the wording and the ideas contained in the Declaration, it becomes clear that the primary influence that shaped that document was the Christian tradition in law and theology." Amos, *Defending the Declaration: How the Bible and Christianity Influenced the Writing of the Declaration of Independence* (Brentwood, TN: Wolgemuth & Hyatt, 1989).
3 Thomas Paine, "The Rights of Man," part 2, in *The Political Works of Thomas Paine*, vol. 2 (London: W. T. Sherwin, 1819), 15. | 4 Ibid.
5 See, e.g., Akil Reed Amar, *America's Constitution: A Biography* (New York: Random House, 2005), 24. Amar notes that the Declaration did not commit colonies to each other, only to independence. But see, Carlton F. W. Larson, "The Declaration of Independence: A 225th Anniversary Reinterpretation," *Washington Law Review* 76 (2001): 701, 721–62, arguing that the Declaration did create "one American nation."
6 John Adams to James Warren, January 9, 1787, *Warren-Adams Letters: Being Chiefly a Correspondence Among John Adams, Samuel Adams, and James Warren*, vol. 2 (Boston: Massachusetts Historical Society, 1917 and 1925), 281.
7 The Articles of Confederation were a failed first attempt. See Barbara Silberdick Feinberg, *The Articles of Confederation: The First Constitution of the United States* (Brookfield, CT: Twenty-First Century Books, 2002), 13. See also Joseph J. Ellis, *The Quartet: Orchestrating the Second American Revolution, 1783–1789* (New York: Alfred A. Knopf, 2015), xi–xvi.
8 *Journals of the Continental Congress, 1774–1789* 5, ed. Worthington C. Ford et al. (Washington, DC, 1904–37): 425.
9 Jefferson to Richard Henry Lee, May 8, 1825, FO-NA. | 10–13 Ibid.
14 Carl Lotus Becker, *The Declaration of Independence: A Study in the History of Political Ideas* (New York: Harcourt, Brace, 1922), 5. | 15 Ibid., 203. | 16 Ibid., 8.
17 Jefferson to Roger C. Weightman, June 24, 1826, in *Works of Thomas Jefferson*, vol. 12, 477.
18 Stephen E. Lucas, "Justifying America: The Declaration of Independence as a Rhetorical Document," in *American Rhetoric: Context and Criticism*, ed. Thomas W. Benson (Carbondale, IL: Southern Illinois Univ. Press, 1989), 67–130.
19 Joseph J. Ellis, *American Sphinx: The Character of Thomas Jefferson* (New York: Alfred A. Knopf, 1997), 292.
20 George Wythe, remarks to Continental Congress, February 16, 1776, in *Journals of the Continental Congress, 1774–1789* 6: 1072.
21 Samuel Adams to Joseph Hawley, April 15, 1776, in *The Writings of Samuel Adams*, vol. 3, ed. Harry Alonzo Cushing (New York: G. P. Putnam & Sons, 1907), 280.
22 *The Colonial Records of North Carolina*, vol. 10, ed. William L. Saunders (Raleigh, NC: Josephus Daniels, 1890), 512.
23 See Becker, *Declaration of Independence*, 129.
24 Stephen E. Lucas, "The Stylistic Artistry of the Declaration of Independence," 1989, National Archives, America's Founding Documents, https://www.archives.gov/founding-docs/stylistic-artistry-of-the-declaration.
25 King George III to Lord North, September 11, 1774, in *The Correspondence of King George III*, vol. 3, ed. John Fortescue (Basingstoke, UK: Macmillan, 1927–28), 131.
26 The text of Henry's speech is based on supposition and was first recorded by William Wirt, who was three years old when Henry gave the speech. Modern evidence suggests the speech was not in Henry's own style but in a style of the man who was Wirt's source, Henry Tucker. See Jim Cox, "The Speech: It May Not Be the One That Patrick Henry So Famously Made," *Colonial Williamsburg Journal* (Winter 2002–3), http://www.history.org/Foundation/journal/Winter02-03/speech.cfm.
27 The first time this appeared in print as attributed to Franklin was 50 years after his death in *The Works of Benjamin Franklin*; vol. 1, ed. Jared Sparks (Boston: Hillard, Gray, 1840), 408. Sparks doesn't cite an original source, instead, it's from Sparks's "continuation" of Franklin's *Autobiography*, in which he "endeavoured to follow [Franklin's] plan, by confining himself strictly to a narrative of the principal events and incidents in his life." xxii. Carl Van Doren didn't think it likely that Franklin said it. Van Doren, *Benjamin Franklin's Autobiographical Writings* (New York: Viking, 1945), 418–19.
28 John Adams to H. Niles, Feb. 13, 1818, in *Works of John Adams*, vol. 10, 283.
29 Jeremy Black, *George III: America's Last King* (New Haven, CT: Yale Univ. Press, 2006), 186.
30–31 Ibid.,195. | 32 Ibid., 207.
33 King George III to Lord North, February 12, 1779.
34 Black, *George III*, 190. | 35 Ibid., 187–88.
36 Jonathan Elliot, *The Debates in the Several State Conventions of the Adoption of the Federal Constitution*, vol. 2, (Washington, DC: J. Elliot, 1827–30), 423.
37 Becker, *Declaration of Independence*, 7.
38 Rom. 13:1–2 (NIV). | 39 Rom. 13:4–5. | 40 Acts 5:29. | 41 Prov. 8:15–16.

42 Jack Jenkins, "Trump's 'God Whisperer' Says Resisting Him is an Affront to God," *ThinkProgress,* August 23, 2017, https://thinkprogress.org/trump-spiritual-adviser-affront-god-d615c512bffc/.

43 John Adams wrote the Declaration of Rights and it was altered very little by the constitutional convention in his state. See, e.g., *Works of John Adams,* vol. 10, 210–26.

44 John Lind, *An Answer to the Declaration of the American Congress* (London: T. Cadell, 1776), 120.

45 Jonathan Boucher, *A View of the Causes and Consequences of the American Revolution, with an Historical Preface* (London: G. G. and J. Robinson, 1797), 534.

46 Ibid., 507–8. | 47 Ibid., 508 (emph. in orig.). | 48 Ibid., 505.

49 Philip Dray, *Stealing God's Thunder: Benjamin Franklin's Lightning Rod and the Invention of America* (New York: Random House, 2005), xvi.

50 Ibid., 66–67. | 51 Ibid., 68. | 52 Ibid., 96. | 53 Ibid., 99. | 54 Ibid., 102–4

55 John Adams, *Diary and Autobiography of John Adams,* vol. 1, ed. L. H. Butterfield (Cambridge, MA: Belknap Press/Harvard Univ. Press, 1962), 61–62.

56 Eccles. 10:20.

57 Harlow Giles Unger, *John Quincy Adams* (Boston: Da Capo Press, 2012), 298–99.

58 Rom. 13:1 (NIV). | 59 Prov. 8:15–16.

60 Matthew Stewart, *Nature's God: The Heretical Origins of the American Republic* (New York: W. W. Norton, 2014, advance review copy), 129. | 61 Ibid.

62 Fascinatingly, this quote of Lincoln's may not be Lincoln's originally. Lincoln may have been borrowing from Wycliffe, or possibly from Theodore Parker, an abolitionist minister. See Daniel Hannan, "150 Years Ago Today, Abraham Lincoln Praised 'Government of the People, by the People, for the People'—But the Words Were Not His," *Telegraph* (blog), November 19, 2013; and William H. Herndon and Jesse W. Welk, *Abraham Lincoln: The True Story of a Great Life,* vol. 2 (New York: D. Appleton, 1892), 65.

63 Becker, *Declaration of Independence,* 62.

64 See, e.g., Ellis Sandoz, *Political Sermons of the American Founding Era: 1730–1805,* 2nd ed. (Indianapolis: Liberty Fund, 1998), http://oll.libertyfund.org/titles/1878.

65 Boucher, *View of the Causes,* 504–5.

Chapter 4 • Referrals: The Declaration's References to a Higher Power

1 See the first comment on the top of p. 299 for sources.

2 Becker, *Declaration of Independence,* 197–200. | 3 Ibid. | 4 Ibid., 197.

5 Richard Henry Lee to Thomas Jefferson, July 21, 1776, in *The Papers of Thomas Jefferson,* vol. 1, 1760–1776, ed. Julian P. Boyd (Princeton, NJ: Princeton Univ. Press, 1950), 471.

6 Geoffrey R. Stone, "The World of the Framers: A Christian Nation?" *UCLA Law Review* 56, no. 1 (2008): 22.

7 Wycliffe's Bible (1380, 1388); Tyndale Bible (1526–30); Coverdale Bible (1535); Matthew's Bible (1537); Great Bible (1539); Taverner's Bible (1539); Geneva Bible (1557–60); Douay-Rheims Bible (1582, 1609–10); King James Version (1611); Douay-Rheims Bible (Challoner Rev.) (1752); Quaker Bible (1764).

8 John Locke, *Two Treatises of Government,* ed. Thomas Hollis, chapter 3, "Of the State of War," § 21 (London: A. Millar et al., 1764), 212.

9 Eccles. 12:1, Isa. 40:28, Isa. 43:15, Rom. 1:25, 1 Pet. 4:19.

10 Reconstruction of Jefferson's draft of the Declaration before it was revised by the other members of the Committee of Five and by Congress, from *Papers of Thomas Jefferson,* vol. 1, 243–47; see http://www.loc.gov/exhibits/declara/ruffdrft.html (emph. in orig.).

11 See, e.g., Annette Gordon-Reed, *The Hemingses of Monticello: An American Family* (New York: W. W. Norton, 2008); Ta-Nehisi Coates, "Thomas Jefferson and the Divinity of the Founding Fathers," *The Atlantic,* December 10, 2012, https://www.theatlantic.com/amp/article/266099/.

12 Reconstruction of Jefferson's draft of the Declaration, from *Papers of Thomas Jefferson,* 186.

13 Jeffry H. Morrison, "Political Theology in the Declaration of Independence," presented at a conference on the Declaration of Independence, the James Madison Program in American Ideals and Institutions Dept. of Politics, Princeton Univ., April 5–6, 2002. Morrison argues the third and fourth references were "intentionally calibrated to the ears of American Calvinists, the largest religious constituency in the colonies, while the first two references were aimed at deistic (or Unitarian) readers."

14 See the Dunlap Broadside, this printer's version of the Declaration, at: http://www.wdl.org/en/item/2716/.

15 Becker, *Declaration of Independence,* 185.

16 Michael Anthony Peroutka, "Evolution is Anti-American," *American View,* November 4, 2011 http://www.theamericanview.com/evolution-is-anti-american/ (audio file).

17 *Black's Law Dictionary,* 9th ed. (St. Paul, MN: West, 2009), "positive law." | 18 Ibid., "natural law."

19 Becker, *Declaration of Independence,* 133–34.

20 Roscoe Pound, *The Formative Era of America* (Boston: Little, Brown, 1938), 29.

21 Voltaire, *The Works of Voltaire,* vol. VI (*Philosophical Dictionary,* part 4), trans. William F. Fleming (New York: E. R. DuMont, 1901), http://oll.libertyfund.org/titles/355#lf0060-06_head_020.

22 *Black's Law Dictionary,* "natural law."

23 Sir William Blackstone, *Commentaries on the Laws of England,* vol. 1 (Oxford, UK: Clarendon Press, 1765), 42. The Christian nationalist claim here is not so clear. Blackstone did distinguish between divine and natural law to an extent: "The doctrines thus delivered we call the revealed or divine law, and they are to be found only in

the holy scriptures. . . . Yet undoubtedly the revealed law is (humanly speaking) of infinitely more authority than what we generally call the natural law. Because one is the law of nature, expressly declared so to be by God himself; the other is only what, by the assistance of human reason, we imagine to be that law."

24 Geoffrey Stone, *Perilous Times: Free Speech in Wartime, from 1798 to the War on Terrorism* (New York: W. W. Norton, 2004), 42–43.

25 Jefferson to Judge Tyler, June 17, 1812, in *Writings of Thomas Jefferson*, vol. 6, 66.

26 Jefferson to Horatio G. Spafford, March 17, 1814, in *Writings of Thomas Jefferson*, vol. 6, 335.

27 See, e.g., Morris R. Cohen, *Reason and Law* (Glencoe, IL: Free Press, 1950).

28 Becker, *Declaration of Independence*, 277.

29 Dershowitz, *Blasphemy*, 126.

30 Jefferson, Opinion on French Treaties, April 28, 1793, in *Works of Thomas Jefferson*, vol. 7, 292. https://oll. libertyfund.org/titles/804#Jefferson_0054-07_619 (emph. added).

31 Jefferson, *A Summary View of the Rights of British America* (1774), in *Works of Thomas Jefferson*, vol. 2, 87 (emph. added).

32 Reconstruction of Jefferson's draft of the Declaration, from *Papers of Thomas Jefferson*, vol. 1, 243–47 (emph. in orig.).

33 Section 1 of the Virginia Declaration of Rights adopted by the Virginia Constitutional Convention on June 12, 1776 (emph. added).

34 Declaration and Resolves of the First Continental Congress, October 14, 1774, http://avalon.law.yale.edu/18th_ century/resolves.asp. *Documents Illustrative of the Formation of the Union of the American States*, ed. Charles C. Tansill (Washington, DC: Government Printing Office, 1927), House doc. no. 398 (emph. added).

35 Samuel Adams, "Massachusetts Circular Letter to the Colonial Legislatures, February 11, 1768," http://avalon. law.yale.edu/18th_century/mass_circ_let_1768.asp (emph. added).

36 See Stewart, *Nature's God*, generally, and specifically 166–75. | 37 Ibid., 183.

38 Thomas Paine, "Discourse," delivered at the Society of Theophilanthropists, Paris, 1798, in *The Theological Works of Thomas Paine* (New York: George H. Evans, 1835), 198.

39 Thomas Young, in *Boston Evening Post*, August 27, 1770; in Stewart, *Nature's God*, 138.

40 John Adams to Jefferson, September 13, 1813, in *Works of John Adams*, vol. 10, 66. | 41 Ibid., 67.

42 Jefferson to John Adams, April 11, 1823, in *The Writings of Thomas Jefferson*, vol. 15, ed. Albert Ellery Bergh (Washington, DC: Thomas Jefferson Memorial Assoc., 1907), 428; see also https://perma.cc/5NN2-HM4E.

43 Stewart, *Nature's God*, 168, quoting François Garasse, *La doctrine curieuse des beaux esprits de ce temps* (Paris: Sebastian Chappelet, 1623), 327, 675, 676.

44 Stewart, *Nature's God*, 168. | 45 Ibid., 172–73.

46 Becker, *Declaration of Independence*, 51.

47 See also Lambert, *Founding Fathers*, 167 (arguing that 'Nature's God' is not the God of the New Testament); Allen Jayne, *Jefferson's Declaration of Independence: Origins, Philosophy, and Theology* (Lexington, KY: Univ. Press of Kentucky, 1998), 9–18 (arguing that natural law is based on enlightenment thinkers such as Locke and Bolingbroke whose ideas conflict with Judeo-Christian principles).

48 See, e.g., Amy B. Wang, "Some Trump Supporters Thought NPR Tweeted 'Propaganda.' It was the Declaration of Independence," *Washington Post*, July 5, 2017.

49 Alan Keyes, interview by Sean Hannity: "It seems to me, either we're going to believe Jefferson's comments about we're endowed by our Creator with certain unalienable rights." *The Sean Hannity Show*, August 27, 2003, on Fox News, http://www.keyesarchives.com/transcript.php?id=268.

50 *The Sean Hannity Show*, April 8, 2009, on Fox News. Transcript by Christine Schwen, MediaMatters.org, "Fox News figures outraged over Obama's 'Christian nation' comment," April 9, 2009, https://perma.cc/9Y5E-5BXZ and https://perma.cc/CP8U-DJS6. See also *The Sean Hannity Show*, September 25, 2009, on Fox News, https:// perma.cc/HLN9-N9Z9; and *Hannity & Colmes*, October 30, 2007, on Fox News, https://perma.cc/9LQJ-VA6V.

51 On BillOreilly.com, his staff wrote a July 2, 2015, article, "Independence from God," that ended: "The left's utopia is a place Thomas Jefferson would find unrecognizable. A place where *our Creator* would be basically forgotten. On this Independence Day, keep in mind that our Founders truly believed independence is a gift to be cherished. A gift from our Creator. A gift from God" (emph. in orig.). See https://perma.cc/8LW9-PKKD.

52 Mac Thornberry, of the Texas 13thh District, wrote: "'***Endowed by our Creator with certain inalienable rights***' – Our worth and our 'rights' come from our Creator – not from government, further establishing the foundational nature of the rights" (emph. in orig.) Mac Thornberry, "The Foundation: The Declaration of Independence," on Thornberry's House.gov website, http://thornberry.house.gov/biography/declarationofindependence.htm.

53 Sen. Sam Brownback, remarks in the *Congressional Record* (Senate), 107th Congress, 2nd Sess., vol. 151, pt. 8 (June 26, 2002): 11550, "Our Declaration of Independence refers to God multiple times including saying that our certain unalienable rights are endowed by our Creator."

54 Lieberman repeatedly made this mistake during a 2008 address to Congress; see *Congressional Record* (Senate), vol. 154, pt. 10 (July 8, 2008): 14208–209; see also "Meet the Press with Tim Russert," October 21, 2001, on NBC. Senators John McCain and Joseph Lieberman were guests along with Dr. Anthony Fauci; transcript at http://www.washingtonpost.com/wp-srv/nation/specials/attacked/transcripts/nbctext_102101.html.

55 See, e.g., Ben Carson, who appeared on Bill O'Reilly's show and said, "Interestingly enough, if you look at our founding document, the Declaration of Independence, it talks about certain inalienable rights given to us by our Creator." *The O'Reilly Factor*, "Impact Segment," October 12, 2015, on Fox News, https://www.foxnews. com/transcript/the-far-left-attacking-ben-carsons-faith.

56 See, e.g., Madison, "Memorial and Remonstrance," ¶ 11.

57 See, e.g., Mark Hulsether, *Religion, Culture, and Politics in the Twentieth-Century United States* (New York: Columbia Univ. Press, 2007), 41.

58 See also Lambert, *Founding Fathers*, 282 (the nonsectarian nature of references leads to universal application).

59 Marco Rubio, remarks, January 18, 2016, Waverly, Iowa. Video at https://youtu.be/gkP9RqPA2PQ.

60 Rev. 2:26–28.

61 Jefferson to Roger C. Weightman, June 24, 1826, in *Works of Thomas Jefferson*, vol. 12, 477. (Original manuscript available at http://www.loc.gov/exhibits/jefferson/214.html. Capitalization and punctuation follow that original manuscript, not the letter in *Works*.)

62 George Orwell, *Animal Farm* (London: Secker and Warburg, 1945).

63 Jefferson to José Corrêa da Serra, April 11, 1820, FO-NA. | **64** Ibid.

65 Madison, "Memorial and Remonstrance," ¶ 8.

66 *Founders' Constitution* online, vol. 1, ch. 14, doc. 10, http://press-pubs.uchicago.edu/founders/documents/v1ch14s10.html (emph. added).

67 Thomas Jefferson, *Notes on the State of Virginia*, query 18 (London: John Stockdale, 1787).

68 John Jay, *Federalist*, no. 2.

69 *Founders' Constitution*, online, vol. 5, Bill of Rights, doc.2, http://press-pubs.uchicago.edu/founders/documents/bill_of_rightss2.html. | **70** Ibid., doc. 5. | **71** Ibid., doc. 6.

72 For an excellent description of these documents and how they compare to the Declaration, see Pauline Maier *American Scripture, Making the Declaration of Independence* (New York: Vintage Books, 1998), 164–66.

73 James Wilson, "Considerations on the Nature and Extent of the Legislative Authority of the British Parliament, 1774," in *Collected Works of James Wilson*, vol. 1, ed. Kermit L. Hall and Mark David Hall, collected by Maynard Garrison (Indianapolis: Liberty Fund, 2007), 4, http://oll.libertyfund.org/titles/2072#Wilson_4140_84.

74 *The Constitutional Convention of 1787*, vol. 1, 219. The top three speakers were: Gouverneur Morris (173 times), James Wilson (168 times), and James Madison (161 times).

75 Wilson, *Collected Works of James Wilson*, 639.

76 An earlier draft of this paragraph and some other ideas in this chapter became an op-ed for the Religion News Service. See, Seidel, "The Bill of Rights, Thomas Jefferson, and the Danger of 'God-given Rights,'" Religion News Service, December 15, 2017, https://perma.cc/F5FX-U2GZ.

77 Robert P. Jones and Daniel Cox, "Clinton Maintains Double-Digit Lead (51% vs. 36%) over Trump." Public Religion Research Institute, October 19, 2016, https://perma.cc/J6H6-J55W.

78 Robert P. Jones, "White Evangelical Support for Donald Trump at All-Time High," Public Religion Research Institute onlinez, April 18, 2018, https://perma.cc/7GBG-PKDG.

79 Jonathan Drew, "Franklin Graham Book Shares Lessons from 'America's Pastor,'" Associated Press, May 4, 2018, https://apnews.com/dbac992f2fab4266a4fc210416145200. Graham said this in the video interview attached to the article but was not quoted in the text: https://youtu.be/F-oFJULEWxM.

80 Franklin Graham, "Clinton's Sins Aren't Private," *Wall Street Journal*, August 27, 1998.

81 Thomas Paine, *Common Sense*, ed. Isaac Kramnick (London: Penguin Classics, 1976), 92.

82 John Fea, *Was America Founded as a Christian Nation? A Historical Introduction* (Louisville, KY: Westminster John Knox Press, 2011), 132.

83 Garry Wills, *Inventing America, Jefferson's Declaration of Independence* (New York: Vintage Books, 1979), xxiii.

84 Steven Green, *Inventing Christian America: The Myth of the Religious Founding* (Oxford, UK: Oxford Univ. Press, 2015), 169.

85 Wilson Carey McWilliams, "The Bible in the American Political Tradition," in *Religion and Politics*, ed. Myron J. Aronoff (New Brunswick, NJ: Transaction Books, 1984), 21.

86 The original language that the House wanted included "so help me God" and another mention of a god. *House Journal*, 1st Congress, 1st Sess. (April 6, 1789): 7. But those two mentions did not make it into the final version. See final here: 1 Stat. 23 (1789), http://memory.loc.gov/cgi-bin/ampage?collId=llsl&fileName=001/llsl001.db&recNum=146.

87 See Becker, *Declaration of Independence*, 197.

88 Jefferson to Roger C. Weightman, June 24, 1826, *in Works of Thomas Jefferson*, vol. 12, 477. (Original manuscript available at http://www.loc.gov/exhibits/jefferson/214.html. Capitalization and punctuation follow that manuscript, not the letter in *Works*.)

89 William C. Kashatus, *Historic Philadelphia: The City, Symbols & Patriots, 1681–1800* (Lanham, MD: Univ. Press of America, 1992), 98.

Chapter 5 • Christian Settlements: Colonizing the Continent, not Building a Nation

1 Ron Swanson, a character played by Nick Offerman on *Parks & Recreation*, in "London Part 1." Directed by Dean Holland. Written by Greg Daniels and Michael Schur. NBC, September 26, 2013.

2 John Adams, *Works of John Adams*, vol. 3.

3 Jefferson, *Notes on the State of Virginia*, query 17.

4 The Declaration of Rights of the Stamp Act Congress, October 19, 1765, in Bruce Frohnen, *The American Republic: Primary Sources*, ed. Bruce Frohnen (Indianapolis: Liberty Fund, 2002).

5 See Fea, *Was America Founded as a Christian Nation?*, 97–100. | **6** Ibid., 79–80.

7 For instance, Gary DeMar has argued that the American "nation begins not in 1776, but more than one hundred fifty years earlier." Gary DeMar, *America's Christian Heritage* (Nashville: Broadman & Holman, 2003), 13. See also DeMar, *God and Government: A Biblical and Historical Study*, vol. 1 (1982; Atlanta: American Vision

Press, 2001), 128 (citing prayer at Continental Congress), 121 ("this lesson will present historical documentation establishing the thesis that America was founded as a Christian nation. Our study will begin with the coming of the Pilgrims in 1620 and continue through"); Eidsmoe, *Christianity and the Constitution*, ch. 1; D. James Kennedy, Jerry Newcombe, *What If America Were a Christian Nation Again?* , 12–36, 207–8; Kirk Cameron, speech at the Family Research Council's Values Voter Summit, September 14, 2012, http://www.c-spanvideo. org/program/308198-1 around 39:15–40:40.

8 See Marsh v. Chambers, 463 U.S. 783 (1983).

9 John Adams to Benjamin Rush, June 12, 1812, in *Old Family Letters: Copied from the Originals for Alexander Biddle*, series A, ed. Alexander Biddle (Philadelphia: J. B. Lippencott, 1892), 392–93.

10 John Adams to Abigail Adams, September 16, 1774, in Adams Family Papers: An Electronic Archive (Massachusetts Historical Society), http://www.masshist.org/digitaladams/archive/doc?id=L17740916ja. Original manuscript from the Adams Family Papers, Mass. Historical Soc. Source of transcription: ed. L. H. Butterfield, *Adams Family Correspondence*, vol. 1 (Cambridge, MA: Belknap Press of Harvard Univ. Press, 1963).

11 Christopher C. Lund, "The Congressional Chaplaincies," *William & Mary Bill of Rights Journal* 17, no. 4 (2009): 1171. See also Chernow, *Alexander Hamilton*, 57 ("Myles Cooper was not the only Anglican clergyman in New York to rail against the Continental Congress. He formed part of a Loyalist literary clique that included Charles Inglis, later rector of Trinity Church, and Samuel Seabury, the Anglican rector of the town of Westchester.")

12 John Adams's September 10, 1774, diary entry in *Works of John Adams*, vol. 2. 377–78.

13 The prayer motion was so unimportant that the Constitutional Convention did not even bring it to a vote; "after several unsuccessful attempts for silently postponing the matter by adjourning," it failed. Franklin himself wrote that "the [Constitutional] Convention, except three or four persons, thought Prayers unnecessary." *The Records of the Federal Convention of 1787*, vol 1., ed. Max Farrand, (New Haven, CT: Yale Univ. Press, 1911), 452 n.15.

14 John Adams to Abigail Adams, September 16, 1774 (emph. added), FO-NA.

15 John Adams to Abigail Adams, October 25, 1777, FO-NA.

16 Edward Duffield Neill, "Rev. Jacob Duché, the First Chaplain of Congress," *Pennsylvania Magazine of History and Biography* 2, no. 1 (1878): 58–73, at 69, http://www.jstor.org/stable/20084327.

17 Rev. Mr. Jacob Duché to General Washington, October 8, 1777, held by the LOC, see http://hdl.loc.gov/loc. rbc/rbpe.04001300. | **18–19** Ibid.

20 Washington to John Hancock, October 16, 1777, FO-NA.

21 Duché to Washington, October 8, 1777.

22 *Journal of the Continental Congress*, vol. 2, 1775, ed. Worthington C. Ford et al. (Washington, DC: LOC, 1904–37): 13 records the next prayer on May 11, 1775. The Articles of Confederation Congress heard sporadic prayers between 1781 and 1789.

23 Brief for the Freedom From Religion Foundation as amicus curiae supporting respondents. Town of Greece v. Galloway, 572 U.S. 565 (2014) (No. 12-696).

24 *Marsh*, 463 U.S. at 791 n.12

25 Elizabeth Fleet, "Madison's 'Detached Memoranda,'" *William & Mary Quarterly* 3, no. 4 (October 1946): 534.

26 *Marsh*, 463 U.S. at 787 n.8.

27 Act of September 22, 1789, ch. 17, 1 Stat. 70.

28 *Marsh*, 791.

29 Stokes, *Church and State in the United States*, vol. 1, 457. | **30** Ibid.

31 Madison to Livingston, July 10, 1822.

32 *Annals of Congress* 950, Sept. 25, 1789. | **33** Ibid.

34 Ibid., "precedents from the late [Continental] Congress."

35 See Andrew L. Seidel, "Wasteful Spending: Congress Pays Clergy $66,000/Hour to Pray," *Freethought Now!*, April 16, 2016, at https://www.patheos.com/blogs/freethoughtnow/wasteful-spending-congress-pays-clergy-66000hour-to-pray/. As of this writing, Congress spends about $800,000 per year on five staffers and two chaplains. The chaplains' sole job under the House and Senate rules is to say the opening prayer; each chaplain's salary is more than $150,000 per year for those prayers. Others at this level on the federal pay schedule include the CFOs of NASA and the EPA, and the CIOs of almost every major federal department and agency. In the House, that prayer duty is farmed out to volunteer guest chaplains 40 percent of the time. The first Congress gave the chaplains $500/year as a salary (about $14,000/year today). Act of September 22, 1789, ch. 17, 1 Stat. 70. § 4.

36 Nancy Isenberg, *White Trash: The 400-Year Untold History of Class in America* (New York: Penguin, 2016), 5–6.

37 See, generally, Fea, *Was America Founded as a Christian Nation?*, 64; Kennedy, Newcombe, *What if America Were a Christian Nation Again?*, 6–11; Dale Summitt, "The United States of America Was Founded As, and Historically Has Been, a Christian Nation," EagleRising.com, January 27, 2015, (since removed); Leon G. Stevens, *One Nation under God: A Factual History of America's Religious Heritage* (New York: Morgan James, 2013), xv ("The Puritans and Pilgrims came to the New World to escape religious persecution in Europe to found a land that they thought could be the new Garden of Eden [and] build a 'new Jerusalem.' Their legacy was one of religious freedom for all. . . . For the past forty-five years our country has taken away the very foundation upon which our country was built. When I heard our national leaders state 'we are not a Christian nation,' I was determined to set the story straight").

38 Jefferson, *Notes on the State of Virginia*, query 17.

39 Madison to Jasper Adams, September 1833 in Daniel L. Dreisbach, *Religion and Politics in the Early Republic: Jasper Adams and the Church-State Debate*, 117–21 (Lexington, KY: Univ. Press of Kentucky, 1996).

40 William Bradford, *History of Plimouth Plantation* (Boston: Wright & Potter, 1898; repr. Carlisle, MA: Applewood Books, 2010), 15. According to Bradford, "seeing them selves thus molested, and that ther was no hope of their continuance ther, by a joynte consente they resolved to goe into the Low Countries, wher they heard was freedome of Religion for all men."

41 Pierre Bayle, *Various Thoughts on the Occasion of a Comet*, trans. and ed. Robert C. Bartlett (Albany, NY: SUNY Press, 2000), § 133, 165.

42 Russell Shorto, *The Island at the Center of the World* (New York: Vintage Books, 2005), 95.

43 Bertrand Russell, *History of Western Philosophy* (New York: Simon & Schuster, 2008), 559.

44 John Mason, *A Brief History of the Pequot War: Especially of the Memorable Taking of Their Fort at Mistick in Connecticut in 1637* (Boston: S. Kneeland & T. Green, 1736), 8, electronic text ed. Paul Royster, http://digital-commons.unl.edu/cgi/viewcontent.cgi?article=1042&context=etas. | 45 Ibid., 9.

46 Pedro Menéndez de Avilés, in *Encyclopædia Britannica* online (2014), http://www.britannica.com/EBchecked/topic/374916/Pedro-Menendez-de-Aviles.

47 Pope Pius V to Menéndez de Avilés, on "The Expulsion of the French Colonists, in 1565, from Florida, on His Return to Spain" in *Historical Collections of Louisiana and Florida . . .* 2nd ser., ed. B. F. French (New York: Albert Mason, 1975), 222–23.

48 Shorto, *Island at the Center of the World*, 45–46.

49 John Adams, "Memorial to Their High Mightinesses, the States-General of the United Provinces of the Low Countries," Leyden, April 19, 1781, in *Works of John Adams*, vol. 7, 400. | 50 Ibid., 3.

51 Shorto, *Island at the Center of the World*, 107.

52 Ibid., 276–77, citing Thomas Dongan, *Report to the Committee of Trade & Plantations (London) on the Province of New York*, February 22, 1687, https://perma.cc/WE3C-7K8N.

53 J. Hector St. John Crèvecoeur, *Letters from an American Farmer*, letter 3, repr., (New York: Fox, Duffield, 1904), 54, http://xroads.virginia.edu/~HYPER/crev/letter03.html. | 54 Ibid., 64.

55 *Religion and Public Life in the Middle Atlantic Region: The Fount of Diversity*, ed. Randall Herbert Balmer and Mark Silk (Lanham, MD: Rowman Altamira, 2006), 74.

56 Shorto, *Island at the Center of the World*, 273.

57 Thomas Paine, *The Rights of Man (Founders' Constitution* online, vol. 5, Amendment I (Religion), doc. 57, quoting *The Life and Works of Thomas Paine*, ed. William M. Van der Weyde, Patriots' ed. (New Rochelle, NY: Thomas Paine National Historical Assoc., 1925).

58 Washington to the Hebrew Congregation in Newport, Rhode Island, August 18, 1790, in *The Papers of George Washington*, Presidential Series, vol. 6, July 1, 1790–November 30, 1790, ed. Mark A. Mastromarino (Charlottesville, VA: Univ. Press of Virginia, 1996), 284–86.

59 Shorto, *Island at the Center of the World*, 85. | 60 Ibid., 274. | 61 Ibid., 275.

62 Ibid., citing Urian Oakes, in Thomas Jefferson Wertenbaker, *The Puritan Oligarchy: The Founding of American Civilization* (New York: Charles Scribner's Sons), 33.

63 Ibid. See also Jeremiah Chaplin, Samuel Dunster, and Edward Swift Dunster, *Life of Henry Dunster: First President of Harvard College* (Boston: James R. Osgood, 1872), 185.

64 This is how Thomas Shepard Jr., a Puritan preacher and contemporary of Cotton, characterized John Cotton's sentiments in *The Bloudy Tenent Washed* in his own work, *Eye-Salve*. See Alan Heimert, *The Puritans in America* (Cambridge, MA: Harvard Univ. Press, 1985), 258.

65 Christian nationalist David Lane uses this language to argue forbible readings and school-organized prayer back in public schools: "America was a Christian nation. The Mayflower Compact declared . . ." Lane, "The Plan to Put Bible, Prayer Back into Schools," WND.com, December 19, 2012, https://perma.cc/N8PD-SPEX.

66 Mayflower Compact, http://avalon.law.yale.edu/17th_century/mayflower.asp.

67 Shorto, *Island at the Center of the World*, 159. See also *Documents Relating to New Netherland, 1624–1626*, vol. 1, trans. A. J. F. Van Laer, (San Marino, CA: Henry E. Huntingdon Library and Art Gallery, 1924), 305. See also Adrian van der Donck, *Remonstrance of New Netherland* (Albany, NY: Weed, Parsons, 1856), 37.

68 See Juliet Haines Mofford, *The Devil Made Me Do It!: Crime and Punishment in Early New England* (Guilford, CT: Globe Pequot, 2011).

69 Madison, "Memorial and Remonstrance," par. 11.

70 Jefferson, *Notes on the State of Virginia*, query 17.

71 Hamilton (as Publius), *Federalist*, no. 1. | 72–74 Ibid.

75 Jefferson, First Inaugural Address, March 4, 1801, *in The Inaugural Addresses of President Thomas Jefferson, 1801 and 1805*, ed. Noble E. Cunningham (Colombia, MO: Univ. of Missouri Press, 2001), 4.

PART II: UNITED STATES V. THE BIBLE

1 Paine to Mr. Erskine, in *The Age of Reason*, in *Paine's Complete Works* (Boston: J. P. Mendum, 1878), 3:179.

2 John Adams, letter to Thomas Brand Hollis, April 5, 1788, FO-NA.

Chapter 6 • Biblical Influence

3 Jefferson to William Short, Monticello, April 13, 1820; original at http://hdl.loc.gov/loc.mss/mtj.mtjbib023789.

4 Paine, *The Age of Reason*, in *The Complete Religious and Theological Works of Thomas Paine*, vol. 1 (New York: Peter Eckler, 1922), footnote at 178.

5 William Shakespeare, *King Henry VI*, Act 5, Scene 6; *Hamlet*, Act 1, Scene 3.

6 Mark Noll, "The Image of the United States as a Biblical Nation, 1776–1865," 39–58, in *The Bible in America*, ed. Nathan Hatch and Mark Noll (Oxford, UK: Oxford Univ. Press, 1982), 43.

7 Abraham Lincoln, "A House Divided Speech," Springfield, IL, June 16, 1858, in *Collected Works of Abraham Lincoln*, vol. 2, ed. Roy P. Basler (New Brunswick, NJ: Rutgers Univ. Press, 1953), 461–69.

8 Henry Herndon, *The History and Personal Recollections of Abraham Lincoln*, ed. Paul M. Angle (1888; New York: World Publishing, 1965), 325. Lincoln read the address to his friend and law partner, Henry Herndon, who retells the story and confirms that Lincoln's biblical allusions were less a product of piety than a desire to communicate. See Mark 3:25, Matt. 12:25, Luke 11:17.

9 John Langdon Kaine, *Lincoln as a Boy Knew Him* (New York: Century, 1913), 5; see also *Recollected Words of Abraham Lincoln*, ed. Don Fehrenbacher and Virginia Fehrenbacher (Palo Alto, CA: Stanford Univ. Press, 1996) 273.

10 Michael Burlingame, *At Lincoln's Side: John Hay's Civil War Correspondence and Selected Writings*, (Carbondale, IL: Southern Illinois Univ. Press, 2006), 137.

11 Stewart, *Nature's God*, 47.

12 US Religious Knowledge Survey, Pew Research Center's Forum on Religion & Public Life, September 28, 2010, https://perma.cc/YV5Y-AT7M, finding that atheists and agnostics outscore every other group on religious knowledge. See also Barna Group survey, "The Books Americans are Reading" (2013) at https://perma.cc/99DX-RPYL showing that only 1 in 5 Americans claim to have read the bible start to finish and that about 40 percent of Christians have not. This number may be skewed heavily by a self-reporting bias.

13 Isaac Asimov was correct when he observed that, "properly read, [the Bible] is the most potent force for atheism ever conceived." Janet Asimov, *Notes for a Memoir: On Isaac Asimov, Life, and Writing* (Amherst, NY: Prometheus, 2006), 58.

14 Herndon, *History and Personal Recollections of Abraham Lincoln*, 325.

15 David Barton remarks on his *WallBuilders Live* radio program on May 4, 2017. See Kyle Mantyla, "David Barton: There is a 'One-to-One Correlation' Between Clauses in the Constitution and the Language in the Bible," Right Wing Watch online, May 4, 2017, https://perma.cc/Y2VS-R4NR.

16 See, e.g., David Barton, *The Myth of Separation* (Aledo, TX: WallBuilder Press, 1989), 196; William Federer, *America's God and Country: Encyclopedia of Quotations* (St. Louis, MO: Amerisearch, 2000), 453; William Graves, "Evolution, the Supreme Court, and the Destruction of Constitutional Jurisprudence," *Regent Univ. Law Rev* 13 (Spring 2001): 513, n. 144.

17 *The New Oxford Annotated Bible with Apocrypha: New Revised Standard Version*, 4th ed. (Oxford, UK: Oxford Univ. Press, 2010), 966.

18 Kurland and Lerner put it best: "Without separation of persons there cannot be a meaningful separation of powers." *The Founders' Constitution*, vol. 1, Major Themes, ed. Philip B. Kurland and Ralph Lerner, (Indianapolis: Liberty Fund, 2000), 312.

19 Jefferson, *Notes on the State of Virginia*, query 13 (1784), in *Works of Thomas Jefferson*, vol. 4, 20.

20 Madison, *Federalist*, no. 47.

21 See Montesquieu, *Spirit of the Laws*, Book 11.

22 Madison, *Federalist*, no. 47.

23 Thomas Jefferson to Francis Adrian Van der Kemp, July 30, 1816, FO-NA. See also *Jefferson's Extracts from the Gospels: The Philosophy of Jesus and The Life and Morals of Jesus*, ed. Dickinson W. Adams (Princeton, NJ: Princeton Univ. Press, 1983), 374–75 at 375.

24 For Jefferson's thoughts on the trinity, see Ibid. For John Adams's thoughts on the trinity, see John Adams to Jefferson, September 14, 1813, FO-NA. For those advancing the argument that the trinity is the source of the separation of powers, see, e.g., Giorgio Agamben, *The Kingdom and the Glory: For a Theological Genealogy of Economy and Government* (Palo Alto, CA: Stanford Univ. Press, 2011); Nadirsyah Hosen and Richard Mohr, *Law and Religion in Public Life: The Contemporary Debate* (Abingdon, UK: Routledge, 2011), 45–49; and Mark Riffle, *The Miracle of Independence*, 237–38 (self-published, Xulon Press, 2009).

25 Franklin to the Federal Convention, September 17, 1787, in *Records of the Federal Convention*, vol. 2, ed. Farrand, 641–43, at 643.

26 John Adams to Richard Price April 19, 1790, in *Works of John Adams*, vol. 9, 564.

27 Alexander Pope, *An Essay on Criticism* (London: W. Lewis, 1711), 30.

28 2 Tim. 3:16. See also Rev. 22:19.

29 John Wesley, sermon, "The Means of Grace," 1872, https://perma.cc/M5P6-WU4Y.

30 More than 200 evangelical Christian leaders, including Christian broadcaster and Coral Ridge Ministries founder D. James Kennedy, signed the Chicago Statement on Biblical Inerrancy (1978) recognizing "the total truth and trustworthiness of Holy Scripture" and affirming its inerrancy. See https://perma.cc/Y3ZM-RAPH.

31 Frank Newport, "One-Third of Americans Believe the Bible Is Literally True," Gallup (May 25, 2007), http://www.gallup.com/poll/27682/onethird-americans-believe-bible-literally-true.aspx; Jeffrey M. Jones, "In U.S., 3 in 10 Say They Take the Bible Literally," Gallup, July 8, 2011, http://www.gallup.com/poll/148427/say-bible-literally.aspx.

32 Donald S. Lutz, "The Relative Influence of European Writers on Late Eighteenth-Century American Political Thought," *American Political Science Review* 78, no. 1 (1984): 189–97, http://www.jstor.org/stable/1961257.

33 Dr. James Hanley, a political science professor at Adrian College and a fellow of the Institute for Social Policy and Understanding. Dr. Hanley did some quick math with Lutz's numbers. His work, "How Much Did the Founders Quote the Bible?," July 9, 2008, on the Uncommon Liberty blog, https://perma.cc/SK5V-Y2T4, was important to

understanding the issues and flaws with Lutz's study. Hanley explains that "the non-sermon publications contained *less than 1 citation each, on average*. In fact because the mean number of citations per non-sermon is less than .5, the likelihood of a non-sermon political publication from the founding era containing a biblical citation is not even random! The political writings were more likely than not to have no biblical references at all."

34 George Barna and David Barton, *U-turn: Restoring America to the Strength of Its Roots* (Lake Mary, FL: Charisma Media, 2014), 44.

35 Hanley, "How Much Did the Founders Quote the Bible?"

36 Lutz, "Relative Influence of European Writers," at 194, table 4; 9 percent of 364 is 32.76 or, rounding up, 33. 364 + 164 = 528. So 33 citations in 528 publications. | 37 Ibid.

38 Despite this damning evidence, Lutz still pays lip service to "the prominence of biblical sources for American political thought" that "was highly influential in our political tradition." Lutz at 192.

39 Franklin was citing Jethro's advice to Moses, but Franklin actually omitted half of Jethro's advice from Exodus 18:21, focusing on the singular secular aspect of it and ignoring the bit about needing men to fear a god. Using religion, again, to reach his political ends, worked; the motion was defeated. *Records of the Federal Convention*, ed. Farrand, vol. 2, page 249. See also Daniel Dreisbach, "The Bible and the Political Culture of the American Founding," in *Faith and the Founders of the American Republic*, ed. Daniel L. Dreisbach and Mark David Hall (Oxford, UK: Oxford Univ. Press, 2014), 144–73 at 159–60.

40 LaHaye, *Faith of Our Founding Fathers*, 196. See https://books.google.com/books?id=UpBp5pu4YJIC.

Chapter 7 • Christian Arrogance and the Golden Rule

1 Robert Ingersoll, "Lectures on the Great Infidels," in *The Lectures of Col. R. G. Ingersoll . . .* , vol. 1. (Chicago: Rhodes & McClure, 1898), 222.

2 William Federer, *Back Fired: A Nation Born for Religious Tolerance No Longer Tolerates Religion* (St. Louis, MO: Amerisearch, 2005), 88 ("Christian leaders in America advocated Jesus' teaching" citing Madison and Morris, among others. Federer also labels the "very concept" as "Christian Forbearance," at 89); Kennedy and New-combe, *What If America Were a Christian Nation Again?*, ch. 6, (noting that "Christianity gave birth to the good type of tolerance, as summarized in Christ's Golden Rule"); Phyllis Schlafly and George Neumayr, *No Higher Power: Obama's War on Religious Freedom* (Washington, DC: Regnery, 2012), 149 (trying to argue using founders' quotes that "America is a Christian nation" and has "a Constitution designed for a people shaped by the Golden Rule and the Ten Commandments").

3 Lev. 19:17–18. | 4 Luke 10:25–37.

5 Rushworth M. Kidder, *How Good People Make Tough Choices: Resolving the Dilemmas of Ethical Living* (New York: Harper, 2003), 157.

6 John Albert Wilson, *The Culture of Ancient Egypt* (Chicago: Univ. of Chicago Press, 1956), 121.

7 David Wiggins, *Ethics: Twelve Lectures on the Philosophy of Morality* (Cambridge, MA: Harvard Univ. Press, 2006), 181.

8 Jeffrey Wattles, *The Golden Rule* (Oxford, UK: Oxford Univ. Press, 1996), 29, citing Diogenes Laërtius, *The Lives and Opinions of Eminent Philosophers*.

9 Laozi, *The Tao Te Ching*, stanza 49, trans. James Legge, in *The Texts of Taoism*, pt. 1 (Oxford, UK: Oxford Univ. Press, 1891), 91.

10 Analects 15.24; Analects 5.12 and 6.30; see Wattles, *Golden Rule*, 15–20.

11 Herodotus, *Histories*; see John P. Meier, *A Marginal Jew: Rethinking the Historical Jesus*, vol. 4 (New Haven, CT: Yale Univ. Press, 2009), 553–57.

12 *Readings in Classical Chinese Philosophy*, 2nd ed., ed. Philip J. Ivanhoe and Bryan W. Van Norden (Indianapolis: Hackett, 2005), 69.

13 Isocrates, *Nicocles or the Cyprians*, 61; or see the positive formulation of the rule in Meier, *Marginal Jew*, 552–57.

14 Plato, *Crito*, 47c; in *The Apology Phaedo, and the Crito of Plato*, vol. 2, trans. Benjamin Jowett (New York: P. F. Collier & Son, 1909), 38; see also Karen Armstrong, *Great Transformation: The Beginning of Our Religious Traditions* (New York: A. A. Knopf, 2006), 309.

15 *Mahabharata*, bk. 13, "Anusasana Parva," § 113, verse 8, trans. Kisari Mohan Ganguli, c. 1883–96, http://www.sacred-texts.com/hin/m13/m13b078.htm.

16 Tim O'Keefe, *Epicurus on Freedom* (Cambridge, UK: Cambridge Univ. Press, 2005), 134.

17 *Talmud*, Hillel, b. Shab. 31a.

18 Luke 6:31.

19 Steven Pinker, *The Better Angels of Our Nature: Why Violence Has Declined* (New York: Penguin, 2011), 182.

20 Peter Singer, *How Are We to Live?: Ethics in an Age of Self-Interest*, (Oxford, UK: Oxford Univ. Press, 1997), 273.

21 John Adams, August 24, 1796, diary entry in *Works of John Adams*, vol. 3, 423.

Chapter 8 • Biblical Obedience or American Freedom?

1 William Penn, *Fruits of Solitude*, pt. 1, in *The Harvard Classics*, vol. 1, pt. 3 (New York: P. F. Collier & Son, 1909–14).

2 Thomas à Kempis, *The Imitation of Christ*, trans. William Benham, bk. 1, ch. 9, in *Harvard Classics*, vol. 7, pt. 2.

3 Edmund Burke, speech on Conciliation with the Colonies, March 22, 1775, *The Works of the Right Honourable Edmund Burke*, vol. 1 (London: Henry G. Bohn, 1854), 464–71.

4 Albert von Ruville, *William Pitt, Earl of Chatham*, vol. 3, trans. H. J. Chaytor (London: William Heinemann, 1907), 317–18.

5 Thomas Paine, "Thoughts on the Present State of American Affairs," *Common Sense* (1776), in *Writings of Thomas Paine*, vol. 1, 1894, 98.

6 Gen. 22:2.

7 Jon Levenson, *The Death and Resurrection of the Beloved Son: The Transformation of Child Sacrifice in Judaism and Christianity* (New Haven, CT: Yale Univ. Press, 1993), 12. Levenson is a good source for a scholarly discussion on child sacrifice in the bible.

8 Gen. 22:9. | 9 Gen. 22:12. | 10 Gen. 22:17–18. | 11 Gen. 19:17, 19:26. | 12 Deut. 10:12 (emph. added). | 13 Rom. 6:16. | 14 2 Thess. 1:7–8 (emph. added). | 15 Isa. 1:19–20.

16 See, e.g., Carol L. Meyers, *Exodus* (Cambridge, UK: Cambridge Univ. Press, 2005), 5–8; Ernest S. Frerichs, Leonard H. Lesko, and William G. Dever, ed., *Exodus: The Egyptian Evidence* (Warsaw, IN: Eisenbrauns: 1997); Thomas E. Levy, Thomas Schneider, and William H. C. Propp, *Israel's Exodus in Transdisciplinary Perspective: Text, Archaeology, Culture, and Geoscience* (Basel, Switz.: Springer International, 2015).

17 Exod. 19:5. | 18 Exod. 24:5–7. | 19 See, e.g., Deut. 13:6–10. Compare Exod. 5:15 and 32:13. | 20 Num. 20:2–13.

21 Franklin Delano Roosevelt, "A Greeting on the Seventy-fourth Anniversary of the Proclamation of Emancipation," in *The Public Papers and Addresses of Franklin D. Roosevelt . . .* (New York: Random House, 1938), 358.

22 Thomas Paine, "Four Letters on Interesting Subjects. Philadelphia: 1776" in *Founders' Constitution* online, vol. 1, ch. 17, doc. 19. Paine was not originally recognized as the author of this pamphlet; see Alfred Owen Aldridge, *Thomas Paine's American Ideology* (Newark, DE: University of Delaware Press, 1984), 219.

Chapter 9 • Crime and Punishment: Biblical Vengeance or American Justice?

1 Thomas Jefferson, "To Edmund Pendleton," August 26, 1776, FO-NA. Source: *Papers of Thomas Jefferson*, vol. 1, 503–6.

2 https://www.amnesty.org/en/latest/news/2018/04/death-penalty-facts-and-figures-2017/.

3 Stephen Fry, Intelligence² Catholic Church Debate, October 19, 2009, an unofficial transcript at http://www.amindatplay.eu/2009/12/02/intelligence%C2%B2-catholic-church-debate-transcript/.

4 Trop v. Dulles, 356 U.S. 86, 100–101 (1958).

5 See also Lev. 20.14; Jer. 49:2; 2 Thess. 1:7–9; Rev. 14:10–11; Rev. 21:8; Ps. 140:10; Jer. 17:27; 1 Kings 14:9–10. | 6 Deut. 22:19. | 7 Exod. 22:18 (KJV).

8 Mark Twain, *Europe and Elsewhere* (New York: Harper & Brothers, 1923), 392.

9 "The terrible Language [of Jonathan Edwards's sinners in the hands of an angry god] frequently frights the little Children and Sets them a Screaming; and that frights their tender Mothers, and Sets them to Screaming, and by Degrees Spreads over a great Part of the Congregation." Charles Chauncy, *Seasonable Thoughts on the State of Religion in New England* (Boston: Rogers & Fowle, 1743), 106; see also 78. See also the story of Phebe Bartlet; a version appears in Jonathan Edwards, *Thoughts on the Revival of Religion in New England, 1740: To Which Is Prefixed a Narrative of the Surprising Work of God in Northampton, Mass. 1735* (New York: American Tract Soc., 1845), 85, but a more accurate breakdown of the story appears in Stewart, *Nature's God*, 50.

10 Billy Hornsby, *The Attractional Church: Growth Through a Refreshing, Relational, and Relevant Church Experience* (New York: Faithwords, 2011), 120.

11 Gen. 37:35, 42:38, 44:29–31. | 12 Ps. 49:15 (if we assume David wrote this psalm). | 13 Acts 2:24–31. | 14 Job 14:13. | 15 Mark 9:43–48. | 16 Matt. 10:28. | 17 Matt. 13:41–42 | 18 Matt. 3:12. | 19 Matt. 18:8–9. | 20 Matt. 25:41. | 21 Matt. 25:46. | 22 Mark 9:49. | 23 Luke 16:23–28. | 24 Jude 1:7. | 25 Rev. 21:8. | 26 Rev. 20:14–15. | 27 Rev. 14:10–11.

28 J. H. Srawley, *The Epistles of St. Ignatius, Bishop of Antioch* (New York: Macmillan, 1919), 48.

29 *Five Books of St. Irenaeus, Bishop of Lyons, Against Heresies*, trans. John Keble (Oxford, UK: James Parker, 1872), 179.

30 Cyprian, *The Treatises of S. Caecilius Cyprian . . .*, trans. Charles Thornton, vol. 3 of *A Library of Fathers of the Holy Catholic Church . . .*, ed. E.B. Pusey et al. (Oxford, UK: John Henry Parker, 1840), 223.

31 Philip Schaff, ed., *St. Augustin's City of God and Christian Doctrine*, vol. 2 of *A Select Library of the Nicene and Post-Nicene Fathers of the Christian Church* (Buffalo, NY: Christian Literature, 1887), 461. | 32 Ibid.

33 All quotes from this sermon are taken from Jonathan Edwards, "Sinners in the Hands of an Angry God (1739)," *Sermons and Discourses, 1738–1742*, Works of Jonathan Edwards Online, vol. 22, 400–418, Jonathan Edwards Ctr. at Yale, 2008, http://edwards.yale.edu/.

34 Edwards, "Sinners in the Hands of an Angry God," *supra*.

35 Thomas Aquinas, *Summa Theologica*, supplement to pt. 3, q. 94, art. 1, vol. 5 (New York: Cosimo, 2013), 2960.

36 Tertullian, *De spectaculis*, trans. T. R. Glover, Gerald H. Rendall, Loeb Classical Lib. 250 (Cambridge, MA: Harvard Univ. Press, 1931), 298.

37 Ezra Stiles, *The Diary of Ezra Stiles*, vol. 3, January 1, 1782–May 6, 1795, ed. Franklin Bowditch Dexter (New York: Charles Scribner Sons, 1901), 345.

38 Voicemail from unidentified female caller left at Freedom From Religion Foundation office phone number on March 24, 2015, at approximately 7:25 p.m. local time. On file with author.

39 *Trop*, 356 U.S. 86, 99 (1958).

40–42 Ibid.

43 According to the Supreme Court, crucifixion and any other method of execution that causes "torture or lingering death" is a cruel and unusual punishment. *In re Kemmler*, 136 U.S. 436, 446 (1890); see also Furman v. Georgia, 408 U.S. 238, 264; Louisiana ex rel Francis v. Resweber, 329 U.S. 459, 463 (1947).

44 Weems v. United States, 217 U.S. 349 (1910).

45 *Trop*, 356 U.S. at 86. | 46 Estelle v. Gamble, 429 U.S. 97, 104 (1976). | 47 Helling v. McKinney, 509 U.S. 25 (1993).

48 Schaff, ed., *St. Augustin's City of God*, vol. 2, 466.
49 Aquinas, *Summa Theologica*, ed. and trans. T. C. O'Brien, vol. 27, (Cambridge, UK: Cambridge Univ. Press), 25.
50 2 Thess. 1:8–9.
51 For an atheist, the death penalty would be a permanent punishment for a finite crime, but not infinite. And the problem is worse if you are a Christian and believe in the eternal soul. Christopher Hitchens, debate with Peter Hitchens, Hauenstein Center, Grand Valley State University, MI, 2008, http://www.youtube.com/watch?v=D-cDbMklrOBI. Under the Eighth Amendment, death is the end of the punishment; for Christians it is only the beginning.
52 Paine to Erskine, 165.

Chapter 10 • Redemption and Original Sin or Personal Responsibility and the Presumption of Innocence?

1 Christopher Hitchens, *God Is Not Great: How Religion Poisons Everything* (New York: Twelve 2007), 209.
2 See Hamilton, *Federalist*, no. 69; also no. 70 ("But in a republic, where every magistrate ought to be personally responsible for his behavior . . .").
3 Seth Stephens-Davidowitz, *Everybody Lies: Big Data, New Data, and What the Internet Can Tell Us About Who We Really Are* (New York: Dey Street Books, 2017), 260.
4 Judg. 11:30–40. | 5 Num. 25:4. | 6 See, e.g., Gen. 8:20–21, Lev. 23:12–18. | 7 Gen. 7:2, 8:20. | 8 1 Pet. 1:19.
9 Andrew L. Seidel, "Chickens, goats, Jesus and the immorality of vicarious redemption," *Freethought Now!*, October 2, 2014, www.patheos.com/blogs/freethoughtnow/chickens-goats-jesus/.
10 "Kapparah." In *Jewish Encyclopedia*, vol. 7 (New York: Funk & Wagnalls, 1906), 435–36.
11 See, e.g., Todd Venezia, "Fowl Ritual," *New York Post*, August 31, 2007.
12 John Adams claimed to have read all of Bolingbroke's works five times, while Jefferson copied 10,000 of Bolingbroke's words into his personal notebook, known as his *Literary Commonplace Book*—six times as much as from any other author and 40 percent of the whole volume. See Adams's letter to Jefferson, December 25, 1813, in *The Works of John Adams*, vol. 10, 82. For Jefferson, see the LOC, "Bolingbroke's Influence on Thomas Jefferson," http://www.loc.gov/exhibits/religion/rel02.html#obj060.
13 Viscount Henry St. John Bolingbroke, *The Work of Lord Bolingbroke . . .*, vol. 4 (Philadelphia: Carey and Hart, 1841), 301. | 14 Ibid.
15 See, e.g., Alexander Volokh, "*n* Guilty Men," 146 *Univ. of Pennsylvania. Law Review* 146, no 1. (November 1997): 173.
16 Coffin v. United States, 156 U.S. 432, 455 (1895).
17 See, e.g., Thomas Bokenkotter, *A Concise History of the Catholic Church*, rev. ed., (New York: Crown, 2007), 132.
18 *Coffin*, 156 U.S. at 453–4.
19 Benjamin Franklin to Benjamin Vaughan, March 14, 1785, in *Works of Benjamin Franklin*, vol. 11, ed. J. Bigelow, 1904, 13. Franklin may have been quoting Blackstone here, who wrote something nearly identical, though his ratio was 10 to 1. See Scott Christianson, *Innocent: Inside Wrongful Conviction Cases* (New York: NYU Press, 2004), 17. Maimonides put the ratio even higher, at 1,000 to 1, though it seems irrelevant compared to the verses listed. For more, see Volokh, "*n* Guilty Men," 173.
20 Different translations render this differently. Voltaire, *Zadig* (1747) in *Voltaire's Romances* (New York: Peter Eckler, 1885), 35–103 at 53.
21 The Supreme Court, in *Coffin*, discussed the origins of the concept: "Greenleaf traces this presumption to Deuteronomy, and quotes *Mascardus De Probationibus* to show that it was substantially embodied in the laws of Sparta and Athens. Whether Greenleaf is correct or not in this view, there can be no question that the Roman law was pervaded with the results of this maxim." Simon Greenleaf himself mentions the bible in a footnote *after* attributing the maxim to Lord Hale; he mentions Greek and Roman law too. Simon Greenleaf, *A Treatise on the Law of Evidence*, vol. 3, note 1 (New York: Little, Brown, 1853), 31. Several others have half-heartedly attempted to tie this maxim to the bible. See, e.g., Eric M. Kubilus, "Innocent until Proven (Hypothetically) Guilty: The Third Circuit Condones the Use of Guilt-Assuming Hypotheticals in *United States v. Kellogg*," *Villanova Law Review* 53, iss. 4 (2008): 665, http://digitalcommons.law.villanova.edu/vlr/vol53/iss4/2; Volokh, aside, "*n* Guilty Men," 146. None have done so convincingly.
22 Deut. 1:39.

Chapter 11 • The American Experiment: Religious Faith or Reason?

1 Adams, "Defence of the Constitutions of Government," in *Works of John Adams*, vol. 4, 292.
2 Matt. 17:20. | 3 Matt. 21:21.
4 Michael Novak, "Faith and the American Founding: Illustrating Religion's Influence," Heritage Foundation, November 6, 2006, https://perma.cc/2Y6E-DD8M.
5 Heb. 11:1 (KJV).
6 Dr. Peter Boghossian, Lecture, "Faith: Pretending to Know Things You Don't Know," May 6, 2012, https://www.youtube.com/watch?v=qp4WUFXvCFQ.
7 Clinton Rossiter, *Seedtime of the Republic* (New York: Harcourt, Brace, 1953), 440.
8 Martin Luther, Last Sermon in Wittenberg . . . Second Sunday in Epiphany, January 17, 1546, in *Dr. Martin Luthers Werke: Kritische Gesamtausgabe*, vol. 51 (Weimar: Hermann Böhlaus Nachfolger, 1914), 126.
9 Luther, *Table Talk*, 353, trans. W. Hazlitt (London: David Bogue, 1848), 164.
10 Thomas Jefferson, *Notes on the State of Virginia*, query 17, in *Works of Thomas Jefferson*, vol. 4, 294. This section is often misread by people unfamiliar with Jefferson's religious beliefs and with his work editing the supernatural

out of the bible. In this work, Jefferson also wrote that "reason and free inquiry are the only effectual agents against error. Give a loose to them, they will support the true religion by bringing every false one to their tribunal, to the test of their investigation. They are the natural enemies of error, and of error only." Ibid., 293. Other passages on the history of Christianity in Rome in this work may even sound pro-Christian nationalist, but they are really a call to reason and free inquiry—a call to test all our beliefs in light of facts.

11 Adams, "Defence of the Constitutions of Government," in *Works of John Adams*, vol. 4, 292.

12 See generally Dray, *Stealing God's Thunder*; Walter Isaacson, *Benjamin Franklin: An American Life* (New York: Simon & Schuster, 2004); Hal Marcovitz, *Benjamin Franklin: Scientist, Inventor, Printer, and Statesman* (New York: Chelsea House, 2009). See also http://www.ushistory.org/franklin/info/inventions.htm.

13 See, e.g., Jefferson to William Drayton, January 13, 1788, FO-NA. [Original source: *Papers of Thomas Jefferson*, vol. 12, 507–8.]; *Monticello as Experiment: "To Try All Things,"* permanent exhibit, https://perma.cc/V73N-5CZQ.

14 See generally I. Bernard Cohen, *Science and the Founding Fathers: Science in the Political Thought of Thomas Jefferson, Benjamin Franklin, John Adams & James Madison* (New York: W. W. Norton, 1997), 65–72, 293; Tom Shachtman, *Gentlemen Scientists and Revolutionaries: The Founding Fathers in the Age of Enlightenment* (New York: Palgrave Macmillan, 2014).

15 Chernow, *Washington*, ch. 13.

16 Alan M. Fusonie and Donna Jean Fusonie, *George Washington: Pioneer Farmer* (Mount Vernon, VA: Mount Vernon Ladies' Assoc., 1998).

17 Office of the Surgeon General, Borden Institute, and the Department of Defense, *Textbooks of Military Medicine: Recruit Medicine,* ed. Col. Martha K. Lenart et al. (Washington, DC: Government Printing Office), 208–9; Shachtman, *Gentlemen Scientists*; Elizabeth A. Fenn, *Pox Americana: The Great Smallpox Epidemic of 1775–82* (New York: Macmillan, 2002).

18 Madison to Jefferson, April 27, 1785, in *Writings of James Madison*, vol. 2. 134–35; see also Alec Foege, *The Tinkerers: The Amateurs, DIYers, and Inventors Who Make America Great* (New York: Basic Books, 2013), 19.

19 Madison to Jefferson, ibid.; Gaillard Hunt, *The Life of James Madison* (New York: Doubleday, Page, 1902), 97.

20 See generally Chernow, *Alexander Hamilton*.

21 Jefferson to Dr. Joseph Willard, March 24, 1789, in *The Writings of Thomas Jefferson*, vol. 7, ed. Andrew Lipscomb and Albert Burgh (Washington, DC: Thomas Jefferson Memorial Assoc., 1903), 327–28. See generally Moncure Daniel Conway and William Cobbett, *The Life of Thomas Paine: With a History of His Literary, Political, and Religious Career in America, France, and England*, vol. 1 (New York: G.P. Putnam's 1892), 241.

22 Shachtman, *Gentlemen Scientists*, xi, 131.

23 Ibid., 40–47, 71–89, 130–42.

24 US Const. art. 1, § 8, cl. 8.

25 Hamilton, *Federalist*, no. 9.

26 Madison to John G. Jackson, December 27, 1821, in *Writings of James Madison*, vol. 9, 76.

27 "This constitution was formed when we were new and unexperienced in the science of government." Thomas Jefferson, *Notes on the State of Virginia*, query 13, in *Works of Thomas Jefferson*, vol. 4, 17.

28 "Politicks are the divine science, after all. . . . The divine science of politicks is at length in Europe reduced to a mechanical system." John Adams to James Warren, June 17, 1782, in *The Adams Papers: Papers of John Adams*, ed. Robert Joseph Taylor (Cambridge, MA: Belknap Press of Harvard Univ. Press, 2006), vol. 13, 128. See also Adams, "Against a Government in a Single Assembly," in *A Defence of the Constitutions of Government*, 299. ("They all had experience in public affairs, and ample information respecting the nature of man, the necessities of society, and the science of government.")

29 John Adams to Mercy Otis Warren, January 8, 1776, in *Adams Papers*, vol. 3, 1979, 397–99.

30 John Adams to Abigail Adams, May 12, 1780, Adams Family Papers: An Electronic Archive.

31 Madison to John G. Jackson, December 27, 1821, in *Writings of James Madison*, vol. 9, 72. ("In the eyes of all the best friends of liberty a crisis had arrived which was to decide whether the Amn. [American] Experiment was to be a blessing to the world, or to blast forever the hopes which the republican cause had inspired.")

32 Franklin to Jonathan Shipley, February 24, 1786, in *Works of Benjamin Franklin*, vol. 11, 232–33.

33 Franklin, who proposed the prayer, wrote in his notes for that day: "The Convention, except three or four persons, thought Prayers unnecessary." *Records of the Federal Convention of 1787*, ed. Farrand, vol. 1, 452, n. 15.

34 John Adams to Richard Price April 19, 1790, FO-NA ("The Constitution is but an experiment, and must and will be altered"); John Adams to Jefferson, July 16, 1814, FO-NA ("The vast variety of experiments which have been made of the constitutions in America, in France, [etc.] can never be forgotten.")

35 John Adams to the Comte de Sarsfield, February 3, 1786, in *Works of John Adams*, vol. 9, 546. | 36 Ibid.

37 John Adams, Inaugural Address, March 4, 1797, in *Works of John Adams*, vol. 9, 106.

38 Jefferson, Inaugural Address, March 4, 1801, in *Works of Thomas Jefferson*, vol. 9, 196.

39 Madison to unknown recipient, March 1836, in *Writings of James Madison*, vol. 9, 607–10 at 610.

40 See, e.g., Hamilton and Madison, *Federalist*, no. 18 ("Very different, nevertheless, was the experiment [of the Greek Amphictyonic council] from the theory. . . . It is much to be regretted that such imperfect monuments remain of this curious political fabric. Could its interior structure and regular operation be ascertained, it is probable that more light would be thrown by it on the science of federal government, than by any of the like experiments with which we are acquainted"); Madison, *Federalist*, no. 14 ("But why is the experiment of an extended republic to be rejected, merely because it may comprise what is new?"); Hamilton, *Federalist*, no. 16 ("The tendency of the principle of legislation for States, or communities, in their political capacities, as it has

been exemplified by the experiment we have made of it, is equally attested by the events which have befallen all other governments of the confederate kind"); Madison, *Federalist*, no. 37.

41 Madison, *Federalist*, no. 39.

42 George Mason to George Mason Jr., June 1, 1787, Philadelphia in *Records of the Federal Convention*, ed. Farrand, vol. 3, 32–33. | 43 Ibid., 33.

Chapter 12 • A Monarchy and "the morrow" or a Republic and "our posterity"

1 *Records of the Federal Convention*, ed. Farrand, vol. 3, 85.

2 Ibid., vol. 2, 125. | 3 Ibid., vol. 1, 413. | 4 Ibid., 422, 431. | 5 Ibid., vol. 2, 452.

6 Matt. 6:26–6:34 (KJV). | 7 Matt. 24:34. | 8 Matt. 16:28. | 9 Matt. 10:23.

10 See, e.g., Rev. 1:1–2, 22:12, 22:20, which are not cited for the truth of the proposition but to show that Christians writing during the first century believed the claims.

11 Pew Research Center, "Life in 2050: Amazing Science, Familiar Threats," June 22, 2010, 10, https://perma.cc/KP39-ST8D. Another international survey was completed by Ipsos Global Public Affairs, "One in Seven (14%) Global Citizens Believe End of the World is Coming in Their Lifetime," May 1, 2012, https://perma.cc/64QG-2KK8.

12 Anthony Ashley Cooper, 3rd Earl of Shaftesbury, *Characteristics of Men, Manners, Opinions, Times*, ed. Lawrence Klein (Cambridge, UK: Cambridge Univ. Press, 1999), 46–47.

13 Harper Lee, *To Kill a Mockingbird* (1960; repr. ed. New York: Grand Central Publishing, 1988), 61.

14 Eccles. 8:2. | 15 Gen. 17:6; 35:11. | 16 Deut. 17:14–15. | 17 1 Tim. 6:15. | 18 Luke 1:32. | 19 1 Cor. 15:24. | 20 1 Sam. 8:19–22. | 21 See, e.g., 1 Macc. 1:10–15.

22 Thomas Jefferson, *Notes on the State of Virginia*, query 14 (1785) in *Works of Thomas Jefferson*, vol. 4, 270. Jefferson was in Paris during the Convention, though he and Madison communicated about the proceedings extensively.

23 Arthur Henry Walker, *A Primer of Greek Constitutional History* (Oxford, UK: B. H. Blackwell, 1902), 11.

24 BibleGateway.com offers excellent resources for searching most English language versions of the bible.

25 Walker, *Primer of Greek Constitutional History*, 11.

26 John Adams, "Dissertation on the Canon and Feudal Law," in *Works of John Adams*, vol. 3, 445.

27 In fact, Adams was pretty upset with religion and the power it had over the centuries. He vilified tyrants and despots of all kinds, including religious ones. In a July 9, 1813, letter to Jefferson in *Works of John Adams*, vol. 10, 50–51, he summed it up: "If you ask my opinion, who has committed all the havoc? I will answer you candidly. Ecclesiastical and imperial despotisms have done it to conceal their frauds."

28 *Records of the Federal Convention*, ed. Farrand, vol. 3, 85.

29 In Lincoln's Gettysburg Address. As discussed in n. 62 to chapter 3, Lincoln may have been borrowing from Wycliffe's first English translation of the bible, or possibly from Theodore Parker, an abolitionist minister. As discussed in chapter 3, using religious language does not necessarily indicate religious influence.

30 Madison, *Federalist*, no. 19.

31 "Sparta, Athens, Rome, and Carthage, were all republics; two of them, Athens and Carthage, of the commercial kind." Hamilton, *Federalist*, no. 6; see also Madison, *Federalist*, nos. 18, 63 (several references to Sparta, and "Sparta, Rome, and Carthage").

32 "Minos, we learn, was the primitive founder of the government of Crete . . . Theseus first, and after him Draco and Solon, instituted the government of Athens. Lycurgus was the lawgiver of Sparta. The foundation of the original government of Rome was laid by Romulus; and the work completed by two of his elective successors, Numa, and Tullus Hostilius." Madison, *Federalist*, no. 38

33 Catherine Drinker Bowen, *Miracle at Philadelphia: The Story of the Constitutional Convention, May to September 1787* (Boston: Little, Brown, 1966, 1986 ed. with Warren Burger foreword), 143; see also Mathew R. Sgan, *The Boston Book of Sports: From Puritans to Professionals* (Bloomington, IN: Xlibris, 2009), 9.

34 Thomas Cuming Hall, *The Religious Background of American Culture* (Boston: Little, Brown, 1930), 184–86.

35 Ruth Hurmence Green, in ed. Annie Laurie Gaylor, *Women without Superstition: No Gods—No Masters* (Madison, WI: Freedom From Religion Foundation, 1997), 469.

PART III: THE TEN COMMANDMENTS V. THE CONSTITUTION

1 Robert Ingersoll, *About the Holy Bible: A Lecture* (New York: C. P. Farrell, 1894), 17–18.

2 Cato's letter no. 31, May 27, 1721, "Considerations on the Weakness and Inconsistencies of human Nature," in John Trenchard and Thomas Gordon, *Cato's Letters, or Essays on Liberty, Civil and Religious, and Other Important Subjects*, ed. and ann. Ronald Hamowy (Indianapolis: Liberty Fund, 1995), vol. 1.

3 Blaise Pascal, *Pensées* (1670) (New York: E. P. Dutton, 1958), polemical fragment #894, 265.

Chapter 13 • Which Ten?

4 Mel Brooks, *History of the World: Part I*, directed by Mel Brooks (1981; Los Angeles: Brooksfilms).

5 Rick Perry, interview by Jennifer Wishon, Christian Broadcasting Network, posted August 5, 2011, https://goo.gl/5ocEgB.

6 Gen. 9:21–27.

7 I am not entirely satisfied that this is an original Mencken. But see H. L. Mencken, *A Little Book in C Major*, pt. 2 § 20 (New York: John Lane, 1916), 33.

8 The commandments are orally given to Moses in Exod. 20:2–17; Moses communicates them to the Israelites and

assembles the stone tablets in 24:3–8. The stone is inscribed in 31:18.

9 Three months, Exod. 19:1; manna, Exod. 16; water from rocks, Exod. 17; camped, Exod. 19:2; climbing and hearing a voice, Exod. 19:3.

10 Exod. 32:16 ("The tablets were the work of God, and the writing was the writing of God").

11 Exod. 32:19 ("Moses' anger burned hot, and he threw the tablets from his hands and broke them at the foot of the mountain"). | 12 Exod. 32:27. | 13 Exod. 32:28. | 14 Exod. 32:27. | 15 Exod. 34:1; Exod. 34:10–28. | 16–17 Exod. 34:10–11. | 18 Exod. 34:19–20.

19 The NRSV Bible does not capitalize Sabbath and, in recognition of its accuracy, I follow suit.

20 Exod. 34:26. | 21 Exod. 34:1. | 22 Deut. 5:6–21. | 23 Deut. 27:1–2, 10–26. | 24 Deut. 27:15–16. | 25 Deut. 27:20–23.

26 Chart adapted from *New Oxford Annotated Bible*, 110 and 260.

27 Deut. 27:23. | 28 *New Oxford Annotated Bible*, 110, n. for Exod. 20:1–17. | 29 Exod. 20:7. | 30 Exod. 20:7 (KJV). | 31 Exod. 20:4. | 32 Exod. 20:4 (KJV). | 33 Exod. 20:13 (KJV) | 34 E.g., Exod. 20:13 (NIV).

35 Diarmaid MacCulloch, *Christianity: The First Three Thousand Years* (New York: Viking, 2009), 442–56.

36 Catholic Canon Law, Can. 752, http://www.vatican.va/archive/ENG1104/_P2H.HTM#G8.

37 MacCulloch, *Christianity*, 545. | 38 Ibid.

39 Bart D. Ehrman, *Jesus, Interrupted: Revealing the Hidden Contradictions in the Bible (and Why We Don't Know About Them)* (New York: HarperCollins, 2009), 74. | 40 Ibid.

41 Madison, "Memorial and Remonstrance," 83.

42 Jefferson, *Notes on the State of Virginia*, query 17, in *Works of Thomas Jefferson*, vol. 4, 295.

43 Chart adapted from the *New Oxford Annotated Bible* at 110 and 260.

44 MacCulloch, *Christianity*, 442–45.

45 Deut. 17:19–20. | 46 Deut. 28:58–59. | 47 Deut. 32:46. | 48 Deut. 16:22. | 49 Lev. 19:31. | 50 Deut. 18:10. | 51 Lev. 19:28. | 52 Lev. 19:19. | 53 Lev 19:27; Det. 22:11. | 54 Matt. 5:17–19 (emph. added).

55 See Edward Countryman, "In Texas Textbooks, Moses Is a Founding Father," *Daily Beast*, September 22, 2014, https://perma.cc/348D-754V. Article based on his report: "Complying with, Getting Around, and Bypassing the TEKS History Standards: A Review of Proposed Texas, U.S. and World History Textbooks in Texas," commissioned by the Texas Freedom Network Educ. Fund, September 2014, https://goo.gl/zYmnqQ.

56 Circuit Court Judge of Covington County Ashley McKathan. See "Judge's Robe Bears Ten Commandments," Fox News, December 15, 2004, https://www.foxnews.com/story/judges-robe-bears-ten-commandments.

57 James Fenton, "Federal Judge Rules Ten Commandments monument in front of Bloomfield City Hall violates First Amendment," *Farmington Daily Times* (NM), August 4, 2014, https://perma.cc/8WT2-NUWM.

58 Hannah Grover, "N.M. city may go online to help raise $700K for legal fees in Ten Commandments case," *Farmington Daily Times* (NM) (February 15, 2018), https://www.usatoday.com/story/news/nation-now/2018/02/15/legal-fees-ten-commandments-case/343987002/.

59 See, e.g., William J. Federer, *The Ten Commandments & Their Influence on American Law: A Study in History* (Fort Myers, FL: Amerisearch, 2002); Eidsmoe, *Christianity and the Constitution*, discussing "covenant theology" and influence of commandments; Freethought Society of Greater Philadelphia v. Chester County, 334 F.3d 247, 267-8 (3rd. Cir. 2003) ("The Ten Commandments have an independent secular meaning in our society because they are regarded as a significant basis of American law and the American polity, including the prohibitions against murder and blasphemy") and collecting precedent (see, e.g., Bertera's Hopewell Foodland, Inc. v. Masters, 428 Pa. 20, 236 A.2d 197, 200-01 (1967) (noting that the Sunday closing laws "trace an ancestry back to the Ten Commandments fulminated from the smoking top of Mt. Sinai. . . . This divine pronouncement became part of the Common Law") Anderson v. Maddox, 65 So.2d 299, 301-302 (Fla.1953) ("Thou shalt not steal' and 'thou shalt not bear false witness' are just as new as they were when Moses brought them down from the Mountain") (Terrell, J., concurring specially); State v. Gamble Skogmo, Inc., 144 N.W.2d 749, 768 (N.D.1966) ("Thus, for temporal purposes, murder is illegal. And the fact that this agrees with the dictates of the Judaeo-Christian religions while it may disagree with others does not invalidate the regulation. So too with the questions of adultery and polygamy. The same could be said of theft, fraud, etc. because those offenses were also proscribed in the Decalogue") (internal citations omitted).

60 *McCreary*, 545 U.S. 844, n. 12.

61 Bosley Crowther, "The Good Book Is a Great Script," *New York Times Magazine*, December 31, 1961, 10.

62 Ibid.

63 2012 marked the first year that Protestants were not the majority at 48 percent of the population. Pew Research Center, "'Nones' on the Rise: One-in-Five Adults Have No Religious Affiliation," October 9, 2012, http://www.pewforum.org/2012/10/09/nones-on-the-rise/.

Chapter 14 • The Threat Display: The First Commandment

1 Pope Pius IX, *Syllabus of Errors* encyclical (December 8, 1864), in *Religion from Tolstoy to Camus*, ed. Walter Kaufmann (1961; repr. ed. New Brunswick, NJ: Transaction, 1961), 163; see also https://perma.cc/D2V6-9DR7.

2 Madison, "Memorial and Remonstrance," ¶ 4.

3 William Jennings Bryan, *The First Commandment* (New York: Fleming H. Revell, 1917), 7.

4 US Const. amend. I.

5 Justice Thomas Clark, speech at the Commonwealth Club, San Francisco, August 3, 1962, in *Chicago Daily Law Bulletin* (August 17, 1962), 3. See also Bernard Schwartz, *Super Chief: Earl Warren and His Supreme Court—A*

Judicial Biography (New York: New York Univ. Press, 1983), 441–42.

6 John Locke, *A Letter Concerning Toleration and Other Writings*, ed. and with an introduction by Mark Goldie, 22–23 (Indianapolis: Liberty Fund, 2010). | 7 Ibid.

8 Robert G. Ingersoll, *Trial of C. B. Reynolds for Blasphemy, at Morristown, N.J., May 1877: Defence* (New York: C. P. Farrell, 1888).

9 Thomas Fitzsimmons of Pennsylvania being the other.

10 *Annals of Congress*, House of Representatives, 1st Congress, 1st Sess., August 15, 1789, 757.

11 "Since the Reformation, when or where has existed a Protestant or dissenting sect who would tolerate A FREE INQUIRY? The blackest billingsgate, the most ungentlemanly insolence, the most yahooish brutality is patiently endured, countenanced, propagated, and applauded. But touch a solemn truth in collision with a dogma of a sect, though capable of the clearest proof, and you will soon find you have disturbed a nest, and the hornets will swarm about your legs and hands, and fly into your face and eyes" (emph. in orig.), John Adams, "Discourses on Davila: A Series of Papers on Political History," *Gazette of the United States*, no. 31 (1790–91) in *Works of John Adams*, vol, 6, 517.

12 Madison, "Memorial and Remonstrance," ¶ 11. The "torrents of blood" language was probably influenced by theist and encyclopedist Baron D'Holbach, who 13 years earlier wrote, "In all parts of our globe, fanatics have cut each other's throats, publicly burnt each other, committed without a scruple and even as a duty, the greatest crimes, and shed torrents of blood. For what?" in his preface to *Le bons-sens, ou idées naturelles opposées aux idées surnaturelles* (1772). See Paul Henri Thiry Baron d'Holbach, *Good Sense, or, Natural Ideas Opposed to Supernatural . . .* (New York: Wright and Owen, 1831), viii.

13 Jefferson to Danbury Baptist Assoc., January 1, 1802.

14 Exod. 19:21–25. In verse 24 there's a command that Aaron ascend the mountain as well, but it's not clear if this is followed and does little to add veracity to the tale—surely Aaron's account would back up his brother's.

15 Paine, *Age of Reason*, 8.

16 Christopher Hitchens, "The New Commandments," *Vanity Fair*, March 4, 2010.

17 "Monotheism." In *Jewish Encyclopedia*, vol. 8, 659–61.

18–19 Ibid. Special thanks to Joseph Lewis, *The Ten Commandments* (New York: Freethought Press Association, 1946), 174–75, for pointing me to the *Jewish Encyclopedia* and its riches.

20 US Const. art. VI (emph. added).

21 Reynolds v. United States, 98 U.S. 145, 166–67 (1878).

22 Madison, *Federalist*, no. 49. | 23 Hamilton, *Federalist*, no. 22 (emph. in orig.).

24 Franklin, remarks during the Constitutional Convention, July 25, 1787, in *Records of the Federal Convention*, vol. 2., ed. Farrand, 120 (emph. in orig.).

25 James Monroe, "Views of the President of the United States on the Subject of Internal Improvements" (May 4, 1822), in *Founders' Constitution* online, vol. 2, Preamble, doc. 20, http://press-pubs.uchicago.edu/founders/documents/preambles20.html.

26 Adams, "Defence of the Constitutions of Government," in *Works of John Adams*, vol. 4, 293. | 27 Ibid., 292.

28 "We formed our Constitution without any acknowledgement of GOD; without any recognition of his mercies to us, as a people, of his government, or even of his existence. The Convention, by which it was formed, never asked, even once, his direction, or his blessing upon their labours. Thus we commenced our national existence under the present system, without GOD." Timothy Dwight, *A Discourse in Two Parts: Delivered July 23, 1812 . . .* (New Haven, CT: Howe and Deforest), 46.

29 US Const. art. VI, § 3. | 30 US Const. amend. I. | 31 Ibid.

32 Seidel, "Dating God," 129–51.

33 Stone, *Perilous Times*, 7.

34 Pope Leo XIII, *On the Nature of Human Liberty* encyclical (June 20, 1888), https://perma.cc/AH87-C5TC.

Chapter 15 • Punishing the Innocent: The Second Commandment

1 Exod. 20:4 (KJV, which interprets the term *idol* as "graven image.")

2 John Calvin, *Institutes of the Christian Religion*, bk. 2, ch. 8, § 20, trans. Henry Beveridge (Peabody, MA: Hendrickson, 2008), 245.

3 John Hodgson's shorthand notes, *The Trial of William Wemms, James Hartegan, William M'Cauley, Hugh White, Matthew Killroy, William Warren, John Carrol, and Hugh Montgomery . . . for the Murder of Crispus Attucks, Samuel Gray, Samuel Maverick, James Caldwell, and Patrick Carr . . .* (Boston: J. Fleming, 1770), 149.

4 Smith v. People of the State of California, 361 U.S. 147 (1959).

5 Joseph Burstyn, Inc. v. Wilson, 343 U.S. 495, 504–5 (1952).

6 The two 1,500-year-old monumental statues were carved into a cliff on the Silk Road and were listed as a UNESCO World Heritage site. According to the *New York Times*, the Taliban "decided that the statues were idolatrous and should be obliterated." Barbara Crossette, "Taliban Explains Buddha Demolition," *New York Times*, March 19, 2001. See also W. L. Rathje, "Why the Taliban Are Destroying Buddhas," *USA Today*, March 22, 2001.

7 Origen, *Contra Celsum*, bk. V7, ch. 65, http://www.newadvent.org/fathers/04167.htm.

8 Ibid., ch. 62; See, e.g., Tacitus, *The Histories*, bk 5, trans. Alfred J. Church and William J. Brodribb (London: Macmillan, 1905), 195.

9 MacCulloch, *Christianity*, 442–56. | 10 Ibid., 443–44.

11 The full text of the Canon is available in Henry R. Percival, *The Seven Ecumenical Councils of the Undivided*

Church . . ., vol. 14 in *A Select Library of the Nicene and Post-Nicene Fathers*, 2nd ser., ed. Philip Schaff and Henry Wace (Grand Rapids, MI: William B. Eerdmans, 1979), 401, https://perma.cc/6DVK-4B93.

12 John Calvin, "On Suffering Persecution," *The World's Greatest Orations*, vol. 7, ed. William Jennings Bryan and Francis W. Halsey (New York: Funk & Wagnalls, 1906).

13 *New Oxford Annotated Bible*, 1427. | 14 Ibid., 1361.

15 Wisd. of Sol., 14:25–27. | 16 Ibid., 14:12.

17 Franklin D. Roosevelt, Address at the Dedication of the National Gallery of Art, March 17, 1941, https://www.presidency.ucsb.edu/documents/address-the-dedication-the-national-gallery-art. | 18 Ibid. (emph. added).

19 Wisd. of Sol., 14:25.

20 US Const. art. III, § 3.

21 Korematsu v. United States, 323 U.S. 214, 243 (1944) (Jackson, J. dissenting).

22 Madison, *Federalist*, no. 43.

23 Story, *Commentaries on the Constitution*, 705.

24 *Korematsu*, 323 U.S (Jackson, J. dissenting). | 25 Ibid., (Murphy, J. dissenting).

26 Gen. 19, 19:8. | 27 Gen. 19:29.

Chapter 16 • Suppressed Speech: The Third Commandment

1 George Orwell, "Politics and the English Language," *Horizon*, no. 76 (April 1946): 252–65 at 262, http://www.unz.org/Pub/Horizon-1946apr-00252.

2 J. K. Rowling, *Harry Potter and the Sorcerer's Stone* (New York: Scholastic, 1999), 298.

3 Exod. 6:3. | 4 Lev. 24:10–16.

5 "Blasphemy." In *Jewish Encyclopedia*, vol. 3, 237.

6 Mark 3:28–29. See also Matt. 12:31–32, Luke 12:10. | 7 2 Sam. 12:14–18.

8 Aquinas, *Summa Theologica*, 2nd Pt. of the 2nd Pt., q. 13, art. 1, http://www.newadvent.org/summa/3013.htm.

9 James Wilson, "A Charge Delivered to the Grand Jury in the Circuit Court of the United States, for the District of Virginia, in May, 1791," in *Collected Works of James Wilson*, vol. 1, ed. Kermit L. Hall and Mark David Hall (Indianapolis: Liberty Fund, 2007), 326, http://oll.libertyfund.org/titles/2072#Wilson_4140_1597.

10 Wilson, "Of Crimes Immediately against the Community," in *Collected Works of James Wilson*, vol. 2, 1149, http://oll.libertyfund.org/titles/2074#Wilson_4141_1600.

11 Madison, *Federalist*, no. 37.

12 Ambrose Bierce, "Decalogue" entry, in *The Devil's Dictionary, Tales, and Memoirs* (New York: Library of America, 2011).

13 Lewis, *Ten Commandments*, 238. Lewis wrote, "Do you want me to tell you why appeals in the name of God are uttered in vain? Do you want me to tell you why prayers are not answered? I will tell you. *There is no such thing as a God who answers the prayers of man.* The sooner we come to that realization, the sooner the human race becomes cognizant of this fact, the sooner will man set about to accomplish for himself all that he has appealed to God for in vain. 'Thou shalt not take the name of the Lord thy God in vain. . . .' Thou canst not take the name of God in any other way" (emph. in orig.).

14 Musser v. Utah, 333 U.S. 95, 97 (1948).

15 Papachristou v. City of Jacksonville, 405 U.S. 156 (1972).

16 John Adams to Jefferson, January 23, 1825, in *Works of John Adams*, vol. 10, 415–16.

17 See, e.g., Ben Hubbard, "Saudis Begin Public Caning to Punish a Blogger," *New York Times*, January 9, 2015, telling the story of Raif Badawi.

18 For more on Raif Badawi, see his book: *1000 Lashes: Because I Say What I Think*, trans. Constantin Schreiber (Vancouver, CAN: Greystone Books, 2015). And his wife's book, Ensef Haider and Andrea Hoffman, *Raif Badawi: The Voice of Freedom: My Husband, Our Story* (Boston: Little, Brown, 2016).

19 Jefferson to N. G. Dufief, April 19, 1814, in *Jefferson: Writings*, ed. Merrill Peterson (New York: Library of America, 1984), pages 1333–35 at 1334.

20 Joseph Burstyn, Inc. v. Wilson, 343 U.S. 495, 505 (1952). | 21 Ibid.

22 Ingersoll, *Trial of C. B. Reynolds*.

23 See Freedom From Religion Foundation v. Morris County Board of Chosen Freeholders, No. 079277, 2018 WL 1832631 (NJ April 18, 2018).

24 Leigh Eric Schmidt, *Village Atheists: How America's Unbelievers Made Their Way in a Godly Nation* (Princeton, NJ: Princeton Univ. Press, 2017), 175–84.

25 Ingersoll, *Trial of C. B. Reynolds*, 10–11. | 26 Ibid., 31–32. | 27 Ibid., 45.

28 New Jersey Revised Statutes 237, § 22 (1874). The two prior sections made it a crime to practice witchcraft and to impersonate "our Savior Jesus Christ." See *Revision of the Statutes of New Jersey*, vol. 2 (Trenton, NJ: John L. Murphy, 1877), 238.

29 Leonard Williams Levy, *Blasphemy: Verbal Offense against the Sacred, from Moses to Salman Rushdie* (Chapel Hill, NC: Univ. of North Carolina Press, 1995), 511.

30 Ingersoll, *Trial of C. B. Reynolds for Blasphemy*, 9.

Chapter 17 • Forced Rest: The Fourth Commandment

1 Thomas Paine, "Of the Sabbath Day in Connecticut," in *Writings of Thomas Paine*, vol. 4, 324.

2 Exod. 31:14. | 3 Num. 15:32–36.

4 Sandoz, *Political Sermons*, vol. 2, 1123.

5 Pascal, *Pensées*, § 7, no. 425.

6 David N. Laband and Deborah Hendry Heinbuch, *Blue Laws: The History, Economics, and Politics of Sunday-Closing Laws* (Lexington, MA: Lexington Books, 1987), 30.

7 Braunfeld v. Brown, 366 U.S. 599, 602 (1961), citing McGowan v. Maryland, 366 U.S. 42, at 437–40 (1961).

8 Virginia Statue for Religious Freedom (1786). Maclear, *Church and State in the Modern Age*, 64.

9 *Braunfeld*, 366 U.S. at 437–40.

10 Soon Hing v. Crowley, 113 U.S. 703, 710 (1885).

11 Senator Richard Johnson made the Sunday Mails report to the Senate on January 19, 1829, the 20th Congress, 2nd Sess. In *American State Papers . . . of the Congress of the United States, from the first session of the First to the second session of the Twenty-Second Congress* (Washington, DC: Gales & Seaton, 1834), class 7, Post Office Dept., no. 74, 211–12; see also Sunday Mails report to the House of Representatives, no. 75, 212–15, https://books.google.com/books?id=cAdFAQAAMAAJ.

12 *McGowan*, 366 U.S. 42, at 420, 453.

13 Frederick Douglass, *The Life and Times of Frederick Douglass: From 1817–1882, Written by Himself, with an Introduction by the Right Hon. John Bright*, ed. John Lobb (London: Christian Age Office, 1882), 110–11.

14 Exod. 21:2.

15 "Slaves and Slavery," in *Jewish Encyclopedia*, vol 11, 403.

16 Exod. 21:7–8. | 17 Exod. 21:9–11. | 18 Luke 12:47–48. | 19 Eph. 6:5–8; Col. 3:22; Titus 2:9–10; 1 Pet. 2:18.

20 James Madison, *Records of the Federal Convention*, ed. Farrand, vol. 2, 415.

21 Edmund Randolph, debate in the Virginia Convention, June 21, 1788, in *Records of the Federal Convention*, ed. Farrand, vol. 3, 334.

22 Justice Thurgood Marshall, Bicentennial Speech, remarks at the Annual Seminar of the San Francisco Patent and Trademark Law Association, Maui, Hawaii, May 6, 1987, http://thurgoodmarshall.com/the-bicentennial-speech/.

23 Deut. 5:15. | 24 Exod. 20:10.

Chapter 18 • On Family Honor: The Fifth Commandment

1 Hitchens, *God Is Not Great*, 53. Hitchens was slightly wrong here. Islam says Ishmael, not Isaac, was to be sacrificed. It does not alter the point.

2 Hitchens, "The New Commandments." | 3 Ibid.

4 Anne Nicol Gaylor, *Lead Us Not into Penn Station* (Madison, WI: Freedom From Religion Foundation, 1983), 11.

5 Gen. 19. | 6 Gen. 19:36.

7 Gaylor, *Lead Us Not into Penn Station*, 11.

8 Deut. 32:46 | 9 Eph. 6:4.

10 Martin Luther, Large Catechism, in *Triglot Concordia: The Symbolical Books of the Evangelical Lutheran Church*, ed. Friedrich Bente (St. Louis, MO: Concordia, 1921), 565–773 at 627. The fourth commandment section of the Large Catechism begins on 611 and ends on 629.

11 Robert Tilton, "What is a Vow?," Robert Tilton website, last accessed July 30, 2018, at http://www.roberttiltonlive.com/vowing.html. See also *Understanding Evangelical Media: The Changing Face of Christian Communication*, ed. Quentin J. Schultze and Robert H. Woods Jr. (Downers Grove, IL, InterVarsity Press, 2009) 300, n. 32.

12 Psalm 89:26; Mal. 2:10.

13 To pick one book from the New Testament, John 1:18, 5:18, 6:27, 6:45–46, 8:41, 8:42, 10:36, 13:3, 16:27, 20:17.

14 Matt. 23:9.

15 Daniel Cox, "White Christians Side with Trump," PRRI, November 9, 2016, https://perma.cc/TJ5K-NVEU.

16 Mark Setzler and Alixandra B. Yanus, "Evangelical Protestantism and Bias against Female Political Leaders," *Social Science Quarterly* 98, no. 2 (2017): 766–78. "Even after controlling for partisanship, evangelicals are nearly twice as likely (as other voters) to believe that men make better political leaders than women," http://onlinelibrary.wiley.com/doi/10.1111/ssqu.12315/epdf.

17 D. F. McCleary, C. C. Quillivan, L. N. Foster, and R. L. Williams, "Meta-Analysis of Correlational Relationships between Perspectives of Truth in Religion and Major Psychological Constructs," *Psychology of Religion and Spirituality* 3, no. 3 (May 23, 2011): 163–80.

18 Ann Coulter, interview by Lloyd Grove, "Ann Coulter Might Dump Her 'Emperor God' Trump over Bannon," the *Daily Beast* (August 18, 2017), https://perma.cc/CT6V-CNXZ.

19 Hitchens said something like this on several occasions. This particular quote comes from his debate with Alister McGrath, "Poison or Cure? Religious Belief in the Modern World," October 11, 2007, Georgetown Univ., Washington, DC. In this instance, Hitchens was speaking of Josef Stalin.

20 Gregory Smith and Jessica Martinez, "How the Faithful Voted: A Preliminary 2016 Analysis," November 9, 2016, Pew Research Center, https://perma.cc/6DPJ-9B88.

Chapter 19 • Unoriginal and Tribal: The Sixth, Eighth, and Ninth Commandments

1 George Carlin, *When Will Jesus Bring the Pork Chops?* (New York: Hyperion, 2004), 17 (emph. added).

2 Stefan C. Reif, *Problems with Prayers: Studies in the Textual History of Early Rabbinic Liturgy* (Berlin: Walter de Gruyter, 2006), 115.

3 F. C. Burkitt, "The Hebrew Papyrus of the Ten Commandments," *The Jewish Quarterly Review* 15 (1903): 392–408, https://perma.cc/UMN6-48YL.

4 Mark 10:19. See also Luke 18:20, Rom. 13:9, and James 2:11.

5 See, e.g., Andreas Sofroniou, *Moral Philosophy: The Ethical Approach Through the Ages* (Swindon, UK: PsySys, 2003), 74; Murray N. Rothbard, *The Ethics of Liberty* (New York: New York Univ. Press, 2002), 170.
6 Ibid.
7 Christopher Hitchens, debate with Alister McGrath, "Poison or Cure? Religious Belief in the Modern World," Georgetown Univ., Washington, DC, October 11, 2007.
8 *McCreary*, 545 U.S. 844.
9 For other, earlier legal codes see David Wright, *Inventing God's Law: How the Covenant Code of the Bible Used and Revised the Laws of Hammurabi* (New York: Oxford Univ. Press, 2009); Kenneth A. Kitchen and Paul J. N. Lawrence, *Treaty, Law and Covenant in the Ancient Near East*, pts. 1–3 (Wiesbaden, Ger.: Harrassowitz, 2012).
10 John Hartung, "Love Thy Neighbor: The Evolution of In-Group Morality," *Skeptic* 3, no. 4 (1995): 86–99, http://strugglesforexistence.com./pdf/LTN.pdf.
11 The earliest version of this story I could find is in Liz Murray, *Breaking Night: A Memoir of Forgiveness, Survival, and My Journey from Homeless to Harvard* (New York: Hachette, 2010), 291; she attributes it to one of her English teachers, Perry Weiner.
12 See Hector Avalos, *The Bad Jesus: The Ethics of New Testament Ethics* (Sheffield, UK: Sheffield Phoenix Press, 2015), 32–34; Hartung, "Love Thy Neighbor." This is the minority interpretation and many, if not most, scholars disagree. See, e.g., Richard Elliott Friedman, "Love Your Neighbor: Only Israelites or Everyone?," *Biblical Archaeology Rev.* (September/October 2014), https://perma.cc/PEB6-PUR2. | 13 Ibid.
14 Lev. 19:18 (emph. added). | 15 Lev. 19:16 (emph. added). | 16 Deut. 15:1–3 (emph. added). | 17 Deut. 15:3.
18 I was first made aware of this in Richard Dawkins's *The God Delusion* (New York: Mariner, 2008), where he, in turn, cited Hartung, "Love Thy Neighbor."
19 See, e.g., Exod. 23:23 (6 races of people); Exod. 23:27–29; Num. 21:3, 21:34–35; Num. 31:7–11, 31:17, 31:35; Deut. 7:1–2 (seven nations), 16, 20; Deut. 13:15; Josh. 6:21; Josh. 8:22, 8:24; Josh. 10:28, 10:30, 10:31, 10:33, 10:35, 10:37, 10:38, 10:40; Josh. 11:1–9 (13 kings and their people), 11:11, 11:14, 11:20, 11:21; Josh. 12:7–24 (31 genocides); Judg. 1:8, 1:17, 1:25; Judg. 3:29; Judg. 6:16; Judg. 8:16, 17; Judg. 9:45, 49; Judg. 18:27; Judg. 19:22–30 (just a horrific story of slavery, rape, and murder, but not a genocide); Judg. 21:10–12.
20 Pinker, *Better Angels of Our Nature*, 10.
21 Babylonian Talmud: Tractate Sanhedrin, folio 79a, ed. Isidore Epstein, trans. Jacob Shachter and H. Freedman (London: Soncino Press, 1935), http://www.come-and-hear.com/sanhedrin/sanhedrin_79.html. | 22 Ibid.
23 "Gentile." In *Jewish Encyclopedia*, vol. 5, 619.
24 Matt. 10:5–6. | 25 John 13:34. | 26 John 13:35. | 27 1 John 2:9–11; 3:10–17; 4:20, all discussing love for brothers or brothers and sisters, but in terms that refer to fellow believers, i.e. brothers in Christ, not in terms that indicate the love is for all fellow humans. See also 2 John 1:5 and 10, which says to "love one another," but was written to a Christian congregation and then points out that no non-Christians should be given hospitality or allowed to enter Christian homes. | 28 1 John 2:9–11.
29 *New Oxford Annotated Bible*, 2140, notes for 1 John 2:9–11.
30 1 John 3:11–17 (emph. added). | 31 Matt. 15:21–28. See also Mark 7:24–30. | 32 Matt. 5:44. | 33 Rev. 22:15. | 34 Rev. 9:4–5. | 35 Matt. 25:41; Mark 9:43–48; Luke 16:22–24; John 3:18, 36; 2 Thess. 1:8–9; Rev. 14:10–11, 20:10. | 36 Gal. 3:28.
37 Orwell, *Animal Farm*.
38 Gal. 3:26–29 (emph. added).
39 Daniel Carey, *God: The Original Segregationist* (privately published, 1955), https://perma.cc/9DA5-JQHW.
40 Ibid. See also Dr. Bruno Bettelheim, "The Fearmongers," *Life*, February 7, 1964, 75.
41 Guy T. Gillespie, *A Christian View on Segregation* (Winona, MS: Assoc. of the Citizens' Councils, 1954). See also Charles Marsh, *God's Long Summer: Stories of Faith and Civil Rights* (Princeton, NJ: Princeton Univ. Press, 1999) 232, n. 124.
42 Bob Jones Sr., *Is Segregation Scriptural?* (Greenville, SC: Bob Jones Univ., 1960), 19. Originally a sermon given as a radio address on WMUU, April 17, 1960, later published in pamphlet form.
43 "Statement by Montgomery Commissioners Vows to Continue Legal Fight for Segregation," *Montgomery Advertiser* (AL), December 18, 1956, 7.
44 Neil R. McMillen, *The Citizens' Council: Organized Resistance to the Second Reconstruction* (Urbana, IL: Univ. of Illinois Press, 1971), 177. | 45 Ibid.
46 Patrick Allitt, *Religion in America Since 1945: A History* (New York: Columbia Univ. Press, 2003), 53. See also Matt. 10:5.
47 2 Cor. 6:14–17.
48 Inaugural address of Governor George Wallace, Montgomery, Alabama, capitol, January 1, 1963 (ellipses in original), http://digital.archives.alabama.gov/cdm/ref/collection/voices/id/2952.
49 See, e.g., Matthew Fowler, Vladimir E. Medenica, and Cathy J. Cohen, "Why 41 Percent of White Millennials Voted for Trump," *Washington Post*, December 15, 2017 (citing a GenFoward/*Washington Post* survey finding that, for millennial Trump voters, employment and income were not significantly related to that sense of white vulnerability but that racial resentment was); Daniel Cox, Rachel Lienesch, and Robert P. Jones, "Beyond Economics: Fears of Cultural Displacement Pushed the White Working Class to Trump," PRRI/*The Atlantic* Report, Public Religion Research Inst., May 9, 2017 (finding that besides partisanship, fears about immigrants and cultural displacement were more powerful factors than economic concerns in predicting support for Trump among white working-class voters); Brian F. Schaffner, Matthew Macwilliams, and Tatishe Nteta,

"Understanding White Polarization in the 2016 Vote for President: The Sobering Role of Racism and Sexism," *Political Science Quarterly* 133, no. 1 (March 25, 2018), 9–34 (finding that sexism and racism were more highly correlated with support for Trump than economic dissatisfaction).

50 Stephanie McCrummen, "Judgment Days: In a Small Alabama Town, an Evangelical Congregation Reckons with God, President Trump and the Meaning of Morality," *Washington Post*, July 21, 2018. | 51 Ibid.

52 Andrew L. Seidel, "The White House Bible Study Group that Influenced Trump's Family Separation Policy," *ThinkProgress*, June 19, 2018, https://perma.cc/2CV6-2LMX.

53 *McCreary*, 545 U.S. 844.

Chapter 20 • Perverting Sex and Love: The Seventh Commandment

1 Arthur Miller, *The Crucible* (1953; repr. New York: Penguin, 2003), 33.

2 Regina v. Mawgridge (Queen's Bench, 1706. Kelyng, 119), in William E. Mikell, *Cases on Criminal Law: Selected from Decisions of English and American Courts* (St. Paul, MN: West, 1908), 371.

3 *Law of the State of Indiana Passed at the Fifty-Second Regular Session of the General Assembly* (Indianapolis: Carlon & Hollenbeck, 1881), 195; *Revised Statutes of Wyoming* (Laramie, WY: Chaplin, Spafford & Mathison, 1899), 1256. The rationale was that masturbation was learned by instruction from others and that "it was appropriate for the law to punish those who irresponsibly sought to pass their vice on to the innocent." Geoffrey P. Miller, "Law, Self-Pollution, and the Management of Social Anxiety," *Michigan Journal of Gender & Law* 7, no. 2 (2001) at 262, https://repository.law.umich.edu/mjgl/vol7/iss2/6.

4 Md. Code Ann., Crim. Law § 3-322. | 5 Mich. Comp. Laws Ann. § 750.29-30.

6 Mike Pence, on *The Mike Pence Show*, May 23, 1997, https://politi.co/2CkkOMz.

7 See Richard Wightman Fox, *Trials of Intimacy: Love and Loss in the Beecher-Tilton Scandal* (Chicago: Univ. of Chicago Press, 1999).

8 "Adultery." In *Jewish Encyclopedia*, vol. 1, 216–18. | 9 Ibid.

10 Eve Levavi Feinstein, *Sexual Pollution in the Hebrew Bible* (Oxford, UK: Oxford Univ. Press, 2014), 47–48.

11 David Instone-Brewer, *Divorce and Remarriage in the Bible: The Social and Literary Context* (Grand Rapids, MI: Wm. B. Eerdmans, 2002), 151.

12 Luke 1:28, Matt. 1:20.

13 Alfred Brittain and Mitchell Carroll, *Women of Early Christianity* (Philadelphia: Rittenhouse Press, 1907), 22.

14 1 Cor. 6:18. | 15 Lev. 18:22. | 16 Deut. 22:5. | 17 Lev. 18:19, 20:18. | 18 Gen. 38:9–10. | 19 Deut. 22:20–21. | 20 Deut. 22:23–27. | 21 Lev. 20:15–16. | 22 Lev. 12:2. | 23 Exod. 21:10. | 24 Exod. 21:7–11. | 25 Num. 31:7–18. | 26 Deut. 22:28–29. | 27 Deut. 25:5–6. | 28 1 Sam. 18:25–26. | 29 Gen. 17:10–14. | 30 Lev. 12:3. | 31 Acts 16:3. | 32 1 Cor. 7. | 33 Matt. 10:35.

34 George Orwell, *Nineteen Eighty-Four* (1949; repr., New York: Houghton Mifflin Harcourt, 1983), 26.

35 Ibid., 152. | 36 Ibid., 152–53. | 37 Ibid.

38 Catholic Canon Law, Can. 277 § 1, http://www.vatican.va/archive/ENG1104/_PY.HTM (emph. added).

39 Cardinal Cláudio Hummes, "Reflection on the 40th Anniversary of the Encyclical *Sacerdotalis Caelibatus* of Pope Paul VI: The Radical Importance of the Graced Gift of Priestly Celibacy," *Vatican Congregation for the Clergy* (February 24, 2007), https://perma.cc/EK98-366X.

40 Matt. 5:28.

41 Loving v. Virginia, 388 U.S. 1, 6 (1967).

42 Walter Wadlington, "The Loving Case: Virginia's Anti-Miscegenation Statute in Historical Perspective," *Virginia Law Review* 52 (1966): 1189, 1191.

43 *Loving*, 388 U.S. 1 at 3.

44 Stewart v. United States, 364 A.2d 1205, 1208 (D.C. 1976).

45 Bowers v. Hardwick, 478 U.S. 186, 196 (1986) (Burger, C.J., concurring).

46 Lawrence v. Texas, 539 U.S. 558, 571 (2003).

47 William N. Eskridge Jr, "*Hardwick* and Historiography," *Univ. of Illinois Law Review* 1999, no. 2 (1999): 631, 646.

48 Lawrence v. Texas, 539 U.S. at 571. | 49 Ibid. at 578.

50 United States v. Windsor, 133 S. Ct. 2675, 2693 (2013) (citing H.R. Rep. No. 104–664, 16 (1996)).

51 *Bowers*, U.S.186, at 211–12 (Blackmun, J., dissenting).

Chapter 21 • Misogyny, Slavery, Thoughtcrime, and anti-Capitalism: The Tenth Commandment

1 Madison to Jefferson, January 22, 1786, in *Writings of James Madison*, vol. 2, 216.

2 Again, thank-you to Mr. Hitchens for pointing this out. Hitchens, "The New Commandments."

3 Abigail Adams to John Adams, March 31, 1776, in *Adams Family Correspondence*, vol. 1, 370. Founding Families: Digital Editions of the Papers of the Winthrops and the Adamses, ed. C. James Taylor (Boston: Mass. Historical Soc., 2015), http://www.masshist.org/apde2/.

4 Simone de Beauvoir, "Woman's Situation and Character," *The Second Sex* (1949; trans. and ed. H. M. Parshley, New York: Alfred A. Knopf, 1952); Quote from (New York: Vintage Books ed., 1989), 621.

5 Exod. 20:10–11. | 6 Col. 3:18; 1 Pet. 3:1; Eph. 5:22–24. KJV, NIV, and NLT all render the command as "submit." NRSV has it as "be subject to." See also 1 Pet. 3:1.

7 1 Tim. 2:11–15. | 8 Deut. 24:1. | 9 Gen. 2:21–23.

10 Roland de Vaux, *Ancient Israel: Its Life and Institutions* (Grand Rapids, MI: Wm. B. Eerdmans, 1997), 40.

11 Elizabeth Cady Stanton, "The Degraded Status of Woman in the Bible," *Free Thought Magazine* 14 (September 1896): 541. | 12 Ibid., 26.

13 Gen. 31:15. | **14** Gen. 3:16. | **15** Sarai/Sarah, Gen. 11:30, 16:1, 21:2-3; Rebekah, Gen. 25:21; Rachel, Gen. 29:31, 30:22–25; Manoah's wife, Judg. 13; Hannah, 1 Sam. 1:6–20; Elizabeth, Luke 1:5–25. | **16** Judg. 13. | **17** Luke 2:22–24. | **18** Lev. 15:19–31. | **19** Ibid. Men are unclean if they get particularly ill and after sex (Lev. 15:1–16), as are women. But women are banished for one of every four weeks simply for being women under this law. | **20** Luke 2:23.

21 *The Complete Artscroll Siddur (Artscroll Mesorah)*, ed. Nosson Scherman and Meir Zlotowitz (New York: Mesorah Publications, Brooklyn, 2001), 19 (emph. added).

22 1 Cor. 14:34.

23 Nicholas Clapton, *Moreschi and the Voice of the Castrato* (London: Hans, 2008), 10–11.

24 Reginald Magee, "Deriving Opera from Operation," *ANZ Journal of Surgery* 69 (April 6, 2002): 672–74, doi:10.1046/j.1440-1622.1999.01662.x.

25 See, e.g., Bradwell v. State of Illinois, 83 U.S. 130 (1873).

26 Glanville L. Williams, "The Legal Unity of Husband and Wife," *Modern Law Review* 10 (January 1947): 16–31, at 16.

27 *Bradwell*, 83 U.S. 130. | **28** Ibid., at 141.

29 Stanton, "Degraded Status of Woman in the Bible." | **30** Ibid., 540. | **31** Ibid.

32 National Woman Suffrage Association, "Declaration of Rights of the Women of the United States," July 4, 1876, in *The Selected Papers of Elizabeth Cady Stanton and Susan B. Anthony: National Protection for National Citizens, 1873 to 1880*, ed. Ann Gordon (New Brunswick, NJ: Rutgers Univ. Press, 2003), 239.

33 Donald Trump, interview by Nancy Collins, *Primetime Live*, ABC News, March 10, 1994, http://abcnews.go.com/Politics/donald-trump-1994-putting-wife-work-dangerous-thing/story?id=39537935.

34 See, e.g., Mike Pence speech on House floor, *Congressional Record* (House), 109th Congress, vol. 152, pt, 11 (July 18, 2006), 14796; speech at 2008 Conservative Political Action Conference, Omni Shoreham Hotel, Washington, DC, February 8, 2008.

35 Mike Pence, "Day-Care Kids," *Indianapolis Star*, April 9, 1997, 11.

36 Aaron Blake, "GOP Congressman's Book: 'The Wife Is to Voluntarily Submit' to Her Husband," *Washington Post*, January 22, 2014.

37 Report of Committee on Baptist Faith and Message, Final version of the report presented and approved at SBC, June 9, 1998, http://www.utm.edu/staff/caldwell/bfm/1963-1998/report1998.html.

38 Republican Presidential Candidates Debate in Myrtle Beach, South Carolina, January 10, 2008. Online at APP.

39 Orwell, *Nineteen Eighty-Four*.

40 Wooley v. Maynard, 430 U.S. 705, 714 (1977).

41 Cantwell v. Connecticut, 310 U.S. 296, 303-4 (1940). Hate crime or bias intimidation crimes are not thought-crimes. Most crimes require two things: an act and an intent. We punish criminal intent differently in our criminal justice system. First-degree and second-degree murder, justifiable homicide, manslaughter, negligent homicide, and so on, all depend on the killer's mental state or intent. While we *do* punish action without examining intent (statutory rape, drunk driving, speeding), we *do not* punish intent without the action (even attempt crimes require taking action to complete the crime, though not the ultimate act). Hate crimes are no different. If you simply hate someone based on race, sexuality, or creed, that thought is not punishable. Only the thought combined with an illegal action is criminal.

42 Valerie Tarico, "Religion May Not Survive the Internet," *Alternet.com*, January 16, 2013, http://www.salon.com/2013/01/16/religion_may_not_survive_the_internet/.

43 Christopher Hitchens, debate with Peter Hitchens, April 3, 2008, Hauenstein Center, Grand Valley State Univ., MI, http://hauensteincenter.org/hitchens-vs-hitchens-faith-politics-war/, 34:50. Hitchens concluded, "But at least you can fucking die and leave North Korea. Does the Koran or the Bible offer you that liberty? No. The tyranny, the misery, the utter ownership of your entire personality, the smashing of your individuality only begins at the point of death. This is evil, this is a wicked preachment."

44 2 Cor. 10:5.

45 Martin Luther King Jr., "A Witness to the Truth," Eulogy for James J. Reeb, March 15, 1965, repr. in *UU World* 15, no. 2 (May/June 2001): 20–23, http://archive.uuworld.org/2001/02/feature2.pdf. See also King, Letter from Birmingham Jail, April 16, 1963, https://perma.cc/UY4N-8NZR.

46 Catholic Canon Law, Can. 752, http://www.vatican.va/archive/ENG1104/_P2H.HTM#G8.

47 John Adams, "Dissertation on the Canon and Feudal Law," in *Works of John Adams*, vol. 3, 449.

48 Council of Trent: *The Fourteenth Session, The Canons and Decrees of the Sacred and Oecumenical Council of Trent*, ed. and trans. J. Waterworth (London: Dolman, 1848), 98, http://history.hanover.edu/texts/trent/ct14.html.

49 Ibid.

50 Matt. 5:28. | **51** Matt. 5:21–22.

52 Lon L. Fuller, *The Morality of Law* (New Haven, CT: Yale Univ. Press, 1969), 70–71.

53 Hitchens, *God Is Not Great*, 212.

54 Jefferson to Danbury Baptist Assoc., January 1, 1802.

55 United States v. Balsys, 524 U.S. 666, 714 (1998).

56 Model Penal Code § 2.01 (1), commentaries, comment to § 2.01 at 214–15 (1985).

57 *American Communications Assn. v. Douds*, 339 U.S. 382, 443 (1950) (Jackson, J. concurring in part, dissenting in part).

58 Ibid., 438.

59 *United States v. Schwimmer*, 279 U. S. 644, 654–55 (1929) (Holmes, J., dissenting).

60 *American Communications Assn.*

61 Catholic Canon Law, Can. 752, http://www.vatican.va/archive/ENG1104/_P2H.HTM#G8.

Chapter 22 • The Ten Commandments: A Religious, not a Moral Code

1 Steven Weinberg, speech, American Association for the Advancement of Science, Conference on Cosmic Design, Washington, DC, April, 1999).

2 Arthur Schlesinger Jr., "The Opening of the American Mind," *New York Times*, July 23, 1989.

3 See, e.g., Roy Moore's dedication speech when he unveiled the Ten Commandments monument at the Alabama Supreme Court in 2001: "To restore morality we must first recognize the source from which all morality springs. From our earliest history in 1776 when we were declared to be the United States of America, our forefathers recognized the sovereignty of God"; Mark Niesse, "Chief Justice Unveils Ten Commandments in Supreme Court building," Associated Press, August 1, 2001; Dennis Prager, "In Moral Absolutes: Judeo-Christian Values: Part XI," TownHall.com article, May 03, 2005, https://perma.cc/B48D-TGSJ.

4 Ignatius Loyola to Fathers and Brothers in Portugal, March 26, 1553, in *Personal Writings*, ed. Joseph Munitiz (London: Penguin UK, 1996), 255.

5 There has been some dispute in certain circles over whether or not Dostoevsky actually said this, but it seems clear he did. Andrei I. Volkov, "Dostoevsky Did Say It: A Response to David E. Cortesi," Internet Infidels, Inc., Secular Web, 2011, http://infidels.org/library/modern/andrei_volkov/dostoevsky.html.

6 "America's Changing Religious Landscape," Pew Research Center, May 12, 2015, https://perma.cc/D87J-MM49, notes that 35 percent of Americans born after 1981 consider themselves nonreligious. Betsy Cooper, Daniel Cox, Rachel Lienesch, and Robert P. Jones, "Exodus: Why Americans Are Leaving Religion—and Why They're Unlikely to Come Back," PRRI, September 22, 2016, https://perma.cc/Y3FB-C3KE.

7 *Atheism Doubles Among Generation Z*, The Barna Group (Jan. 24, 2018), https://perma.cc/5U9D-JGDB.

8 Deut. 13:6–11. | 9–11 Ibid.

12 For a full catalog, see Dan Barker, *God: The Most Unpleasant Character in All Fiction* (New York: Sterling, 2016).

13 Gen. 4:8. | 14 Gen. 4:19. | 15 Gen. 20:12, the incest is even blessed by God in 17:16. | 16 Gen. 12:13–17, 20:2. | 17 Gen. 19:30–38. | 18 Matt. 10:34–39. | 19 Luke 14:26–27. | 20 Matt. 8:21–22. | 21 John 2:3–4; Matt. 12:46–50; Mark 3:31–34.

22 Yes, he had brothers and sisters, though we never really hear about them. Mark 6:3, Matthew 13:55–56, and Galatians 1:19.

23 Matt. 19:10–12.

24 John 3:16; see also the perverse, warped attempt to bring god into love in 1 John 4:7–21.

25 Daniel C. Dennett, *Intuition Pumps and Other Tools for Thinking* (New York: W. W. Norton, 2014), 56. Dennett defines a *deepity* as something that sounds profound simply because it is ambiguous.

26 Gen. 22. | 27 Judg. 11.

28 Va. Code Ann. § 18.2-371.1(C); W. Va. Code Ann. § 61-8D-2(d); Iowa Code § 726.6(1)(d); Ohio Rev. Code Ann. § 2919.22 (A); Miss. Code. Ann. §§ 43-21-105 (l)(i), 97-5-39; Ark. Code Ann. § 5-10-101 (a)(9)(B); Wash. Rev. Code Ann. § 9A.42.005; Idaho Code Ann. § 18-1501(4).

29 The exemptions were passed so that states could access federal programs and funds and were a requirement of the Federal Child Abuse Prevention and Treatment Act, which President Nixon signed into law in 1974. That law is no longer in force, but the exemptions remain.

30 Judith Inglis Scheiderer, "When Children Die as a Result of Religious Practices," *Ohio State Law Journal* 51, no. 5 (1990): 1429–46, http://hdl.handle.net/1811/64118.

31 Nigel Duara, "An Idaho Sheriff's Daunting Battle to Investigate When Children of a Faith-Healing Sect Die," *Los Angeles Times*, April 18, 2017. | 32–33 Ibid.

34 Canyon County Sheriff Kieran Donahue in Duara, "Idaho Sheriff's Daunting Battle."

35 Nicholas Ray, *Lesbian, Gay, Bisexual and Transgender Youth: An Epidemic of Homelessness* (New York: National Gay and Lesbian Task Force Policy Institute and the National Coalition for the Homeless, 2006).

36 Laura E. Durso and Gary J. Gates, *Serving Our Youth: Findings from a National Survey of Service Providers* . . . (Los Angeles: Williams Inst. with True Colors Fund and the Palette Fund, 2012).

37 Caitlin Ryan, *Supportive Families, Healthy Children: Helping Families Support Their Lesbian, Gay, Bisexual, and Transgender (LGBT) Children* (Washington, DC: National Center for Cultural Competence, Georgetown Univ. Center for Child and Human Development, 2009), 4.

38 Ann Coulter, Twitter post, October 15, 2013, https://twitter.com/anncoulter/status/258068513506328576.

39 Mollie Reilly, "Rob Portman Reverses Gay Marriage Stance After Son Comes Out," *Huffington Post*, March 15, 2013.

PART IV: AMERICAN VERBIAGE

1 Sir James George Frazer, *Psyche's Task: A Discourse Concerning the Influence of Superstition on the Growth of Institutions* (1913; repr. London: Macmillan, 1920), 169.

Chapter 23 • Argument by Idiom

2 William Davie to James Iredell, January 22, 1788, in *Life and Correspondence of James Iredell* . . . , ed. Griffith J. McRee, vol. 2 (New York: D. Appleton, 1858), 217.

3 "Comte de Moustier, Description of the Inauguration," in *Documentary History First Federal Congress*, vol. 15, Correspondence: First Session, March–May 1789, ed. Charlene Bangs Bickford, Kenneth R. Bowling, Helen E. Veit, and William C. diGiacomantonio (Baltimore: Johns Hopkins Univ. Press, 2004), 403–6, at 404. See also Lengel, *Inventing George Washington*, 103.

4 Tobias Lear, April 30, 1789, diary entry, in *The Writings of George Washington*, ed. Jared Spark, vol. 10 (New York: Harper & Brothers, 1847), 463 (emph. in orig.).

5 William Maclay, April 30, 1789, diary entry, in *Journal of William Maclay*, ed. Edgar S. Maclay (New York: D. Appleton, 1890), 9.

6 *Senate Journal*, 1st Congress, 1st Sess., April 30, 1789, 18.

7 Cathy Lynn Grossman, "No Proof Washington Said 'So Help Me God'–Will Obama?," *USA Today*, January 7, 2009.

8 Ibid.

9 Peter R. Henriques, "'So Help Me God': A George Washington Myth that Should Be Discarded," *History News Network*, January 11, 2009.

10 Lengel, *Inventing George Washington*, 105.

11 William Maclay, April 30, 1789, diary entry, 7.

12 George Washington, *Rules of Civility: The 110 Precepts That Guided Our First President in War and Peace*, ed. Richard Brookhiser (New York: Free Press, 1997), 78.

13 *House Journal*, 1st Congress, 1st Sess., April 27, 1789, 21. | **14** *Senate Journal*, 1st Congress, 1st Sess., May 5, 1789, 22.

15 Rufus Griswold, *The Republican Court; or, American Society in the Days of Washington* (New York: D. Appleton, 1856), 141. | **16** Ibid., 142.

17 Lengel, *Inventing George Washington*, 105.

18 Arthur did not take the oath in the way familiar to modern readers, repeating the oath, clause for clause. Instead, the chief justice read the oath and Arthur replied, "I will, so help me God." See "The New Administration," *New York Times*, September 23, 1881, 5.

19 The most thorough report of the private March 4, 1917, oath is detailed enough that it mentions the words of the bible and the chapter and verse where Wilson's thumb lay when taking the oath. Wilson did not add "so help me God," according to this report. "Wilson Is Sworn in for Second Time at Simple Ceremony," *Washington Times*, March 4, 1917, Sunday Evening ed., 1 and 5, https://perma.cc/9J9D-DBX8; https://perma.cc/MHX6-GT3L. "Following administering of the oath, the Bible, the property of President Wilson, was taken to one side of the room by Chief Clerk Maher and opened at the fly leaf for the signature of the President and the Chief Justice. On the fly leaf was written, with colored ink, in old English script, the oath administered today. At the bottom of the oath President Wilson affixed his signature." Ibid at 5. I obtained a scan of the flyleaf of Wilson's inaugural bible from the LOC and the oath ends where the Constitution dictates; "so help me God" does not appear. Further evidence that Wilson didn't say it. Two other descriptions of the private oath, from his wife and his chief clerk, agree that Wilson did not add "so help me God." See Edith Bolling Galt Wilson, *My Memoir* (Indianapolis: Bobbs-Merrill, 1939), 130; Thomas W. Brahany, March 4, 1917, diary entry, in *The Papers of Woodrow Wilson Digital Edition* (Charlottesville, VA: Univ. of Virginia Press, 2017). Conversely, several sources say that Wilson added "so help me God" to the public oath on March 5. See, e.g., *Second Inauguration of Woodrow Wilson . . .*, March 5, 1917 (Washington, DC: Government Printing Office, 1918), 41.

20 There have been far more presidential oaths than presidents. Through Donald Trump's 2017 oath, presidents took the oath 75 times. Circumstances forced some to do so in private ceremonies—Arthur, Teddy Roosevelt, Coolidge, and more. Others did so in private Sunday ceremonies that were repeated later in public—Wilson, Eisenhower, Reagan, and Obama. Still others took multiple oaths to erase any doubt or question as to the validity of the initial oaths—Coolidge, Obama. Of the first 40 presidential oaths in US history (1789 through March 4, 1917), only Arthur's 1881 and Taft's 1909 public inaugurations featured the words "so help me God." There is conflicting evidence about Taft's oath. Two newspapers report that the words were added: "Now in Office," *Washington Herald*, March 5, 1909, https://perma.cc/T2E5-9X3U; "Oath Administered by Aged Jurist," *Washington Times*, March 4, 1909, late ed., 2, https://perma.cc/5XL7-DMPC. However, the oath recorded in Taft's bible and signed by both the president and chief justice does not include the words. See *Presidential Inaugural Bibles: Catalog of an Exhibition: November 17, 1968 through February 23, 1969* (Washington, DC: Washington Cathedral, 1969), 38.

21 Hoover's 1929 inauguration is the exception. Coolidge himself did not say the words in 1925, but did respond "I do" to Chief Justice Taft's prompting, and Taft did use the words: "Chief Justice Taft . . . administered the oath, as follows: 'Calvin Coolidge, do you solemnly swear … protect and defend the Constitution of the United States, so help you God?' The President bowed his head. 'I do,' he replied in a voice that was barely audible." *New York Times*, March 5, 1925, 3.

22 John Milton Cooper Jr., "Politics and Wilson's Academic Career," in *The Educational Legacy of Woodrow Wilson: From College to Nation*, ed. James Axtell (Charlottesville, VA: Univ. of Virginia Press, 2012); see also Niels Aage Thorsen, *The Political Thought of Woodrow Wilson, 1875–1910* (Princeton, NJ: Princeton Univ. Press, 1988), 142.

23 Woodrow Wilson, *George Washington* (New York: Harper & Brothers, 1903), 269–70.

24 Germany resumed unrestricted U-boat warfare on January 31, 1917; the US ended diplomatic relations with Germany on February 3, 1917.

25 The Zimmerman telegram came to light March 1, 1917, and was confirmed March 3.

26 See, e.g., Frederick S. Lane, *The Court and the Cross: The Religious Right's Crusade to Reshape the Supreme Court* (Boston: Beacon Press, 2008), 25–47; Sarah Palin, interview by Bill O'Reilly, May 7, 2010, *The O'Reilly Factor*, Fox News, http://www.foxnews.com/story/0,2933,592422,00.html; Kennedy and Newcombe, *What If America Were a Christian Nation Again?*, 3; F. LaGard Smith, *The Daily Bible Devotional: A One-Year Journey through God's Word in Chronological Order* (Eugene, OR: Harvest House, 2008), 235; Rev. Dwayne Byerly, *Today's Democrats & Christianity* (Rev. Dwayne Byerly, 2008), 58-9; Christian Smith, *Christian America?: What Evangelicals*

Really Want (Berkeley: Univ. of California Press, 2002), 21–60 (explaining a survey of evangelicals and their beliefs); John J. DiIulio, *Godly Republic: A Centrist Blueprint for America's Faith-Based Future* (Berkeley: Univ. of California Press, 2007), 1–3 (explaining but not making the claim); William Henard, "America: Essentially Christian," in *Christian America?: Perspectives on Our Religious Heritage*, ed. Daryl C. Cornett (Nashville, TN: B&H, 2011), 168, quoting Rep. Randy Forbes's May 6, 2009 speech in the House to support his "American Spiritual Heritage Week resolution"; Paramount-Richards Theatres v. City of Hattiesburg, 210 Miss. 271, 278 (1950).

27 Geoffrey Stone, "The Story of the Sedition Act of 1798: 'The Reign of Witches,'" in *First Amendment Stories*, ed. Richard Garnett & Andrew Koppelman (New York: Foundation Press, 2012), 13–38.

28 At press time, the investigations into President Donald Trump, his family, his campaign, and his businesses, tied to Russian election meddling and possible collusion, remain incomplete.

Chapter 24 • "In God We Trust": The Belligerent Motto

1 Robert Ingersoll, interview by *Secular Review*, London, 1884, in *Works of Robert G. Ingersoll*, ed. C. P. Farrell, vol. 8, 186.

2 Mark Twain, "Education and Citizenship," May 14, 1908, speech, in *Mark Twain's Speeches* (New York: Harper & Brothers, 1910), 147–48.

3 I owe Mike Newdow for his work uncovering the religious purpose behind the addition of "In God We Trust" to our coinage. Much of the history and citations contained herein were his work.

4 J. David Hacker, "A Census-Based Count of the Civil War Dead," *Civil War History* 57, no. 4 (2011): 30748. https:// muse.jhu.edu/. Hacker's estimate is higher than the previously accepted 620,000 and accounts for about 2.4 percent of the country's population of 31 million. Applied to roughly an American population of 327,000,000 in 2019 yields 7,848,000 dead. The lower figure, 620,000, would be about 6.5 million dead in 2019.

5 Walt Whitman, *Memoranda during the War*, "The Million Dead, Too, Summ'd Up," in *The Complete Prose Works* (Philadelphia: David McKay, 1892), 79–80 (emph. in orig.), http://www.whitmanarchive.org/published/ other/CompleteProse.html#leaf043r1. A special thanks to Ric Burns and PBS for bringing this haunting piece to my attention in Burns's *Death and the Civil War* on PBS's *American Experience*.

6 As Paul Finkleman pointed out to me, the Haitian Revolution may be the exception to this statement. Though perhaps there is a distinction to be made between slaves revolting and the nonslave class warring against itself.

7 Wood Gray, *The Hidden Civil War: The Story of the Copperheads* (New York: Viking, 1942), 115.

8 Abraham Lincoln, *Abraham Lincoln Papers*, ser. 3, Gen. Correspondence, 1837–1897, Second Inaugural Address, March 4, 1865, endorsed by Lincoln, https://www.loc.gov/item/mal4361300/. See also Mark Noll, "'Both . . . Pray to the Same God': The Singularity of Lincoln's Faith in the Era of the Civil War," *Journal of the Abraham Lincoln Assoc.* 18, no. 1 (Winter 1997): 1–26, http://hdl.handle.net/2027/spo.2629860.0018.103.

9 William Lloyd Garrison, remarks at the fifth national woman's rights conference, Philadelphia, October 18, 1854, in *History of Woman Suffrage*, ed. Elizabeth Cady Stanton, Susan B. Anthony, and Matilda Joslyn Gage, vol. 1, 1848–1861 (New York: Fowler & Wells, 1889), 382–83.

10 David Goldfield, *America Aflame: How the Civil War Created a Nation* (New York: Bloomsbury, 2011), 1. Special thanks to NPR's ongoing series with librarian Nancy Pearl, who recommended this book. | 11 Ibid., 3.

12 Quoted in John Dean, *Conservatives without Conscience* (New York: Viking, 2006), xxxiv. | 13 Ibid., 5.

14 David Goldfield, "Evangelicals, Republicans and the Civil War," *New York Times*, July 7, 2011.

15 Goldfield, *America Aflame*, 37, citing Richard J. Carwardine, *Evangelicals and Politics: Antebellum America* (New Haven, CT: Yale Univ. Press, 1993), 137.

16 Austin Willey, *The History of the Antislavery Cause in State and Nation* (Portland, ME: Brown Thurston, 1886), 260.

17 Goldfield, *America Aflame*, 125.

18 As quoted in *Congressional Globe*, 31st Congress, 1st Sess. (March 4, 1850), 477.

19 Ibid.; Goldfield, *America Aflame*, 65–66. | 20 Ibid. | 21 Ibid., 4–5.

22 Joint Resolution #4 to Establish a Seal for the Confederate States, approved by the 1st Congress of the Confederated States, Sess. 3, April 30, 1863, in *The Statutes at Large of the Confederate States of America* . . . ed. James M. Smith (Richmond, VA: R. M. Smith, 1863). For various translations, and there are more, including "an assenter, a defender, protector, deliverer, liberator, a mediator, and a ruler or guardian," and "avenger or punisher"; see the speech by CSA senator Thomas Jenkins Semmes of Louisiana describing the phrase in detail in "Seal of the Southern Historical Society and the Great Seal of the Confederate States of America," *Southern Historical Society Papers*, vol. 16, ed. R. A. Brock (Richmond, VA: Southern Historical Society, 1888), 416–22, at 419–22. See a lithograph of the original engraving of the seal at https://lccn.loc.gov/2014645208.

23 Ibid., *Southern Historical Society Papers*, vol. 16, 420.

24 Goldfield, *America Aflame*, 8.

25 James D. Richardson, *A Compilation of the Messages and Papers of the Confederacy Including the Diplomatic Correspondence 1861–1865* (Nashville, TN: United States Publishing, 1905), 37, https://bit.ly/1t5FwVc.

26 Mason I. Lowance Jr., ed., *A House Divided: The Antebellum Slavery Debates in America, 1776–1865* (Princeton, NJ: Princeton Univ. Press, 2003), 60.

27 Gen. 16:1–5.

28 For the best exposition of the bible's support for slavery see Hector Avalos, *Slavery, Abolitionism, and the Ethics of Biblical Scholarship* (Sheffield, UK: Sheffield Phoenix Press, 2011).

29 *Annals of Congress*, House of Representatives, 1st Congress, 2nd Sess., February 11, 1790, 1229. | 30 Ibid., 1506.

31 See, e.g., Joseph Wilson's sermon "Mutual Relation of Masters and Slaves as Taught in the Bible" in the First Presbyterian Church, Augusta, GA, January 6, 1861: "The Holy Spirit . . . has included slavery as an organizing element in that family order which lies at the very foundation of Church and State," http://docsouth.unc.edu/imls/wilson/wilson.html.

32 Rev. Frederick A. Ross, *Slavery Ordained of God* (Philadelphia: Lippincott, 1857), 5 (emph. in orig.).

33 Large excerpts of the address were printed in Daniel Lee's *The Genesee Famer* (Rochester, NY) 15 (1854): 26, https://bit.ly/2F9NtWE, though I was first made aware of the address in Goldfield, *America Aflame*, 108.

34–39 Ibid.

40 Thomas Cary Johnson, *The Life and Letters of Benjamin Morgan Palmer* (Carlisle, PA: Banner of Truth Trust, 1906), 212–13.

41 Frederick Douglass, "American Slavery, American Religion, and the Free Church of Scotland: An Address Delivered in London, England, on May 22, 1846," in *American Slavery: Report of a Public Meeting . . . to Receive Frederick Douglass, the American Slave . . .*, eds. John et al. (London, 1846), 12–13; John W. Blassingame et al., ed., *The Frederick Douglass Papers: Series One—Speeches, Debates, and Interviews*, vol. 1 (New Haven, CT: Yale Univ. Press, 1979), 269.

42 Mark A. Smith, *Secular Faith: How Culture Has Trumped Religion in American Politics* (Chicago: Univ. of Chicago Press, 2015), 57. | 43 Ibid., 27. | 44 Ibid., 58.

45 Aleksandr I. Solzhenitsyn, *The Gulag Archipelago, 1918–1956: An Experiment in Literary Investigation*, vol. 1 (1973; repr. New York: Basic Books, 1997), 173.

46 Jefferson, *Notes on the State of Virginia*, query 18. "For in a warm climate, no man will labour for himself who can make another labour for him. This is so true, that of the proprietors of slaves a very small proportion indeed are ever seen to labor. And can the liberties of a nation be thought secure when we have removed their only firm basis, a conviction in the minds of the people that these liberties are the gift of God? That they are not to be violated but with his wrath? Indeed I tremble for my country when I reflect that God is just: that his justice cannot sleep for ever."

47 Goldfield, *America Aflame*, 10.

48 Herman Melville, "Shiloh: A Requiem (April 1862)," http://www.poetryfoundation.org/poem/175176. Melville is referring to the religious lies and the lies of glamorous war.

49 Margaret Mitchell, *Gone with the Wind* (1936, Macmillan; repr. ed. New York: Warner Books, 1993), 229.

50 Harold Adams Small, *The Road to Richmond: The Civil War Memoirs of Major Abner R. Small . . .* (New York: Fordham Univ. Press, 1939), 85. Small takes a kinder view of the chaplains, thinking them untrained. See also Gerald Linderman, *Embattled Courage: The Experience of Combat in the American Civil War* (New York: Simon & Schuster, 2008), 253–54.

51 Linderman, *Embattled Courage*, 254. | 52–54 Ibid.

55 Roy Morris, *The Better Angel: Walt Whitman in the Civil War* (Oxford, UK: Oxford Univ. Press, 2001), 109.

56 Full text of the letter can be read at https://perma.cc/L3A3-P7SN. | 57 Ibid. (emph. added).

58 *Baptist Missionary Magazine* (Massachusetts Baptist Convention, Boston) 30 (1850): 304, lists a Mark R. Watkinson as a Baptist in Philadelphia.

59 Stokes, *Church and State in the United States*, vol. 3, 601.

60 Rep. Herman P. Eberharter remarks, US Congress, House, Committee on Banking and Currency, 84th Congress, 1st Sess., in *Miscellaneous Hearings* (Washington, DC: Government Printing Office, 1956), 53.

61 Theodore Roosevelt to William Boldly, November 11, 1907, repr. in Ted Schwarz, *A History of United States Coinage* (San Diego, CA: A. S. Barnes, 1980), 230. See actual letter at: https://perma.cc/B8CN-MZAX.

62 During the reinstatement debate in 1908, 42 Cong. Rec. 3384-91 (1908) at 3385.

63 H.R. Rep. No. 662, at 3 (1955).

64 *Proceedings of the National Convention to Secure the Religious Amendment of the Constitution of the United States* (Philadelphia: James B. Rodgers, 1872), iv, https://bit.ly/2W0Zrrf. (The vice presidency is noted at 2.)

65 *Report of the Director of the Mint*, in *Report of the Secretary of the Treasury on the State of the Finances Year Ending June 30, 1863* (Washington, DC: Government Printing Office, 1863), 190–91, https://bit.ly/2Tyk5Cd.

66 H.R. Rep. No. 662, at 3 (1955).

67 An Act in amendment of an Act titled "An Act relating to Foreign Coins and the Coinage of Cents at the Mint of the United States," 38th Congress, 1st Sess., *Statutes at Large*, 54–55. Congress did not vote specifically on the "in God we trust" language until 1865: "it shall be lawful for the director of the mint, with the approval of the Secretary of the Treasury, to cause the motto 'In God we trust' to be placed upon such coins." An Act to Authorize Coinage of Three-Cent Pieces, 38th Congress, 2nd Sess., *Statutes at Large*, 517–18.

68 "Elihu," *American Mercury*, February 18, 1788 (arguing against an acknowledgement of a deity in the new Constitution).

69 *Journals of the Continental Congress*, vol. 32, 1774–1789, ed. Worthington C. Ford et al. (Washington, DC, 1904–37), 223–25. | 70–71 Ibid., 303–5.

72 Eric Newman, *The Early Paper Money of America* (Atlanta: Whitman, 1967), 20, 33, 46. | 73 Ibid.

74 1 Stat. 246 (1792) Section 10.

75 Technically, the US had no official motto until the 1950s, but this served as the de facto if not the official motto.

76 See generally John Adams to Abigail Adams, August 14, 1776 [electronic edition], in *Adams Family Papers: An Electronic Archive*. Source of transcription: *Adams Family Correspondence*, vol. 2, 1963. The *E pluribus unum* motto survived on Simitiere's sketch of the seal. See, *The Papers of Thomas Jefferson*, 1:550. | 77–78 Ibid.

Chapter 25 • "One nation under God": The Divisive Motto

1 Edward R. Murrow, "A Report on Senator Joseph McCarthy," *See It Now*, CBS, March 9, 1954, http://www.lib.berkeley.edu/MRC/murrowmccarthy.html.

2 Newdow v. US Congress, Elk Grove Unified School District, et. al., 292 F.3d 597 (9th Cir. 2002). The Supreme Court overturned this 2002 decision, not because the legal conclusion was incorrect, but because the father challenging the pledge did not have full custody of his daughter. See p. 281.

3 Adam Smith wrote that if the government does not aid religion, "Each teacher [of religion, i.e., a preacher] would no doubt have felt himself under the necessity of making the utmost exertion and of using every art both to preserve and to increase the number of his disciples. . . ." See Adam Smith, *An Inquiry into the Nature and Causes of the Wealth of Nations*, bk. 5, ch. 1, pt. 3, art. 3 (1776) in *Founders' Constitution*, vol. 5, Amendment I (Religion), doc. 31. Madison wrote, "It was the Universal opinion of the Century preceding the last, that Civil Govt. could not stand without the prop of a Religious establishment, & that the Xn. [Christian] religion itself, would perish if not supported by a legal provision for its Clergy." See Madison to Robert Walsh, March 2, 1819, in *Writings of James Madison*, vol. 8, 431–32.

4 Kevin Kruse, *One Nation Under God: How Corporate America Invented Christian America* (New York: Basic Books, 2015), xiv.

5 Ibid. generally. | 6 Ibid., 4. | 7 Ibid., 12. | 8 Ibid., 13. | 9 Ibid., 7–8. | 10 Ibid., 132. | 11 Ibid., 132–3. | 12 Ibid., 134.

13 Harry S. Truman: Radio Address as Part of the Program "Religion in American Life," October 30, 1949. Online at APP.

14 Kruse, *One Nation Under God*, 138. | 15 Ibid., 137–38.

16 A. Roy Eckardt, "The New Look in American Piety," *Christian Century* 71 (November 17, 1954): 1396.

17 "God in the White House," *God in America*, PBS, 2010, http://www.pbs.org/godinamerica/god-in-the-white-house/.

18 J. Ronald Oakley, *God's Country: America in the Fifties* (New York: Red Dembner, 1986), 320–21.

19 Or "Jesus Christ, we forgot the prayer!" depending on who is doing the retelling. Norman K. Risjord, *America, a History of the United States: Since 1865* (New York: Prentice Hall, 1988), 361; Nancy Gibbs and Michael Duffy, *The Preacher and the Presidents: Billy Graham in the White House* (New York: Hachette, 2007), 43.

20 Kruse, *One Nation Under God*, xiii, 88–92.

21 Patrick Allitt, *Religion in America since 1945*, 31.

22 Oakley, *God's Country*, 325, citing a 1951 Gallup poll.

23 Pew Research Center's Forum on Religion & Public Life, Religious Knowledge Survey 2010, 22 ("Slightly less than half of those polled [45 percent] can name all four Gospels [Matthew, Mark, Luke and John]. An additional 6 percent correctly name between one and three of the Gospels"), https://perma.cc/264H-SPV7.

24 Rep. Wingate Lucas read Graham's sermon into the Congressional Record on February 18, 1952. *Congressional Record* (House), vol. 98, pt. 8, January 8, 1952 to July 7, 1952, A910.

25 Kruse, *One Nation Under God*, 54–56.

26 66 stat 64; 36 USC Sect 169h; Public Law 82-324.

27 Richard A. Harris and Daniel J. Tichenor, ed., *A History of the U.S. Political System: Ideas, Interests, and Institutions: Ideas, Interests, and Institutions*, vol. 1 (Santa Barbara, CA: ABC-CLIO 2009), 129.

28 Kruse, *One Nation Under God*, 75–81.

29 Jonathan P. Herzog, *The Spiritual-Industrial Complex: America's Religious Battle Against Communism in the Early Cold War* (Oxford, UK: Oxford Univ. Press, 2011), 104.

30 Oakley, *God's Country*, 320–21; Kruse, *One Nation Under God*, 95; Leo Pfeffer, *Church, State, and Freedom*, rev. ed. (Eugene, OR: Wipf and Stock, 2018), 242.

31 "Stamp Dedicated by the President," *New York Times*, April 9, 1954.

32 H. Con. Res. 60, Doc. No. 234, 84th Congress, 1st Sess.

33 Pub. L. No. 396, Ch. 297, 68 Stat. 249 (1954).

34 Pub. L.84-140, 69 Stat. 290, H.R. 619, enacted July 11, 1955.

35 *History of the Bureau of Engraving and Printing, 1862–1962* (Washington, DC: Treasury Dept., 1962), 177.

36 Pub.L.84-851, 70 Stat. 732, H.J.Res. 396, enacted July 30, 1956.

37 Kruse, *One Nation Under God*, 140–48.

38 Freedom From Religion Foundation, Inc. v. Obama, 705 F. Supp. 2d 1039 (W.D. Wis. 2010), vacated and remanded, 641 F.3d 803 (7th Cir. 2011). | 39 Ibid.

40 Elk Grove Unified School District v. Newdow, 542 U.S. 1, 18 (2004).

41 Ibid. at 26–27, (Rehnquist, CJ concurring). | 42 Ibid. at 28, 29.

43 Andrew L Seidel, "The Christian Hypocrisy of 'In God We Trust,'" *Freethought Now!*, April 13, 2016, http://www.patheos.com/blogs/freethoughtnow/the-christian-hypocrisy-of-in-god-we-trust/.

44 See H. R. Rep. No. 83-1693, at 3 (1954).

45 Amy Crawford, "How the Pledge of Allegiance Went from PR Gimmick to Patriotic Vow," *Smithsonian*, September 2015, https://bit.ly/2eCmur0. | 46 Ibid.

47 Kruse, *One Nation Under God*, 102–3.

48 Robert Griffith, *The Politics of Fear* (Amherst, MA: Univ. of Massachusetts. Press, 1987).

49 Oakley, *God's Country*, 2.

50 Fred J. Cook, *The Nightmare Decade: The Life and Times of Senator Joe McCarthy* (New York: Random House, 1971), 152–56.

51 William Shirer, *Midcentury Journey: The Western World Through Its Years of Conflict* (New York: Farrar, Straus & Young, 1952), 275.

52 Mike Miller, "50 Years Ago, Fear Ruled Fourth: Reporter's Petition Measured Effect of McCarthy," *Capital Times* (Madison, WI), July 4, 2001; Dave Zweifel, "Plain Talk: Remembering Joe McCarthy, We Need to Fight Smears and Fears Anew," *Capital Times*, June 29, 2011.

53 Miller, "50 Years Ago."

54 Oakley, *God's Country*, 74.

55 Earl Warren, "Blessings of Liberty," *Washington Univ. Law. Quarterly* 105, iss. 2 (1955), http://openscholarship. wustl.edu/law_lawreview/vol1955/iss2/1. Chief Justice Earl Warren delivered this address February 19, 1955, as the keynote speaker at the opening assembly of WU's Second Century Convocation.

56 Allitt, *Religion in America since 1945*, 23.

57 Joseph McCarthy, Address to the Sons of the American Revolution, Claridge Hotel, Atlantic City, NJ, May 15, 1950, in *Congressional Record*, 81st Congress, 2nd Sess., A3786-3789 at 3787, https://bit.ly/2TzkpAM. See also McCarthy's May 25, 1950, remarks to the Catholic Press Assoc. in Rochester, NY, quoted in Martin E. Marty, *Modern American Religion: Under, Indivisible, 1941–1960*, vol. 3 (Chicago: Univ. of Chicago Press, 1996), 357–38 ("You have been engaged in what may well be the final Armageddon foretold in the Bible—that struggle between light and darkness, between good and evil, between life and death, if you please.")

58 Allitt, *Religion in America since 1945*, 25; Kruse, *One Nation Under God*, 148–49. | 59 Ibid.

60 Peter Lewis, *The Fifties* (New York: J. B. Lippencott, 1978), 73–74.

61 Allitt, *Religion in America since 1945*, 24.

62 Oakley, *God's Country*, 324, quoting Harry C. Meserve, "The New Piety," *Atlantic Monthly* 195, June 1955, 35.

63 Ibid., 184, citing Samuel Stouffer, *Communism, Conformity, and Civil Liberties: A Cross-section of the Nation Speaks Its Mind* (New Brunswick, NJ: Transaction, 1955), 161, 176, used to refine and expand quotations in this cite.

64–65 Ibid., 26. | 66 Ibid., 72.

67 Dan Lewerenz, "50 Years Ago, Sermon Spurred Putting 'Under God' in Pledge," Associated Press, February 6, 2004.

68 Rev. George M. Docherty, sermon at the New York Avenue Presbyterian Church in Washington, DC, February 7, 1954, 9, http://www.nyapc.org/wp-content/uploads/2014/01/Under_God_Sermon.pdf.

69 H.R. Rep. No. 83-1693, at 1–2 (1954), repr. in 1954 U.S.C.C.A.N. 2339, 2340.

70 Dwight D. Eisenhower, Statement by the President upon Signing Bill to Include the Words "Under God" in the Pledge to the Flag, June 14, 1954. Online at APP.

71 Zorach v. Clauson, 343 U.S. 306 (1952).

72 Ibid., 323 (1952) (Jackson, J. dissenting). | 73 Ibid., 313 (1952).

74 William Cohen, "Commentary: Douglas as Civil Libertarian," in *He Shall Not Pass This Way Again: The Legacy of Justice William O. Douglas*, ed. Stephen L. Wasby (Pittsburgh, PA: Univ. of Pittsburgh Press, 1990), 121–28 at 123. (Cohen also points out that Douglas never explained his doctrinal and verbal inconsistencies between this opinion and his later opinions on state-church separation and calling the opinion "puzzling," at 124.) See also Nadine Strossen, "The Religion Clause Writings of Justice William O. Douglas," in ibid., 91–108 at 92, 100–101 (noting that this was the only Douglas opinion rejecting an Establishment Clause challenge, calling it anomalous).

75 See, e.g., Bruce Murphy, *Wild Bill: The Legend and Life of William O. Douglas* (New York: Random House, 2003), 310–11.

76 *McGowan*, 366 U.S. 42 (Douglas, J., dissenting). Douglas continued, "second, that no one shall be interfered with by government for practicing the religion of his choice; third, that the State may not require anyone to practice a religion or even any religion; and fourth, that the State cannot compel one so to conduct himself as not to offend the religious scruples of another. The idea, as I understand it, was to limit the power of government to act in religious matters, not to limit the freedom of religious men to act religiously nor to restrict the freedom of atheists or agnostics."

77 Watkins v. United States, 354 U.S. 178 (1957).

78 John F. Kennedy, speech, Greater Houston Ministerial Association, Rice Hotel, Houston, TX, September 12, 1960. https://www.jfklibrary.org/learn/about-jfk/historic-speeches/address-to-the-greater-houston-ministerial-association.

79 Torcaso v. Watkins (1961); Engel v. Vitale (1962); Abington v. Schempp (1963); Epperson v. Arkansas (1968).

80 "Atheism Doubles Among Generation Z," Barna Group, January 24, 2018, https://www.barna.com/research/atheism-doubles-among-generation-z/. | 81 Ibid.

Chapter 26 • "God bless America": The Diversionary Motto

1 George Carlin, *It's Bad for Ya*, HBO special, March 1, 2008.

2 Edward Abbey, *Postcards from Ed: Dispatches and Salvos from an American Iconoclast* (Minneapolis: Milkweed, 2006), 71.

3 Kruse, *One Nation Under God*, 256; Edward Fiske, "'Underground' Church Started Right in Nation's Capital," *Day* newspaper (New London, CT) September 6, 1969, 6.

4 President Richard Nixon's televised address to the nation on the Watergate investigation, April 30, 1973, http://watergate.info/1973/04/30/nixons-first-watergate-speech.html.

5 David Domke and Kevin Coe, *The God Strategy: How Religion Became a Political Weapon in America* (Oxford, UK: Oxford Univ. Press, 2008), 61–62. See also Domke and Coe, "Happy 35th, 'God Bless America,'" *Time*, April 29, 2008.

6 Nixon, Remarks at the Grand Ole Opry House, Nashville, Tennessee, March 16, 1974. Online at APP.

7 Andrew L. Seidel, "Trump Pushes Bible Classes in Public Schools, Backs Project Blitz," *Freethought Now!*, January 28, 2019, https://www.patheos.com/blogs/freethoughtnow/trump-pushes-bible-classes/.

8 Ronald Reagan: Address Accepting the Presidential Nomination at the Republican National Convention in Detroit, July 17, 1980. Online at APP.

9 Domke and Coe, "Happy 35th, 'God Bless America.'"

10 *Founders' Constitution* online, vol. 5, Amendment 1 (Religion), doc. 66; Madison, *Writings of James Madison*, FO-NA; Madison to Livingston, July 10, 1822, FO-NA.

11 Donald Trump, speech at Liberty Univ., Lynchburg, VA, January 18, 2016.

12 Eugene Scott, "A Revealing Aside in the Trump Tape Sheds Light on the Limits of His Outreach to Black Voters," *Washington Post*, July 25, 2018, https://wapo.st/2mEUaWy. The full exchange was as follows:

    TRUMP: And, your guy is a good guy. He's a good —

    COHEN: Who, Pastor Scott?

    TRUMP: Can't believe this. No, Pastor Scott. What's, what's happening —

    COHEN: No —

    TRUMP: Can we use him anymore?

    COHEN: Oh, yeah, a hundred — no, you're talking about Mark Burns. He's, we've told him to [UNINTELLIGIBLE].

    TRUMP: I don't need that — Mark Burns, are we using him?

    COHEN: No, no.

13 Madison, "Memorial and Remonstrance," ¶ 5.

14 *The West Wing.* "In God We Trust," Season 6, Ep. 20. Dir. by Christopher Misiano. Written by Lawrence O'Donnell Jr. NBC, March 23, 2005.

15 37 percent of Americans could not name a right protected by the First Amendment in 2017. See 2017 Annenberg Constitution Day Civics survey by the Annenberg Public Policy Center, "Americans Are Poorly Informed About Basic Constitutional Provisions," September 12, 2017, https://perma.cc/SRN7-BHRC.

Conclusion • Take alarm, this is the first experiment on our liberties

1 Madison, "Memorial and Remonstrance Against Religious Assessments," ¶ 3.

2 As an atheist attending my first Catholic wedding, I noticed early on that the focus was not on the couple and began counting. I repeated the experiment at other Catholic weddings I attended. I counted the number of times the wedding officiant refers to the couple or individuals in the couple, and the number of mentions of a god or the church. The final tally at the wedding referred to above was 60 to 238.

3 See, e.g., Shane Idleman, "America—Then vs. Now. It's Almost Unbelievable," *ChrismaNews.com*, April 6, 2015 ("*Newsweek* magazine, on December 27, 1982, in an article titled, 'How the Bible Made America,' made this revealing statement: 'Historians are discovering that the Bible, perhaps even more than the Constitution, is our Founding document'"); Gary DeMar, "The History Con May be Over," Americanvision.org, June 1, 2010 ("A 1982 article in *Newsweek* Magazine stated, '[F]or centuries [the Bible] has exerted an unrivaled influence on American culture, politics and social life. Now historians are discovering that the Bible perhaps even more than the Constitution, is our founding document'"); Barton, Original Intent, 226; Mark A. Beliles and Stephen K. McDowell, *America's Providential History* (Charlottesville, VA: Providence Foun., 1989), 186.

4 Kenneth L. Woodward and David Gates, "How the Bible Made America," *Newsweek*, December 27, 1982, 44–51.

5 Tim Minchin put it nicely in *Storm*, his "epic beat poem." See an animated version at https://bit.ly/2TyIqbd.

6 See, e.g., Jerry Coyne, *Faith vs. Fact: Why Science and Religion Are Incompatible* (New York: Viking, 2015); John William Draper, *History of Conflict between Religion and Science* (New York: D. Appleton & Co., 1875); Andrew Dickson White, *A History of the Warfare of Science with Theology in Christendom* (New York: D. Appleton & Co, 1901).

7 Green, *Women Without Superstition*, 469.

8 Such as Congress printing bibles (a misrepresentation), language in the Northwest Ordinance (passed in 1787 by the Confederation Congress while the leading founding fathers were at the Constitutional Convention), and irrelevant Supreme Court dicta issued in cases involving an alien labor law. See, e.g., Church of the Holy Trinity v. United States, 143 U.S. 457, 471 (1892).

9 Franklin to Richard Price, October 9, 1780, in *Works of Benjamin Franklin*, vol. 8, "Letters and Misc. Writings, 1779–1781," 311.

10 Jefferson, *Notes on the State of Virginia*, query 17.

11 Madison, "Memorial and Remonstrance," ¶ 3. | 12 Ibid.

Index

Note: Page numbers in *italics* indicate illustrations.

on natural law, 76, 77
on object of Declaration of Independence, 54
on reason in government, 147
on religion as seen in actions, 42
on religious coercion and violence, 167
on religious fervor, 268
on religious intolerance, 106, 107
rewriting of New Testament by, 43
as scientist and inventor, 148
on Sedition Act, 258
on separation of church and state, 36, 175
on slavery, 82–83
as suspicious of organized religion, 82
on trinity, 113
Virginia Statute for Religious Freedom and, 36, 196
Jesus
adultery and conception of, 222–23
commandments and miracles of, applicable to believers only, 215–17
death of, and personal responsibility, 139
on faith, 145
family values and, 245–46
on future, 153
as giver of political authority, 82
Golden Rule and, 119, 121
hell and, 132, 133, 134, 137, 217
ideals of, 41
Jefferson's excision from bible, 43
Jewish views on, as savior and son of God, vii–viii, 4
name of, 188–89
name of god and, 187
obedience to, 125, 130, 137
omission of, in founding documents, 35, 70, 81
on public prayer, 112
on punishment, 130, 132–33
slavery and, 200
vicarious redemption through, 117, 139–42
Washington's references to, 28, 42
The Jewish Encyclopedia, 176, 199, 214, 222
Jones, Bob, 218
Judaism. *See also* Religion
views on Christianity and Jesus, vii–viii, 3, 4
mitzvot and, 168
Judeo-Christian principles. *See also* Myth(s)
erroneous claims of Declaration of Independence as embodiment of, 53, 67, 68, 70
elitism as ideal of, 242
Golden Rule, 119–22
guilt and punishment, 129–32

irrelevance of "Judeo" part to Christians, 4
meaning of term, 2–3
morality and immorality of, 248–49
origin of term, 3
as oxymoronic term, vii–viii
separation of powers and, 113
as "un-American," 17, 117, 228, 236, 295–96
and women, 230
Justice system
guilt in, 142–43
personal responsibility as basis, 138
punishment in, 128, 129, 135–36
US Constitution and, 128

Kasich, John, 10
Kennedy, John F., 15, 287–88
King, Steve, 10–11
Kingdom Coming: The Rise of Christian Nationalism (Goldberg), 4
Kingdom of God, 154–55
Kleindienst, Richard, 289
Knights of Columbus, 282
Kruse, Kevin, 277, 278

LaHaye, Tim, 9, 117
Lamborn, Doug, 10
Law(s)
apply to all, 220
blasphemy, 189–93
categories of, 75
Constitutional requirements for, 189
regulating sex, 221–28
religious exemptions to child abuse and neglect, 247
resemblance of, to Ten Commandments does not mean influence, 209–10
secular reasons as necessary for, 227
Sunday closing, 195–98
vagueness of, 187–88
Laws of nature
as category of law, 75
Christian view of, as atheist, 79
as legal basis to justify revolt, 76–78
natural rights and, 37
people cede rights to government, 83–84
Lear, Tobias, 252–53
Lee, Harper, 154
Lee, Richard Henry, 54, 70
Legislative initiatives, 7–8
Lengel, Edward G., 27, 28, 253
Leo III (Byzantine emperor), 181
Leo XIII (pope), 178
Letters from an American Farmer (Crèvecoeur), 102–3
Liberty Party, 262, 263

Lieberman, Joe, 80
Life of Washington (Irving), 255
Lincoln, Abraham, 111, 261–62, 281
Lind, John, 61
Livingston, Robert, 69
Locke, John, 48, 59, 71, 174
Lot, 125, *184*, 185, 204
Loving v. Virginia (1967), 226
Loyola, Ignatius, 242
Lucas, Stephen, 56
Lund, Christopher C., 94–95
Luther, Martin, 147, 205
Lutz, Donald, 115–16
Lyman, Theodore, 269

Maclay, William, 253
Madison, James, *175*
American Philosophical Society and, 148
on chaplains for Congress, 96, 97
on concentration of power, 113
on Constitution as experiment, 150–51
on Constitution to endure, 152
on duty of citizens, 297
"infidel principles" of, 38
intolerance of Christianity, 106
on meaning of god's words, 188
models for US government, 156
morality as distinct from religion, 47
on need to battle all infringements on liberty, 15–16
on people as legitimate source of power, 177
on political tyranny in name of religion, 175
on preventing consequences of guilt beyond author of, 183
on protection of slave trade, 201
on religion in Holland, 99
on religious coercion and violence, 167
as scientist and inventor, 148, 149
on separation of church and state, 37–38, 39, 291
as suspicious of organized religion, 82
Virginia Statute for Religious Freedom and, 37
Marshall, Thomas, 64
Marshall, Thurgood, 202
Marsh v. Chambers (1983), 96–97
Mason, George, 77, 150–51, 152
Mason, John, 100–101
Massachusetts Constitution, 84
Matlack, Timothy, 73
Mayflower Compact, 105
McCain, John, 4
McCarran Internal Security Act (1950), 285
McCarthy, Joseph, 283, 284, 287
McGuffey, William Holmes, 27
McHenry, James, 156

INDEX

Meade, William, 38
Melville, Herman, 268
"Memorial and Remonstrance
against Religious Assessments"
(Madison), 15–16, 37–38, 175
Mencken, H. L., 161
Menéndez de Avilés, Pedro, 101
Mill, John Stuart, 47
Miller, William Lee, 279
Monolatry, 176
Monroe, James, 177
Montesquieu, 49
Morality
Christianity as requirement
for, 44
code of, 242
as evolving, 242–43, 245
Golden Rule and, 119
Judeo-Christianity as final
authority on, 129
national, 44–45
personal, as absolute, 85–86
religion and, 41, 44–47, 49,
242–45, 248, 249
universality of, 209–10
Moral Majority, 8
Morris, Gouverneur, 43–44, 45, 47
Morrison, Jeffry H., 73
Mosaic Law, 168
Moses, xii, 1, 3, 113, 126, 130,
139, 161–65, 168, 170, 175–76,
180, 205, 209, 211–13, 222
Murder rates and religion, 49, 50
Murphy, Frank, 183
Murray, John Courtney, 284
Myth(s). See also
of Christian nationalists, 41,
295, 296
as enemy of truth, 15
"God bless America" phrase,
258, 259, 289–90, 290–91
"In God we trust" phrase,
258, 259, 260–61, 260–74,
270–72, 278–80, 285
Judeo-Christian principles as
basis of America's founding,
1–2, 3, 5, 9. 10, 11. 14,
16–17, 20, 31, 38, 49, 80, 93,
116–17, 169, 220
"one nation under God" phrase,
258, 259, 285
only Christians are moral, 44
refutation of, that America is
Christian nation, 16–17
secular America as, 5
"so help me God" phrase,
252–57, 259
Washington praying at Valley
Forge, 2, 27–28, 29, 280

Napolitano, Andrew, 12
National Day of Prayer, 112, 279,
280–81
National morality, 44–45
National Prayer Breakfast, 279

Natural law, 37, 74–5, 76–78, 79,
81–84, 268
Nature's God: The Heretical Origins
of the American Revolution
(Stewart), 78
Neely, Sylvia, 26
Neff, Lawrence, 219
Netherlands, 99–100, 101–2, 106
New Deal, 277–78
New Hampshire's Bill of Rights, 84
Newsweek, 3, 295
New York Times, 8–9
Nineteen Eighty-Four (Orwell),
224–25
Nixon, Richard, 258, 289–90
Noll, Mark, 111
Nollett, Abbe, 63
Notes on State of Virginia
(Jefferson), 82–83, 155
Novak, Michael, 12, 146

Oakes, Urian, 105
Oakley, J. Ronald, 282, 285
O'Donnell, Lawrence, 292
One Nation Under God: How
Corporate America Invented
Christian America (Kruse), 277
"One nation under God" phrase,
258, 259, 285
On the Nature of Human Liberty
(Leo XIII), 178
Opinion on the French Treaties
(Jefferson), 76
O'Reilly, Bill, 12, 80
Origen, 180
Original sin, 21, 43, 117, 125
Orwell, George, 224–25
"Our Country's Religious
Heritage" bills, 7

Paine, Thomas, 51
on absolute power and freedom,
127
American Philosophical Society
and, 148
on authority of Ten
Commandments, 176
as deist, 47, 78
on forgiveness of sin, 51
on freedom and government,
123–24, 127
on importance of independence,
53
quotations from bible in
Common Sense, 112
as scientist and inventor, 148
slavery and, 265
on toleration/intoleration, 103
on tyranny and religion, 137
Palmer, Benjamin, 266
Paul (epistle to the Romans), vi,
59–60
Peale, Norman Vincent, 284–85
Pence, Mike, vi–vii, 12–13, 221,
235

Pennsylvania's Constitution, 84
Pequots, 100–101
Perkins, Tony, 4
Peroutka, Michael, 74–75
Perry, Rick, 10
Personal responsibility, 138–42
Pilgrims, 98, 99–100, 105–6
Pinker, Steven, 121, 213–14
Pitt, William, 123
Pledge of Allegiance, ix, 2, 9, 258,
276, 280, 281, 282
Polk, James K., 262
Pollock, James, 271–72
Poor Richard's Almanack
(Franklin), 42
Portman, Robert, 248
Positive law, 75, 76, 77
Pound, Roscoe, 75
Prayer, 27–28, 29, 112
Project Blitz, 6–8, 12, 16
Punishment
in bible(s), 128, 129–32, 135–
37, 136, 183–85, 184, 195
in Christianity, 128, 132–35,
136, 136–37
US Constitution and, 128, 129,
135–36, 183
Puritans, 98, 99, 100–102, 105, 106

Quakers, 265, 267–68

Rabaut, Louis C., 282
Racism and religion, 218–20, 226
Randolph, Edmund, 201
Reagan, Ronald, 290–91
Reason, 10, 17, 295–96
Reason: The Only Oracle of Man
(Allen), 112
Redemption, vicarious, 117, 139–42
Religion. See also bible(s);
Christianity; Judaism;
Separation of church and state
absence of regulation respects, 35
abuse of civil power in name
of, 174
authoritarianism and, 206–7
beliefs cannot take precedence
over Constitution, 176
Civil War and, 261–62
code of, 242
coercing attendance at worship
services, 195
in colonies, 91–92, 99, 100–106
creator-gods in, 71
current affiliations of Americans,
288
different contain universal
human principles, 297
education and, vi, 14, 286–87
exemption from laws and, 247
faith and, 145–46
First Amendment to
Constitution and, 173–75
founders kept beliefs to selves, 41
George III and, 58, 73

336

Picture Credits

Courtesy of author: 1
Getty Images/kickstand: 243
Internet Archive: 274
Library of Congress: 29, 45, 51,
63, 72, 175, 192
Rijksmuseum: 136

Shutterstock/Zvonimir Atletic: 181
University of Notre Dame/
Reproduced from the original
held by the Department of Special
Collections of the Hesburgh
Libraries of Notre Dame: 273

Courtesy of Wikimedia
Commons: xii, 140;
The Indian Reporter: 114;
NYPL: 230,
Wellcome Collection: 184